TWENTY TUMULTUOUS YEARS: INSIGHTS INTO INDIAN POLITY (1973-1994)

TWENTY TUMULTUOUS YEARS

INSIGHTS INTO INDIAN POLITY

(1973-1994)
(In 2 Volumes)

DEMOCRACY MY FOOT !
(Volume I)

Ayub Syed

Edited by
Dr. Anees Syed
Dr. Shri Prakash

GYAN

GYAN PUBLISHING HOUSE
NEW DELHI–110 002

TWENTY TUMULTUOUS YEARS: INSIGHTS INTO INDIAN POLITY (1973-1994)

(Political Science)

Rs. 1800 (Set)
Rs. 900 (Each Volume)

ISBN: 81-212-0804-1 (Set)
ISBN: 81-212-0821-1 (Vol. 1)
ISBN: 81-212-0822-X (Vol. 2)

Published in 2003 in India by
Gyan Publishing House
5-Ansari Road, Daryaganj
New Delhi-110 002
E-mail: gyanbook@vsnl.com
Visit our website at: http//www.gyanbooks.com

Lasertypesetting by: Varsha Graphics, Delhi
Printed at: Mehra Offset Printers, Delhi

Contents

2. The Janata Experiment

A. Janata Ideology—Janata Prime Ministers

B. Janata Leaders and Ministers—Many Voices

C. Two Years of Janata Rule

3. Return of Indira Gandhi

A. Indira Confronts Government Suppression

C. CONGRESS ON THE THRESHOLD OF ITS 2ND CENTURY

Preface

Societies and nations live on primarily because their thought processes seek to better the world they find themselves in and the experience they seek to get from the time spent here. A critical analysis of reality in its multifarious aspects is integral to progress and change. In essence a journalist's job is not much different from that of a social scientist. Both seek to draw conclusions of wider applicability from their observations about social, political, economic and other behaviour at the individual as well as institutional levels. A more perceptive journalist or social scientist doesn't look only at the immediate socio-political events that occupy the nation's attention. Nor does he only take a step further to identify the relationship between seemingly unrelated events. He goes beyond and broadens his vision to understand the concerns and desires of the thousands of groups and communities that form the underlying reality of our country. A successful journalist is then able to convey, in his stories and articles about immediate events, this deeper awareness to his audience. This, Ayub Syed did.

These reports, articles, interviews and editorials contained in this book weave a moving picture that brings to life the events and personalities that have shaped the destiny of our country while simultaneously bringing to the surface the larger picture of India's underlying reality.

This book, probably the first of its kind, represents a new approach to the history of modern Indian politics. The contemporary interviews, articles, reports and editorials are a chronological reportage of the events and personalities that have shaped the political history of post-Nehru India. The analysis and perspective provided by the author and the political players contribute to giving the reader a valuable insight into the politics of those important years. The editors have sifted through some eleven hundred articles published in the *Current* weekly. The material thus gleaned is not just a presentation in a chronological order, but an organised and thematic sequence, which brings forth a body of thought and analysis about the burning issues of the day.

Newspapers often represent the first draft of history—they reflect the varied strands of Indian polity and preserve contemporary history. And when the major thrust of any one of them is to focus on issues relating to governance, defined by the leading political, public and governmental personalities of the day, then a collection of such interviews and articles becomes not only a contemporary record but also an objective and critical analysis of the existing system. The author and the subject, the interviewer and interviewee are no longer interlocutors separately articulating mere monologues. They are actors with a personal involvement in what they say and write. Their statements then become a significant interpretation transcending time and place. It is this characteristic, which makes this contribution by the late Ayub Syed, both publishable and readable in print.

Dr. Anees Syed
Dr. Shri Prakash

Acknowledgements

We owe a debt of gratitude to Mr. Inder Malhotra the eminent journalist, whom we are proud to count as a friend, for his valuable advice during the preparation of the book and associating with it by writing the foreword.

To justice P.B. Sawant former chairman of the Press Council of India, our heartfelt thanks for writing a very incisive introduction in spite of his extremely busy schedule.

Our thanks to Mr. Sumit Chakravartty, for allowing us to include the article which Ayub Syed wrote for *Mainstream* in 1970.

We are grateful to Mr. Asif Syed and Mr. Faisal Syed, Directors, *Current* Publications for making available to us all the issues of *Current* weekly for this publication. Our special thanks to Mrs. Jalu Kodia and Mr. Wilson of *Current* Publications for their essential help with computers and preparing the manuscript.

We appreciate and thank Mr. Zohar Furniturewala for designing the covers for both volumes of the book.

Last but not the least our thanks go to Mr. B.P. Garg and Mr. Amit Garg, proprietors of the Gyan Publishing House for doing all in their power to bring out the book. Their colleagues Mr. Preetamji and Mr. Guru Dutt also deserve a special mention for their patient labours in producing the book, as do all others whose names being many cannot be mentioned individually.

—Editors

For

Asif Syed

and

Faisal Syed

Foreword

Few countries in the world are so preoccupied with politics as India is. Way back in 1946 the great British journalist James Cameron had come to this country to cover the Simla Conference of political leaders that the last but one Viceroy, Field-Marshal Lord Wavell, had called to "settle India's future". In one of his earliest dispatches, a memorable one that had also forecast the failure of Wavell's initiative, Cameron had described India as "A Political Place". Four decades later, an American scholar specialising in South Asia was to remark to me that "except for the area within Washington beltway" there was no place in America as intensely political as "even the smallest Indian town".

This may have something to do with the long and hard freedom struggle, under the tremendously inspiring leadership of such titans as Gandhi, Nehru, Patel, Azad et al, as also the parallel movement in the later stages for Pakistan. But whatever the reasons, the material point is that the massive sway of politics in national consciousness is inevitably reflected in its predominance also in journalism. Today, newspapers and magazines cover a host of areas and issues - ranging from environment to human rights and from bonded labour to unbounded corruption, to say nothing of the plight of women and children - that they had generally neglected in the past. "Free market" and the halting advance towards globalisation also claim more than their fair share of newsprint. This may be in keeping with the spirit of the times, encapsulated by Bill Clinton's famous phrase, "it's the economy, stupid". Far more depressing is the print media's descent to prurience and porn, with even the premier papers of yesteryear publishing pictures of scantily clad starlets and fashion models. Of the Page Three journalism, unashamedly propagating the cult of hedonism and consumerism, the less said the better.

However, all this having been said, the fact remains that news and views on politics retain their paramount importance in the eyes of serious readers constituting the bulk of those who buy the paper or the weekly, fortnightly or whatever. And that is where the value of the two volumes of Ayub Syed's selected writings over a period of more than two decades comes in. For Ayub was an archetypal political journalist, both as a correspondent in Delhi and as the forceful and dynamic Editor of the Bombay-based Current. It was there that he made, impressively and with aplomb, a mark that was the envy of many a cognoscenti.

For me to write this brief foreword to the two volumes is not a duty to a departed friend -a rare capacity to offer warm, deep, loyal and lasting friendship was one of Ayub's endearing attributes -.but a privilege. It also gives me an opportunity to stress, especially to the younger readers, the importance of his writings as a source material for future historians in a country that, in spite of being an ancient civilisation, remains appallingly indifferent to history.

Ayub's articles and editorials most painstakingly selected and edited by his historiographer wife, Dr. Anees Syed along with Dr. Shri Prakash and reproduced on the pages that follow - add up to a panoramic portraiture of Indian politics in an extremely important era that was full of high drama, low comedy, vile chicanery and searing tragedy. The story starts with the period in 1973 when Indira Gandhi, after scaling the Olympian heights of power and glory, was on a dismal downhill slide that eventually led to the Emergency, her hammer-blow to Indian democracy. After the 19-month nightmare she called a General Election apparently on her own volition, not under pressure, and predictably lost it humiliatingly.

Exit the Empress and Crown Prince Sanjay, enter the Janata under the leadership of Indira's arch rival, Moraiji Desai, a *bête noire* turned into Nemesis. Few governments have come to power on the crest of such a tidal wave of goodwill as Morarji's; fewer still have collapsed so ignominiously and so fast as it did. It was almost literally crushed by the staggering weight of its incompetence, manic compulsion to persecute rather than prosecute Indira and, above all, the clashing ambitions and implacable hatreds of its three top leaders, riding the party, like old men of the sea. Within 30 months flat, the woman who, in Atal Behari Vajpayee's contemporaneous words, was supposed to have been "consigned to the dustbin of history" was back in power spectacularly.

Ayub has chronicled and commented on these and every other subsequent landmark event, turning point or defining moment forthrightly and sometimes with passion right up to his premature death 24 hours before Republic Day in 1995. To a few of these matters, I will return presently but first a word about the man, his life, time and approach and my own very pleasant association with him is called for.

He was only marginally younger than I am but he joined the troubled and yet exciting trade of journalism considerably later than I did. The reason for this was simple. I had to earn a living immediately after appearing for my BA examination in a good but unknown college in Punjab. He, after his studies in Jamia Millia Islamia Delhi, went to Aligarh Muslim University and then to the Khartoom University in Sudan to research on the Sudanese national movement and then on to the famous Al Azhar University in Cairo. Unlike, Midnight's Children our generation was lucky enough to have witnessed both the last phases of the freedom struggle and the "substantial" redemption of the tryst with destiny. This translated into the ecstasy of independence accompanied by the agony of partition though the latter had the merit of being mutually agreed to. It was not an imposition by any outside power. Bliss was it in that dawn to be alive, but to be young was very heavenly.

Another remarkable feature of that age, not sufficiently remembered, was the attractiveness of what can only be called the Leftist school of thought. It was not necessarily allegiance to the Communist ideology but more a commitment, like Nehru's, to Fabian socialism and to the doctrine of equality, egalitarianism and concern for the poor and the exploited. The magic of this message - now routinely derided - had captivated the youth.

This should explain why Ayub started his career as a journalist with Patriot, a Left-leaning paper that bore the stamp of its remarkable Editor, Edatata Naryanan, just as Ayub was to put his own stamp on Current later. I was then Political Correspondent of The Statesman and he and I met off and on, usually in the company of the much respected Nikhil Chakravartty, the founder-editor of Mainstream. Like Ayub, he too is no more. I was quickly struck by Ayub's friendly and genial personality and by what Nikhil used to call his "instant warmth" in his dealings with "one and all - irrespective of age or position". To which I will add that the sharpest of differences over politics or anything else made no difference to his personal relationships. Sometimes, though only sometimes, he was even respectful of the contrary opinion.

What I found even more remarkable was the ease with which he had taken to political reporting, rather like fish to cool, blue water, the number of friends he had made during a short time and achieved almost free access to political leaders across the political spectrum. I should have known that politics was in Ayub's blood. His father was a freedom fighter. (Ayub volunteered to me the information that the elder Mr. Syed was a regular reader of The Statesman and would be angered by even the slightest delay in the paper's delivery.) One of his uncles was a Congress MP for 20 years. Ayub's own political potential had evidently come to Indira Gandhi's attention. For, one day we suddenly heard that she had given him a Congress ticket for the membership of the M.P. Vidhan Sabha election in 1972.

His Editor, Eadatata, wasn't pleased. He gave Ayub a choice between joining politics and staying in the paper. He chose politics. At that time I found this surprising but not in retrospect. However, call it fate, chance or vagaries of life, but when Ayub went to file his nomination, his name was missing from the electoral rolls. He decided not to return to Patriot but to fly to Bombay where some Congressmen were trying to buy Current from its founder owner and editor, D. F. Karaka, once a doughty fighter whose health was failing by then. Worse, his weekly's circulation and fortunes had by then been virtually destroyed by the formidable and flourishing rival tabloid, Russi Karnjia's Blitz. In one of his eminently readable articles, Ayub has recounted the hilarious story of Current's sale but it is best read in original.

The gloss of whatever ambiguous association some Congressmen might have had on the journal soon wore off and since then Current became "Ayub's own weekly". In Nikhil Chakravartti's words, he "played with the paper as he thought fit. It had an extraordinary career under Ayub. In fact, it reflected the whole spectrum of his interests - from politics to trivialities'. It is a tribute to Ayub's skills that in a relatively short time he not only brought his weekly back to health but also beat Blitz hollow to make Current the country's premier tabloid newsmagazine.

Since I was also in Bombay at that time we saw a lot more of each other, and I enjoyed his gracious and ample hospitality that was becoming something of a legend in the prosperous metro. His home became a meeting point of friends and acquaintances of all political hues and social background. The high and mighty had to rub shoulders with the lowbrows, and the irreverent in the gathering often punctured their inflated egos.

Let me not make the mistake of giving the impression that Ayub was perfect and flawless. None of us ever is. He was human and had his shares of failings, flaws and foibles. A minor one of these was a proclivity to waste his great talent and greater opportunities by getting too closely involved with the fate of an individual politician rather than concentrate on the wider issue at stake. Also, sometimes he could be less than punctilious in the choice of his methods to pursue his perfectly legitimate objectives. To quote Nikhilda again, during his partnership in the course of the Emergency with Rajni Patel - Indira's subedar in Bombay until his inevitable fall from grace - Ayub's circle of "political and financial friends" included the "well-known as well as the notorious -indeed the entire Bombay circuit".

All of us, of course, change our opinions depending on the change in circumstances. In Ayub's case such changes could sometimes be volatile. For instance, he had supported the Emergency and almost everything Indira and Sanjay did then to the hilt. After her defeat in the 1977 poll that he had foreseen clearly, his criticism of her become a tad too sharp, even wounding. In one issue of his weekly, underneath a picture of Indira, he published, in a type so large as to cover half of the front page, just one word: 'LIAR'.

This was the only occasion when I gently remonstrated with him. I told him that the statement she had made had certainly economised with the truth, but surely there were different ways of pointing this out. Ayub gave me his usual, infectious smile, looked me in the eye and said, "Inder, if anything needs to be said, it has to be said loud and clear. Your urbane writing is fine for the editorial columns of The Times of India, but I am fighting a different kind of battle".

It is perhaps needless to say that Indira and Sanjay were not pleased with what Ayub had done. And yet not much later when Ayub had concluded - and said so in his weekly - that the Janata Must Go, he picked up the phone and rang up Sanjay. Indira immediately invited him to the "unkempt, desolate 12 Willingdon Crescent for a talk" that lasted more than two hours.

The decade of the Eighties was exceedingly turbulent, climaxed by Indira Gandhi's assassination and the horrific anti-Sikh riots that followed. Rajiv succeeded his mother within a few hours and soon won a majority in the Lok Sabha that neither Indira nor even Nehru had ever attained. Ayub had the prescience to declare, "Indira Wins Election for Rajiv".

One can go on and on but let me stop after mentioning just one more revealing incident. By 1988, Rajiv had got inextricably embroiled in the allegations about Bofors bribery. He had parted company with not only V. P. Singh but also his two closest confidants, cousin Arun Nehru and crony Arun Singh. V. P. had by this time become the rallying point of all those wanting to oust Rajiv. In that year Ayub instituted an award for the Most Honest Politician. He invited me to join the jury to select the winner. It was headed by Nikhil and included Romesh Thapar.

At the jury's meeting over a sumptuous meal, Ayub was present as both the host and an observer. He did mention though that he would like us to consider, along with other candidates, V.P. Singh. We did not agree and gave the award to Jyoti Basu. Far from being unhappy or disappointed, Ayub applauded the decision and honoured Jyoti babu at a glittering function.

If the Almighty has a "hit list" it is unclear why He put Ayub's name on it. Cancer took his life at a time when he had miles to go and scale even greater heights than he had. V.P. Singh, going to see Ayub after the latter had returned from the United States where he had undergone medical treatment, was startled to find that the man with a "thick flock of hair and full of dynamism" had gone bald and weak. But he was amazed by the keen interest that Ayub showed in current political developments. "His body may have gone sick but Ayub himself was the old lovable self with all his zest", wrote V.P.

This zest permeates all of Ayub's writings included in the two volumes and although journalism can sometimes be ephemeral, most of his work retains its relevance and resonance—and freshness, rather like his memories. Anyone, particularly if interested in politics or journalism or both, will find a rewarding read.

New Delhi, November 19, 2002 — Inder Malhotra

Introduction

What is journalism? What is ideal journalism? Is there a role model for a journalist? These and similar questions will be adequately and positively answered by the varied contents of this book which bring alive the dramatic happenings of the period which has proved a watershed in the history of this country and the life its people. The reporting of the events adequately, commenting on them instructively and educating the reader sufficiently in lucid appealing language, which are the hallmark of good journalism, were the forte of Ayub Syed's writings. They came to him naturally as a part of his born-self and were not acquired either through instruction or imitation. Superficiality, casualness or pedantic ostentation were not of his ilk. He abhorred them as much as he did the non-serious and flippant attitude to any subject. He believed in probing in depth the issues and the events, in collecting first hand information and having authentic version of the things he quoted about, to do which he spared no pains and considered no obstruction as formidable. This straightforward, penetrating and no-nonsense approach though clothed in his amiable personality and suave manners, helped him in getting what he needed without even a demur from widely disparate and even warring sources. His in-depth knowledge of Indian politics from the national to the grass-root level, his intimate grasp of the problems facing the country and the issues involved, his constant touch with the flow of events, and the deep awareness of the past, keen observation of the present and hopeful vision of the future are fully reflected in all his writings and interviews. His penetrating interviews, to say the least, are masterpieces of his insight in the minds and thoughts of the principal actors on the central stage of the times. More than anything else they revealed the current reality and the things to come. His searching, confrontationist and sometimes even accusatory questioning of such diverse personalities as Indira Gandhi, Morarji Desai, Charan Singh, Bahuguna, Jayaprakash Narayan, Bhindranwale, Longowal et al., manifest many of his innate qualities most prominently - the courage of his conviction, the transparency of his heart, the fearlessness in the attempt to find out the truth, the readiness to appreciate the contra positions with equal ease, and yet be amiable to all. It speaks volumes in his favour that even knowing his past and the present views the interviewees never doubted his bonafides and all were accessible to him at any time at his request.

His constant concern for the poor and the down trodden, his devout belief in democratic values and principles and his relentless crusade against corruption and communalism were a part of his character and became more and more ingrained as days passed. He pinned hopes in certain individuals and welcomed and supported governments led by them expecting the much-needed deliverance of the masses from poverty, ignorance and disease, and of the country from authoritarianism, corruption, criminalisation and communalism. But when they failed, and they all did - he was sorely disappointed and spared none from his devastating criticism. He could accurately analyse the current developments and gauge their consequences. Being always abreast of the ground realities, his prognosis rarely failed. He was almost always first to ring the warning bells with his political forecasts scarcely going off the mark.

A journalist need not be learned. He has to be correct. For that, he must have some convictions, and moral and intellectual integrity. Ayub Syed had all this and something more - independence of mind, courage and fearlessness. Money did not lure him, adversity did not deter him and authority did not cower him. He never compromised his principles and conventions. On the other hand, he lambasted those who did it for one or the other gain. All his ideal qualities came to the fore during his stewardship of the Current and were on test when it was going through the vicissitudes on its journey onward. Unfortunately his tribe is rare and is fast dwindling.

The editors have done well to select the contents for Twenty Tumultuous Years: Insights into Indian Polity (1973-1994) from the *Current* published between 1973-1994. They recreate in vivid images, the fast developments of the period through Ayub's pen and his interviews with the main actors on the scene during those momentous times, which shaped the history of the country. Those who lived through this period will be helped to recall to their mind every little happening of the days while the student of history will be happy to find here in one place all he needs to know about the period so lucidly presented to him by an insider's insight and a critic's objectivity. The contents are a rich authentic source of material for the scholar and the layman alike.

The first volume focuses on the years when the difficulties confronting the Indian State's ambitions to develop and modernise a country of many hundred of millions were beginning to surface in an open manner.

The Congress, which during the struggle for independence from British rule had provided a coalitional umbrella for various nationalist currents to combine on a relatively unified platform, had after 1947 acquired a more distinct identity and role as the governing party of India. Between 1947 and 1967 the Congress won a series of national elections on the strength of its reputation as the premier nationalist organisation as well as its strategy of economic development, which was a distinct improvement over the century and a half of British rule over India.

However, while the 3.5 or 4 percent rate of growth which characterised the Nehru years and the subsequent short-lived period of Lal Bahadur Shastri's government was several times more than the 1% average, characteristic of the period of British rule, it was not adequate to mount a decisive attack on poverty in India. Despite the desired egalitarianism of Nehruvian Socialism the fruits of development never did get fully divided amongst the various sections of Indian society. The inequality in the distribution of the gains of economic growth was further exacerbated by the manner in which the ruling interest groups – the domestic industrialists, traders, Kulaks, the administrative bureaucracy, the political parties and mainly the ruling Congress party – creamed off the major share for themselves. And the Congress, which had an unbroken run of election victories until the Samyukta Vidhayak Dal displaced it in some of the States in 1967 and which had been in power for more than two decades at the Centre had become complacent in its habit of ruling, or as the opposition said of 'misruling' India.

By 1969, with the break out of the industrial crisis, it had become clear that the Nehruvian programme had yielded all the gains it could in India's given situation. The immediate response of the State was to try and further extend the home market through measures designed to improve the credit of local industry, the purchasing power of all income earners and enhanced investment in agriculture. However, as the main financier was the State, which had centralised national finance in its hands through Bank Nationalisation and deficit financing, it could not restrain increases in money supply, which fuelled inflation.

Indira Gandhi's radical programme of overcoming or lessening poverty mainly through state-controlled redistribution of existing social wealth by ever higher taxation of the urban rich, trade tariffs, job creation in the public sector and deficit financing resulted in predictable stagflation of the economy and unintentional social unrest. Rising inflation and unemployment caused by the population growth being faster than the economic growth rate needed to generate adequate employment provided the grass root causes for social unrest and political agitation.

It is not at all surprising that the liberal democratic and even the right wing opposition parties made a central issue of the fact that the Congress had failed to ensure that benefits meant for the poor reached the poor. They united under the banner of Jayaprakash Narayan's movement for bringing about a 'Total Revolution', to abolish corruption, casteism, capitalism and the Congress.

The fact that the opposition to Mrs. Gandhi's regime and policies came mainly from parties characterised as Rightist was due mainly to the support she was able to mobilise from the Left as well as the State oriented nature of her policies.

The movement led by Jayaprakash Narayan which mobilised mass protest precisely on the issues of official corruption, authoritarianism and non-implementation of programmes also facilitated the entry of new layers of social groups from among the Backward Classes into protest politics and the electoral arena. This mass protest later gave rise to the Janata Party, which reflected the far-flung and sometimes inchoate nature of the ideas and policies of JP's Total Revolution.

Confronted with a popular reaction to her government's shortcomings, Indira Gandhi failed to put together an alternative social support structure. Perhaps she did not think it was necessary. Instead in a counterproductive attempt to restore her credibility Indira Gandhi imposed a National Emergency. Guided in part by her younger son Sanjay Gandhi's desire for a loyal personal following Indira Gandhi demanded and in large measure obtained, what she termed a committed judiciary and bureaucracy. The golden rule of Gandhian politics – means are as important as the ends sought – was forgotten in the rush of outmanoeuvering an aggressive opposition.

Autarchy, blinkered economic policies, corruption and inept administration had blunted the government's attack on poverty, and burgeoning unemployment now provided an army of discontents with the motivation to take part in opposition organised agitations. The imposition of Emergency only made matters worse because it diverted more resources for maintaining law and order, and Mrs. Gandhi relied much more on the bureaucracy to implement development and welfare programmes. The sort of excesses, which marked the Nasbandi or the Population Control programmes, could happen only because the bureaucracy had enhanced its own powers and also muzzled the media through the imposition of censorship, shutting both its own eyes and ears to the grim situation.

Fortunately for India and Indian Democracy, Mrs. Indira Gandhi never intended to institutionalise the Emergency Powers she had appropriated. Once her intelligence agencies assured her that Emergency had restored discipline, improved the implementation of anti-poverty measures and also had made her popular, she was willing to call elections, which she no doubt hoped to win.

However, this is exactly how she became the victim of her own information system, which had shut out the independent and the critical media. The logic of imposing state control over all and sundry undid her government at the Centre. This misjudged experiment succeeded in doing what even India's defeat in the 1962 war with China had not done – a non-Congress government was elected at the Centre for the first time since 1947.

There can be no denying the truth that the Janata Party was born from the womb of a dynamic Indian democracy wherein the people exercised their right to protest their grievances, to build a political alternative to the Congress party and to provide themselves with economic succour and new social and political leadership. It was equally true that as a product of a tremendous social and political ferment, the Janata Party brought together many political stalwarts from different social groups and ideologies, opening up possibilities of liberation from traditional inequalities and giving hope of a new political order based on equality and justice.

The defeat of the Congress, it was hoped, would provide an occasion for the maturing of the democratic processes in India and it was expected that the elected non-Congress government at the Centre would complete its term for five years and take the country forward. However the diverse social groups that the Janata Party encompassed, ensured that as a political formation it would function according to several common denominators concerning various issues.

As with most political formations of a large size, the process of producing a consensus was an involved one within the Janata Party. Moreover, there was little assurance that a consensus once formed would prevent leaders from speaking in different voices.

The conflicting views within the Janata leadership on the question of how to deal with Mrs. Indira Gandhi in the post-emergency scenario ranged from Jagjivan Ram's statement that he was 'against witch-hunting' to that of Charan Singh's proclamation that, 'Indira will be arrested on criminal charges'. Also the difference of perceptions on the major economic and governance issues between Prime Minister Morarji Desai and ministers like Charan Singh, Raj Narain, Jagjivan Ram and H.N. Bahuguna made decision-making difficult.

Absence of both, a cohesive long-term programme and a short-term strategy made the Janata Party a house far more divided than the Congress ever was.

The phenomenon of electoral victors being concerned about the early return of the politically vanquished is a rare one. Apprehensions entertained by the Janata leaders vis-à-vis Indira Gandhi and Indira Congress were because they could see that she was down but not out. In retrospect, sending Mrs. Gandhi to jail turned the tide in her favour once again. It was one thing to defeat her on the strength of the anti-Congress wave in 1977. It was another to keep her contained by using those very means that the Janata leaders had earlier vehemently criticised her for using against them.

The Indira Congress made it amply clear that it did not consider losing one election as a major blow and intended to return to power soon. What is more, Mrs. Gandhi blamed the excesses committed during the emergency on the over-enthusiasm of bureaucrats and claimed that she had of her own accord ended the Emergency and called for elections.

The very instability of the Janata-Jansangh coalition, the absence of consensus on a common programme and the lack of a Parliamentary majority which made the minority Janata government dependent on Left support from the outside to remain in power undermined the self-confidence of the first non-Congress government at the Centre. Two years of Janata rule had also taken the shine off their newness and exposed the fallacy that a mere change of government could by itself reform or change the system for the better. This required an effort of a different magnitude.

The Janata party's ideological moorings were tied to a very liberal and decentralising notion of Federalism and the autonomy of the states. Yet once it had formed a government at the Centre, the Janata government used Article 356 to dismiss the Congress governments in the states and install its own men to hold mid-term elections.

In the Indian situation all new economic thinking must enhance growth quickly to enlarge the cake, which the government can help to distribute to the poor. This is one dictum no government can forget. The Janata Party persisted with policies of deficit financing, creating conditions for inflation. This is one of the major reasons for its inability to prevent the return of Mrs. Gandhi to power. Within a short time the government's unstable policies saw a change of Prime Minister but no real change of direction in economic policy.

It is natural for any new party, inexperienced in governance and yet desirous of securing its social and political base to concentrate on fulfilling its main promises and rewarding its supporters. If the supporters are numerous, disparate and also new to power, the rewards expected would naturally far exceed the rewards granted. However, if the promises are as grand as the Total Revolution – a society without inequality and injustice, a state without a bureaucracy and a nation without corruption – their non-performance brings about proportionately greater disillusionment. The disillusionment of Jayprakash Narayan with the way his Total Revolution was forgotten once the Janata Party was in power was in fact 'the tragedy of being J.P.'

The Congress (I) managed quickly to become a factor in the coalition politics of those days and finally found its way to holding mid-term elections. The astute politician that she was, Mrs. Indira Gandhi sided with one Janata faction against another until their shortcomings and their lack of unity were exposed for all to see. Coming to power proved more expensive for the Janata than staying in the opposition.

Being out of power for a few years tested Indira Gandhi's political acumen. Her objective of winning the election was made easier by the divisions in the Janata Party. At the same time, the firm stand she adopted on issues of opposing casteism and communalism helped her to overcome the opprobrium she had earned by imposing Emergency. She criticised the new regime for not being able to protect law and order and fight fundamentalism as well as terrorism. At the same time she depended too much on Sanjay Gandhi to build a disciplined organisation. This was too huge a task to be completed in a short time and certainly not by the means adopted by Sanjay Gandhi, who loved mainly to gather together a lot of dedicated personal followers rather than pursue a developmental agenda of his own. Mrs. Gandhi at any rate made it clear that when and if she took charge of the government, she did not intend to return simply to a state centred agenda, but begin to give more room for the private sector to play its part in development. However, she still had to work out a strategy to tackle nepotism, black marketing and corruption. Even while the Cong (I) was pondering on these problems the Charan Singh government fell, and elections were on the way once again.

Victory in mid-term elections in 1980 brought Mrs. Gandhi back to power and she ran her full term. It is easier getting into power than staying there or making use of it effectively. It was the latter issue, which occupied the days of Mrs. Gandhi's government when she returned to power. Once in power the Congress also slowed down on efforts at revamping the party at the organisational level.

By 1984 however, the principal problem of managing the contradictions of the Congress Party became too acute to handle. Not only were there revolts by state units and within state units in Andhra Pradesh and Karnataka; the rise of regional leaders, parties and coalitions started eating at the local power base of the Congress. The issue of further redistribution of power between the centre and the states cropped up. Khalistanis in

Punjab and the Terrorists in Kashmir were becoming extremely active. The Assam Gana Parishad and the All Assam Students Union were leading a militant movement in Assam. And finally the use of force against Sikh fundamentalists - Operation Blue Star again highlighted the foolhardiness of using wrong means to achieve the right goals.

After the death of Sanjay Gandhi, the question of a young leader for the Congress (I) became an important one. Rajiv Gandhi would not be accepted as a leader until he himself won a Parliamentary election both for himself and the Congress Party as a whole. The first condition he fulfilled by winning the election to the Lok Sabha from Amethi. He also prepared to lead the Congress by becoming one of its General Secretaries. Being tested in electoral politics before getting recognition as a leader gave a stamp of authenticity to Rajiv Gandhi's political efforts and undermined his detractors who only saw the triumph of the dynastic principle in his elevation.

Indira Gandhi's death at the hands of her own Sikh security guards further added to the trauma of the Congress setting the stage for the arrival of Rajiv Gandhi as Prime Minister and Congress leader. Giani Zail Singh decided to invite him to take over as Prime Minister, the Cabinet and the Congress approved and Rajiv Gandhi, the leader, was very much on his own.

The saga and spectacle of sacrifice has not only provided inimitable substance to Indian folklore but can become a candid political force in contemporary times. This was more than evident in the ground swell of sympathy for the Congress during the General Elections held in the aftermath of the assassination of Mrs. Indira Gandhi. Her Party led by her son scored the most impressive electoral victory achieved by any political party since Independence – almost a two-thirds majority in the Lok Sabha, 400 out of 543 seats and slightly more than 50% of the votes cast.

The Congress (I) during the tenure of Rajiv Gandhi as Prime Minister decided to use its electoral majority to launch its own programme of liberalisation. The struggle to renew and rebuild the Congress organisation at the grassroots was to be handed over to a new generation of leaders, which would rely less on State control and more on market forces and consensus building. When it did so its expectation was that liberalisation would yield quick economic growth and rich political dividend by stealing the thunder from parties like the BJP who had long demanded a greater role for the private sector in the Indian economy.

Basking in the glow of appreciation in the local and international media, the Congress thought that issues like the fight against corruption and poverty did not need to be highlighted as much as during the days of Indira Gandhi. Whether or not Rajiv Gandhi had anything to do with the Bofors scandal and several others – the mere fact that these happened while his government was in power, turned media and public opinion as well as some of his key ministers against him. The reaction to the Bofors scandal, the sudden and massive rise in petrol prices announced by Rajiv Gandhi's government, the sharp deterioration in his relations with President Giani Zail Singh, all contributed to the major electoral defeats of the Congress in Kerala and West Bengal. This made more and more Congressmen hostile to the idea of the liberalisation platform. Any strategy of development which could not at the same time win elections and keep the Party in power was bound to earn the ire of those who were in the business of "politics" and not the campaign for nation-building and national integration. Given the cancerous spread of corruption, a social environment existed in which the Prime Minister could be and in fact was held accountable for a scam involving the Central government. The media and public ire at the Bofors scandal showed up the popular impatience with corruption in high places and rightly condemned it as the source of all other corruption afflicting the administrative system.

The phenomenon of 'criminalisation' of politics that was later to cost him his life and which afflicted the Congress as well provoked extreme reactions to Rajiv Gandhi's efforts at promoting economic and political reforms. As these articles and interviews in the present work show, one Congress leader was quoted as comparing a socially progressive leader like V.P. Singh being "just like a Cobra. He was fed on milk by the Congress but is now injecting poison into the body politic of the country only a man like me can kill him." [*Current,* 9.9.1989, p. 2] Rajiv Gandhi's reforms challenged "political" interests at a fundamental level, they sought to consolidate the hold of a small politico-administrative-economic elite spread over the Indian State, and these steps drew an incredulous criticism cutting across party lines.

The end of Volume I brings to a close what legitimately can be called – The Indira Era. From 1989 a new and innovative phase begins in Indian politics, which is dealt with in Volume II.

Volume II deals with the ongoing political processes that challenged the political order built around a system of one-party dominance and the maturing of electoral democracy leading to the emergence and establishment of a coalition state at the centre.

This wide ranging transformation is to be seen in the growing regionalisation of the national polity, radical democratisation of the national question and the consequent shift towards federalism, decentralisation and grass-roots assertion of the mass of the people.

Already in 1956, the victory of a left front in Kerala and the formation of the Samyukta Vidhayak Dal governments in the states since 1967 while the Congress government ruled at the Centre had demonstrated that the Indian electorate could install different governments according to local aspirations and national ideological perceptions as they evolved.

The basis for the rise of regional parties was definitely laid by the people's reaction to the 'Congress System' – An over centralised, highly bureaucratic control of the state apparatus from Delhi. This was aided, in no small measure, by the non-emergence of an all-India Opposition or a national alternative to the Congress party.

The CPI (M) led Left Front had attained the sheen and attributes of a national phenomenon and a national party because of its two-decade hold over West Bengal and Kerala. However, to make its presence felt on a national level the Left had to fit into equations with other parties on the basis of a common minimum programme. This involved a large dose of political pragmatism and compromise on its economic agenda. It also lifted the curtain on the Left's weaknesses and its inability to break out of its regional sequestration.

The political preferences of the states and their democratic movements have been conditioned by the emergence of a distinct political make up that centres around their linguistic, cultural and regional specificity. These ground realities and the ambitions of regional leaders and their fledgling regional parties come alive through interviews done with Dev Raj Urs, Sharad Pawar, N.T.R., Rama Krishna Hegde, Jyoti Basu and his ministers in Bengal. These leaders translated their political and economic aspirations into demands for federalism as enshrined in the Indian Constitution and asserted that the strong states ensured a strong centre. Others, like Bal Thackeray, organised political parties on narrow regionalism combined with communal and sectarian politics.

Democratic experiments and regional aspirations for greater autonomy by Punjab, Assam and Kashmir merit a separate chapter consisting of articles, editorials and interviews taken on the frontlines of the action. The politics of manipulation getting the better of the politics of fulfilling the inherent logic of democracy and justice, denial of a just distribution of economic development and social enrichment led to a growing lack of confidence in the performance of the parliamentary and party institutions. The decline of secular and modernising beliefs produced a major detraction in the name of religion, culture, ethnicity and the like. The Punjab question is embedded in the growing political and cultural resentment of the Sikh community, which is distinctive in a religious sense. However distasteful may be the language in which extremists have chosen to couch them, their various demands particularly those affecting employment opportunities were genuine. Instead of taking steps to mitigate poverty and solve the political tangle the State looked at social and political issues as law and order problems and became increasingly repressive. The armed attack on the Golden Temple and the genocide of the Sikhs following Mrs. Gandhi's assassination did not solve the problems. Guns do not solve the problem.

Kashmir represents a complex of problems – dwindling resources for economic development, demand for different degrees of relative autonomy being pursued by people and restructuring of relationship between the Congress elite and the emergent non/anti Congress elite. It was the arrogance of the state that ignored Mir Qasim's plea that 'by our behaviour and conduct we must reassure the people that their identity and democratic aspirations expressed through the ballot will be respected in full measure'. Democracy is a participatory system based on the principles of equality, freedom, justice and reason – unfortunately this was ignored. A purely political problem cannot be solved by military or para-military forces and a durable solution of the situation in Kashmir remains a mirage.

'Little nationalism turned chauvinist' is an apt description of the Assam politics and society during these two decades. By the mid 1970s, reorganisation of North East India cost Assam its tribal regions and position of Greater Assam. The extensive demographic changes in the Brahmaputra valley, the shrinking home land made elite Assamese increasingly apprehensive of the possible Bengali domination politically and economically. The recurring ethnic conflicts, perceived danger to ethnic Assamiya culture, anger against Delhi further fuelled the turbulent politics of North East. The role played by the militants, student and political groups – All Assam Students Union, United Liberation Front, the Bodo Movement in the agitation that lasted for six years. They are opening the nationality and 'Foreigners' question, demanding detention, disenfranchisement and deportation of Bangladeshi and Nepali migrants - and that the movement remained steadfast comes out alive from these interviews and reports.

Since the mid 1980's there were signs of fundamental transformation in the terrain of democratic governance, of the shifting basis of national politics and changes in the ground rules of electoral democracy. Sections of the urban middle class with their liberal democratic consciousness were getting alienated from the Congress Party and its leadership on the issues of political authoritarianism, corruption and criminalisation of politics.

Segments of Semi-Urban and rural voters with their changing social combination and new socialist awareness were turning away from traditional centripetal policies and were looking for an alternative political agenda; further various groups coming from marginal/subaltern strata of Indian society were surging forward for their place in the political arena of national politics.

Added to it was the clear and definitive assertion of regional consciousness, which was demanding a federal restructuring of the political landscape. The national scene represented challenges for democratic and radical forces to get into the act.

The rise of V.P. Singh had galvanised the opposition to the Congress and prepared the ground for a new political order – the coalition state. The National Front emerged as a new political alternative, the standard bearer of coalition politics. The elections of 1989 were in a way a referendum for an alternative agenda of democratic governance, which would be people oriented, secular and linked with distributive justice. The coalition state would be a principal mechanism of coordinating the "Pro-People" politics of various regional groups and parties representing the socially disadvantaged section. V.P. Singh failed to achieve all this as his government fell after ten months. The crucial decisive step that V.P. Singh took to implement the Mandal Commission Report was a masterstroke and is a tangible gain for the people. It created a trend towards the overcoming of social injustices – rights for Dalits and backward classes, now has the support of practically all political parties – and for diminishing the gap between social reality and political power.

One of the key dimensions of the new phase of coalition politics is the growing demand for and accord of decentralisation and autonomy and financial powers to the states and a broadening of the basis of Indian democracy. Midterm elections held more often, although expensive give the people a greater say in the running of their own affairs. The instability of the Indian state on the political surface reflects nothing else but the inner morphology of growing and unsatisfied social expectation, the need for much greater development and the just distribution of its benefits to the people. "The B.J.P. will also change and most likely in the right direction. It will remain an important rightist force but may drop the Ram Card in favour of Roti and more Roti – It will certainly make an attempt to broad-base itself by attempting to woo the minorities and the Harijans into its fold." (Why be coy about coalitions? Edit 4.5.1991). This simple truth has more force behind it than much complex speculation about coalition politics being a product of the rejuvenations of caste and communal politics.

The key to the riddle of unstable and volatile coalition politics in India lies in going down on the straight economic road of development, social welfare & secularism. This indeed is the message of Ayub Syed's writings as a journalist.

The political culture of "Public Functionaries" becoming a threat to the rule of law by exploiting the social and economic insecurities of the marginal sections of society is not the only sordid aspect of contemporary Indian polity; the deliberate introduction of religious fundamentalism as a powerful deteriorating agent into the body politic being the other. For winning an election most democratic parties have made compromises with religious fundamentalists and the consequences of this politics of compromise has been the growing communal divide in the country. The "pragmatic" communalism of the Congress and the programmatic communalism of the RSS-BJP combine have played havoc with the secular content of Indian Democracy.

The last two chapters provide thumbnail sketches of this politics of obscurantism, hate and fear. Illustrated by the shameful compromise on the elementary rights of indignant Muslim women in the Shah Bano affair and above all the malignancy of the Ram Janam Bhoomi - Babri mosque crisis.

Only a passionate and keen student of social, political and economic life of this country could have dealt with the panorama of the developments during the eventful period so ably. While reading this account whether through the editorials, or the interviews, one constantly carries the impression that Ayub was almost an aorta of the happenings and one of the actors in the field. He takes the reader with him, infecting him with his excitement, curiosity, hope as well as disappointment. The arrangements of the contents make the book readable like a novel with the successive unfolding of one dramatic event after another, narrated in inimitable style that was Ayub's. It is a live history made livelier and absorbing by a model of a journalist. What the world of journalism and the people thirsty for authentic in-depth information of the developments that affect their life have lost in his death, will be much piquantly realized by them by a reading of this most imaginative compilation and collation of the fascinating, yet penetrative pouring of the head and the heart of one who comes alive and kicking through them. No, Ayub Syed is not dead. He lives with us and will forever live with us through these vivacious writings.

December 4, 2002 P.B. Sawant

I

DEMOCRACY MY FOOT!

1

Indira Gandhi: Issues Before and During the Emergency Years

A. Agenda for government and Party

Choices before Indira Gandhi

I have been closely following the various theses advanced by my esteemed friend Dr. Jai Dev Sethi regarding the current state of affairs in the country.

The major weakness of his argument is his intense concentration on attaching too much importance to an individual who happens to be the leader of the largest political party and also the Prime Minister of the country at a time when its political future appears uncertain.

The snag is that he holds her the central cause of this uncertainty or what he calls 'instability'—by deliberately ignoring the interplay of forces. It has gone beyond the control of an individual or a single party.

There is so much gloom and intellectual demoralisation in his cliche-ridden cataloging her failure that an accepted balanced approach cannot be easily discerned. After reading his indictment of Smt. Gandhi one sees ominous and dark clouds hanging low over the unfortunate country and its hapless people.

Dr. Sethi is apprehensive of "polarisation" yet he is keen to see a period of 'consolidation' agreed upon by the warring Centrist political parties. How can these be consolidation in the absence of some sort of polarisation. Moreover, the Centrist factions are bound to face elimination whether it is consolidation or polarisation. Only the parties of the Left and the Right can accelerate such a process and Dr. Sethi has conveniently ignored this very important factor.

He has brushed aside the nationalisation of banks as an insignificant act which is outside the general pattern of political activity. Only an ivory tower academician can afford to ignore the tremendous impact of one of the most drastic economic steps taken so far. It has undoubtedly set a certain political pattern so much so that even the Rightist parties like the Jana Sangh are obliged to remodel their economic policies.

That a radical economic step can stir the masses of the country has been taken note of by the Rightist parties with a mass base and aspirations to share power. It is a fact that some of the fundamental or startling political and economic changes have been made in democratic countries including India when the rulers were pushed to the wall.

What he poses as popular questions and seeks their indirect answers are in fact no posers. They are just queries. First reshuffling of the cabinet is a democratic process and a Prime Minister cannot have the same cabinet especially at a time when group loyalties are in a state of flux. In fact, the British Prime Ministers have been more ruthless with their cabinet colleagues than any of ours. The reshuffle of the cabinet is not a major policy decision. It is made with a view to execute the policies decided by the leaders of the ruling party. A minister who holds views contrary to the one held by the Prime Minister has no choice but to quit.

Secondly, Dr Sethi's insistence on her formulating "new economic policies", betrays his ignorance of the background of the 10-Point Programme. If implemented honestly and thoroughly, it can bring about a desired change or at least pull the country out of the economic stalemate. Both economic and political changes are slow, though what we need is some sort of intensification and a will to see them through.

Our misfortune has not been a lack of planning but the bureaucratisation of the plans at the execution level. The plans ought to have come as the result of popular acceptance. They ought not to have been given the impression of imposition. No plan can attain its object in the face of popular apathy.

Dr. Sethi's arguments are the reflection of his intense academic approach to a very stimulating situation in the country. With Jawaharlal Nehru's death, a historic phase came to an end. The one significant development is that the process of decision making has undergone a basic change. Nehru did not face the multiple ideological challenges.

The process of fragmentation had begun in the Congress the day it assumed power. The split could not become inevitable as the prospects of sharing power or losing power at the centre or in the states did not exist. Powerful individuals who disagreed with Nehru's policies dropped out and were lost in the wilderness.

Smt. Gandhi took to, what he calls, the 'balancing game' as soon as she realised that the prospects of losing power had compelled the groups with various denominations to search for allies outside the framework of the parent organisation. She alone cannot be held responsible for the split of the party, though she was not keen to preserve the dead, amorphous body in its original shape.

Smt. Gandhi is not a saint. Had she been one, the country would have got rid of her long ago. But she is perhaps the one politician who could anticipate the events in order to perpetuate her leadership. The act of perpetuating leadership is again no sin in politics, provided it does not entail coercion or lead to violence.

The split in the Congress was thus the logical outcome of the changing pattern of our politics and not as Dr. Sethi would like us to believe, the direct result of the contradictions between her strategy and the interest of the power structure. And what is this mythical 'power-structure'? Can it be located in precise terms?

Further political fragmentation is inevitable, but to contend that it will be entirely due to her 'strategy of manipulating balances' is to attach too much importance to an individual. A clash between her and the 'Young Turks' might take place if she fails to maintain the 'balance', but its shape cannot be so easily predicted. However, one fails to understand why and how will it be the graveyard of the entire political elite?

Dr. Sethi's charge that violence or instability in the country is generated due to her 'strategy' is an academic imagination run wild. The causes of violence and instability have rather deeper roots than the sheer creation of an individual. Has India been free from the threat of violence or instability in the pre-Indira period? I believe she has done a unique service to her party and the country by destroying what he calls 'the established consensual and plural system at the top' which, to borrow his terminology, represented the 'static power-structure'.

It was a highly undemocratic, authoritarian system. It had culminated in 'bossism'. A political party facing popular democratic challenge can ill-afford to stick to obsolete methods. The Congress is no more the national movement. It has been reduced to the status of a political party and as such it has to bring about certain organisational changes. That Smt. Gandhi has so far been unable to achieve desirable results is a different matter. The important thing to note is that if the Congress does not keep pace with the changing political pattern it will die a fragmented death.

To assume that the split and her 'strategy' have unleashed the forces of 'populism' or 'violent pluralism' is to indict an individual for the ills of the systems. Dr. Sethi is no doubt exercising his democratic right by accusing her of enlisting Leftist support not because 'she is progressive' but because they have certain ulterior motives.

His strident anti-leftism has led him to despise the Communists for favouring her 'populist' policies. He appears to be deliberately avoiding to enlighten us on the extremely grave consequences of the similar populist designs of the Rightist parties. What would he call the collection of half a million people from all over the country on the streets of Delhi for a totally superfluous issue of cow? Which is better: to enlist mass support on the issue of bank nationalisation or herding the naked Sadhus and invoking them to go violent?

The Communists have held larger demonstrations in front of Parliament and the newspaper reports were that they were disciplined, peaceful and dignified despite the legitimacy of their demands. But were it not the Rightists who attempted to enact a *Reichstag* at the very first opportunity? Smt. Gandhi has perhaps an elementary political sense in choosing her allies.

Mainstream, 02.05.1970.
pp. (35-36)

Revamp Congress as tool for progress
Indira alone can save us

The country is in the throes of an unprecedented popular discontent. The common man, the architect of the ruling party's massive victory in 1971, is fast losing faith in the government's capability to fulfill the promises made four years ago. The dream that the people of India saw with the unequivocal ascendancy of the post-split Congress has shattered. Or was it a hallucination?

The credibility gap between the people and the government is widening, it is becoming unbridgeable. The ominous shadows of inflation loom over this great country with tremendous resources. Spiralling prices, acute shortage of essential commodities, dislocation of the public distribution system, hoarding, corruption, blackmarket and the parallel economy that black money runs with impunity have brought the country to the verge of a virtual collapse.

It has bred frustration. There is tension in the minds of men. Uncertainty pervades the national ethos. The industrialist is sore and indignant. The shortage of raw material, hackneyed financial policies, high taxation, and the seething labour unrest have blighted production. The small entrepreneur smarts under a sense of insecurity. The desired protection he needs from the official agencies is lacking. He is apprehensive of being gobbled by the big sharks. Hundreds of small industrial units have ground to a halt.

Strikes, bandhs, lockouts, power shortage, lack of coordination among various economic ministries and organisations, red tapism, erratic licensing policies and the devil—may care attitude of the woodenheaded bureaucracy have resulted in stagnation on the industrial front. Our rate of growth hovers around the freezing point, the foreign exchange reserves have touched rock bottom. With four-fifths of the total export earnings spent on importing petrol, the foreign exchange reserves are likely to be soon wiped out.

The working class nurtures a grievance of being let down, ignored and sold to what its professional leaders call 'perpetual capitalist bondage." The atmosphere of hostility between the employer and the employee has increased.

While the urban sector is facing ruin, rural India has also been antagonised. The landowner is defiant, he is in a violent mood. The Khedut Sangh has intensified the class war in Gujarat and it will have its repercussions elsewhere. The landless have not received the land promised to them. They feel cheated. Half-hearted land reforms have proved a big hoax. The government failed to carry conviction with the producer of the soundness of its grain procurement policy. Powerful elements in the ruling party openly sabotaged the nationalisation of the grain trade and forced the party High Command to go back on the issue of rice trade takeover. The Food Corporation of India, one of the largest public sector organisations, stinks with corruption.

The banks, whose nationalisation gave a great fillip to the sagging Congress morale in 1969, have become dens of corruption and nepotism. Bank managers have become like grand Moghuls. A thorough probe would reveal the extent and depth of corruption in this core sector. The functioning of the nationalised banks needs drastic changes and stricter control by the political authority.

Students and youth are yet another major segment of the population which nurse a grievance. They feel let down and ignored. Despite the realisation that the present education system is the legacy of the colonial era no effective steps have been taken to replace it with a system in tune with the growing needs of modern India. The universities are no better than teaching shops; some of them are worse than the badly managed factories. They churn out millions of Young men to whom life outside the campus is a pathless desert.

The number of unemployed youth has touched the astronomical figure of 80 millions. It is nearly 15 per cent of our total population. This will increase to 100 million by the end of the next year.

There is no end to our economic woes. We are undoubtedly passing through the worst economic crisis since independence. Our social and economic life is hanging by a thread.

The policies laid down by the ruling party are basically sound. The concept of mixed economy is not the gift of one person. It has emerged over the years through a national consensus. Despite pressures from the Right and the Left it should be admitted that the only alternative to this policy is either fascist dictatorship or totalitarianism.

We have failed only in the implementation. The party which framed these policies lacks the will to implement them. In a recent interview Mrs. Gandhi expressed her awareness of this basic and most vital factor. She agreed that the post-split Congress could not rise to the expectations of the people. It continues to "function in a rather flabby way".

The one and the most effective way to refurbish the government image and rejuvenate the ruling party is to purge it of elements who have no faith in its policies. The careerists, the blackmarketeers, the speculators, the *thugs* and the opportunists will have to be weeded out. So far, the party has relied on the bureaucracy to implement its policies. It will have to place great reliance on its activists and trained cadre to shoulder the gigantic task of fulfilling its promises.

Ultimately the responsibility is that of the unquestioned leader of the party and the country, Mrs. Indira Gandhi. The people may have lost faith in the Congress but she continues to enjoy their confidence. She is their only hope and she alone can perform this major operation.

Current, 19.01.1974.
pp. (1)

Explosive situation
we are perched on a powder keg

Seething mass discontent has created an explosive situation in the country. Galloping prices, non-availability of essential commodities, hoarding, black-marketing and black money have given rise to a political and economic crisis of vast dimensions.

The government has singularly failed to rise to the expectations of the people to provide them with the bare minimum. The ruling party, which won a massive mandate from the people, is cracking under its own weight. Factionalism and groupism have torn it asunder. Congressmen out of power have been challenging congressmen in power. The lust for power has made them totally oblivious to the disaster ahead.

Gujarat has provided the spectacle of an internecine war among congressmen. The worst enemy of a congressman today is a congressman. It is balderdash to accuse the weak, disunited, frustrated and rudderless opposition. The ruling party should own up its responsibility for its sins of omission and commission. Its leaders should show the courage of the Mahatma; they should admit that they blundered.

What has shocked the country most is the involvement of the ruling party in giving protection to the Guilty Men, who have played havoc with the nation's economy. The situation has not, we feel, still gone beyond control. If the party in power does not act soon, India will be embroiled in a turmoil.

As we said two weeks ago, Mrs. Indira Gandhi alone can act and save the nation from the impending disaster. There is strong indication that she will not allow the country to sink. She will act with the boldness and courage for which the people hold her in high esteem.

In this issue, two controversial Congress leaders, both with a radical, socialist background, speak to 'Current' readers. Both appear disillusioned.

Mr. Mohan Dharia, Union minister of state for Planning, has threatened to resign his office if the situation does not improve soon. He has suggested certain concrete steps to arrest further deterioration in the economy.

Mr. Rajni Patel, President of the Bombay Pradesh Congress Committee, and of late the target of vehement attacks by his antagonists, has also made confessions. He has expressed apprehension about the explosive situation in Bombay, the metropolis of India.

Bombay is perched on a powder keg. The ruling party has hardly taken note of the grim warnings which are being hurled at it from the chawls and dens of poverty. It has found a traditional method of facing the challenge—the ruthless and brutal use of force by the most hated element of society—the police.

Mr. Rajni Patel admits "that the Maharashtra government has allowed the impression to gain ground that it has been lax in the enforcement of law. There is an impression created that the administration is prone to adopt double standards in the use of force to maintain order."

Bombay must remain the exemplary cosmopolitan city that it has been, as a symbol of the progress and advancement we have attained since independence, he said.

"Stringent action to curb *goondaism* against minorities and greater protection to the weaker sections who are subjected to a reign of terror is called for."

Goondaism is no substitute for political action. "The harassment and open intimidation of petty traders, hawkers and even householders leading a peaceful life, has been reported in increasing numbers. In suburbs like Vikhroli and Bhandup, there have been large-scale terrorisation of peaceful citizens merely on the ground that they hail from South India. Unruly elements have made travel in suburban trains at night a nightmare for some people."

"All this hardly rebounds to the credit of the administration in Bombay which had till now earned the reputation of one of the best in the country."

"All the good name it has earned is likely to be besmirched if it fails to ensure minimum protection to its citizens, to enable them to lead a peaceful life without humiliation and fear," he said.

"The intolerance that is shown to South Indian communities in Bombay, is a slur on the traditional large-heartedness and generosity of the people of Bombay and Maharashtra. This state, and more particularly, Bombay city, has prospered with the unstained cooperation and active participation of people from all parts of India. The events of the past few weeks have tarnished the profound image of Bombay as the model for the rest of the country in every walk of life."

Mr. Rajni Patel conceded that the government had its own difficulties "and a host of pressures to resist and mollify." It could not, however, ignore the fact that various sections of people in the city have been agitated over various problems they have had to face in recent months.

"Seething discontent threatens to erupt in various ways in different pockets," Mr. Patel warned. While it may be impossible for the administration to take care of all these factors simultaneously "the bare minimum any civilised government could do is to ensure that peace-loving citizens should be enabled to lead a life free from fear and want."

Asked if he could suggest a solution to the intimidation faced by the linguistic minorities in Bombay, Mr. Patel said: "only stringent action by the administration could check hooliganism and violence. But it is really the people who must come together and organise to protect the people, especially the minorities. All progressive, democratic people must think in these terms," he stressed.

Referring to the frequent clashes in the Worli chawls between Scheduled Castes and Caste Hindus, Mr. Patel said it was not merely a law and order problem. The Harijans have been suffering indignities and social ostracism for centuries. They are now in revolt against the perpetration of grave injustices and atrocities. They are in revolt against the reformist ideas.

The Dalit Panthers, he pointed out, are a bunch of conscious youths with the right ideas. They do have a real sense of grievance and efforts must be made to remove the cause of their grievances, rather than tackling the symptoms.

"It is no use merely talking about the weaker sections: greater effort must be made to ensure social and economic justice to them, which alone will ensure real equality for them."

Asked to what extent he or the BPCC could go to ameliorate their grievances, Mr. Patel said: "I am prepared to help them. They have my sympathy, though sometimes I feel that their energies are misdirected."

"What have you to say about the Congress defeat in the Lok Sabha by-election from the city?" We asked.

"It was symptomatic of the vehement voter protest against high prices, shortages, and the daily irritations faced by citizens. There was also the suspicion among the people that the Congress had, against its own declared principles, entered into an alliance with the Shiv Sena. The boycott of the poll by the Harijans at the behest of the Dalit Panthers was a contributory factor."

"Wasn't there a tacit understanding with the Shiv Sena?"

Mr. Patel: "We have made it clear that there was no understanding with the Shiv Sena at all. The public declarations made by some leaders of that organisation, soliciting help for the Congress candidate as being the best of the worst in the constituency, did strengthen the people's suspicions. True, the BPCC did not spurn the offer of support from that organisation. It would not have been strategically advisable to reject voluntary offers of support."

The BPCC President warmed up: "The BPCC, as a socialist, democratic and secular organisation is against any form of parochialism, fascism or narrow vested interests. It can have no truck with communal and parochial organisations."

Speaking about the acute shortage of essential commodities, he said. "It is an irony that we have had a bumper harvest, and yet not enough food to go round."

His solution was: "The state must come down with a heavy hand on hoarders and blackmarketeers. At no other time was the exhortation of Jawaharlal Nehru to hang all blackmarketeers on the nearest lamp-post more relevant."

Vacillation and weakness in dealing with rich farmers can be suicidal in a situation as we have today.

Extra effort would also have to be put in, Mr. Patel said, to ensure that the distribution machinery was geared up to face the task. It stands to reason that a deficit state can expect help from the centre, after it has put its own house in order. "The state must garner its resources and intensify its procurement drive."

It is time we woke up to the realities of the situation. "Instead of searching for secondary causes and scapegoats, we have to tackle the root causes of the people's discontent."

This can come about only if radical, long-range and long-term measures are formulated and implemented with zest and sincerity, Mr. Patel pointed out.

Symptomatic of the unrest within the party is the bombshell dropped by the Union minister of state for Planning, Mr. Mohan Dharia last week, that unless drastic remedial measures to correct economic distortions are taken, he might be forced to resign his office. Several other ministers, at various levels of the government, are similarly in a desperate mood.

Mr. Dharia has circulated his views and suggestions on major steps that should be adopted without delay. He has called for "basic decisions and urgent measures to be implemented with courage and determination."

According to Mr. Dharia, the basic reasons for the distortions in our economy could be traced to the glaring economic disparities, deficit financing, black money, conspicuous consumption, low rate of savings, inefficiency in the performance of some public sector undertakings, negligible revenues from the agricultural sector, wrong emphasis on the production of luxury goods as against essential commodities of mass consumption, huge margins of profit, foreign debt service charges and dearth of foreign exchange. To remedy the situation he had suggested that:

1. Deficit financing should be stopped for the next four or five years.
2. Wealth Tax and Income Tax measures should be introduced to ensure that no family can hold unproductive property (movable or immovable) above Rs. 2 lakhs (excluding a reasonable residential house or flat) and a net monthly income above Rs. 2,500.

3. Employment Tax be levied on all wage-earners, both urban and rural, with a monthly income above Rs. 250.
4. Import of all luxury items should be banned.
5. Unproductive expenditure and conspicuous consumption should be taxed heavily. Registration fees on private cars, television sets, big radio sets, air conditioners, refrigerators, big electrical machines and such other articles beyond the reach of the common man should be enhanced considerably.
6. No individual should be allowed to build a residential flat or building worth more than Rs. 1 lakh. Loans from public finance institutions for this purpose should be limited to Rs. 25,000 per unit.
7. Building of skyscrapers throughout the country should be banned for the next five years in view of the shortage of cement and steel.
8. States should be persuaded to introduce or enhance tax on agricultural income and water supply.
9. Ceiling on property and income and a ceiling on gold holdings to the extent of 10 tolas per married couple and five tolas for each daughter in a family, will help mop up the black money in the country.
10. All property transactions above Rs. 5 lakh during the past 15 years should be scrutinised and appropriate action taken against those who have deceived the government.
11. Audit institutions should be nationalised and audit through private chartered accountants should be stopped.
12. Government should make available essential articles and commodities of mass consumption through a massive distribution machinery.
13. Greater emphasis should be given to productivity, workers' active participation in management, curbing of monopolistic trends and production-cum-employment-oriented small industries and village industries, removal of regional disparities and balanced development.

Mr. Dharia points out that it would be improper to curtail the outlay of Rs. 51,000 crore on the Fifth Plan if the growth rate of 5.5 per cent is to be maintained. "It may perhaps be necessary to have more outlays for agriculture, irrigation, fertilizers, power and small and village industries," he feels.

The measures he suggests, would, Mr. Dharia feels, help bring down prices and also introduce a Wage Income Price policy in the country.

Gold worth Rs. 6,000 to Rs. 7,000 crore had been smuggled into the country in the last 25 years, Mr. Dharia assesses. "It may not be possible for us to be as rigorous and harsh as China" in view of the religious feelings, sense of security, love of women for ornaments and also the problems of unemployment of goldsmiths. He has, however, suggested restrictions on the possession of gold ornaments.

The Gold Control Order brought in after the Chinese invasion was basically sound, but the large-scale unemployment it caused among the goldsmiths was its undoing. Mr. Dharia says.

He suggests banning all repatriation of capital, dividends or any other payment in any form beyond 10 per cent of the total invested foreign capital by foreign concerns, during any financial year.

Mr. Dharia also points out that it would be "unfair to treat residents of Indian origin abroad on par with foreign investors. An appropriate scheme to fetch investments from Indians abroad should be formulated . . . to provide a constant flow of free foreign exchange and also of the new science and technology."

"An approach ensuring social justice, equality of opportunity and elimination of disparities based on the spirit of *swadeshi* and patriotism can actively involve millions of our masses and can generate tremendous resources for our development."

He suggests that "all offences of tax evasion or wrongful declaration should be treated as major offences and should merit conviction of not less than five years and confiscation of all property and also cancellation of licences or permits or quotas, if any."

Current, 09.02.1974.

pp. (1 + 4)

People's call for action
Congress at the crossroads

The AICC, the highest policy-making body of the Ruling Party, is meeting at a time of unprecedented crisis. The crisis has been aggravated by the challenge thrown by Mr. Jayaprakash Narayan at the Establishment.

Emboldened by the Sarvodaya leader's virulent attacks on the established system, certain powerful forces have picked up courage to undermine our democratic roots and the basic principles on which the entire edifice rests—democracy, socialism and secularism.

Mr. Jayaprakash Narayan, leading a motley crowd of discredited and disgruntled elements is spearheading a queer 'movement' over which he does not seem to have any control. From his strident pronouncements it appears he has lost faith in the Constitution and the very fabric it has established in the country.

He has not only opposed the present electoral system but has had the temerity to brand the democratically elected leader a 'dictator'.

The forces he has unleashed cannot be checked by armed might. They will have to be met by those congressmen committed to the Party's basic principles. The majority of the people, it has been proved five times since independence, are with the Congress. In 1971 they gave a massive mandate to Mrs. Indira Gandhi. Subsequent events have proved that she still enjoys their unshaken faith. Hers, still remains the most powerful voice of this nation.

Mr. Narayan is neither against corruption nor the corrupt. He is merely exploiting a feeling among the people that congressmen having acquired power, do not appear to be aware of the crisis the country is facing. The long spell of power the Party has enjoyed has made them complacent.

Congressmen of all hues—leftists or rightists, socialists or sarvodayists, pragmatists or sectarians—must realise that slogans alone will no longer keep them in power.

The question whether the party should be what it is or be made into a cadre-based mass party has to be decided by its leaders, but allowing all and sundry to come in is bound to prove disastrous. Mrs. Indira Gandhi has more than once alluded to this abnormal growth. Honest and committed congressmen expect her to cleanse it of its flabbiness.

No other leader in the party has the capacity and the courage to take this bold step. The operation is necessary for the very survival of the party and the government it runs.

Despite our enormous unexploited wealth, the vast majority of the people still live in squalor and privation. The economy has grounded to a halt. Our foreign reserves have shrunk to rock-bottom. We do not have enough foreign exchange to import oil. Coal is not reaching its potential users. The public distribution system is in total disarray. Due to sharp decline in production, topsy-turvy planning, profiteering and accumulation of unaccounted money, prices are galloping.

The Fifth Five Year Plan is in the doldrums. Congressmen helplessly watch these ominous trends and the mounting crisis. The Party's slogans are about to be drowned in the tidal wave of mass frustration and anger.

The gap between the rich and the poor has widened. Land reforms have been sabotaged by the very congressmen pledged to implement them. Various mechanisms have been fabricated by the Party and the bureaucracy to protect the interests of the rich farmers. The Party has forgotten its power base—the peasants, the workers and the have-nots.

Our economic and industrial sector is not only thoroughly disorganised, but is on the verge of chaos. Since the Party has neglected its trade union base, the working class has become an easy tool in the hands of adventurers and factional powerseekers. The lust for power among congressmen has made them totally oblivious to the problems on the labour 'front'. The Railway strike, which paralysed the country, could have been averted if congressmen had been more alert.

Our public sector is in shambles, run as it is by wooden-headed bureaucrats with no commitment to the basic philosophy. Initially, its growth suffered because strident slogan mongers in the party cried wolf. Industrialists were dubbed blood-suckers and exploiters.

The MRTPC hung as a sword of Damocles over their heads. Expansion was restricted and growth marred. Red tape and corruption played havoc with them. Curbing the growth of the private sector, without providing alternatives in the public sector proved calamitous.

It has been belatedly realised that warring factions in the Party have done enormous damage to the morale of the growth-oriented industrialists. Let the country first grow. Mere nationalisation does not mean socialism.

In all this ideological confrontation and experimentation, what was overlooked was that there could be no compromise with corruption.

Like many other bad things in the economy and social life, corruption too proliferated. It has attained a Frankensteinian proportion where the people are no longer prepared to take it lying down. If Mr. Jayaprakash Narayan's challenge has to be met, the Congress should first purge itself and the administration it runs of corruption, nepotism and favouritism.

Congressmen, the general feeling is, think that so long as there is no alternative to their party the people will have no choice but to let them enjoy absolute power.

There is an element of truth in this impression. The post-1971 complacency is dangerous, it may prove disastrous. The people have learned through bitter experience how to assert themselves. They did it in 1967. It can be repeated. 1976 is not very far off.

The members of the AICC should therefore bear in mind some of these grim aspects of the prevailing situation in the country if they are sincere in preserving the policies enunciated by their leader, Jawaharlal Nehru.

Current, 20.07.1974.
pp. (1 + 4)

Snap Poll

The Licence Scandal Session of the Lok Sabha, prorogued on December 20, was perhaps the last. The President of India is likely to be advised to dissolve Parliament and order a fresh poll most probably in March 1975.

Arrangements at the organisational and governmental level are being finalised to plunge the country into a battle of the hustings, both for the Lok Sabha and some state Assemblies.

Prime Minister, Mrs. Indira Gandhi, has held intensive discussions in the last few days to work out strategies, plan details and the issues to be highlighted in the election campaign.

Top leaders in the party have been assigned specific duties to conduct the campaign.

Mrs. Gandhi's personal assessment is that the situation in the country is most auspicious for the Congress. The *rabi* crop has been excellent, prices are generally on the decline. The opposition is in total disarray.

Mrs. Gandhi is confident that rural India will back her to the hilt.

She feels that Mr. Jayaprakash Narayan's movement is a peculiarly urban phenomenon which has failed to touch the core of the country. Despite his best efforts, the Sarvodaya leader has not been able to extend his agitation beyond a few pockets of discontent.

Mrs. Gandhi is not likely to leave out any chances to her calculations going wrong. If necessary there would be a spectacular display of a more sophisticated nuclear energy than the May 18 explosion at Pokharan. It is 'something' that will literally stupefy the advanced members of the nuclear club.

The Prime Minister dropped a veiled hint at the valedictory address to the Congress Parliamentary Party of the impending mid-term poll, when she talked about the need for revision of electoral rolls.

It is significant that in the course of his extensive tours of the states, Congress President Mr. D.K. Borooah, has been discussing in detail with local leaders methods of rejuvenating the party units and keeping them in trim for a possible snap poll. Without disclosing to any Chief minister or PCC President that elections are round the corner, he has been asking them to be fully prepared.

Mr. Barooah, like Mrs. Gandhi, has realised that the opposition will not succeed in forging a united front. Even J.P. has not been able to put them together for the limited purposes of dissolution of the Bihar Assembly. The opposition has no common objective, programme, or credibility to gain the confidence of the people.

Mrs. Gandhi is confident that with proper organisation and direction, the Congress can still sweep the polls making mincemeat of the opposition.

But she is also aware of the drawbacks she has to contend with within her organisation. Some of the leaders who have disgraced her name and distorted the image of the Party are likely to pay a heavy price. They may be asked to step down immediately. High on the list of those who would have to quit is Railway minister, Mr. Lalit Narayan Mishra, who suddenly became the focal point of bitter attacks by the opposition.

In the states too some Congress leaders are likely to be jettisoned to improve the image and performance of the government. Chief minister of Maharashtra, Mr. V.P. Naik may be the first to go. His removal, the Prime Minister's close advisers feel, will improve the chances of a landslide victory for the Congress in Maharashtra.

In Gujarat, the High Command has already decided to isolate the old guard, who disgraced the Congress and the government. Mr. Barooah's search for new faces in the state has yielded positive results. He is likely to pull out more rabbits from his hat than is generally suspected.

The Congress President is credited with the view that only young blood, with an unblemished public image, can save the party in Gujarat.

Orissa Chief minister, Mrs. Nandini Satpathy agrees with the view that the time has never been so propitious for a poll in her state with the Bhartiya Lok Dal and its leader, Mr. Biju Patnaik, so thoroughly exposed.

With the unity that has been forged in the Youth Front in West Bengal and with the Marxists in utter ideological confusion, Chief minister, Mr. Siddhartha Shankar Ray, has promised to rout the Marxists.

Only two states where the Congress will face difficulties are Uttar Pradesh and Tamil Nadu.

In Lucknow, Chief minister, Mr. H.N. Bahuguna, is involved in a fierce factional fight. He is being asked to give up his intransigence to accommodate various groups within the party clamouring for representation in the Cabinet.

In Tamil Nadu, the Congress leadership has failed to make any dent in the DMK and ADMK strongholds. Chances of an alliance with Mr. K. Kamaraj have receded as he is fast losing ground.

Such a poll will evidently suit the CPI close ally of the Congress. The Communists have decided to extract their pound of flesh. In Bihar, West Bengal, Uttar Pradesh, Tamil Nadu, Kerala and Orissa, they are demanding poll adjustments in more seats.

The nation should get ready for the hustings.

Current, 28.12.1974.
pp. (1 + 4)

B. Testing Time for Democracy

Bihar on a volcano

I was in Bihar last week the day a student was shot dead and another had his nose chopped off because they wanted to concentrate on their studies.

I spent two and a half hours with Mr. Jayaprakash Narayan, who has taken on himself the mantle of leadership of what he calls a crusade against corruption. Another four hours were spent with Mr. Abdul Ghafoor, Chief minister of Bihar, who is bearing the brunt of the unholy alliance allegedly fighting corruption.

Mr. Narayan and Mr. Ghafoor answered a common set of questions with varying emphasis. The former edited his own dictated script. Mr. Ghafoor spoke off the cuff.

Two days in Bihar are enough to convince anyone that the state is perched on a volcano. Mr. Narayan has been diligently stoking the fires of revolt among the youth and students of this appallingly poverty-stricken state.

The ruling party presents a pathetic sight. Congress leaders have neither the guts nor the political credibility to face Mr. Narayan's massive challenge. The party rank and file is thoroughly demoralised. Ministers dare not go in public without armed police escorts. They squander their time in conspiring and in jockeying for power.

Dr. Jagannath Mishra, younger brother of Railway minister, Mr. L.N. Mishra, is compared to Brutus. He is considered to be the chief conspirator and the main target of attack by the people and a large number of congressmen.

Two years ago, he was an ally of the Jana Sangh. His sudden rise to power is not only considered out of proportion but also as an ominous portent of money power.

Local leaders sling mud at each other to their heart's contenι. A diatribe against the BPCC President, Mr. Sitaram Kesri, also a member of the Rajya Sabha, who spends most of his time in Delhi appeared in a recent issue of a local journal, "BOMSEL".

It said: "Strange are the ways of politicians, especially the "King Makers". One who should have been nowhere in public life is BPCC President today—on the gaddi of Dr. Rajendra Prasad and other saintly patriots who set examples for the whole country. What a degradation for the Congress and shame for the prestigious chair!

"Self-styled Chief-minister-in waiting—Sitaram Kesri, popularly known as "Khuddi Chor" for having been convicted for stealing "Khuddi" (broken rice) and dragged on the streets of Dinapur with a rope tied round his waist, is learnt to be an expert in WT (Without ticket travel) and is also alleged to have escaped the Aiyer Commission. As a class friend of Rama Jain, Kesri has been true and loyal to S.P. Jain, but this loyalty may prove very costly for the state, it is feared. No wonder the Congress is fast losing prestige and facing so critical a situation in Bihar today!"

BOMSEL is not an opposition paper. It is allegedly financed by a congressmen. Mr. Gauri Prasad Singh, who is also Deputy Chairman of the prestigious Agro-Industries Corporation. The paper also enjoys the support of a local senior Cabinet minister.

A rival journal, SPLINTER, writes: "If all wishes end in success, Mr. Ghafoor's repeated wish to drop Dr. Jagannath Mishra may turn him into a Sultan. But would he like to be an "Ek Din Ka Sultan" and issue like Humayun his leather coin in politics . . . ?"

"The common 'L.N.-Jagannath bogey' suits him. Ghafoor may try to upturn the applecart of political truce imposed by the High Command which itself would last till mid-August. The Brutus of Bihar is under pressure by his adviser, Mr. Daroga Rai and hence Caesar may die but there are Antonys to take revenge and are itching to fight."

Splinter is edited by the wife of a local District Magistrate. It is financed by yet another Cabinet minister. Thousands of free copies of these two journals were distributed at the last AICC session in New Delhi, providing an insight into the behaviour of Bihar congressmen.

Corruption has been institutionalised in Bihar. Mr. Ghafoor, whose integrity and honesty is unquestioned, finds it an uphill task to fight it. The more he fights it, the greater the opposition to him from his own party men. He has dismissed or suspended over a hundred senior officials on charges of corruption. His plans to drop ministers with a bad image in the next reshuffle are being fought with the tenacity and vigour which corrupt ministers are capable of mobilising.

Former ministers, Mr. L.P. Sahi, who built four huge houses in Patna, and Ram Lakhan Singh Yadav, who was found guilty of rank corrupt practices by the Aiyer Commission and several others known to be dishonest, have formed themselves into a phalanx in his fight against corruption.

Most of the ministers and ex-ministers have built political houses for themselves. The former ministers, whose number is legion, refuse to vacate ministerial bungalows. Officers with private houses continue to occupy official bungalows on the plea that the politician should set the example.

The Youth Congress has suggested that these defiant officers should be suspended and that there should be an open inquiry against ministers and ex-ministers who have built houses using their concealed wealth.

Retired bureaucrats grab appointments as Chairman or Managing Directors of public sector organisations. One of them, Mr. Harnandan Thakur, ex-Development Commissioner, against whom there were strictures in the Aiyar Commission Report, is today the Chairman of the Tubewell Corporation, a gold-mine in Bihar.

The state has gone financially bankrupt. The entire administration has been geared to meeting the law and order situation created by Mr. Narayan's agitation. Over Rs. 10 lakhs are being spent daily to maintain law and order.

The ministers and bureaucrats seem to be under an illusion that the storm will blow over.

If JP succeeds in his movement, it will not be because of his moral or political authority. Congressmen are, in fact, offering him Bihar on a silver platter.

JP: Total Revolution

Syed: *Could you elaborate your concept of partyless democracy? Will it be necessary to destroy the present system in order to implement your ideas?*

JP: It will take too long to elaborate my concept of partyless democracy. Some idea of my concept can be gained from a study of my previous writings on this subject. However, the point to emphasise here is that as far as the present Bihar movement is concerned, it is not partyless democracy that I am aiming at but the evolution of some organs of people's power which may exercise strict vigilance over the democratic process—elections, for instance—and the institutions of democracy—for instance, the legislators and legislatures.

I am hoping that the Chhatra Sangharsha Samitis and Jana Sangharsha Samitis together will be able to play this role provided they continue to function even after the dissolution of the state Assembly. I do expect them to do so because these committees have to struggle not only against the government and the administration, in as much as there is corruption and mis-government in them, but also against blackmarketing, hoarding, *benami* and fictitious transfers of land in order to evade ceiling laws; also to protect the rights of the weaker sections, particularly the Harijans and Adivasis; and generally to fight against social injustices and evils of all kinds.

The aim of the movement, as far as I am concerned, is total revolution—social, political, economic, cultural, educational and above all moral. For that, human beings will have also to be reformed but that is a task not for persons like me or for political leaders, but for saints and Mahatmas. What I am concerned with is reform of, or revolution in, institutions, laws, procedures, systems, etc.

I cannot say if all these, including the students, who are involved in the movement will follow me to the ultimate goal. But as far as it lies in my power, I shall try to take everyone with me. If I fail, somebody else will have to make the attempt at some other time.

Syed: *Is it possible to fight corruption or the other evils without the help of an organised group or a party especially when the ruling party can fight back with its might and resources?*

JP: It was after a fairly long experience with seminars, discussions, including with those in power, that I came to the conclusion that if corruption had to be fought it is the people who must do so. But it was not very clear to me even then how the people could fight against corruption. Students, closely followed by the people of Gujarat showed the way. Though their movement ended abruptly, their achievement should not be underestimated. It happened for the first time since *Swaraj* that a major political change was brought about by youth and people's power.

The Gujarat lead was taken up by the students of Bihar, who really started this movement on their own initiative. I came into it later. It is no doubt true that in Gujarat as well as in Bihar the students did say that they were responding to my call, but I think the credit for conceiving and leading the movement must go to the students of Gujarat and Bihar.

As for the ruling party, whichever it may be, fighting back "with its might and resources", all I can say is that in a democracy no ruling party can afford to fight the whole people.

Syed: *In what way is the crusade against corruption interlinked with the dissolution of the elected bodies and the closure of educational institutions? Will it not create anarchy?*

JP: In Gujarat the link between corruption and the "dissolution of the elected bodies" was clear from the very beginning. Rightly or wrongly, the students of Ahmedabad and later of other places in Gujarat demanded the resignation of the Chimanbhai Patel Ministry on the ground that it was too corrupt to be tolerated. After the ministry's resignation the demand for the Assembly's dissolution was a natural step.

In Bihar neither the resignation of the Bihar ministry nor dissolution of the state Assembly formed part of the original twelve demands of the Bihar Pradesh Chhatra Sangharsha Samiti. It was when the state government did not respond satisfactorily to the Sangharsha Samiti's demands that the Samiti decided to *gherao* the Assembly House on the day it was to meet. (18th March).

One event followed another, beginning with the Bihar state administration's monumental failure in Patna on March 18, on which day at least for two and a half hours Patna town was at the mercy of the *goondas* while thousands of armed Police stood watching the Legislative House and the Raj Bhavan.

As for the closure of educational institutions it is not all of them that we are demanding to be closed—schools and high schools have been excluded and the closure applies only to the universities and colleges. This is essential in order that the students may remain unaffected and their movement—it is necessary to stress that it is their, i.e., the student's movement—may succeed.

This need not lead to anarchy because there is so much to do, both constructive and combative, that almost every college student who wants to participate actively will have his hands full. I hope to issue after consultation with Chhatra Sangharsha Samiti and Jan Sangharsha Samiti leaders a full programme of activities to which not only students but also teachers and ordinary citizens would address themselves.

Talking of anarchy, has there not been anarchy enough in the universities of Bihar and U.P. in the past years? Have not examinations been delayed before, sometimes for months together. A twelve-month delay is not unknown. This is for the first time that an attempt is being made to channelise the student's discontentment and anger to revolutionary and constructive purposes.

At the same time I have urged the educationists of the state to utilise the closure period to evolve a more meaningful system of education. This is impossible in the rush of routine work when the institutions are open. I am also thinking of starting some experiments in education during this movement. I am having this matter studied. And the most important point in this connection is: who can stop anarchy if a peaceful and purposeful outlet is not provided to the pent-up discontentment, anger and frustration of the youth and the people?

Syed: *What about corruption among traders and investors, leaders of opposition parties and academicians? It is alleged that a number of people with concealed sources of income have joined you or are extending help to you?*

JP: Of course, there is corruption among traders, investors, opposition parties, academicians and, if I may add, students and many others too. I have spoken repeatedly about this at my public meetings and also written about it. The Bihar movement, for instance, is not only concerned with political and administrative corruption, but also with corruption among traders and businessmen.

And as time passes this part of the programme will gather momentum with the help of the thousands of volunteers from the ranks of the students. In Patna alone, we estimate that a thousand volunteers would be needed to keep watch on the ration-shops, ferret out hoarded essential commodities, fix reasonable prices for such commodities and other similar tasks.

One point regarding corruption which I have been stressing in the past and I should like to stress here is that though corruption is all-pervasive in our society its root lies in the political and administrative spheres. And if this evil has to be rooted out, the cleaning up must begin with those spheres.

Syed: *How do you justify calling an elected leader a dictator? What is your concept of dictatorship?*

JP: Dictatorships may be of different kinds. Even an elected leader, if he or she, concentrates too much power in his or her hands, becomes a virtual dictator. As I see it, if all important decisions are centralised in the Prime Minister's hands there is fear of dictatorship. This is very different from the concept of "the first amongst equals", *primus inter pares.* Further, I find that democracy within the Congress Party and Provincial autonomy (wherever Congress is the ruling party) is a formal affair. It is for these reasons and in this sense that I have called "an elected leader a dictator".

Syed: *You have praised Mr. Ghafoor as an honest man and there is an impression that he has taken certain drastic measures to fight corruption. Would you like to help him in his struggle against corruption?*

JP: I have commended Mr. Ghafoor's effort to deal with corruption in the administration almost every time he has told me of the measures he was taking. I have reminded him that unless he removed his corrupt colleagues in the Ministry all his efforts would be ineffectual. At that point Mr. Ghafoor either invariably fell silent or smiled the matter away.

I should add that it is not for me to tell Mr. Ghafoor or anyone else which minister is corrupt or not. They have their bureaus of intelligence and other organisations to find out the facts. I believe the facts are not unknown, but either the will is lacking or there is fear that drastic action against influential ministers might lead to disastrous results for the Congress Party or the Chief or Prime Minister concerned.

Ghafoor: 'it will fail'

Syed: *Do you agree with Mr. Jayaprakash Narayan's idea of partyless democracy?*

Ghafoor: Through his concept of partyless democracy, Mr. Jayaprakash Narayan is playing a deep political game. He wants to destroy the fibre of our democratic society. His concept aims at negating our Constitutional and parliamentary achievements.

Mr. Jayaprakash Narayan is a confused politician. His plans are to confuse and misguide the younger generation. His charge that the Prime Minister, Mrs. Indira Gandhi is as good as a dictator is merely a smoke-screen under which he would like to set himself up as a dictator. Recently in Bombay he drew a distinction between the concentration of power in the hands of the Prime Minister and the absolute power wielded by Hitler and Mussolini.

I charge Jayaprakash Babu with strengthening fascist tendencies in this country. His agitation in Bihar is manned and organised by the RSS and the Jana Sangh. Something is gone wrong with this once Gandhian and Sarvodaya leader. If he has any illusions about the non-violent nature of his movement he is living in a fool's paradise.

A student was killed last week when he wanted to appear at examinations. Another student's nose was chopped off. Young boys are dragged out of their classes at the point of a dagger and prevented from attending classes. Bombs and crackers are used freely. JP calls it a non-violent movement. If this is his concept of non-violence then I will certainly face his challenge on the same grounds.

Syed: *Mr. Jayaprakash Narayan says you are an honest congressman, that you are incorruptible. What are your plans to fight corruption at the political and administrative level?*

Ghafoor : I am thankful to JP for his certificate. I had met him in the beginning and asked him for his specific plan to root out corruption. I offered him my full co-operation. I broadcast an appeal on All India Radio, urging people and parties to help me fight corruption. I said I would support JP's agitation against corruption which was being launched in Bihar. I would have been the happiest man if Bihar had shown the light for the whole country. Later I found that JP had some other motives. His call for an anti-corruption drive was a ruse to destroy the democratic fabric and now his campaign has degenerated into a dangerous political agitation.

The day I became Chief minister I decided to clean the state of corruption. During my short stay I dismissed and suspended more than a hundred officers including IAS, superintending engineers, doctors and collectors. I meant to intensify this process and I am still determined to fight corruption single-handedly, if necessary.

In this crusade, I am prepared to seek help from any quarter, including JP. I have planned to set up small Committees of honest men-officials and non-officials, who will visit districts and at lower levels to register complaints from the people against officials. If any official is found guilty he will be suspended on the spot and if the report of the Committee confirms his guilt, he will be dismissed. In this drive I will invite the students and the youth to help us.

Syed: *Who is financing the movement?*

Ghafoor: Money is collected by threats and force. Youngsters carrying knives and daggers go to shopkeepers and demand Rs. 500. If they refuse, they brandish their weapons and raise their demand to Rs. 800 and then to Rs. 1,000. If the shopkeeper resists, they loot the shop. This has happened in several parts of the state. Our duty is to protect the shopkeepers and when we protect them, JP brands us as fascists.

A lot of blackmarketeers and people with concealed wealth have joined the JP bandwagon because I have been trying to unearth their misdeeds.

It is not out of love for JP but out of fear of me that they have sought his protection.

The manner in which JP has been hurling threats is hardly the way of a Sarvodaya leader or a follower of the Mahatma. It reveals the thought process of a clever politician. He draws his inspiration from what happened in Gujarat. It was the students who paved the way for the dissolution of the Assembly in Gujarat. I will not let this happen here. Bihar Chhatra Sangharsh Samiti forwarded 12 demands. Many of them were justified and I accepted most of them. The students were happy at their victory and were about to return to their classes when JP entered the scene.

The students were provoked by him. They threatened not to let the Governor deliver his address to the Assembly on March 18. We took precautions and the Governor did address the Assembly. This frustrated JP and his moves. They resorted to violence, burnt down the 'SEARCHLIGHT' and attacked the 'INDIAN NATION' and looted hotels and shops. It was clear from this move that JP wanted to throw Bihar in the cauldron of chaos and anarchy.

We cut short the Assembly session to avoid tension. They raised a hue and cry and demanded that the Assembly be reconvened. When we called the Assembly they offered *dharna* in front of the Assembly gates.

Fearing trouble, we closed the educational institutions from March 18. They demanded that the colleges be reopened. When we reopened the colleges they demanded that they should be closed down. On the day press reports appeared about the reopening of the colleges, JP issued a public threat that the government was taking a risk and would have to face the consequences.

What does all this mean? Is it a method of a Sarvodaya worker or a politician who plans to paralyse the government and the state? JP's threat touched off large-scale disturbances.

Syed: *Do you think JP's call for dissolution of the Assembly and closure of all educational institutions for a year will help the fight against corruption?*

Ghafoor: JP is a frustrated and disillusioned politician. His call for the dissolution of the Assembly has been a failure. Only 30 out of 318 MLAs have resigned so far. Half of the Jana Sangh legislators have revolted and formed another party. Barring two or three, those who have resigned are now repenting. They are dazed. They are thoroughly disillusioned by his theory of partyless democracy. JP has been going round the country asserting that he has the Jana Sangh. SSP, PSP and others supporting him. Why don't these parties then dissolve themselves and give concrete shape to his new thesis?

His first phase was a failure. In the second phase he claims that he has linked his fate with the students. I have been a student leader myself and I also know the mind of the students. By linking his fate with that of the students of all varieties, irrespective of their ideological affiliations, he is out to destroy the very fabric of democracy in this country. He is deepening the crisis that we are facing today.

Syed: *Do you plan to take workers and peasants into confidence for meeting the JP challenge?*

Ghafoor: The working class in Bihar is absolutely against his agitation. The workers have refused to come out in his support. The peasants have not cast their lot with him, despite the grievances they have against the government.

I will put an end to *benami* transactions in this state. If there is any resistance to our plans for the redistribution of land to the landless, I will not hesitate to use MISA and other legal powers. All *benami* land will be taken over and redistributed to the landless.

Syed: *Are you planning similar steps against corrupt politicians?*

Ghafoor: Yes, very much so. I am planning to set up a committee of inquiry to go into charges of corruption against politicians right from 1952. I have informed JP of this also but there was no response from him. I want to let the people of Bihar know through judicial inquiries, who the corrupt politicians are.

Then there is the Lok Ayukt who is ready to receive complaints with affidavits from the people. In fact, it is enquiring into charges against politicians including ministers. As soon as this report is submitted, I will take action.

Syed: *Mr. Jayaprakash Narayan has said that you have not fulfilled your promise to remove some corrupt ministers from your government.*

Ghafoor: He was never clear about these ministers. In the last reshuffle, I dropped a large number of ministers. Not because all of them were corrupt, but it is a fact that some of them earned a bad name.

I believe JP has a particular minister in mind. He wants me to remove him but I just cannot follow the dictates of JP. As Chief minister it is my duty to fully satisfy myself if this particular minister is corrupt or not. I am watching his conduct and performance. I will not take any action against him unless I have positive proof.

Syed: *Do you have any means to get positive evidence?*

Ghafoor: Yes. The Lok Ayukt is there. Such allegations are dealt with by him. His report will soon be submitted to the government.

Syed: *The Prime Minister has been branded a dictator. Do you agree with this charge?*

Ghafoor: It is a slur upon Mrs. Gandhi. In fact, JP is more dictatorial in his functions than any living politician today. He formulates his rules and policies and is not answerable to any elected or representative body.

I have not come across a single instance where Mrs. Gandhi dictated anything to me as Chief minister. I always posed my state's problems before her and sought her guidance. Never once have I or anyone else I know got the impression that she is a dictator. Maybe JP, like his policies has also formulated his own concept of a dictator.

Current, 03.08.1974.
pp. (1 + 4 + 16).

Make Congress an instrument of change people's upsurge

The Allahabad judgement has divided the nation vertically. Never in history have we witnessed such a sharp division among its people—the intelligentsia, the urban classes—on the issue whether Mrs. Indira Gandhi should stay or quit.

We expressed our firm views last week in favour of her continuing as the leader of the country irrespective of the judgement.

The mass upsurge that the country witnessed since then has further strengthened our conviction. The mammoth rally of June 20, described as the largest political gathering in the world—was a reflection of the peoples' will for change. The rally confirmed that she unequivocally symbolises the nation's aspirations for stability, progress and determined march towards the ultimate goal.

It was this realisation that impelled the Congress to assert, with a rare display of unity that she should continue to lead the world's largest democratic party and also a resurgent nation. The pledges of support have assumed the form of mass assertion. People from every corner of the country are demanding that she should not step down.

The law may take its own course but it cannot and should not trample the democratic will of the people.

Her detractors apprehend that the whole process might lead to the cult of personality. It is not true. In a democracy like ours no 'cult' is permitted to emerge. The Father of the Nation was criticised, his disciple, Jawaharlal Nehru was assailed in Parliament and in the press almost every day; Indira Gandhi is perhaps the most ruthlessly criticised politician and yet the bogey of the 'cult' is being spread.

The fact is that in the queer turn of events, she is no more taken as an individual. She has become a symbol, the strident voice of the oppressed millions in the country.

The mass upsurge in her support has understandably upset JP. In it he finds the symptoms of the beginning of an era of totalitarianism and the emergence of the 'cult'.

The Sarvodaya leader is known for a remarkably short memory. His denigration of Congress President D.K. Barooah for calling her a 'symbol of victory' is a wilful attempt to malign a trusted colleague of the Prime Minister. JP should know that she has received more effusive praise from her harshest critics than from her partymen.

"You are the honour of this country. You are a *Devi*. The nation is proud of you." The adulator was none other than the firebrand Jana Sangh leader Atal Behari Vajpayee. The praise came from him the day Bangla Desh was liberated.

On the same day, Mr. Morarji Desai pronounced: "We must thank God for this day of rejoicing. But we thank more the nation's leader and its representative Prime Minister Mrs. Indira Gandhi under whose leadership the whole country rallied together."

The unparalleled awakening as shown by the one-and-a-half million sea of humanity which converged on the heart of the capital predictably unnerved the opposition. Criticism has therefore been replaced with hate, animus and invectives. The language has become abusive. This is what soft spoken JP said about her:

"Her continuation in power would debase further not only the political coinage but also everything else that the ordinary citizen still holds dear . . . The Congress parliamentary party's resolution was yet another instance of unabashed political immorality of the Congress leadership and of its mischievous attempt to mislead the people. But the people, in their own interest, should beware of this Goebbelsian propaganda and save our cherished values of life and democratic institutions from fascistic machinations."

This is not the language of a Gandhian. This kind of language invariably leads to tension, hatred and violence. His Leftist and Rightist disciples have used similar language in denouncing her.

CPM's Jyotirmoy Bosu has branded her a power-maniac "sticking to office like a leech". BLD's Piloo Mody has likened her to "the Godmother, whose unsatiable lust for power and position would make her cling to office even if it destroyed the nation of 600 million people."

The invectives reflect desperation, a sense of despondency. The June 20 rally has sent shivers down the opposition's spines. It could not mobilise one-fourth of the June 20 number for its rally. The combined opposition has been unable to convince the masses that its faith in the legal process is more deep-rooted than that of the Congress.

The opposition has no cause. Its approach is negative. Now even JP has failed to add to its 'Indira *Hatao'* movement the moral strength it thought he commanded, and which it needed.

But the failure of the opposition to make political capital out of the judgement should not make the Congress complacent. Some of its leaders have been shining for long in her reflected glory. It has once again been proved that she commands greater faith from the people than the organisation she leads.

The people have given the Congress yet another lease of life. This opportunity should be used to transform the party into an instrument of change. Even now it is not too late for the Congress to emerge as a dedicated body true to its words and promises and as a protector of the weaker sections.

The Allahabad verdict has its positive factors. The Congress should recognise and utilise them to implement its promises and policies. The Party has to realise that the underprivileged and the oppressed are gradually losing faith in its capacity to fulfil its pledges.

But 1969 should not be repeated and vague and undefined radical slogans should not be considered the sole weapons of the battle.

Commitment to the leader is not enough. The AICC, the only policy-making body, should be convened immediately, for a full-fledged debate on the Narora Programme.

Rural India should no more be ignored. All the instruments of economic power must be mobilised on a massive scale to wipe out poverty, hunger and misery. It is time that the financial might of the nationalised banks is harnessed to liquidate rural indebtedness.

The very sincerity of congressmen about the policies and programmes of the party is being questioned. Unless some immediate practical steps are taken to translate these policies into reality, fresh promises of radicalism and change will only be taken as a ruse to perpetuate power.

The gap between promises and performance can be narrowed if the current political turmoil can be given a new direction. Instant slogans should not be permitted to once again degenerate into shielding the status quo.

We said this before; we repeat it, because a sense of urgency in adopting such a course is called for right now.

Current, 28.06.1975.
pp. (1 + 4).

Indira: I stand by democracy
'Emergency to save majority from the tyranny of minority'

In the first incisive interview after the Emergency, Prime Minister Indira Gandhi asserted that nobody else had done more to try and strengthen democracy in India than herself. Her faith in Parliament and democratic institutions remains undiminished.

The Prime Minister received me in her austere South Block office with a broad, warm smile. She looked fresh. The storm which had blown over the capital of the world's largest democracy during the last two months, had left no trace of strain or fatigue on her.

The atmosphere in her office was relaxed. Throughout the day, she had received a stream of visitors, including a delegation of journalists, some of them known for their sympathies for disruptive forces.

The Prime Minister replied to my questions with rare equanimity. Even my most provocative questions did not ruffle her.

The answers exploded the sinister insinuations of her detractors that she is out to establish a personalised rule and promote a cult of personality.

I asked: Madam, reactionaries at home and their friends abroad say that you have finished democracy in India?

There was a pause. Then she looked far beyond my shoulder and replied:

Well, I cannot think of anybody else who has done more to try and strengthen democracy in India. The people who are today criticising us or accusing us are the same people who supported not in India but abroad—Yahya Khan in 1971. Now, I do not know whether they would say that is a perfect democracy.

Today they are fully supporting China. Do they think there is democracy there? So one cannot take very seriously their feeling for democracy in other countries we do not want certificates from them.

I have always said, I still believe that democracy is the only system which gives strength to the people and, therefore of all the available systems, it is the best. But democracy does mean certain responsibilities on the part of the government to allow freedom of expression and so on, but equally it enjoins responsibility on the opposition to allow the government to function.

Now I feel that our democracy had gone somewhat off the rails, that is the very local minority was trying to suppress the majority. This is not democracy in any country or any language.

The manner in which the multi-party system has worked in India appears to be at the root of the present crisis. It has resulted in irresponsible and erratic political competition and harmed the national interest. Do you think the system should be allowed to continue in its present form or does it need change?

Well, this question was raised by the opposition—that the system is not working and it is a matter which could be debated and people's opinion taken. I would not say the multi-party system has failed, but somehow a sense of frustration is brewing among some leaders and the desire is to have power by any means.

Or to grab power?

It does not make much difference what word you use, but the last few years have been years of extreme hardship for the people. So they tried to exploit the situation. This was not unique to India; it was there practically in every country of the world. In fact, India was one of the first countries to be able to curb inflation.

What should we do with these parties now?

We have to see how to bring about more responsible functioning.

Are you envisaging some practical steps to give some kind of direction to the people?

This is really something which the people themselves should learn to correct. Now this Emergency has brought a new sense of awareness, a sense of discipline and if we can maintain it, then I am sure that the opposition parties will also be influenced by it.

You mean the Emergency or the sense of discipline?

The sense of discipline.

You said a few had been trying to trample upon the democratic rights of the many. How do you propose to prevent recurrence of such tendencies after the Emergency is lifted?

Well, we have to try and prevent situations which they can exploit and perhaps I was too tolerant and as I have said, when you have freedom of the road, it does not mean that you can drive on the right side and thereby endanger the life of somebody else. So, it is the same in political life that you have freedom, but it should not be such as will prevent the freedom of other people which is what was happening here.

The question now is what kind of political system you are going to evolve. We are at the crossroads . . .?

My wishes are for a democratic system. But I think, if you ask any country, democracy can exist only if there is a corresponding sense of responsibility amongst the opposition. Election should be fair and if they win, they form the government. But whoever is in the government, or whoever in the opposition, once the elections are over, there must be a certain amount of co-operation in functioning.

Now, if we had wanted, we could have prevented the functioning of the opposition governments. But, we have not. The Tamil Nadu government has been functioning for all these years. In between, we had these coalition governments in many states. And when they fell, it was not because we made an effort but because of their internal quarrels and rivalries.

Now in Gujarat, there is a government. We certainly will do nothing to upset it.

But if they do not follow the centre in certain matters. . .

That is a hypothetical question because I think they will co-operate if they do not, then it is very difficult. It is not only the centre, but we have to deal with so many states and the centre is something that comes to their help. The centre does not hamper state governments. On the contrary, it tries to help them, when they have problems with other states. Had there not been a strong centre, then the weaker states would be nowhere at all.

The attitude in Gujarat at the moment is not to carry out the orders of the centre.

Well, I do not know. I think they want to protest a bit about the Emergency and so on. But otherwise, I do not think . . .

Are you aware that there are Jana Sangh members in the Gujarat government whose affiliations with the RSS is no secret?

I do not know if this is true, but normally the Jana Sangh insists that when it forms part of the government, it should be with the RSS.

The ban on the RSS and other extremist organisations had been announced the previous evening. The morning papers had led with it. I congratulated the Prime Minister on this bold, but long-overdue step. I thought she would be rather too happy to reply to the question on one of her greatest achievements.

The ban on the RSS and the organisations of the extreme right and the adventurer left has been widely hailed by the people. But, the Jana Sangh is a by-product of the RSS and its leaders are also members of the Jana Sangh. Will it be possible to eliminate these forces from the political arena?

Well, those that are RSS, even if they are in some other organisations, will obviously be covered by this. If anybody else is acting in a manner prejudicial to communal harmony, then we will have to see.

Is it true that largescale RSS infiltration has taken place in the government services and public sector organisations?

To some extent, that is true and we have to look into this.

Will you take steps to purge them?

Well, strictly speaking, steps should have been taken long ago, because government servants are not supposed to take part in politics. But the RSS has been taking part in political work and even in governments, when there have been coalition governments in the states.

The economic programme announced by you has been widely welcomed by all sections of the people. It constitutes a landmark in our struggle for economic advance. The question is whether the existing administrative machinery is adequate enough to translate your great dream into reality. Is it therefore necessary to have a committed bureaucracy? If so, do you plan to re-educate at least the younger elements in the bureaucracy to recognise the new outlook?

Generally, the younger elements are good. It is only when they come in contact with certain others that they sometimes adopt the same habits.

This word "committed" has been misinterpreted and misused. What we meant was, under our system—and you know we had largely adopted the British system—the bureaucracy has to carry out the orders of the government of the day. The government's policy is what is passed by Parliament, so in that sense they have to do what the ministers tell them. When we used the word "committed" it had been in a much larger sense, that is, they should be committed to the national interest.

And, obviously, there are certain policies for instance, the policies of the RSS or of the Naxalites which are not in the national interest. They cause disorder and they want to take the country toward anarchy, when the greatest need for the country is stability and strength. So, anything that divides the people, either in the name of religion or something else, is a weakening factor.

Who will execute these new economic steps that you have announced at the district level? Officers or . . .

Well, it has to be a joint endeavour. While the responsibility is to a considerable extent with the government officials and with the government of the states, we have said that they should associate citizens, all those who believe in the policy either of our party or other senior citizens, youth and so on.

We think the involvement of the people is very important in any programme. For instance, unless the workers feel involved, production cannot go up. So at every level, every group of people must be involved in making a success of our programme.

Should I repeat that the goal is socialism, as you have been mentioning frequently, and we are happy that now the vision is clear. Shouldn't the bureaucracy also feel involved in the process, the kind of socialism you want to bring to this country?

We have adopted this policy not because of any whim or because we like a particular word. It is because we believe that in the existing conditions—poverty and economic backwardness—it is essential to have greater equality economically and socially, that is among the people of different religions, castes and so on. This alone can bring about socialism.

Our concept of socialism?

Yes, our concept. If a person has to carry out the policy, obviously he has to understand it first.

Are you thinking of involving the Congress Party from the grassroots level in the implementation of the new economic programme?

That is our effort.

Will the Congress Party again hold camps to educate the grassroots workers?

I don't know whether camps are necessary or what method will be found, because we have discussed all this with the Chief ministers. Now, they should take it down at different levels and we should have some machinery in the centre, which will be vigilant to follow up these programmes.

Can this vigilance be maintained by the Party workers at the lower level?

I think it should be.

Should it be in coordination with the district-level officials because ultimately the programme has to be implemented at the district level?

As I said, we want the party to be involved, but we would like to give it as broad a base as possible. If there are other citizens, young people, who believe on the programme and want to participate, well, their help will be taken. Just as in production, we are taking the help of all trade unions who would like to co-operate.

The success of your post-Emergency economic policies depends on the states. Would you fix time limits for the Chief ministers in this regard?

We have many times announced time-bound programmes and we know the time limit is not always kept. So, I don't think a time limit as such makes any difference. But we should be very vigilant to see that the programmes go on. We have asked the people to keep directly in touch with us also, so that if something is not moving in a particular state, we can follow it up.

Time limit, I think, gives a sense of urgency as was done at Narora.

Obviously, they do not have all the time in the world. I mean they have to speed up all their activities

A section in the Congress feels there should be a moratorium on lock-outs and strikes during the Emergency. Will your new scheme for 'workers participation in industry' keep this aspect also in view?

We are talking with the trade unions. They say that they would like to voluntarily evolve some methods. That is much better. Then you do not have to declare a moratorium.

A consensus among the trade unions can be of great help . . .

Yes, three trade unions met me this morning and they assured me that they would like to help in every way to increase production and soon—the INTUC, AITUC and HMS. The only thing they want is that there should be some machinery so that if there is a grievance it could be immediately redressed. The management should not take advantage of this. Just because the workers are saying they won't strike, it does not mean that the management should do something that is against the workers' interests. So it has to be a co-operative effort of all concerned.

I understand there was a suggestion that the workers' representatives be taken on the management?

Well, we have said that before. But the real problem has been the multiplicity of unions. Now, we will have to see in what way we can have greater participation. But I think it is more important to have it in the production programme, at the shop floor level and so on.

Do you expect that with the co-operation of the trade unions, industrial peace would be maintained?
We certainly hope so.

What about the smaller trade unions?
Well, there are some which are not co-operating.

Are steps being taken to persuade them?
Let us see how this works.

Has a change in attitude taken place?
Change in the attitude of the workers—that is what will produce results. After all, unions consist of workers and today there is a change in outlook.

I conveyed my impression that the workers had largely welcomed the new measures. They now feel they have a stake in this policy. The only thing is the management; it should also be persuaded to be responsive to the economic measures.

Some people ask, if the new measures could not have been taken without arresting the opposition leaders and invoking the Emergency.
Well, yes. You see, all these opposition groups were planning a kind of programme for seizing power, bypassing our democratic methods. There were some amongst them who believed in non-violence, but there were also some who did not believe in it. It was necessary, in order to avoid any trouble, because it would have been their effort to provoke violence. That would not have created a good situation. So, it was more to keep the peace.

Will they be kept in for long?
Well, I cannot say at all.

Are you taking any steps to severe the links between the reactionaries at home and those abroad?
I should have thought that any patriotic person would not have such links and certainly if there are any, we should do our best to severe them.

A section of the press, you have said, has persistently tried to suppress truth and facts in the pre-Emergency days. Is censorship the only way to tackle them?
No. At this moment we had to have censorship. But I think that certain codes of conduct should be evolved and then we should see that people stick to them.

Yes, we know you have implicit faith in democracy and a free press. You have been saying that you believe in a free press. In fact, we have learnt to believe in a free press from you. I understand some press delegations have already met you and the expectation is that some formula will be evolved in which the press becomes responsible and the government becomes responsive to the press.

The press itself should see to it. Now they say it was only a few papers that did this and the rest are penalised. I think the others should have woken up to the fact that some of them were not bringing a good name to the press, if I can put it that way.

But the papers that have been aware of the situation should not be penalised.

Well, I hope something will be worked out.

Now the last question, which is on a personal note. The nation is really agog at your tremendous courage, determination and stamina. We would like to know the secret of this.

I am afraid I have no secrets at all. My life has been an open book since I was small. It is when you are doing something which you think is right, which you believe to be right and which you believe is for a larger cause, not for yourself, I think that is what gives you the strength.

As you said, you get strength from the people. Whenever you meet the people, they give you strength. Will you continue to meet them in the same manner.

Yes.

Addressing public meetings and so on?

Certainly.

She spoke softly but firmly, throughout the interview, she never raised her voice; sometimes her voice was not even audible.

There was a look of relaxed contentment on her face—a sense of achievement.

Current, 12.07.1975.
pp. (1 + 4 + 16)

Social change now or never

The Congress President, Devkant Barooah, takes a long range view of the Emergency. The Prime Minister's initiative, he firmly believes, has brought about a qualitative change in politics. Henceforth, the very style of functioning in our public life will be shaped in a different pattern, with greater discipline.

Mr. Barooah, who works nearly 18 hours a day, manages to look fresh. His soft but meaningful laughter has not lost its captivating charm.

His Tughlak Road residence overflows with visitors. The reception office, his personal office, the living room, the bed room, the dining room and the verandahs are filled with people, from Chief ministers, Cabinet ministers, MPs, MLAs to district and taluka level workers. There is no distinction among visitors and Mr. Barooah shakes hands and talks to all of them in the same manner.

When a visitor wants to have an exclusive audience, he is taken into the bed-room which Mrs. Barooah has often to vacate. A big shamiana has been put up in the lawns to accommodate the visitors.

The Congress President agreed to give me an interview at 6 p.m. But then, 15 minutes later, there was a call and the Prime Minister wanted to see him urgently. We decided to meet at 7.30 p.m. but at 7.35 p.m. tall and smiling Siddhartha Shankar Ray barged in and took him away to an unknown place for important discussions.

We ultimately managed to sit down to a serious question-answer session at about 10 p.m.

I asked him: "Aren't you tired?"

The room reverberated with laughter: "I have just begun my day."

With the Emergency, the work-load has increased. I asked: A new situation has arisen and as head of the ruling party, your responsibilities have increased. What steps are you planning to attain the objectives enshrined in the declaration of Emergency?

Mr. Barooah looked at the almirahs stuffed with books on religion, philosophy, philology, ethics, politics, economics and oil, then he fixed his eyes on the ceiling and began:

The Emergency has brought about a new situation. It has introduced a qualitative change in the politics of this country. Till now, we were trying to implement a number of economic and political measures to bring about social changes based on social justice.

This was resisted by our bureaucracy, which was interested in maintaining status-quo. Some sections were helpful, though.

Secondly, in our own party ranks, some had become cynical because programmes and policies, already accepted, had not been implemented.

Thirdly, the opposition also created difficulties, in legislatures and outside. In the last two years we had our hands full in dealing with the law and order situation at all levels.

All this created a piquant situation in the country, economic and political. Now we need a period of stability, a period of discipline, that has been so aptly described by Acharya Vinoba Bhave as a *Anushasan Parva* (Era of Discipline). It has also been highlighted by our Prime Minister, when she said, "without a sense of discipline nothing can be achieved in this country." With this sense of discipline it will now be easy for us to implement our economic objectives.

The 20-point programme is not the last word, it is only a continuing process. More restrictions will be imposed and more measures taken, till such time as we are able to bring about basic social changes, based on social justice.

Perhaps a little more dynamism and more awareness will be able to achieve the objective.

But, can the Congress Party be the instrument of change?

Basically, the Congress organisation from the beginning has been the instrument of change. It is only when the objective situation was not helpful or where our awareness has sagged or where we had weakened, that the Congress found itself in difficulties.

With a little streamlining and the involvement of the younger generation, it would be possible to convert the Congress into a potent instrument of social change.

The Prime Minister has said the Congress Party has become flabby and something must be done to streamline it and to make it more effective. Are you thinking on those lines?

In a mass organisation like the Congress, we have points of strength and weakness. Our strength is that we can involve the masses more readily than any other party because we really represent the organised strength of the masses. Our weakness is that we are a very big—too big—an organisation. Therefore, the Congress has to be streamlined. The flabbiness comes from lack of purpose and a sense of destiny to attain certain things, then, and then alone. Would this organisation be able to meet the challenges facing us.

In what way will the party help the government to implement the 20-point programme?

Till now we haven't been able to find out very effective means of co-operation at the lower levels. At the national levels, yes, and the state levels also. But when we come to specific levels, we have to go into them in detail, in the states, the districts and the talukas.

At the grass-root level?

Yes, at the grass-root level, we are now planning to associate the Congress at all levels, from the taluka to the state level, for perfect co-operation within the Congress and with the government.

Are you planning to purge political elements who had to be accommodated merely to neutralise their nuisance value?

That is a very important question. You see, the Congress is a mass organisation, with sections which are useful, and some that are undesirable. There have been historical processes of getting rid of them. Whenever some programmes crop up or some progressive revolutionary situation arises, in which we have to function more effectively, many of these party critics drop out.

Now when we have a plan of action, a number of these critics will drop it.

Those who are against the Congress principles, who have no faith in the Congress ideology or the leadership of the Prime Minister, will inevitably have to go.

You mean the opportunists have to go?

Yes, opportunists are there some of them right at the top, hostile to the party programme and the political leadership.

Are you planning to expel them?

It is obvious, a climate will be created so that they will find themselves completely isolated from the rank and file of the party. This will soon follow.

The Prime Minister has referred to the need for a far more healthier political behaviour and a sense of responsibility. What can the Congress Party do to inculcate such an attitude among congressmen?

It is very important. Take for example, the land ceiling. Unless congressmen conform to the requirements of the Land Ceiling Act, how do they expect others to do so? Charity begins at home. And in this case, people know about the amount of land a man has, so, unless he sheds what he is not entitled to under the law, people won't have any confidence in him and if a large number of congressmen behave in this manner, they will impair the credibility of the Party which has to great extent been restored by Emergency.

We will have to ask congressmen to discipline themselves and behave and follow a code of conduct for themselves. We will have to impose it on at least the leadership at both the state and the national levels. That will provide a model for all workers to follow.

Party members have been regularly violating Congress Principles,

particularly on the economic front. Are you envisaging some action against them?
Certainly, we will ask them to disclose their assets. But I would expect them to show a streak of conscience about this, rather than impose it on them. I am having discussions with Chief ministers and others. We will ask them to surrender excess land. We will start with land and then go to other items.

The Prime Minister has been insisting that discipline has to be inculcated in the people. This can be done best through the party, not the government, because the Party is the best instrument for this.
My idea of discipline is not exactly regimentation. What I would like to create is a sense of inner discipline which accepts certain norms of behaviour—political and social. In fact, we inherited great things from the days of Gandhiji. One of them is a willing acceptance of certain norms of discipline—political, personal and social.

As it was during Gandhiji's time . . . .
That is true, certain discipline, certain norms, personal, political and social.

Are you planning more Narora-type camps to re-educate the ranks and to make them fully conscious of their responsibilities in the new situation?
We are not starting camps now, because no decisions are arrived at such camps, but we are now organising Congress workers at the district level, so that they can meet and discuss specific problems in co-operation with the government.

It means you are launching a massive course of re-educating party workers?
That is right. The Congress organisation also must engage itself in a continuous process of education and re-education.

The apprehension is that if the party is not active, the bureaucracy might have an upper hand.
You are right, compared to the performance of the last few years, there is greater unity in the party now. There is greater awareness and a far better sense of fulfillment. I am sure that congressmen will respond to our call, the Prime Minister's call.

So you are planning co-ordination between the bureaucracy and the party workers at the district level?
Yes, there will have to be some discussions, some arrangements to function within the government. Bureaucrats are also social beings, they also represent different social strata in the country. I am sure we will get support from them.

There may be diehards and reactionaries, and I think they should be weeded out soon.

My impression is that a fairly large number of bureaucrats are not attuned to the situation you want to create in the country. Don't they need re-education?

If you mean only the senior officers, that is a different story. But where the vast masses of government employees are concerned, I don't believe they are reactionaries. They may not have the correct awareness of the problem. But from the point of view of their own interest. I do not think they are reactionaries and I am sure they will welcome any change that will benefit society. In fact, the increase in the exemption limit of income tax, benefit to the students, the matter of subsidising textbooks—all this will help. Many students are children of government employees.

The CPI has been the only non-Congress Party to whole-heartedly welcome the Emergency and extend co-operation to the Prime Minister. Could you throw some light on the factors leading to such identity of views between the two organisations?

Some other parties have also welcomed the measures. The CPI is the major party which supported us. Ever since 1969, the CPI has been co-operating with the Congress and the Prime Minister's policies and programmes. The Congress would welcome the support of any progressive party. But I'll make it very clear, the main burden of carrying the masses would be ours, because we are genuinely the organised strength of the masses.

My impression is that the understanding with the CPI is at the national level. Are you envisaging some sort of co-ordination at the district or the state level?

At the national level it is a question of acceptance on principle. But the main activity of any political party is in the states and the districts. And that will vary from place to place. In certain places there is no CPI unit. In Gujarat, there is hardly any CPI. But in Kerala, the CPI is in the government. We are supporting them and working together. In West Bengal, they are a big party and we co-operate. In Bihar also, by and large we will be able to work together.

Will this kind of co-ordination lead to greater understanding between the two parties?

We have certainly an understanding about the programmes and ultimate objectives.

You think in this manner the social goal will be attained earlier?
The point is how effective is the government in implementing this programme. The Emergency has given us a chance. We have to be firm about our commitments.

Secondly, we have to utilise this occasion to implement these measures which give relief to us. So if we succeed in both these objectives, I am sure this will be acceptable to the people. They will support us in implementing measures of socialistic development. In fact, social change can come about only with the participation of the masses.

Do you identify socialism with nationalisation?
Not always necessarily. Eighty per cent of our people live in the villages. Their livelihood is in agriculture, cottage industries and village crafts. Socialism to them cannot mean nationalisation of their means of livelihood. They will not be benefited by nationalisation. In nationalising industries, you curtail the power of the vested interests to stall social changes.

Could you define socialism in a nutshell, your concept of socialism?
My concept of socialism is the same as was laid down in the Congress constitution, by Pandit Nehru. It means voluntary acceptance of socialism.

I am asking you a personal question. People who know you, talk of your deep knowledge of history, culture and religions. Some suggest that had you not been in politics you should have been either an eminent philologist or a historian. Do you regret being a whole-time politician?
I started my life as a freedom fighter. After freedom was attained, I stayed on because to me, freedom was only a step to social change. That is why I continue in public life: a fighter for social change, rather than an administrator. In fact as you know, I left a cabinet post to take up this party post only because I am convinced that the Congress is the only instrument for social change. If this objective is fulfilled my life would have been worth living.

You have no regret in life?
I have no regrets. I have had an opportunity to use the knowledge acquired in my youth to bring about social change.

Who has been the main source of inspiration in your academic and political life?
Pandit Jawaharlal Nehru and he continues to do so.

Academically?
Academically also, because Pandit Nehru's contribution to Indian History is unique. I wonder whether any other person has done as much.

The impression is that you have been deeply influenced by Buddha.
Buddha wanted to create a society based on rationality . . . that is more of an intellectual exercise for me. But as a living example, I think Pandit Nehru influenced me more than any other person I know.

Current, 19.07.1975.
pp. (1 + 4 + 16)

Congress destined to change policy: no going back, asserts Ray

Mr. Siddhartha Shankar Ray, "Manu-da" to his cabinet colleagues and friends, bestrides West Bengal like a giant. His benign shadow looms over the once strife-torn state.

Though the people have yet to recover from the traumatic experience of the Naxalite and CPM terror, the remarkable absence of fear now is a tribute to the outstanding leadership of the soft-spoken and urbane Chief minister.

A woman can now walk without fear in the night on the streets of Calcutta. Bombs no more explode in the college campus. Schools and universities are once again centres of academic activity. Factories and mills operate in full swing.

"Yes, peace prevails. Now our problem is how and where to expand," a top executive of a multinational business organisation told me. The same gentlemen, three years ago, was planning to fold up his business and leave Calcutta for good.

Siddhartha Ray has grown from an unsure and shaky Chief minister into an unchallenged leader of West Bengal. He is adored by his people, though his frequent visits to Delhi cause anxiety to his colleagues. The Bengalis, by and large, however, have a great sense of pride in the fact that their Chief minister enjoys the confidence of Mrs. Indira Gandhi.

I met him in his Writers' Building office. The meeting lasted two hours.

Siddhartha Ray's politics is commitment to ideals and policies. To him the 20-point economic programme is an article of faith. "If we fail to implement the programme, the people will never forgive us," he emphasised.

A blunt, outspoken man, Siddhartha Ray talks in measured words. He said: "A great danger existed to the integrity of the nation before June 26. Some of the opposition parties were secretly supported by certain foreign agencies. The aim was to create chaos. Had the Prime Minister not acted in time and declared Emergency, the country might well have lost its independence."

In recent months, Siddhartha Ray has emerged as one of the key men in Indian politics, whose views and opinions help formulate policies and national patterns. He was relaxed, precise and clear in his mind as we discussed the post-Emergency situation.

The questions ranged over the qualitative change in the political situation in the country to "arrogant and overbearing" bureaucrats. With his characteristic incisiveness and perception, Mr. Ray dissected the problem, analysed it and then offered an explanation and rationale for it.

Taking a broad-range view of the situation as it has developed, since June 26. Mr. Ray sounded prophetic: "Unless we can implement the programme fully, we shall lose face and posterity will blame us for not having been able to implement a programme our leader—Mrs. Indira Gandhi—had announced in all earnestness."

The Emergency has brought about a qualitative change in the political situation. This has been welcomed by people all over. The Prime Minister has received heaps of telegrams and letters congratulating her for having brought about this change.

The first impact of the Emergency has been the raising of expectations of speedier change for the all round good. If these expectations are not fulfilled, we shall be found wanting, Mr. Ray stressed.

The students, youth and the common people, who have pinned great faith in the economic programme announced by the Prime Minister, have to be actively involved in the task of implementing them. Mr. Ray pointed out. "The Jagjivan Ram Committee report on the most effective manner of implementing the programme is awaited. Meanwhile, his own government has gone ahead with administrative steps to implement the 20-point programme."

What administrative steps?

In respect of some of the most important points in the programme—distribution of land to the landless; distribution of house-sites to the homeless; wiping out rural debts of the marginal farmers, the small farmers, the landless, the share croppers and the artisans. An ordinance has been issued for staying the recovery of debts from these people in the lowest strata of society.

Mr. Ray pointed out that a conference of officials and financial institutions from all over the state was held in Calcutta to find out methods of granting loans to these sections of people through the co-operatives. "This will require a large sum of money; so it would take some time to begin with."

What about the distribution of house-sites?

We have set a deadline for it—October 2 this year. The same deadline holds good for distribution of land to the landless. Greater attention has to be paid to the recovery of lands in the excess of the ceiling. This can be done effectively only after the Jagjivan Ram Committee Report comes in. Then again, popular committees will have to be set up to push through the programme.

How do you plan to impose the ceiling on urban lands? This question assumes significance, since next to Bombay, Calcutta has to face the brunt of the problem.

A central legislation is coming soon in this respect, which will be applicable to Calcutta as well as to Bombay and other major urban areas. We have had elaborate discussions about the socialisation of urban and urbanisable land and the consensus is that no one should be permitted to have more than seven cottahs as vacant lands . . . the rest should be distributed properly.

What about compensation?

Compensation no longer exist . . . it is no longer in vogue. The word now in use is the "amount" to be paid. This should be fixed very carefully by the Union government.

Equally important for you, in West Bengal, is the question of a public distribution system. What have you done in this respect?

Fortunately in West Bengal, every man, women and child is covered by a ration card. That is, everybody is entitled to a card, and if any, one hasn't it's no fault of ours. We have a legal obligation to provide a fixed amount of ration to everyone holding a statutory ration card. About a crore of people are covered by this scheme.

Unfortunately West Bengal is not a producing state. We do produce paddy, wheat and some other commodities, but not in sufficient quantities. We have to depend upon other states for our supplies of mustard oil, sugar, salt—in fact all essential commodities.

If the supply from other states is regular and adequate, there is no difficulty with the Public Distribution System. The distribution system is completely streamlined.

Mr. Ray pointed out that the public distribution system was an important part of the programme and it should not only be made to work properly, but expanded, particularly in the modified rationing areas."

What about the problem of expansion of irrigation facilities to improve agriculture?

Orders have been issued by my government to bring large areas under minor irrigation. We have sanctioned Rs. 7 crore for this, without depending upon the centre. We are distributing mini-pumps to the farmers, besides seeds, insecticides and fertilisers to ensure a better *aman* crop. We have also distributed highyielding seeds as an experiment for the *aman* crop.

We have sanctioned funds for the sinking of hundreds of shallow tubewells to tap underground resources. The problem, so far as we are concerned is not water, but land. We have water, but not enough land. So we are planning to make one-crop areas into two-crop or three-crop areas.

What about cloth for the poor?

We are awaiting instructions from the centre regarding the quality of controlled cloth. You see, in many of these matters we have to depend upon the centre for directions. What we can do on our own. We are going ahead with, for example, the distribution of land—they can't do it; we have to do it ourselves. It is our responsibility.

Can you throw some light on what shape the new political and economic system will take?

That is a tricky question. The political system that we want is one where the citizens should have democratic rights, not licence. Democracy does not mean that you have only rights and no obligations. In legal parlance, there can never be a right without a concomitant obligation. If you have a right to do certain things, you have an obligation to do certain other things. Democracy is meaningless if you have only rights and no obligations. Rights carry with them some obligations and duties to perform. If these obligations are not honoured, rights become meaningless. The political system that we envisage is one where obligations have to be honoured and duties have to be performed. No system can work unless there is greater discipline.

What about the press? Why this pre-censorship?

That's it! All you have to do to find an answer to your question is to read the newspapers published during the one month before June 26. What they did was not freedom of the press—it was indulging in some sort of licence. It was not freedom at all.

Can you define the role of the Congress in the changed circumstances?

The Congress has to fashion itself in such a manner that it can really deliver the goods. If we depend entirely on the bureaucracy and congressmen are allowed to sit at home and do nothing—nothing can be achieved . . . no, even one of the 20 points of the programme. We also have to work with like-minded parties.

The Congress is the largest Party in India; without it you cannot have any progress. It is the only party that can deliver the goods. New responsibilities and new duties have devolved on congressmen. If the Congress is able to discharge its responsibilities and perform its duties, we shall come out of this difficult history quite successfully and honourably.

The Congress has changed beyond recognition in the last 90 years of its existence. The change has always been for the better. It has changed with the aspirations of the people—it has advanced and it has always been in the forefront.

Today, it has brought in a new social condition. The Congress has changed since 1971 considerably. It was necessary to change, since it symbolised India and since the aspirations and desires of the people changed. In its own way, the Congress also has given a lead in changing the desires and aspirations of the people.

Would the change be more effective if the Congress is transformed into a cadre-based party?

The Congress has been partly a cadre-based partly and party a mass-based party. We have in effect made it a cadre-based party, but the main strength of the Congress lies in its rank and file, which comprises of the masses. The cadres are meant to initiate the masses into the philosophy of the Congress and its objectives.

The aims and objectives of the Congress are synonymous with the aspirations and objectives of the people of India. Fortunately for us, from time to time, it has also led us to the right aspirations and the right goals. A new goal, a definite goal, has now to be found for the Congress.

What role do you envisage for the organised youth of the country in the changed circumstances?

The youth and students have to play a more important and purposeful role in the changed circumstances, particularly in implementing the economic programme. Youth camps should be organised all over the country to make them partners in the change that we so earnestly earn for. After all, it is they who have a larger stake in tomorrow.

What about the role of the CPI and like-minded parties in all this?

The CPI has written to us offering their co-operation. Details are being worked out. The CPI and the Congress should work together in certain fields with certain specific programmes. If the economic programme has to be a success, there has to be coordination in various places and the youth and students who believe in this programme, irrespective of their party affiliations, should work together.

In West Bengal, the Youth Congress and the Chhatra Parishad will give the lead in this respect, because they are mass organisations.

There has been considerable criticism of our bureaucracy. Do you think it will help in implementing the programme?

The bureaucracy has to change to become more involved in the social philosophy of the government. I have already had two meetings—one with the secretaries and the other with the ministers. I have made it clear that they have to understand the social philosophy behind the 20-point programme and also the motivations of the government as a whole. If we find any official negligent in implementing the programme, we shall do away with him.

I have asked all top officials of the state government to be humble and never arrogant. In the present circumstances, not even ministers should be arrogant. Our approach has to be as humble as possible. The people expect this from the bureaucrats and also from the politicians.

What about corruption? How do you plan to tackle this problem?

We have a number of organisations in West Bengal which deal with corruption. We have vigilance organisations. From 1972, when we took charge here, we have taken action against several IAS and IPS officers. We have not spared anyone. In my own secretariat there is a vigilance cell, which entertains complaints. Every complaint is looked into.

I came to the question that almost everyone in the country is asking today: How long will the Emergency last?

Mr. Ray knitted his brows for an instant. Then his rugged face lit up with a self-confident smile.

"The Emergency will continue as long as it is necessary," he seemed to pronounce a verdict. "Whether it will be for a long period or a short period, I think nobody can say now. The intention of the government, however is not to keep it any longer than is essential—that is, till normal conditions come back. Normal conditions do not mean conditions as they existed before June 26. The concept of normal conditions has changed." He did not elaborate. We did not press him either.

Current, 02.08.1975.
pp. (1 + 4 + 20).

Mobilise youth power: say Yuva Congress

West Bengal's stormy petrel, Subrata Mukherjee has a husky voice. With his chiselled features and elegant dress, he can be taken as one of the Calcutta University campus academicians. He was bereft of the Home portfolio but his political status remains the same. He almost single-handedly controls Calcutta the fifth largest city in the world. At 20, he is the youngest member of Siddhartha Shankar Ray's Council of ministers. His weight in West Bengal Politics is much greater than the portfolio he holds—information and public relations.

Subrata Mukherjee's contribution in wiping out left adventurism from West Bengal is next to none. A secret of his success is his very large following among the youth and students. It remains unchallenged. He commands the Chatra Parishad and Yuva Congress with great tact. For the first time after Independence, Bengali students and youth have flocked to these two organisations. And Subrata Mukherjee is the moving spirit behind them.

When we met one morning for a discussion, the study in his modest flat was crowded by his comrades. They included Sudip Bandhopadhyay, president of the Yuva Congress, Tapas Dhar, Chief of the Land Army, Debaprasad Roy, the fiery General Secretary of the Yuva Congress and Atanu Mukherjee, Treasurer of the Chatra Parishad.

Sudip and Debaprasad sport flowing black beards and long hair. I mistook them for awadhoots. "These beards appear rather interesting", I commented.

"Yes, they are nature's gift," Sudip replied.

Tapas Dhar, the commander of the Land Army, appeared tense. He would not even smile. He had come after addressing a meeting of share-croppers. "The jotedars . . . yes the jotedars . . . . something will have to be done about them. The land must be given back to the tillers. This is the gist of the Congress ideology."

Dhar was interrupted by Subrata: "Yes, without a comprehensive agrarian revolution the task of the Congress will remain unfinished."

I asked Subrata how the youth could be guided in the implementation of the 20-point economic programme as the government may have the tendency to depend on the bureaucracy rather than on the party in these matters.

Subrata Mukherjee: The students and the youth fully support the programme and I have no hesitation in saying that they are ever willing to join hands with the party organisation and the administration in its implementation. But the question is, "How?"

Both in the party and the government there is no discussion on this issue. My suggestion is that the youth should be involved in the implementation Committee. I feel at the district level, atleast one youth and one student should be members.

Secondly, there should be a clear directive to the administration that positive help from the youth may be taken instead of just harassing them. For example, in the work of distributing land for the marginal cultivators, the students can help by recording the distribution of land. Land which is not under record can be recorded.

It is not our duty to go to the administration, instead the administration must approach us. Otherwise we are doing nothing much except building up public opinion in favour of the programme. So positive projects in the implementation depends on the administration itself.

But you are part of the administration?

Subrata Mukherjee: Yes, theoretically. But I am alone. I am only an individual minister, the whole government should be involved to give proper direction.

Recently, your Chief minister suggested that the popular committees will be composed of the people's representatives, government officials and students and youths. Who will select these student and youth representatives?

Subrata Mukherjee: We will. The Yuva Congress and the Chatra Parishad will give the nominations. For implementing certain specific points of the programme we can totally depend on the Chatra Parishad, specially in food distribution and the book bank scheme.

One book bank will cover a particular zone with a certain number of colleges. Our representatives from the student will assist in the actual distribution of books and in deciding cases of who should or should not get books, etc.

In the present situation there is a greater likelihood of the bureaucracy becoming hot-headed and assuming all the powers. I was told that people who had nothing to do with politics have been arrested. What steps will you take to eliminate this?

Subrata Mukherjee: This is called bureaucratic fascism. The major responsibility lies with the government as nothing can be done politically. If the youth and the party give authentic reports of officials misusing powers then steps will immediately be taken and an enquiry conducted.

In what way will the Yuva Congress deal with this?

Sudip Bandhopadhyay: It is our belief that most of the ministers are pro-bureaucracy. We have appealed several times to the leaders of the states to remove certain officials holding key positions but unfortunately no proper steps have been taken.

Subrata Mukherjee: At the time of the last harvest and also during the procurement we had submitted a list of 46,000 volunteers and had requested the government to give them official recognition to enable them work in 38,000 villages of West Bengal but we got no reply.

At the moment though the government still says that it is seeking our co-operation we do not know whether we can really get involved properly. The maximum we have done is to pass a resolution that we should go to the aid of the landless cultivator.

Now the urban problem of slums. What is the slum population of Calcutta.

Subrata Mukherjee: 15 lakhs. The Calcutta Metropolitan Development Authority and the City Improvement Trust are involved in the betterment of the slum-dwellers. Students and youth cannot effectively take part because of the present administrative structure.

Mr. Dhar, you're the Chief of the Bhoomi Sena or the Land Army. What is the Sena doing in the present situation?

Tapas Dhar: We work mainly in the rural areas trying to recover land from the big jotedars. We also help poor cultivators to transplant paddy, initiate cultivation, etc., all with our limited resources. The main problem is that while we are ready to cooperate, the government has been slow in extending its co-operation. . . .

Subrata Mukherjee: Particularly in areas where thousands of acres of land have been forcibly occupied by owners of big fisheries. We are also trying to reclaim land but some big jotedars are standing in the way. They take advantage of the law.

Have you acquired any such land?

Tapas Dhar: Yes, 5,000 bighas.

Subrata Mukherjee: But the process is difficult as the present laws protect the jotedars.

Tapas Dhar: I would also like to mention the case of one judge who is himself a big jotedar for he owns 5,000 bighas of land and he looks after these cases!

Subrata Mukherjee: I know of one case where a cultivator went to a jotedar with a petition but the landlord shot him. The landlord said that he did it in self-defence and he was released!

Tapas Dhar: Our struggle is starting, and we will fight to the last for the land that rightfully belongs to the tiller.

The CPI has not only unconditionally welcomed the Emergency but has offered to co-operate with the Congress and they might also serve on the popular committees. What is your attitude?
Subrata Mukherjee: It would be right political thinking to accept their participation.

But to what extent?
Subrata Mukherjee: At all levels, on every point of the programme.

Is there any likelihood of clashes between Congress and CPI?
Subrata Mukherjee: In West Bengal I do not think this will happen.

Are you forming some kind of a co-ordination committee?
Subrata Mukherjee: There is no guidance as yet on this from Delhi but in an isolated way some people are meeting together and discussing things.

There are sections in the Congress who oppose collaboration with the CPI. How would you like to co-operate with this element in the West Bengal Congress?
Subrata Mukherjee: They should realise that they are being irrational and unscientific. At present we should join hands with the CPI to impress upon the people the need for right political action.

In this process won't the Congress lose its identity?
Subrata Mukherjee: I don't think there is any question of our losing our identity. The CPI are joining hands with us for the implementation of a particular programme, aim or objective. They are not giving up their ideology when they do this, and we won't give up ours.

On the workers' front do you think co-operation between the Congress and the CPI would be healthy?
Debaprasad Roy: Yes, it is healthy if it serves the people. We have no prejudice against the CPI or against working with them. Not because of the fact that they are holding the red flag but because they recognise the country's problems as we do.

Earlier the attitude of INTUC used to be opposed to the AITUC?
Debaprasad Roy: Even Atulya Ghosh had formed some rival union against INTUC in the tea plantations, I think. But today the INTUC leadership is not basically anti-CPI. And there are people who are against the INTUC because they feel that the two labour organisations would merge and their interests would be affected.

We are essentially Yuva Congress workers and we keep our aims in mind, not the aims of the INTUC. At the same time we have to be members of INTUC as it is a recognised organisation of the All India Congress Committee.

Is there a possibility of the INTUC and AITUC youth forming a joint committee for the labour front?

Debaprasad Roy: The Yuva Congress is demanding that there should be a big change in the present INTUC leadership. This is fundamental.

Subrata Mukherjee: Our experience is that anti-congressism is wrong politics and blind animosity towards the CPI is also wrong politics.

Debaprasad Roy: With changing times, the Congress has to change its policies and programmes also. 1975 is reality and everybody has to accept it. Today the situation is different, the atmosphere is different and the crisis is different.

Q. What is reality now?

Debaprasad Roy: Reality, which has now been fully identified, is to serve 56 crores of people who are waiting for economic emancipation and the basic things in life.

Current, 16.08.1975.
pp. (10 + 11)

Poll on Time

The decisive judgement of the Supreme Court upholding Mrs. Indira Gandhi's appeal against the verdict of the Allahabad High Court, fully vindicates her stand. It leaves no room for any doubt about her right to continue as the Prime Minister.

The judgement gives legal validity to the moral sanction she has already acquired with the spectacular achievements of the last twenty weeks of Emergency. The tranquillity, peace and progress attained in this period is a foretaste of the benefits that could accrue from a long spell of disciplined work for national good.

Greater discipline increased production.

The Emergency that was promulgated in the wake of the most heinously reactionary conspiracy to subvert democracy and the economic and social progress of the country, has come as a boon.

As Dr. Raj Nigam, Director of the Bureau of Public Enterprises, traces in his article on page 12. "Emergency has ushered in an era of economic emancipation for the vast numbers of our countrymen." The promise is contained in the marked progress seen in the agricultural, industrial and economic spheres. Emergency has enabled us to target for an unprecedented 114 million tonnes of foodgrains, 7.7 million tonnes of steel ingots, 42 million tonnes of iron ore, 98 million tonnes of coal and 1.9 million tonnes of fertiliser.

With greater discipline and increased production, these targets are attainable. They promise a period of prosperity and freedom from constricting shortages.

The strict measures adopted during the Emergency to check inflation have borne fruit. There are no shortages of essential commodities anywhere in the country. Smuggling has been effectively controlled, our foreign exchange earnings have skyrocketed and the sense of despondency that threatened to overwhelm us a few months ago has given way to a feeling of buoyancy, hope and confidence in the future.

Mrs. Gandhi has rightly become the symbol of national resurgence. With the authority she commands, she is in an unassailable position to bring about radical social transformation.

She has already spelt out her vision of social changes for the country. The entire nation is behind her in the fulfillment of this objective.

The 20-point economic programme has created a new atmosphere in the country. There is tremendous enthusiasm everywhere to implement the programme taking full advantage of the Emergency. The abolition of rural indebtedness, provision of house sites for the rural poor, abolition of bonded labour, relief for students, the unemployed and the tax payers and the crackdown on economic offenders are among the significant achievements during this period.

Despite these achievements, there has been a tendency towards slackness and complacency in the bureaucracy. Bureaucrats, taking advantages of the absence of public criticism, have tended to grow arrogant. Under no circumstances can public servants be permitted to assume authoritarian positions.

The political machinery of the government and the ruling party should maintain greater vigil and be ready for corrective action wherever necessary.

There is also need for total involvement of the people at all levels in the effective implementation of the economic programme as also other measures aimed at social transformation.

A review of the achievements of the last six months and formulation of policies and programmes for the future can be undertaken at the forthcoming AICC meeting in December at Chandigarh. The AICC will also be the right forum for chalking out plans for the next general elections due in March 1976.

The circumstances are propitious for holding the general elections on schedule. It is right and proper for the ruling party to seek a fresh mandate from the people after the tumultuous events of the last 12 months.

Mrs. Gandhi has met the challenges of the recent past with a sense of destiny and unflinching faith and confidence in herself.

A fresh election and a fresh mandate is called for, if social transformation is to be effective and radical. No radical and abiding transformation can be possible without far-reaching changes in the present legal and educational systems to suit social needs and conditions. This also presupposes drastic changes in our Constitution.

Our legal and constitutional systems must take note of the changing social and economic order. Economic offences have become more deadly and vicious than individual crimes and should be put down with harsh and deterrent punishment, which are not provided for in our present legal system.

The Prime Minister has already called upon the national sector to bring about greater industrial development. Utilisation of all land for optimum agricultural output and socialisation of all urban land for common good are among other objectives that need to be attained, if social change has to have some meaning.

Socialism of Mrs. Gandhi's concept, accepted by the people cannot be introduced without these changes. The present is the most opportune time for her to push through her programmes and usher in socialism in our life time.

Current, 15.11.1975.
pp. (1 + 4)

People's participation in nation building

The Prime Minister, Mrs. Indira Gandhi, has laid to rest the confusion that enveloped India's industrial economy for several years. She told Parliaments' Consultative Committee on Planning earlier this month that the government stood committed to the concept of mixed economy as a basic tenet of India's industrial policy.

Her assertion came in response to a paper submitted by a Congress Member of Parliament, Mr. V.P. Sathe, advocating greater state control over the private sector. The paper sought the regulation of organised industry so that profits, after disbursement of dividends and wages, accrued wholly to the states.

Mr. Sathe advocated, in his own words, the establishment of a "democratic socialist national sector." It was presumably a retort to the concept of national sector propounded by Mr. T.A. Pai, Union minister for Industry and Civil Supplies. According to Mr. Pai this could be achieved by permitting minority public participation in the equity of public sector companies.

Mr. Pai is backed by weighty recommendations by a number of committees, including one headed by the late Mr. V.K. Krishna Menon. Yet his proposal provoked sharp criticism, especially from some leftist circles which dubbed it as a manoeuvre for a sell-out of the public sector to private industry.

The Prime Minister took up cudgels on behalf of Mr. Pai's proposal emphasising the economic and democratic validity of the idea of inviting public participation in the equity of public sector undertakings. The controversy did not subside.

Some spokesmen of the private sector also twisted Mr. Pai's proposal urging that along with equity participation the management of public sector undertakings should be handed over to the "professionally experienced and competent" entrepreneurs. When joint sector undertakings were first mooted some years ago, a similar misinterpretation of the concept generated a virulent controversy with the result that joint sector ventures made little headway. It dampened popular enthusiasm.

In this controversy two basic factors have been conveniently ignored. Firstly, the large scale investment by financial institutions in the private sector and the consequent regulatory powers they enjoy have imposed on the private sector a greater sense of social responsibility.

Secondly, the involvement of the public sector in nodal consumption areas has made public sector managements more responsive to market forces in order to compete with the private sector. Consequently, bureaucratic approach is yielding place to professionalism.

The steady increase in the generation of internal resource in the public sector in the last three years is evidence that the public sector has a greater sense of economic responsibility.

This should be an ideal framework for a mixed economy in which allocation of scarce resources for optimal utilisation will be based on industrial priorities rather than sectorial precedence, and in which every investment, either in the private or public sector, is deemed a national investment.

No conceivable mode of resource mobilisation can be neglected in the pursuit of such an industrial culture. The underlying idea is to use private entrepreneurial talent to subserve socio-economic objectives.

A logical extension of this principle will be greater mobilisation of private savings to subserve these objectives rather than for private gain. Taxation, the most common method of mopping up private savings for public use is not the answer since the compulsion involved in tax collection and the indirect return benefit provides the taxpayer no sense of participation in nation-building even though that is what he does by paying the taxes.

Inviting public participation in public sector undertakings, in Mrs. Gandhi's words, is to ensure that private savings are attracted to productive investment directly, voluntarily and with a sense of involvement. The classical capital market in developing countries has become an inefficient instrument for mobilising investible funds. Stock market activity too, has become speculation-oriented, affording no opportunity to common people to participate by investing their savings in local undertakings.

The expensive rural sector remains untouched by urban investment motivations. Our entrepreneurs and stock exchanges have hardly made any effort to mop up the substantially increased rural incomes. The field is wide open for the public sector to make a determined bid to mobilise rural savings and channel them into productive investment.

The response to the public issue by Scooters India Ltd., the first public sector undertaking to offer equity participation to the public holds out hope that the common people, who have so far kept out of the urban-biased and often manipulated public issues of private sector companies will willingly invest in public sector undertakings.

The overall performance of the public sector has improved remarkably, with both profits and profitability registering an upward trend. Public confidence in public sector units is rising. The time is ripe for public sector units, particularly the consumer-oriented ones, to woo public participation.

The government is not likely to shed its controlling interest in these concerns. Neither can the capital structure of public sector units be radically altered to disburse their surpluses among private shareholders.

Public participation cannot be equated with industrial investment based on private gain. That would open the floodgates for a total recasting of the monetary and fiscal policies, so consciously framed to subserve the socialist objectives. Sharing the fruits of development and not reaping the monetary returns on investment should be the motivation behind public participation in public sector undertakings.

Current, 29.11.1975.
pp. (1 + 71)

Youth must take over

The Congress Party, with its historic record as the instrument of change, took yet another momentous decision last week when it declared India "a socialist, secular democratic republic."

The recommendation is enshrined in the Swaran Singh Committee report. Prime Minister Mrs. Indira Gandhi, wearing a spotless white Khadi Sari, and in the best of health at 59, declared amidst thunderous applause that the Congress was within its right in taking "far-reaching decisions and yet completely within our declared policy and the mandate given to us by the Indian people."

Her suggestion that the proposed constitutional changes should also include an article on fundamental obligations and duties, which citizens owe to the country, was later accepted as an amendment. The new duties and obligations are to include "sustenance of the unity and integrity of the nation, action in accordance with the Constitution and laws of the land, maintenance of discipline in every sphere, performance of public duties and safeguarding of public property."

The AICC had a record attendance, with 804 of its 966 members participating. The delegates were jubilant over the far-reaching decisions. One of them remarked: "Even Lord Jagannath changes shape every 12 years. Why not the Constitution?"

The Prime Minister and the entire top echelons of the Party sat through the session from morning till evening, hardly moving, even for lunch. AICC General Secretary, Purabi Mukherjee, would give a stern look at the delegates who shuttled between the hall and the spacious dais. So great was the discipline during the session that the Prime Minister profusely complimented the delegates and specially Mrs. Purabi Mukherjee for the commendable performance.

Mrs. Gandhi herself intently listened to the speeches and unlike the earlier sessions (where the delegates would insist on talking to her) she dissuaded even senior leaders from disturbing the solemn atmosphere.

In two days she spoke thrice, deliberating at great length on various points. At one stage she lashed out at religious and obscurantist elements for creating obstacles in the party's determination to curb the population growth.

"No one will be allowed to make political capital out of communal propaganda against such far-reaching programmes," she warned.

She was thunderously cheered. Even stiff-looking security men who guarded the gates joined in the applause.

Explaining the proposed constitutional changes, she declared that they sought to achieve "true justice and true equality for the common man and to give deeper and purposive meaning to democracy."

The changes in the Constitution have been proposed, she said, because "we have to think of some basic matters—what we are fighting against and what we are fighting for."

Raising her voice, and looking the delegates straight in the eye, she said: "Our basic fight is against the entrenched privileges of a few whether in the social or economic field or in international affairs."

"We are fighting for the rights of the common man in India and the common man all over the world. We are fighting for the removal of fear." She added.

The Prime Minister was in a rare and exceptional mood. She chided the delegates who took to the podium and started heaping praise on her: "I do not like being mentioned too often and on every subject." It was not proper to drag her name everywhere. "This shows that you simply want to get rid of the responsibilities by passing the buck on to me," she said.

Mrs. Gandhi also reserved her scorn for the so-called "ideologues" who have been purveying theories of left and right.

"I happen to be not merely the daughter of Jawaharlal Nehru but one who worked with him very closely. So, for people whether of the left or the right to tell me what Nehru stood for is not only funny but also shows to what extent people go."

The Youth Congress leader Sanjay Gandhi, who took a back seat, heard her with rapt attention. He too sat through the sessions from morning to evening but met cabinet ministers, Chief ministers and a very large number of delegates. He went around the spacious lawns and corridors of the Vithalbhai Patel Bhavan where the session was held, inspecting the arrangements.

The Youth Congress and its youthful leaders made their presence felt by distributing a large amount of literature and acquainting the delegates of their activities.

Hundreds of Youth Congress activists had come from all over the country. They kept their President Mrs. Ambika Soni, busy by explaining their problems to her. Mrs. Soni has grassroots approach to problems mixes with the younger crowd with extreme conviviality. She has acquired tremendous grasp of youth problems in a short spell of time. Both Sanjay Gandhi and Ambika Soni have established relations with a very large number of young people.

The Youth was perhaps the most important theme of Congress President D.K. Barooah's speech. The emergence of Sanjay Gandhi, as the youth leader, has electrified the atmosphere in the country. "Our generation is dying out. It is time that the youth take over," the Congress President told the highest policy-making body of the Indian National Congress.

"In this country, youth have done a lot of things, but the old people have taken more credit for it. He gave several examples of young people creating history.

Shankaracharya was 19 when he sought to transform Hindu society; Vivekananda was only 27 when he stormed the citadels of the West and Akbar the Great was in teens when he propounded a new religion—*Din-e-Ilahi.*

The delegates heard the Congress President assert that Jawaharlal Nehru had become a national hero before he was 30.

The time has come, he said, when youth should take over the country and the Party. They should shoulder greater responsibilities in the transformation of the social order. In the past, he said, youth had shied away from the party. Now they have reposed faith in it. "They should not only be soldiers but generals too," his words were drowned in the loudest cheers of the day.

Warming up, he commended the four-point programme given to the youth by Sanjay Gandhi. Partymen should adopt the four points along with the 20-point programme of the Congress. "Thus, we will have a 24-point programme," he added.

Mr. Barooah reminded the delegates that until now they could excuse themselves by saying that they could not implement the policies because of impediments. He paused for a moment, smiled and added: "Now that the impediments are being removed, what excuse will you give to the people? We will now have to implement all our decisions: otherwise, they will not forgive us."

The Prime Minister lustily cheered him when he declared: "We owe only one allegiance. That is the allegiance to the people of India and the destiny of India."

One remarkable speech of the session came from aging Oil minister, K.D. Malaviya, amongst the senior leaders, he was the one who pointedly drew their attention to the state of the Party. The Party, he said will have to totally identify itself with the 20-point programme. The tendency is to leave the implementation to the bureaucrats. This may prove disastrous. Party workers should be in the forefront in championing the cause of the poor and also saving the common man from bureaucratic high-handedness.

West Bengal Chief minister Siddhartha Shankar Ray spoke in similar tone. The constitutional amendments, he said, were absolutely essential to fulfil the aspirations of the people. "If the Congress was not willing to make the changes necessary for the country's socio-economic transformation, the people would themselves bring about the changes, not through constitutional methods but by violent means," he warned.

The Delhi AICC session has once again proved that the Congress has a sense of destiny. It has once again reflected the aspirations of the people.

The session was directed, as Mrs. Gandhi said, to make democratic institutions more meaningful and effective, so that the rights of millions of people, which had been usurped, were restored to them.

Current, 05.06.1976.
pp. (1 + 4)

Indira must contain anti-Congress wave

Congressmen in Bihar, UP, Haryana and Punjab are facing an avalanche of popular anger. I shudder at the idea of this tidal wave of mass hostility sweeping down over the majestic Indo-Gangetic plains towards the lush-green mountains and fields of the South.

Congressmen are demoralised and have surrendered to these powerful tides rushing through the cities, towns, villages and hamlets of North India, the proud bastion of the Congress since its inception.

Indira Gandhi is the only force which can combat this unprecedented anti-Congress wave. She still retains the charisma and the mass popularity required to win over the people.

During my whirlwind tour of this area, I must have spoken to hundreds of men and women—old and young. They unleashed their fury against the Congress, the government, the bureaucrats and the police. But not a word against Indira Gandhi—she is a *devi*, the sins are committed in her home.

Congressmen in power—and out of it—have pinned their hopes on her. Without her the Party would have been bundled out lock, stock and barrel by people seething with rage.

I have witnessed and reported three General Elections and never did I come across such a fouled political atmosphere.

This time it is not an election it is a referendum on what the government did during the 19 months of Emergency—especially forced sterilisation—*Nasbandi*. It is a dirty word all over. It stinks. It provokes.

The anger is so intense that Congress candidates in Patna. Lucknow and Chandigarh are unable to hold even street corner meetings. They are booed and chased. A "giant" like Chaudhury Bansi Lal, who is facing little-known Chandravati in Bhiwani, has sensed the pulse of the people. I heard him speak with folded hands in a public meeting. Words rolled out from his "powerful" mouth: "Never in the future would any compulsion be allowed. Forgive us for our past mistakes and we shall be careful in future."

I rubbed my eyes in disbelief. If this was the condition of Bansi Lal, the Builder of modern Haryana, what about the grassroots congressmen?

Nasbandi seems to have shaken the very foundations of the Congress. The situation is ominous because these areas are largely populated by martial races—Jats and Rajputs who identify manhood with virility. *Nasbandi* is burnt into their minds as a sure way to impotency. The weaker sections who were the special target of the crusade are still cowering with fear. In Patna, I met a young man at a minister's house who had come to complain to him about the cruel treatment meted out to him.

I asked him: "What do you do?"

The frail, emaciated man stared at me : "I was released from jail last week after 16 months. My only fault was that I refused to be sterilised. I also refused to bribe the "daroga" (Head Constable). I was beaten and tortured in jail. My sister was abducted by the Police Inspector. I want my sister back. I want my sister back.

Tears rolled down his coarse cheeks. This was not the only tale of police and bureaucratic excess I heard.

In a U.P. village I met the father of a bridegroom who had jumped from a *tonga* while travelling with his bride when he saw a medical team. "He has not yet come back. Please get my son back." The old man pleaded with folded hands.

"And what about the 'chikona' (butcher)? Another farmer from among the crowd asked me in a Sultanpur village. "He jumped from his shop and ran away as he saw the *Nasbandi* squad. Three months have passed and he hasn't returned."

Numerous tales of horror were related to me in village after village. The proud, brave peasants of the Indo-Gangetic belt are terror-stricken.

The specter of *Nasbandi* still haunts them despite numerous declarations of the withdrawal of F.P. disincentives. They believe that the draconian measures would be reintroduced if the Congress is returned to power.

The *Janata* demagogues have made maximum capital out of this fear. Even the "hijras" have jumped into the fray.

Last week they met at Lucknow and resolved to support the Janata. The Congress policy is for less births and hence less *baksheesh* for them. Their leader, Haji Allarakkha will organise an all-India anti-*nasbandi* campaign.

It is not fear alone, various sections of society have been antagonised. School and college teachers in Bihar and U.P. have not been paid for months. The Bihar government sanctioned Rs. 9 crore for salary arrears of teachers only last week. Teachers in U.P. still remain unpaid.

Government officers' salaries and promotions were withheld till officials fulfilled sterilisation quotas. Teachers and government servants are an important, influential segment of our electorate. Lawyers are angry over the "erosion of the independence of the judiciary," petty traders for the misuse of MISA, peasants for the increase in land revenue and the faulty implementation of land reforms.

A number of *Nawab*s, *Rajah*s and *Rani*s have been fielded by the Congress in this election. In 1971, Congress workers actively campaigned against them. Now they share election platforms with the same feudals. This is an aberration.

Old and moth-eaten politicians have been dug out from political archives and pitted against Janata candidates as "safe bets" much to the consternation of younger elements.

These areas present a frightful picture to Congress campaigners while Janata leaders appear overwhelmed at the unexpected and unprecedented response from the people.

The polarisation is complete. The battle lines are drawn. The people are divided into pro and anti-Congress camps. The fight is straight.

Despite the existence of the Janata and Cong-D as separate parties, the people do not differentiate between their leaders. The Janata means simple and plain anti-congressism. The preponderance of Jan Sangh element has not frightened minority voters including Muslims.

In U.P., Haryana and Bihar with their 149 seats, the "waves" have demolished religious, casteist and even geographical boundaries. The Charan Singh Wave sweeps over Western U.P. and Haryana, the *Babuji* Tide rolls over Bihar and Eastern U.P. and Bahuguna rides the crest in the U.P. heartland.

In Bihar, Ramanand Tiwari, Madhu Limaye and George Fernandes add a touch of glamour and bravado to high-voltage campaigns. A caged portrait of George Fernandes attracts hundreds of people in the *bazaars* of Muzaffarpur. The socialist leader has suddenly become a symbol of revolt for Bihar youth. They shine shoes to finance his election.

In Eastern U.P., Chandra Shekhar and Ram Dhan, are heroes; women do their 'aarti' and garland them with currency notes.

I found dissatisfaction even in Rae Bareli where Raj Narain roams like a Goliath. "Will you improve your position this time?" I asked the bearded socialist. "Improve! This time she'll lose her deposit," he shot back.

Raj Narain has shed 25 kg in jail. Though he was certainly over-optimistic, the political atmosphere was not very pleasing in the Prime Minister's constituency.

Amethi begins where Rae Bareli ends. Sanjay spends most of his time touring U.P. accompanied by Chief minister N.D. Tiwari. But he is new to Amethi and he was fervently advised by wellwishers to take his constituency rather more seriously.

The situation would have been equally bad in Orissa had the Prime Minister not dismissed Nandini Satpathy. She symbolised tyranny and coercion. With her exit, Orissa is safe for the Congress.

This is frankly admitted even by Janata leader Biju Patnaik. Stalwart Hare Krishna Mehtab, who pooh-poohed the Jag-bomb, thought Nandini, despite her enormous ill-gotton wealth, was a liability to Biju.

Chief minister Binayak Acharya showed me the fabulous mansion she has built in the heart of Bhubaneshwar. I also saw the thatched roof of her old house in Cuttack.

The Oriyas have been victims of recurring droughts. Nearly 80 per cent of them live below the Chapati Line. With the lowest per capita income in the country, they have taken poverty as a fait accompli.

People in villages cannot even afford a pair of shoes or a *dhoti.* Yet, most top Oriya politicians and bureaucrats are notorious for corruption, callousness. The Oriyas are, therefore, indifferent to "the politics of change." Binayak Acharya's clean reputation is an asset to the Congress though he is yet to assert himself politically.

The Orissa example shows that the people are not anti-Congress for the sake of being anti-Congress. There are valid reasons which have provoked frayed tempers in the Hindi belt.

Despite the massive anti-Congress wave, the situation is not yet irreversible.

Congressmen should not be apologetic about the Era of Emergency.

If they justify the Prime Minister's June 25 step, they should also feel proud in communicating the major economic achievements in those 19 months.

They should rise to the occasion, gather courage and face the people.

Current, 05.03.1977.
pp. (1 + 2)

C. Authoritarianism and Excesses

Bahuguna believes this government will fall

Bahuguna is the man to watch.

As the most dazzling fall-out from the Jag-Bomb, he is being weighed in silver by his adherents in U.P. towns.

Though he has been a prominent leader of this sprawling state of 10 crore and finally became its Chief minister, he never had it so good.

We worked together in the 1971 Congress campaign. As AICC General Secretary he planned and campaigned vigorously. I never saw him losing his temper. Always laughing and jovial, he introduced a new style of functioning. He has a tremendous capacity to make friends and maintain friendships.

But Bahuguna was a changed man when I met him recently in Lucknow. He spoke, loudly, lost his temper quickly, thumped the table constantly and gave the impression of being in a hurry. It was breakfast time and he finished three thick yellow moong chapatis within minutes.

Outside a large crowd of supporters and admirers waited for him and despite stern instructions to his secretary, the telephone constantly buzzed. Calls from Bombay, Madras, Azamgarh and Benares came asking for his presence in the election campaigns. He has never been so much in demand. He never expected it.

He would not agree to a formal interview: "Let's talk, I want to talk to you, I want to unburden myself. I was hurt. I was humiliated. I was isolated. They tried to kill me politically, to bury me, to erase my name from the political map of the country. Now the time has come for me. The people are with me. The people are my phalanx."

Whenever I tried to intervene he jumped on his wooden chair, pressed my hand and said loudly: "Listen, you must listen to me. I want to open your eyes to the realities. You're blinded by your love for Mrs. Gandhi. Stop this chamchagiri.

Incoherent, strong words rolled out from his wide mouth like pieces of burning coal. Then suddenly he noticed the taperecorder: "Yes, I want you to record each and every word I speak. The era of fear has ended. Emergency has been 'relaxed.' It will have to be demolished."

There was a call from Dr. N.N. Kailash from Bombay beseeching him to rush to the city. " But why to Bombay?" He shouted back.

"The Muslims, the Muslim voters. Only you can influence them." I heard Dr. Kailash's weak voice over the line.

Bahuguna's eyes sparkled with joy. "Look! This is what they've made of Bahuguna. I am the hero of the Muslims. I wept for them when they were hurt. I rushed to their rescue when their lives were endangered. I protested loudly, (censors wouldn't pass the report) When the Imam of a Moradabad Masjid was burnt alive and when there were firings all over U.P.

I made another desperate attempt to ask him a question but he waved his heavy hand in the air almost physically shutting my mouth. This time I shouted: "But you have joined hands with the Jana Sangh and RSS?"

The small 10' × 20' room was quiet. Bahuguna was silenced at last. He stared out of the window and sprang back as though bitten by a bug.

"Mrs. Gandhi has done worse than that. She went to the Swami Sharadanand Centenary celebrations, and said that his way of life is our way of life!"

What's wrong with that? I asked.

You're a child. You better read literature on the Shuddhi movement.

What I am saying is that she may have gone there but basically she's opposed to the RSS philosophy.

Excuse me, she's the worst communalist that one could have in the country.

I think you are angry.

I am not. I am unhappy with you because you've developed an absolute blindspot for Mrs. Gandhi.

You helped me to develop the blindspot. You almost coaxed me to do so in 1970. I countered.

Yes I did. Now I am liberated and you remain where you were.

The small room reverberated with his laughter.

You have developed a blindspot for the Jana Sangh. You have gone into an alliance with known communalists.

This is not an alliance. This is adjustment of a kind. The Editor of *Current* better know the difference between alliance and adjustment. When Churchill embraced Stalin he didn't become a communist nor Stalin an imperialist.

You will ultimately merge with the Janata. The Janata has a hard-core and a base while the Cong-D has none.

You better wait and see. Bahuguna thundered. I didn't want to predict events. But I can tell you that this government will fall. The Home ministry will not come to her rescue. She has blunted the functioning of the government. The Home ministry was pulverised. Intelligence and police appointments were taken away from the Home minister.

That's the Prime Minister's prerogative, I retorted.

Not at all. The Prime Minister is first among equals. Nothing more, nothing less. Let her have the whole Home Ministry, why blunt the instrument? The poor Home minister has to look after only his home! Then the Finance Ministry. It was denuded of two of its most important wings—banking and revenue intelligence. Tell me, which Finance minister does not control banking and revenue?

Well, this is a new system. Each Prime Minister has the right to evolve his or her own system of governance. Why should you object to that?

Yes, the new system is controlled by an invisible hand from behind the scenes—not the ministers. We'll not permit the establishment of a monarchy in this country.

What monarchy? Who's establishing a monarchy? In which monarchy can you have democratic and free elections like this? Under what monarchy will people be allowed to speak so bluntly and loudly?

The issue of monarchy has now been challenged vigorously. Power has gone back to the people. But worse things happened under the Emergency regime. You have no bloody idea of what happened in U.P. She had made it impossible for anyone to know the truth. Voices were throttled. Truth was stifled.

Then suddenly he got up and asked: Do you believe in *Nasbandi?* I mean forced sterilisation?

I do believe in curbing the population growth and it cannot be done without taking certain drastic measures but I don't believe in force and coercion. The population has to be controlled.
It does not have to be controlled. The abnormal growth of population is a reflection of our economic situation. It has grown because the poor live in slums with no alternative entertainment except their wives.

Do you believe in sterilisation with co-operation? I asked pointedly.
I say family planning has to be the people's choice. Our task is to educate them. Is it very necessary that every Indian goes to jail?

Family planning is both the government's and the people's responsibility.
The government is no bloody one to do it. It has no bloody power to do anything under coercion. Coercion is no substitute for persuasion. You think the government has all the wisdom and the people have none? Leave it to the common sense of the people. What does Sanjay Gandhi know of the poverty of the people? What economics has he read? Has he read Marx, Keynes, Marshall, anyone? What does he know of Gandhi? He speaks too much on Gandhi. He is described as the light of Asia! But, he is not even a lamp in a dark corner of the country."

You seem to be getting angry again.
Of course. Anyone who is not angry is a dead person. I did not fight for this freedom. Did I suffer for this day? I've reasons to be angry.

Now be objective. Tell me, do you see any benefits of Emergency?
I am sorry, none. It has ruined the moral fibre of our people. We had no progress whatsoever. Coal worth Rs. 200 crore is lying in coal pits and our people are dying of cold. We have no market for our steel and textiles. Over 4,50,000 textile workers have been thrown out of factories. Two million jute labourers are on the verge of starvation. There were lockouts and strikes; bonus was denied to workers. Yes Emergency has brought enormous profits to a few of the rich, he continued. Birla's profits have gone up from Rs. 82 crore for the same period prior to Emergency to Rs. 135 crore during Emergency. Emergency has done enormously well for the exploiting classes.

What will be your economic policy? Will you go in for rapid land reforms, more nationalisation?
Yes. We will enact land reforms vigorously and go in for more nationalisation. The sugar industry. Yes.

Cement?
I am not talking to you about everything. I'm talking to you about what is

in my mind. I'm not for nationalisation for nationalisation's sake. But sugar, jute and textiles are basically connected to our rural life. If I had my way, I'll nationalise these three.

Who is financing you?

The torrential rain of words suddenly stopped. Bahuguna adjusted his cap, looked straight at me and shot back:

The people. People are collecting money, I am not giving money to anybody. We have given our candidates coupons to sell and asked them to collect money for the elections. I have been the Chief minister of this state. I know my people.

Are some rich people supporting you?

So far I have not met a rich man. The rich are on the other side.

Any companies supporting you?

We have not produced any souvenirs.

But you are an expert on souvenirs. If I remember right, you masterminded the souvenir system.

You are wrong. I never did that.

Why don't you do that? Is not it a proper way of collecting election funds?

No. I believe in straight transactions. Shanti Bhusan has warned companies against this kind of surreptitious transactions.

The crowd outside the Services Hostel in Lucknow had swelled. We had already spent 90 minutes together. People were getting agitated. They wanted to gate-crash.

We'll meet after elections, I said. I have to rush to Rae Bareli.

Bahuguna got up. While shaking hands, he said: "Ask me the last question."

What if Emergency is reimposed? What will you do?

Bahuguna stood motionless, as though petrified. He took some time to recover.

The call for elections has eliminated any such possibility.

Current, 12.03.1977.
pp. (1 + 27)

Sanjay Gandhi: yesterday's bouquets today's brickbats

The elections are over. The Congress and most of its giants have been massacred. Both Mrs. Indira Gandhi and Sanjay have been humbled.

It can be said without fear of contradiction that the past two years were the years of Sanjay Gandhi. For bad or for good he was at the helm of affairs. His spectacular rise to power and his total control over the political as well as the government machine has no parallel in the country's history.

These two years he has been the most feared and sought after politician. During Emergency his were the only public meetings besides those of the Prime Minister. They were described as "large" and "mammoth".

Current was the first paper to recognise his sudden emergence and informed its readers about its political significance. Week after week we covered his and Youth Congress activities in detail. We genuinely supported his 5-point programme and especially the family planning crusade. We believed and we still very firmly feel that political and economic power should be shared by the Youth. They should be given more responsibility.

But in a number of private meetings we had warned Sanjay of the infiltration of communal elements and bad characters into his organisation. We had, however, very little idea of the excesses committed by the bureaucrats with the connivance and patronage of the local Congress politicians including Chief ministers and ministers.

We came to know of them only when we toured the country. The horrifying tales of inhuman behaviour were recounted fearlessly and with a vengeance by the victims.

This would not have happened had the press not been totally muzzled and the bureaucracy not been cowed down by the local political satraps.

It appears that despite all her sources of information, the Prime Minister was kept totally in the dark about these ghastly events.

The MISA was misused. Most Chief ministers got power drunk and behaved like despots. They used Sanjay as an instrument to enhance their political power and in the process completely curbed dissent within the party. Inner-party democracy was stifled.

When Emergency was relaxed and Indira Gandhi called for elections, the nation, phoenix-like rose from its ashes.

Suddenly the country was in the grip of an anger bordering on wrath.

The sycophants, the courtiers and the opportunist vanished. Sanjay stood alone in the sea of hatred.

He was the main target in the epic battle that ended last week. The whole country talked about and against him. The 20-point programme, his five points, Indira Gandhi's political and economic achievements—everything was relegated to the background.

The opposition mercilessly attacked him in public meetings. Congressmen who until yesterday had hailed him as a saviour, were silent. They were overawed by the avalanche of invectives hurled at him and at them.

The braves were peeved. The Chief ministers who had danced around his little finger, were not to be seen. Their only wish, during the election, was that he should not visit their state!

Sanjay was thus the central theme of the fierce political battle witnessed last week.

Current, 26.03.1977.
p. (12)

2

The Janata Experiment

A. Janata Ideology—Janata Prime Ministers

Opposition front will emerge—Ram Manohar Lohia

This interview was taken on the eve of the 1967 elections to the Lok Sabha. It was a crucial period in our parliamentary democracy. The atmosphere was tense. Indira Gandhi was facing a massive challenge from the opposition parties.

The opposition was badly divided and fighting against each other. At that time there were two powerful personalities on the scene—firebrand socialist Dr. Ram Manohar Lohia and the RSS boss Guru Golwalkar . . . .

I had long sittings with them a month before the elections. Dr. Lohia was living in his Gurudwara Rakabganj Road bungalow. I met him early morning. He shut himself in his bedroom, instructed his followers and admirers camping in the verandahs and spacious lawns not to disturb him and told his life-long friend Roma Mitra not to give him any telephone or even important messages.

We sat down for a three hour interview-cum-conversation. His last interview.

If a choice is to be made between democracy and socialism, would you discard democracy for socialism?

In a certain sense democracy as well as socialism are only means to an end. It is human welfare both material equality and spiritual equanimity and that is the end. In order to achieve that, democracy as well as socialism are means. I do not see any theoretical conflict between the two but I concede that there may be occasions when there is such a practical conflict.

In such a situation, I would take good care to see that I do not sacrifice one for the sake of the other but as I do not wish to evade your question.

I would say that my preference would be for socialism rather than democracy but I hope that such an occasion doesn't ever arise when I have to exercise that preference.

Actually, I have been looking upon socialism or equality as a means to the prosperity of my nation. I have quite often thought that if only we could have a national understanding of all vocal opinion that for the next 20 years we utilise the mode, the method of equality to achieve national prosperity. After having done that there is no other mode open to us excepting socialism.

After having achieved national prosperity, I would be prepared to keep the ring open for any encounter between socialism, capitalism, mixed economy and the like but for the next 20 or 30 years I believe there is no other way out except socialism.

After all from the entire national produce, you have a portion for investment in industry and agriculture with which to improve your equipment and if you spend that portion in modernising consumption, in luxury, in imitating the West and Russia and America, then there is so much less left for investment. That is why I would like to put a moratorium on all imitation of European and American standards of living, luxury—what is known as dignity of life.

Do you think socialism can be achieved without regimentation and one party system?

Again my answer is yes. Although practical difficulties would arise, actually the difficulty after the conquest of power is the same as that before it. At the moment we are faced with this great question. Is it possible to destroy evil without destroying the evil doer? I know of no revolution in all mankind which has been able to do one without doing the other Mahatma Gandhi tried to achieve that method of operation. I still believe in it but the more I see of Man, the more I become sceptical about it.

Nevertheless, I have not given up that hope. That hope shall always stay with me that is to have a revolution in India which shall not need the guillotine like the French revolution, which shall not massacre like the Russian revolution, which will perhaps do a little coercion, may be lots of coercion by way of taking away all such private property as is harmful. In the process if certain things get done well, however much I dislike them, they will get done.

But then that is all. Nevertheless, I would want my country and mankind to revive, particularly my country. Our people have been living in a state of stupor, of stagnation all these 10 centuries or may be 15 centuries.

Ever since the disintegration of Kannauj—that stupor has got to be destroyed. If it cannot be destroyed through my methods, well others will come up with their methods.

You stress that civil disobedience or satyagraha should remain a recognised form of resistance to injustice even in a democracy. How can it be ensured that it does not turn out to be a free for all method to advance individual and group interest?

I forestalled your question in my earlier answer upto a certain extent. It is true that any kind of popular action is likely to take the form of violence. Selfish unorganised action may be uprising, may be isolated acts and the like. But if it is civil disobedience, then the chances of such a deterioration are very slight. Because after all, civil disobedience or violence, they are only modes of organisation.

There has so far been a very serious misunderstanding of the problem. People have argued about the use or non-use of violence. That is not the central issue. In the ultimate moment, if for an hour of a day or two violence is used or is not used that is not the central issue. The central issue is how does one organise one's rebellion. Organise over years, over decades and so if a rebellion has been organised on the basis of civil disobedience, then there has been a certain kind of training and civil disobedience is in itself a guarantee against exploitation for selfish ends.

Because in civil disobedience one invites mischief on oneself. One doesn't inflict it on others. That being so, if I am doing it for selfish ends, I will soon be found out. I will have to suffer. Furthermore, if I do it in an extravagant way or sporadic and violent way, then again I will be found out. So if it is real, proper civil disobedience, that is the political leaders, the organisers of that movement are really serious about it, then the chances of deterioration is very slight.

When Gandhiji was leading a civil disobedience movement and satyagraha, whenever the situation got out of hand or there was some sudden eruption of violence he used to confess that he had failed. For instance at Chauri Chaura, he confessed it was a Himalayan blunder. But now opposition leaders, even if they feel that the situation has gone out of control or if the followers have not reacted properly, do not own up their mistakes and blame the government.

Mahatma Gandhi did not do in 1930 and 1932 what he did in 1920 and again he did not do in 1942, not at all, what he did in 1920. A very serious error in the understanding of Mahatma Gandhi has crept in.

Mahatma Gandhi did not write formulas, he evolved his action and therefore, what he did later was corresponding with the increasing maturity of his movement. During the weaker stages, his action was of a different kind. Therefore, the analogy of Mahatma Gandhi confessing to this or that and stopping a movement, because of its violent eruptions, does not hold good. He did not stop his later movements because of these eruptions.

Furthermore, when you talk of opposition leaders of the present moment, very few of them have accepted the Gandhian philosophy if I can call it that. Or, let us say, the Gandhian practice of civil disobedience. And if I blame the present government even more. Because after all there are three types of Gandhian inheritors.

There are the government inheritors, who have always ridiculed the idea of civil disobedience under freedom; then there are the priestly inheritors of Mahatma Gandhi, who go about divesting him of all political action, of all righteous anger, and devote exclusive attention to what was the love element in him; so these two classes of Gandhian followers, the governmental class and the priestly class, have created a situation in which it is almost impossible, for a person of my type the heretic Gandhian, to uphold the banner of civil disobedience, but then, I hope favourable times would come some day.

Does your party's understanding with the Communists to fight the coming elections in consort mean that your theory of equal irrelevance no longer holds good?

My theory of equal irrelevance was formulated in regard to the state of our civilisation. In regard to the conflict between capitalism and communism and then I thought and I still do so that these two systems and their chief opponents like America and Russia are both equally good or equally bad. Therefore, irrelevant to the new human civilisation. Their automatic carrying over of that theory to the political parties in India is not justified.

I never did it and if my opponents do so, then they are changing the terms of the discussion midway which is not fair. As to the awareness of the political parties in the country, communists or us or any other, I have undergone a slight change from the position I held 20 years ago. Twenty years ago, I was opposed both to communism and communists. I perhaps was reacting emotionally to what they had done during the 1942 rebellion against British rule.

Today I continue to be opposed to the doctrine of communism and when I say the doctrine of communism, I don't mean equality, I mean the modes of action, the evil that goes with it, the identifying of the ultimate human good with a particular country or a particular system.

I continue to be opposed to that doctrine same as before. Perhaps in a more determined way, because it is also a cooler way but then towards the communists, I have changed and I believe they are just as good or bad human beings as any other and just as good or bad Indians as any other and my attitude towards political parties is, including my own, improve them or destroy them.

I hope to effect improvements in the position of the Communist party that is individual communist, through our association with them as I hope they will introduce certain improvements in our position if either of us do not achieve those improvements, that party will be destroyed. So, instead of carrying on a frontal direct fight against the evils of communism, or, rather supplementary to that fight, I am conducting a plank operation that treat them as human beings, as you would liked to be treated, by them and associate with them in such action as is desirable and hope for the best.

I have in fact suggested that the communists and us might become one single party for I am absolutely confident, that if we became one party, then this new party would not for a moment accept to have a priest between India and the World. We just do not want a priest between India and the World. Whether that priest is Russian, or Chinese or American. Be done away with priest and it is possible, of course, that the new party may give us, in the earlier stages, occasions to lament, but then if we can persist in our path, I am more or less certain that the new party will give up the right communist approach of Russia and the left communist approach of China.

Once that is done, I hope upto a point, even those other approaches with regard to cultural relationships and violence and evil and identifying of something existing with the ideal human good would also be given up.

Do you have hopes that a purely Indian Communist Party might emerge out of the present situation?

I do not see why you should call it a Communist Party. Again we will get into a battle for names, we might as well call it the Socialist Party. We might call it the Man's party or well anyway these names do not matter. But then when I put forward the idea of a single party, I was talking for myself. I do not think that any Communist leader would dare to support that idea publicity. There might be some in the Communist rank and file of both parties who are fed up with continual wranglings and who might like that idea.

Actually I go further. I do not see why all the opposition—why they should not all come together and merge. What I have said about the Communist Party holds good about the Jan Sangh. The angularities of the Jan Sangh I am perfectly confident, would be removed in course of the operation of this new party.

My faith and hope is sustained not because of that pious belief that the truth ultimately prevails. I believe Indian politics will have to be tolerant. There are so many minorities in the country that they will have to be tolerant. At the same time Indian politics will have to be nationalist however revolutionary we are, however economically radical we are—that the frontiers of the country must be fully preserved. Unless of course we have a world government based on adult franchise.

These are the rock-bottom beliefs of the Indian nation. The prospects of a single opposition party. I wouldn't say prospects, the future of a single opposition party, if it is ever formed, is very bright indeed. But there are innumerable difficulties. Twenty years of continual leadership of small movements has caused the iron to enter their souls and I do not know how long it will still take for the Indian people ultimately to decide as to which one of these parties is on the right way.

People have always told me 'Why is it that you leaders always quarrel among yourselves? To that my answer is 'yes, leaders are to blame, they must get together. But then at some point, the people will have to decide as to which set amongst these leaders has the best policy and has made the best effort to get together and then to vote for it. And then when that party begins growing, I hope the other parties and their leaders will begin to see reason.

In the earlier days whenever there was any suggestion of joint action with the Communist—United Front—some of your people would object that ultimately it might turn out to be a Dhritarashtralingan (Bearhug). Communist being stronger, might destroy the other units. Has the situation changed now?

I think that was an error that lack of confidence should never have been there. One of the reasons why Communists have grown in this country is precisely this. This fear, this irrational fear of them and the corollary that the Congress government has to be protected against Communist attack on the one hand and the Jana Sangh attack on the other. If you recall the Socialist movement in its early stages after freedom, suffered from this kind of unpaid soldiering for the Congress government.

That should never have happened. If we have not done it then the people of India would have looked upon the Socialist Party as the sole or certainly the most dominant instrument of social change in the country. We missed that opportunity and now certainly we should not repeat the mistake. For the sake of a ghost that might appear in the future let us not stop seeing the devil that is there in front of us in flesh, blood and bone.

Lohiaji, could you comment on the three Prime Ministers we have had and has there been an improvement or has the things got worse?

Better! (laughs) How can anything go better under this fantastically evil Congress administration. They have all been evil and I do not blame the individual for it but there is some kind of social law in operation. Each successor has got to be worse than his predecessor. So there it is. Each one of them has been worse than the fellow that preceded him or her and has got to be so.

For instance whoever comes after the present Prime Minister Indira Gandhi will inevitably have to be worst. Because, if I may be forgiven for an analogy from the plant kingdom, when a tree rots and if the tree is old, nothing—not injections nor medicines—can revive it and the Congress is an old organisation. Nothing can revive it. Self-interest has become the only basis for its holding together. No principles hold it together. They never talk about policies. Policies are only tools in their hands for the purpose of getting votes.

Most of the time. I would say 99 per cent of their time is taken up with problems of who is with whom, who is fighting whom, which group is where and how my own particular bread could be buttered. That being so, you cannot expect this organisation to produce any good Prime Ministers, those fellows are all the time bothered about what will happen to them, in case this set up is disturbed and that other set up takes place. I would say this for the succeeding Prime Minister—poor chaps!

It has been a tragedy for them. Each one of them has had a load to carry. The burden of the past. The misdeeds of thc past. Each one of them has had the accumulated sins of his predecessors to carry and so if the present Prime Minister, this women—who still is pretty- if- she- has-earned- the disapprobation, and anger of her people more than any other, I would say this—for her—it is not only her own sins its those of Shastri and Nehru that she has had to suffer. You know that Indian saying—the jar of sins is now full to the brim or almost full. I do not know whether it is going to burst soon, but then that stage is arriving.

Current, 19.08.1978.
pp. (9 + 10 + 12)

No alternative to socialism—Chandra Shekhar

Yesterday's young Turk Chandra Shekhar, is the Janata's Think Tank of today. Though a committed firebrand socialist, he has traces of Gandhism in him. Three-year long, hard, bitter struggle against authoritarianism in the Congress and 19 months incarceration have not left any bitterness in him.

In fact he appears more humble than he ever was, his laughter has the original peasant innocence and his beard has acquired a status quo.

When the elections were announced a number of senior Janata leaders were reluctant to go to the poll apprehending rigging.

They thought Indira Gandhi would not permit fair and free elections and she must have made some arrangements to win them. She was perpetuating the hoax. But Chandra Shekhar perhaps knew the pulse of the people, their aspirations and their intense desire to change the government.

"Do not be afraid," he said, "despite restrictions and constraints, accept the challenge. She will be defeated because this is the will of the people."

As a son of the soil he could feel the vibrations and rumblings of the earthquake.

He was a bit worried about the demands of inquiries into "excesses" committed during Emergency. This might lead to revenge, witch-hunting.

I am not in favour of any inquiry of vague and general charges but the specific charges of corruption, misuse of power and high-handedness should be inquired into. Yet I am not in favour of any vindictive action.

Do you support the idea of an inquiry Commission?

"Commission about what?" He retorted.

"To go into details of alleged excesses," I added.

I repeat, I do not support the idea of Commission without knowing specifically the nature of charges. Mr. Subramaniam Swamy carries a file containing 46 specific charges.

If they are specific charges then the Janata government should inquire about them and take a decision accordingly.

Chandra Shekhar is not known for his soft corner for our bureaucracy yet he rightly absolves the bureaucrats: "If any excesses have been committed, it is at the instance of the politicians. They should be held responsible for all the wrongs committed during Emergency."

In certain cases police and over-zealous officials did exceed their authority on their own.

"Then the government should look into these cases. But I do not think these are such serious matters. The country is not so much exercised over these problems. We are more concerned about the major issues and I would not want the Janata government to waste time on smaller issues and waste its energy."

What are the basic issues?

"Poverty, unemployment and social justice."

In what way your economic policy will be different?

That I don't know. The question is not difference in the economic policy but how to implement it. The Janata government will keep its promises and will try to implement them. If we have problems we will not keep them as a secret and the people will be asked to share them."

As a member of the Congress Working Committee you always insisted on the party being given more importance and weightage in carrying out the policies.

I remember that. But now the implementation of our policies should not be the concern of one party. The whole nation should be involved and on certain issues the ruling party should take the co-operation of the opposition.

What will be the methods of involving the people. The Janata is made up of several parties and their merger is a gradual process. Don't you think you are likely to face ideological problems within the party?

I don't think the Janata is made up of so many parties. It is not a combination of these parties. All these parties put together would not have been able to create so much popular support. The Janata is a movement. The old circumstances and the old areas of division have been eliminated. Anybody who wishes to revive the old pattern will be sadly mistaken.

Within the Janata Party or outside?

Both. Merger is a mere technical matter, a formality to be completed by the four political parties. Take my case. I am not concerned whether these parties merge or don't merge. I am already in the Janata Party. Thousands of young men with no past political association have swelled its ranks."

You seem to be depending too much on the popular support as a main factor of inner-party unity.

I am sure popular support will keep Janata united and those who try to create division will be thrown out of the current.

Are you trying to give some sort of an organisational shape to the Janata? At the moment it is just made up.

Yes, it is just made up. It will take some time to organise itself. Even then it is a movement, it has its own momentum and one who does not follow this momentum will be thrown aside.

How do you propose to keep the pace of the momentum.

"Every popular momentum has its ups and downs. "That will mainly depend on how the Janata government functions. If it does not function properly the momentum cannot be kept up.

In that case the momentum is very likely to turn against the Janata.

Yes. It is likely but there are people within the Janata to watch and see that it does not happen.

Do you apprehend repetition of the SVD governments?

The SVD governments were totally a different thing. To compare them with the Janata government is unfair. Please do not have such illusions.

Have you formulated some major economic steps you plan to take up immediately?

No, to be very frank.

I asked you because economics has been your strong point.

It is true but that will depend upon the priorities to be set up and the assessment of the situation after we take over.

How socialist will be the Janata Party?

If the Janata Party is to survive it has to be socialist. It has no option, no choice.

What brand—Narendra Deo or Nehru or JP or mixture of all these?

"My socialism is based on scientific democratic principles."

I remember your long editorials in Young India passionately advocating the rapid expansion of the public sector, its fortification from the private sector. Any change since you became Janata?

No. The Janata will also have no option if it wants the country's economy to grow.

Choudhary Charan Singh may not agree with you.

"You should ask him."

But is he not an important member of your party?

Whether one likes it or not, the question is what is the option.

You don't see any alternative.

Yes, no alternative to socialism.

Would you like to maintain some political links with similar social elements within the Congress or enter into a dialogue with them. Like the CPI, it has its spokesman in the Congress?

Not specifically but the Janata should keep in touch with all those elements who are willing to extend a helping hand in promoting socialism, whether they are inside the Congress or outside.

Why do you depend so much on politicians for promoting socialism. What about our educated youth and the intelligentsia?

I agree with you. Our mistake and notion has always been that only the politicians are responsible for running the country.

Our politicians think too much of themselves. Are most of them not hypocrites and turncoats?

We should get out of this rut. There are boundaries much beyond our politics. There are greater forces in the country which can be of greater help in socialist advancement than all these political parties put together.

Youth seem to be breaking fresh ground. I agree that the time has come when politicians should begin to look beyond their nose. For instance, the Janata received tremendous spontaneous youth support. Without the youth and their passionate, active involvement in defeating the Congress the Janata would not have been anywhere.

Now the youth have their own expectations, ambitions and desires. How do you propose to fulfil them to formalise, organise and crystallise this youth force: it has to be given a sense of direction, otherwise the Janata is riding a tiger.

True. It is true. A detailed programme of economic and political activities will have to be worked out to consolidate the youth power. Besides there are other areas of activities where the youth force can be utilised purposefully.

It means you have to create a Janata Party youth wing. What will you call it?

Yes. We have been discussing this aspect. This is the first priority on our political agenda.

Will this organised youth force be determined by the RSS cadre?

There may be this fear but I do not apprehend this. Sometimes we exaggerate things too much. When I agreed for elections I was sure that obscurantist forces and those elements opposed to democratic norms will be automatically eliminated in the process. History has reached a stage where there is no going back. This is what I had told Mrs. Gandhi. I had told her not to fight Jayaprakash. At that time friends like you were not very favourable to me.

Yes, I did not favour your stand at that time.

But I saw the writing on the wall because it is a peculiar country. Here if your aim is to gain power only and stick to it, you create limitations around you. Once you decide not to have power alone and you want to do something more concrete, more difficult, then the situation becomes different.

In the Janata Party, for the time being, I do not know how long, it may degenerate, the feeling is that anybody who tries to manoeuvre the party for factional ends he will be, at the moment, sadly disillusioned.

It brings us to the ticklish problem of inner-party democracy. At Simla (AICC session 1969) you fought valiantly for the preservation of democratic norms within the party. The party bosses tried to muzzle your voice but ultimately you won the seat in the working committee. Would you fight in the same manner, for the same purpose in the Janata and where will it lead to?

It may lead to anywhere but I think that is the code of democratic functioning in our society. If there is no inner-party democracy there cannot be democracy in the country. I cannot make any compromise on that.

Have you thought of the consequences?

I don't care. I never cared for the consequences in the past. I do not see any reason why I should care for them now or in the future. Not because I want to do some bravado. I feel that this is the essential, this is the imperative.

I agree, the basic principles of inner-party democracy have to be upheld.

Yes, unless you have inner-party democracy you cannot have parliamentary democracy.

Your stand reminds me of your role of a rebel in the Congress. Will you continue to expose the misdeeds, if any, of the ruling party?

I hope I shall not compromise on issues dear to me. But the question is not exposing or protecting a particular individual. The question is what are we for in politics. If politics is a career then I can make any compromise. But if politics is a creed and social service then I shall have to keep in mind the values which ultimately lead us to the goal.

And if you keep to those ideas. I don't see any other option but to expose those people who take undue advantage of their positions.

There is a feeling that disparate elements within the Janata may not co-exist. For instance what is common between you and Morarjibhai?

They will coexist. I assure you this much and how will they coexist only time will tell. Sometimes people do exaggerate things. Even then I had very little differences with Morarji personally.

Policy differences were there?

Yes and on minor issues compared to the overall picture of the country. Subsequently it was proved that Mr. Desai came around with the same idea and Mrs. Indira Gandhi went far away in the opposite direction.

Yesterday I asked Morarjibhai about his views on prohibition and gold control. He said he had not changed but added that either he would follow the dictates of the party or quit.

I never opposed Morarjibhai on these issues. I am for gold control. I am not opposed to prohibition. But I am against the fad part of it.

Which Morarjibhai has.

No. I have no fad about it but I do feel we should discourage drinking in a country like India.

It can be done by creating popular opinion against evils of drinking, by using the mass media but people should not be prevented physically.

They should be persuaded?

I am against imposition.

I am glad you said that.

Chandra Shekhar felt very strongly about the muzzling of the Press and the Draconian censorship rules, the misuse of the MISA.

"Samachar was a shame and though it should not be wound up, it should be made autonomous."

But he was not sure whether AIR should be made into a corporation.

"That I am not sure about. Because I have not been able to understand the implications. There are two sides of it."

I asked him whether he would prefer the continuation of the kind of discipline brought about during Emergency or let the working class revert to the pre-Emergency days.

We would like neither. "We must create a situation where strikes and lockouts are made impossible. Worker's grievances should be immediately attended to. We should create a system where differences can be resolved amicably. Strikes should not be banned and the only way to avoid them is to attend to the workers' grievances expeditiously."

He is also against banning any political or social organisation irrespective of its sectarian and extremist overtones.

"Ideas cannot be banned. I will fight against these ideas within the party and the people who persist to hold these ideas will have no place in the Janata."

He felt very strongly about some of the large business houses donating to the Congress. The Janata Party will call for an explanation from such groups and the Company Law should take care of them.

He also thought that the use of black money cannot be eliminated in elections.

Every election is fought on black money. We fought the election on popular support, on tremendous small contributions.

But even in our party if there was a donation of over Rs. 1,000 it was most likely black money. The only way to limit the role of black money in our society is to create situations where the use of black money does not create comforts.

My last question was: *Will you try to stop ostentation amongst Janata leaders and ministers?*

I will, if I have the authority, and he laughed vigorously.

That was the last laugh of our first sitting after his release from jail. I have rarely seen a man laughing so vigorously, so full throatedly.

Chandra Shekhar is perhaps the simplest living man among the Janata meteors.

Current, 02.04.1977.
pp. (10 + 13 + 18).

One party rule?
Chandra Shekhar against total Congress rout

The main problem of the newly elected Janata President Chandra Shekhar is the people. There is a sudden outburst. They come like an avalanche and besiege his modest, barely furnished South Avenue Lane house. They come from all over the country in their traditional costumes, speaking different languages.

The small lawn is insufficient to accommodate them. They throng the narrow corridor and overflow into his sitting-room, bedroom and even the kitchen. He shuttles from one place to another talking to a number of them simultaneously. He has no proper secretariat and he simply cannot keep his appointments because every visitor thinks it is his right to meet him.

A telephone rings constantly and as I was talking to him a call came in from Seattle. JP's secretary Abraham was on the line. On the first day, despite his attempts to sit with me for an interview, he could not do so. As we were about to begin, an impressive team of CPM leaders led by Jyoti Basu barged in. We decided to meet next day at six in the morning.

I reached at 6.30. It seemed to be too late. A crowd of over a hundred visitors was already waiting outside. But this time, Chandra Shekhar bolted the doors of his bedroom from within and settled down for a long chat. Tea was served by a small boy who had just perhaps got up from his sleep.

Power had certainly not gone to this young peasant's head who sat on the bed and spoke with brutal frankness. Policies apart, Chandra Shekhar is a great, warm-hearted friend and leads an extremely simple life.

Will you continue your present life-style, I asked him.

I cannot change my way of living even if I want to. The presidentship of the Janata Party cannot change my economic condition. I can't live a 'luxurious' life even if I want. I'm a man with limited economic resources.

What about your total assets? Do you have enough clothes?

I have not counted my *dhotis* and *kurtas*. During elections I had a dozen of them but now I don't think I have more than four pairs.

And your total assets?

I have about three acres of land in my village of Ibrahimpatti in Ballia District, I also have a four-roomed house, in a very bad shape. And we are a joint family with four brothers. I have no other house anywhere. I have a jeep in my village and Rs. 4,000 in the bank.

Is it enough?

I'll be glad if you give me some!

Will you continue writing?

Yes. And the Young Indian will come out . . . yes, I remember I have another Rs. 9,000 which I won from the government for furnishing information on tax-evasion by the Birlas. This I've deposited with a friend. I expect to receive more money.

From where?

From the government of course. My information led the government to reassess the Birlas and get crores. According to the rules I should get 10 per cent as an informer. According to one estimate I should get at least Rs. 90,000. I assure you I don't want to use this money personally but my intention is to promote a trust to help those who furnish information to the government against monopolists and tax-evaders. It should have been done much earlier but I was arrested.

Do you insist on getting this money?

Of course, it is my due I'm not going to use it for bad things.

What about the Rs. 10 lakhs bet you won on the election results?

That shall go for the proposed hospital in my village.

Who was this unfortunate man who lost to you?

Ram Nath Goenka.

The small bedroom reverberated with his laughter.

We had another cup of tea.

The last time we met I had asked Chandra Shekhar how he would feel if he was made the Chief of the Janata. He wasn't sure. He had just returned from Jaslok after seeing JP.

It is not possible, he said. I don't feel very happy at the idea because I'm too small a man.

How do you feel now?

I don't know. I have no different feelings. The responsibility has come on me I feel neither elated nor depressed.

The morning newspaper came carrying Brahmananda Reddy's picture on the front page.

How do you react to this?

It's an internal matter. Only congressmen can decide who their president should be. Reddy is a good friend of mine. I've nothing to say.

As the Janata Chief?

As the Janata President I welcome any decision of the AICC about its President. I hope Reddy will play the role expected of him.

Do you think the Congress could have selected a better man?

It's a matter of opinion. There can always be improvement in selection. So you can't say this is the best selection. But it is not a bad one.

Regarding internal politics of the Congress?

I'll refrain from saying anything.

Being an ex-congressman you know rather a lot about the infighting.

That's why I'm not saying anything. Most of them are my personal friends.

What are your immediate tasks as Janata Chief?

To organise the party to face Assembly Elections. The other task is to have a cohesive team. It's difficult to run a party in a country like India. More difficult now because the Janata is a newly launched party made up of more than one group. So a lot of work is required to assimilate all these elements into one single cohesive force.

The cohesion has to be not only at the leadership level but also at the grassroots.

As you know we're passing through certain historic movements. The people have emerged as a formidable political force and they're guiding us in attaining our goals. We belong to various ideological groups but have joined together, certain basic factors compelled us to unite. The dynamics of unity can no more be ignored though there are certain difficulties. We have friends amongst us with strong prejudices. They can create problems. But the whole thing depends on how strong the Janata wave remains.

You mean to say the people have proved to be more dynamic than the party?

Yes the people have become a real force. There were doubting Thomases who thought the Janata may not come into being: it may not be able to select candidates for the Lok Sabha; after the election they thought the various Janata components may not merge; they talked of the quarrel over the selection of the President and finally the CFD may not join us. All these apprehensions have been proved baseless.

The emergence of the Janata as a political entity is only a step in a certain direction. Basic ideological and economic question will follow. If you remember in our last interview we discussed economic ideas. You had said they were not yet crystallised. You fought the Lok Sabha elections on the issue of Democracy vs Dictatorship. That is over. Now you have to go to the people with your economic policies.

Yes, that is true. But when I talked to you last time about ideas not yet being crystallised. I meant long-term economic policies and ideologies.

The Janata ideology?

Yes, the Janata ideology. But we definitely have an economic programme and we fought the Lok Sabha elections on that basis. That programme still holds good. There are certain economic compulsions in India which we cannot ignore. We've accepted the public sector as part of our economic life and have pledged to narrow social and economic disparities. This is what we call socialism. There's no going away from socialism. We've to fulfill the aspirations of the people. There is very limited scope for maneuverers in the field.

Will you associate some non-party people to help formulate your economic policies?

Yes, we'll discuss our ideas in various forums and we may invite non-partymen to participate.

You are of the view that certain basic changes are discernible in the outlook of the Janata components but the other day RSS Chief Balasaheb Deoras turned down your request to disband the RSS.

It didn't come as a surprise to me because when one is associated with a certain institution he feels bad about it losing its identity. It is more difficult for those who are dedicated in a way to a certain organisation.

Or to a cause?

No. To the organisation or institution. I don't think Mr. Deoras has rejected my appeal. He has just expressed his attachment to his organisation and it is quite genuine. But we'll talk to him and try to understand each other's views. It cannot be done suddenly. It's going to be a long process. I don't know if my view will be acceptable to others but if I have the freedom to express my views Mr. Deoras is entitled to his.

The Jan Sangh has seemingly changed. Its leadership gives the impression of having a quiet and an entirely new outlook. But the RSS has taken different postures. This may lead to a crisis.

I don't think so. But I don't rule out some difficulties. It is over-simplification to say the difficulties will be created by RSS or Jan Sangh alone. There are other elements too. The trouble in the Congress is not created by the Jan Sangh or RSS.

In a democracy these things are expected?

Yes, and one shouldn't worry about them.

Will the Janata carry JP's call for Total Revolution to its logical conclusion?

I can understand JP's concern about Total Revolution. He is committed to certain ideals, certain basic principles. Whether the Janata can fulfill his dream, I don't know. But it will surely have to move in a direction where people feel it reflects their aspirations.

There is danger of the country once again falling under one-party rule. The Congress is likely to be routed again in the Assembly elections and the Janata may emerge as the only party. This will be dangerous. Can this calamity be avoided?

I don't know whether the calamity, as you put it, can be avoided but the total elimination of the Congress will be an unfortunate development. It's always good to have some balance in political life. If the Janata gets an overwhelming majority I will make every effort to maintain inner-party democracy. That would serve our purpose to a certain extent. The Congress ruled the country for 25 years without difficulty because it permitted inner-party democracy. It was during the last four years that the democratic process was scuttled within the Congress and the great organisation collapsed. As President of the Janata Party. I strongly feel that the Congress should provide a healthy opposition.

But if it fails?
Then the Janata will have to keep its forum open for criticism. That's the only way to keep democracy alive and functioning.

I apprehend a great influx of sycophants, racketeers and opportunists in the Janata. Can you prevent this?
Your apprehensions may be justified. If people come in large numbers to the ruling party this kind of infiltration cannot be avoided. In a big country like India one cannot rule out the possibility of undesirable elements creeping in despite our best efforts. The main consideration is whether such elements will be allowed to dominate and direct policy. Some powerful elements in the Congress came to believe in money-power and to get money they made compromises with those who had nothing to do with ideologies. Expediency became the guiding factor. We can avoid these mistakes.

The Congress was dominated by some influential Big Houses. They caught hold of some members of the Ruling Caucus and influenced policies. I see the same people hanging around the Janata leaders. I wonder if they will influence Janata Policies, too.
I cannot say I do not make tall claims. I'll try and prevent them. I do not know if I will succeed. I think in the present mood it'll be easy to counter them and restrain them. Ultimately this is to be seen only with experience. So let's wait.

Now the elections are coming. You are bound to raise funds. Last time you told me that any donation over Rs. 1,000 is black money. Can you prevent the use of black money for elections?
Total elimination of black money is not possible in the present situation but it can be checked to a certain extent. You know I had demanded a ban on company donations. I genuinely felt it would remove corruption from public life but it didn't. More money has flowed into party coffers through

questionable means. Now I feel it'll not be wrong if we revise our stand and allow companies to donate to political parties. They will at least be accountable.

And you shall know who is giving how much to whom.

Yes. Then honest people will be able to collect funds. In the past the collectors of funds also became the controllers of the Congress. They became influential because they dealt with questionable money.

It also led to vulgar display of wealth and ostentatious living among congressmen. They started behaving like potentates. Will you be able to prevent this ugly spectacle in the Janata?

There was some talk of laying down a code of conduct for the Janata Working Committee but I tell you it is impossible to compel people to be austere.

Can't you lay down certain rules?

No. For the last 10 years I have been associated with the formulation of these rules in every AICC session but they were only observed in the breach. I think the people at the top should set the pattern.

Morarjibhai has set the pattern.

Yes he has. Others should emulate him.

I was surprised at the Janata ministers' anxiety to acquire larger bungalows. The idea of limiting them to 3,000 sq. ft. seemed to have been thrown to the winds. There seems to be a scramble for posh houses. What's the difference between them and the Congress ministers?

The whole thing is that sometimes we react to a particular situation beyond the limit. We get overwhelmed by a large groups of visitors and feel we need bigger bungalows. There has been pressure on me, too, to move to a bigger place.

Will you yield to the temptation?

Not temptation exactly, but one can make temporary arrangements. I have put up some tents and a shamiana to receive visitors.

Would you advise your party colleagues to shun ostentation?

I don't want to pontificate. It should be discussed in a committee.

You have gone back on the issue of defections. It'll vitiate the political atmosphere. Are you personally in favour of an anti-defection bill?

I am. But you cannot lose sight of a particular situation. There are congressmen who are feeling suffocated. During Emergency they were not allowed to express themselves. Now the climate is free. Should they not be allowed to speak freely?

They should. But should they also change parties?

No, not changing parties. But I'm as good a congressman as a Brahmananda Reddy, if not better. If certain congressmen chose to side with Reddy why should not others be given the freedom to side with me?

Has your attitude to monopolists changed?

It continues to be the same.

There are elements in the Janata Party who . . .

Yes. But there are elements in the Congress too who tried to influence me. I refused to yield.

Then you were an ordinary Working Committee member, now you are the head of a party. There is a difference between the two positions.

These issues are not decided by changing your political position. There are certain commitments in life, certain basic convictions. I still strongly feel that if the monopolists continue, other entrepreneurs have no scope. Also it'll not be possible to get the co-operation of the larger section of the toiling masses for the economic development of the country.

Current, 14.05.1977.
pp. (1 + 3 + 20)

Janata should destroy the caste system

Madhu Limaye has the persistence of a spider. He has been fighting battles single handedly for certain principles and causes. His doggedness and ability to probe deep into any issue he picks up has made him one of our ablest Parliamentarians.

Socialism has been the primary commitment in Madhu's life. But after the Janata victory, he gives it second priority. The first goes to the success and stability of the first non-Congress government at the centre. To him the Janata victory is the realisation of his guru, Ram Manohar Lohia's dream.

He is one of those politicians who resolutely shuns power but keeps a firm eye on the people in power. He is basically an organisation man, a studious revolutionary. As General Secretary of the Janata, he is aware of his herculean task.

When we met him for a three-hour in-depth discussion in the lounge of Western Court, he was in a retrospective mood. The picture of Madhu the revolutionary, the crusader, the destroyer of any fake gods and deities was saliently absent. He spoke in a calm, firm voice with a research scholar's approach to the subject under discussion.

The emergence of the Janata Party was the culmination of a long process, which was initiated by some of us in 1974. The student agitation in Gujarat and the involvement of JP, who had kept away from active politics since 1955, gave a tremendous fillip to the movement for opposition integration. Then came the U.P. elections where Congress secured a near majority on the basis of only 32 per cent of the total votes. That brought into sharp focus the need for opposition consolidation.

Subsequent to this came the Bihar movement which assumed a mass character after JP took over the leadership. Most opposition parties except the CPI supported JP.

I asked JP since you are seeking dissolution of the assembly, if your demand is conceded or if large number of MLAs resign or if the government is forced to accede to this demand, what will be your attitude in the elections that will eventually be held, will you abstain or take part in those elections? He said, having secured dissolution he would not keep away from elections. They would have to be contested.

Then I asked him if he would work for adjustments among the opposition parties and their youth wings. He said there would have to be one candidate for each constituency and the people of that constituency should have a decisive say in the selection of candidates. A United Legislature Party could emerge with a common programme, constitution, discipline and leader.

Our idea was not to destroy or remove parliamentary democracy but to enrich it and expand it. And gradually JP realized that without the formation of a new opposition party, this country had no future. He cautioned me. I remember in June when I met him at Allahabad. He asked why he was expected to offer solutions. He agreed that the general direction was towards the creation of a new party. That was his attitude.

In the formation of a united party?

Yes. But he realized that ultimately there has to be a single united party. . . In October 1974, he had a three-day bandh in Bihar and the movement was at its climax. After that he found that the solution to the Bihar problem could not be found at the state level.

National scope?

He would have to extend the movement to other states also. The reason was the local government could not cope with the problem. So increasingly

Abdul Ghafoor's government came to rely on force. And the force was supplied by the centre. I think there were about 60 battalions of CRP.

In Patna city alone?

And the Border Security Force. So JP realized it had now become an all-India fight. Ultimately he was persuaded to call a conference of all political parties, non-party individuals, sarvodaya workers, academicians and intellectuals in Delhi. This conference was held on November 25 and 26.

We took two important decisions. One was to hold a demonstration in Delhi. And for that purpose we decided to draft a charter of demands. Several meetings were held to finalise this. When attention generally focussed on the Emergency provisions in the constitution. One of the demands was withdrawal of the 1971 Emergency. We realised that the provisions are likely to be abused.

In February 1975, there were big changes in Bangladesh. A new constitution. Sheikh Mujibur Rahman took over as President. The old parties were abolished. They not only had a presidential system but a one-party system.

One person rule.

An authoritarian regime. This was an eye-opener and we had several sittings among ourselves and also with JP.

You also gave a statement.

So it was demanded that Emergency should be removed. In fact JP started taking interest in active politics since 1971 itself. I remember that I persuaded him.

That is after the general elections?

Yes. When the Bangladesh issue came to the fore. I persuaded him to organize an international conference.

Which he did.

Unfortunately I was not present at the conference. I went abroad. He told me you put this idea into my head and now you are running away. But anyway, for JP that was an important departure from his attitude of not taking part in active politics.

The second landmark in 1973 with the suppression of the three judges of the Supreme Court JP's faith in the democratic credentials of Mrs. Gandhi was shaken. So he circulated a letter to leading MPs suggesting that they should apply their mind to the question of judicial integrity and independence. And he wanted a new arrangement to be made whereby if the seniority principle is to go, he said let us have another principle where the choice of the Chief Justice will not be left exclusively to the government.

The third was of course of the Gujarat and Bihar movement and at one point he remarked that 'I was groping for life. And I found that the Gujarat movement was the answer.' Both the Gujarat and Bihar movement according to me, in the initial stages, were essentially urban movements.

Particularly in Gujarat.

Also in Bihar, in the initial stages. In Bihar when he came out in the streets with that silent procession, he took on active leadership. We told JP to give a call like Mahatma Gandhi. Don't depend upon parties, all these organisations because their ambitions are more electoral. They are more interested in winning the elections. But they don't seem to be interested in intensifying the movement. Several times this question was discussed but no final decision could be arrived at.

And there were differences also in the initial stages.

This was the main difference. People were looking forward to the elections to the Lok Sabha to be held in 1976. So instead of starting a struggle, a general atmosphere in favour of a struggle was created. But no one action programme was undertaken. Then came the Gujarat election and the decision of the Allahabad High Court.

The same day.

Yes. And the pace of events was accelerated. We called a meeting of the National Executives of the four parties and a decision was taken to establish a joint front.

That was a signal for Mrs. Gandhi to act. She was not prepared to resign. It is my personal view that if she had resigned instantly, she would have been able to stage a comeback.

Yes with much more popularity.

But by deciding to stick to power at any cost and by clamping down this new Emergency. She destroyed the very foundations of the democratic system.

During the pre-Emergency months there were attempts to unify the political parties. The question arose as to what should be the basis of this unification. Without a policy and programme, unification was not possible. So a small committee was set up with myself as convenor to formulate a draft programme. And we had several sittings and ultimately a programme was drawn up. I revised and circulated it.

There were three propositions for consideration. After the success of the Janata morcha in Gujarat, people felt that consolidation on the lines of Janata morcha was all right. Others felt this was not enough. So the idea of a federal party was floated where parties would maintain their identity but a national committee would be set up.

With one platform?

This was something more than an ordinary morcha or united front. The idea was to have a national committee, a common symbol and programme. But Choudhury Charan Singh, the leader of the BLD was not in favour of this half-way answer. He suggested outright merger of all the parties. The socialist party met in Poona after the judgement.

Allahabad High Court judgement?

. . . was delivered. Some people favoured the *Janata morcha* set up. George Fernandes and I were for a federal party as a first step, leading to outright merger before the Lok Sabha elections.

Merger or leading to a federal party?

Federal party leading to total unification. But the merger, according to us, was to take place before the Lok Sabha elections. So we go into the elections as a unified party. But there was some internal opposition both in Congress-O as well as our party and the Jana Sangh. So at that time, only a few individuals and Choudhury Charan Singh and his party were in favour of merger.

But the majority was against it. They were prepared to go only upto the federal structure. Then came Emergency. And we always held the view that it is only common suffering and common experience which will bring the parties together and fuse them into a unified whole.

What JP could not do Indira Gandhi did?

In a way what we should have done we were able to, thanks to Emergency and the suffering. So you can say although she did not intend it, this was the result.

She precipitated the merger?

Unwittingly. When we were in jail during the 20 months, there were discussions in the various jails. And all of us felt that nothing short of merger would do.

Who were with you in jail?

Not many people because I was arrested in Raipur. I spent about 2 months in Raipur, then they transferred me to Nasik.

Nice place.

The climate is excellent. The water was also very good. But there was a lot of political harassment. The arrest of JP, Morarjibhai, Choudhury

Charan Singh. That completely shook up opposition ranks but it united the rank and file.

Then Emergency was relaxed and elections were announced. We did not get much time to think. I feel that if Mrs. Gandhi had started a dialogue with the opposition and if she had continued this dialogue for six or seven months, our reputation would have been hurt, we would have compromised ourselves. There again Mrs. Gandhi came to our rescue instead of holding a dialogue . . .

She has been helping you in this?

Unintentionally. You see I was afraid. When I was in jail I wrote to my friends, Piloo Mody, JP and several others that I don't understand this talk about dialogue. There is nothing in common between Mrs. Gandhi and us.

And Chandra Shekhar was talking of national reconciliation?

But that was before Emergency. But some leaders who had been released came together and issued a statement, Piloo Mody, Biju Patnaik and some others.

If Mrs. Gandhi, with her usual shrewdness had gradually relaxed Emergency and all that, ·ve would have been hopelessly compromised in the eyes of those in jail. Luckily, she did not hold any dialogue and went in for elections.

So under these circumstances, and the experience of jail and this suffering, traumatic experience it was, the Janata Party was launched. It was to be something like the Swaraj party and a parliamentary party. But people you know, rallied around the Janata banner. The people just took over. The Janata idea. It was an idea. It was floated. And the people seized it.

People took the initiative?

You know, during Emergency there was suppression. They underwent all sorts of suffering. And when the Janata idea was floated, they rallied around the Janata banner.

Don't you think Madhu that you were also united under the pressure of the people?

But at that time the people were not articulate. I would not say that the people forced us. It was the common suffering. And the destruction of democracy. We felt here is Mrs. Gandhi who is busing herself upon certain calculations. That people have been effectively terrorised, opposition organisation, has been shattered and she was advised that she will get about 400 seats.

Shankar Dayal Sharma said: "This time we shall not be satisfied with anything less than 400 seats."

So this was a terrible miscalculation. She came to the rescue of the opposition in a negative kind of way. Instead of holding the dialogues she held the election.

Originally they were thinking in terms of some other name. 'Rashtriya Loktantrik', 'National Democratic', Congress and so on. I would call it a goods train type. But this Janata party appealed to the people. And nearly 90 million people have voted Janata and its allies.

It is a very massive mandate you know.

It was so massive, that many allies were carried with the tide. So the first thing we did after the victory was to prepare a Janata Party membership in which we reaffirm our faith in secularism, democracy, socialism.

Secondly, we reaffirmed our faith in the values and goals set before the country by Mahatma Gandhi.

Mahatma Gandhi identified socialism or 'swaraj' with 'dharitri'. Another tradition of the national movement was the idea of social equality,' economic justice. These were the noble traditions. Apart from that the Congress in the pre-independence days had always sympathised with the aspirations of the suppressed colonial peoples.

We have also reactivated our faith in peaceful methods. And the potency of *satyagraha* as an effective method of social change. Now people ask us how can you function with the Jana Sangh people. This is a heterogenous crowd and the Janata Party will just not work . . .

When we were in jail, when I was brought to Bhopal, at the end of 1976, I found that there were several Jamiat leaders. They lived under the same roof. They stayed together round the clock for 19 months. Wherever responsible Jana Sangh leaders were there like L.K. Advani in Bangalore or Balasaheb Deoras of the RSS in Yeravada and Kushabhao Thakre in Bhopal they superbly handled the question of relations with the Muslims. And it made an impact.

You have seen Balasaheb's statement. Do you think the RSS can be more useful to the Janata Party by remaining outside? My own feeling is the Jana Sangh has made adjustments. Have they agreed to socialism, secularism and democracy. Have they also adopted non-violent resistance, and Gandhism also?

They have adopted Gandhism. The Jana Sangh was accused of being anti-Mahatma Gandhi. But the people did not hold them responsible for the Mahatma's assassination. Everybody knew that they belonged to a school of thought which had become anti-Mahatma. Let's trace the history of this divergence. Hedgewar was the founder of this movement. He was a nationalist and in his early youth he was also a revolutionary. He had connections with Bengal revolutionaries and he was a great admirer of Lokmanya Tilak . . .

He was a militant and a nationalist. He was also part of the mainstream. In those days, even Muslim League leaders and Hindu Mahasabha leaders were also members of the Congress because Congress was anti-imperialist.

So upto 1934, Hedgewar and his friends were part of the mainstream. It was only after 1934 that a section of Hindu opinion started drifting away from the mainstream.

It was the starting point of this divergence. Ranadi and Malaviya formed a Nationalist Party of their own because of that. As you know the founders of the RSS were mainly from Maharashtra. So the events in Maharashtra also greatly influenced their thinking.

After the communal war, changes took place in the leadership of the Maharashtra Congress and the old leadership of N.C. Kelkar was ousted and Shankarrao Dev, N.V. Gadgil, Keshav More became the leaders of the Maratha peasants. They came to the front.

An increasingly powerful Kelkar made use of the Hindu Mahasabha to oppose the Congress. And in VDS he found a leader who had mass appeal because of his revolutionary past. Under Savarkar's leadership, this section of Hindu opinion, drifted away from the mainstream.

But Savarkar never joined the RSS?

No, not the RSS. But Savarkar's ideas have shaped the outlook of the RSS.

There was an affinity between the two.

This was the history of the divergence with the result that while Savarkar took part in the Satyagraha movement, after the divergence of 1934, a gulf appeared between the mainstream and the RSS and he left the Nagpur session where the co-operation resolution was adopted in 1948. Under Savarkar's influence, the Hindu Mahasabha developed this militant Hindu philosophy. They did not participate in the 1942 movement. They might have been stray individuals, but the bulk of them kept away from it completely. There was another development in the RSS. While Hedgewar was a politician, the new Chief. Govalkar was more of an optimist and he played the Hindu ideal of mukti of liberation in the RSS cadres.

But why did Jawaharlal and Indira try to isolate the RSS?
You see it was the result of certain historical evolutions. Once they fell away from the mainstream, they began drifting apart. It was Dr. Lohia who made the first attempt to bring the Jana Sangh into the mainstream. He succeeded only partially. But his incomplete work was more than completed by the Janata Party.

It was Dr. Lohia as you pointed out earlier who developed this idea of an anti-Congress movement. He said that as long as the opposition remains divided it will not be able to throw out the Congress. And the Congress will continue to dominate indefinitely on the basis of a minority vote—minority not in the sense of religious minority but the total minority. He started this idea and he backed it up by a series of struggles in 1964 and 1965 with the result that Congress was defeated in 8 states. This was the beginning but the experiment of the SVD government failed. So we had to relearn our lesson and in the crucible of fire through which we passed during the last three years, we were drowned.

Are you trying to elaborate the changes in their outlook and strategy?
Jana Sangh at one stage was in favour of manufacturing nuclear weapons. But upon coming to power they realised that this was not the main interest of the party.

Did the Jana Sangh realise this or did the other components of the party tell them?
No. They came face to face and they gradually realised that some of their ideas will have to be revised.

That's a great improvement.
Yes. So we have the nuclear weapons question that you have referred to, the Indo-Soviet treaty and the public sector.

You were talking about Nana Deshmukh. You were describing how the change had come?
He said that we have to carry our rank and file with us, and I agree with him.

You mean that the acceleration should not be so fast?
Yes. We should not force their hands. They should be allowed to adjust.

He said he wants a family in which . . .
He said that for 50 years we had given them a certain training and they shall have to be re-trained. And he said that his own vision of India was an India in which one family will encompass a devotee of Hinduism, Islam, and Christianity. All in one family, as my friend George Fernandes

said: "most people are not aware of your vision. So you have to speak of these things publicly so that people will get to know your views."

Bala Saheb has said that RSS may not merge?

Personally, I feel that these issues are premature. Earlier in the ad hoc committee some of us suggested that discussions should be held with RSS. It will necessarily be a long-term process.

What is the final outcome?

As I visualise it, all volunteer organisations which have some spiritual or ideological . . .

Or religious?

No. I am not talking in the religious sense. I am talking about the spiritual affinity with the Janata Party spiritual affinity in the political sense. For instance there is the Rashtra Seva Dal . . .

The Sarva Seva Sangh is also there.

The Sarva Sangh is not a volunteer organisation. It's a service league. All these voluntary organisations will adjust their relations. In a few years I would want them to merge. And a new volunteer organisation would emerge.

You want the Jamiat-e-Islami also?

I don't think it is a volunteer organisation. However, the volunteer organisation should not be in a subordinate position to the Janata. That much is clear. It should be an independent autonomous body. Whatever affiliations or affinity there is, it should be in the realm of ideas.

But no physical affiliation?

We should not impose our views on them or interfere in their organisation.

But if it takes a critical view of the party?

It will not be a political party. So it will function in their own sphere. Secondly, this organisation which I visualise, should be open to all citizens of the country. It should also take steps to enlist them. And this they will be able to do only if they accept secularism. There is no other basis for uniting this country.

Janata is again becoming a single party government and we are facing the danger of one-party democracy in this country! Ultimately it seems that Janata is going to be the only party.

There is a difference. We will ensure that there is freedom of press, association and speech and all the other fundamental freedoms. We will restore all fundamental rights. We are committed to the preservation of these freedoms. There is a guarantee that there will be democratic ethos in this country.

Because we have a hierarchical society, whichever be the power centre, everybody gravitates toward it. That is the danger inherent in our society. We have to destroy this hierarchical society and create an egalitarian order.

Again I come to the noble traditions of the nationalistic forum. Take the caste system. Unless the caste system is destroyed all will gravitate towards the upper caste.

You mean the Janata Party will take steps to destroy the caste system?

It should. But whether the party can do it or not. I do not know.

Current, 21.05.1977.
pp. (10 + 11 + 18)

I am not a dictator

Morarji Desai, the first non-Congress Prime Minister, has been a congressman of 47 years standing.

His spectacular rise to power was as sudden as his dismissal from Deputy Prime ministership. Eight years in wilderness have not brought an iota of change in his views, though he has mellowed and may not be as inflexible as before.

Age does not show on him and incarceration and public humiliation have not left any traces of bitterness. He is bland, straightforward, alert.

The one thing he has not learnt is to smile. But does it matter?

When I flew with him from Mumbai to New Delhi on the March 20 Airbus, he did not know he was so close to power. He sat on my right. On my left was Mr Y.B. Chavan. Throughout the journey they did not even look at each other though. I spoke to both of them separately.

The whole aircraft studied them with great amusement. They exchanged pleasantries only when the plane landed and they were disembarking.

"How were your elections?" Chavan asked Morarji, rather hesitantly.

He gave him a dry look and said: "Fear, I came across a lot of fear. Too much fear had been created."

Chavan did reply with a vague smile and both went their separate ways.

Next morning, when I met Morarjibhai at his modest Duplex Road bungalow, a huge crowd of admirers was milling in the corridor and compound carrying garlands, "gulal". I could spot some top industrialists who until yesterday had managed Mrs. Gandhi's election funds.

The interview began as soon as we sat down. He would reply to my question even before I could finish them.

I said: The constitution . . .

Yes, he shot back, we shall amend it in a way so that Emergency cannot be inflicted like this on the people at any time. Nor can it be amended at the sweet will of the Prime Minister or anybody else. Or censorship levied on newspapers. Or the judiciary be interfered with. Their independence must be safeguarded.

I wanted him to allay the apprehensions about retaliation and vindictiveness.

I hope you will not permit vindictiveness and . . .

He again cut me short: "There is no question of vindictiveness or retaliation. We must treat them well. We must treat them with courtesy. We must do all that."

That is what is expected of you.

Yes, otherwise there shall be no difference between that government and this government and what will the people get out of it? Therefore, we have got to be humble. We must work in humility. This is responsibility. It is not intoxication. If we get intoxicated, we would behave like them. That must not happen.

Intoxication reminds me of prohibition, I said.

Morarjibhai did not even blink before stating: "Prohibition is the constitution's Policy, which I did not frame. You see, all you people try to run away, locate one man and blame him. That is wrong. That's what I had told Moraes (the late Frank Moraes of *Indian Express*). I asked him if I was rigid in prohibition. He said he couldn't say that as he was rigidly anti-prohibitionist himself."

This means you are determined to bring back prohibition.

It is there in the constitution. The constitution must be amended or it should be implemented.

Would you prefer amendment or implementation, I asked.

I'd certainly want implementation. I do not want you to drink.

Why don't you want me to drink?

The journalists, I am not talking of you particularly, I do not know whether you drink, but most journalists do drink.

What's the harm?
Because they get the drinks free. That's why journalism has gone wrong. That is why you have all become cowards.

But if they buy their own drinks?
No. That can never happen. They cannot afford it.

If they want to buy cheap drinks?
They cannot afford it.

What about industrialists, businessmen?
Even then it harms, he retorted.

But it harms their personal life!
Then . . . then, why should we have the Indian Penal Code? Cancel it. What is the meaning of this freedom? It is nonsensical freedom. It is something which goes against you, against your family, against society. How can it be freedom?

This will create a lot of problems.
Oh no. It does not. There are no economic problems involved. On the contrary it will benefit the people more.

Bootlegging will surely raise its ugly head ahead.
Is there no bootlegging when there is no prohibition?

People will die as they did in Tamil Nadu and Gujarat.
Why? Because they are lax. Because it is these very people who are running the government. They were making them drunk for their votes.

Don't you remember Bombay's prohibition days? Didn't it bring enormous difficulties to the people?
No, no, no. There were European journalists who had come there. I told them to go about, do a survey and find out if it had done good or harm. They returned and said it did a lot of good.

To the people!
Yes. To the people concerned. The poor people.

Well, this is a matter which the Janata Party will have to discuss broadly and decide, I suggested.
I am not a dictator. I cannot be a . . . Even if I am the Head of a government I cannot dictate to it.

Correct. But if the Janata decides against prohibition?
I may even resign and get out.

On this issue?

I may. I do not say that I would. It all depends on what is done and how it is done.

You mean to say that you will take a stand on this issue?

For the first time he raised his voice, looked straight at me and said: I am bound to have a stand on every issue. Why on this issue alone?

Because, I said, prohibition will be one of the crucial issues.

That shows your attitude.

Well, yes. I am against prohibition.

You are anti-prohibitionist. That's what I see.

Try to convince me.

We will discuss it. You come for that a second time. Because I have discussed this with foreigners and they have had to agree with me.

I attempted to digress, *it was felt you were a changed man. You drew a new picture of humility and flexibility. During these two-and-a-half months. You have also given the impression that vindictiveness can never pay dividends. There is, however, a strong feeling that you plan to set up Inquiry Commissions into excesses committed during Emergency. What kind of excesses would you like to be inquired into?*

The octogenarian paused for a while. While he was staring into the vacuum, he looked like a statue carved in teak. He can manage to appear absolutely motionless. Then suddenly he looked around and said:

When you say I'm a changed man. I'm changing all the while. Even now I have to change. One is not perfect until one realises God. This language you will not understand, because you don't believe in that kind of thing. Probably you have no faith in God. Otherwise you would not have said all these things.

I have recently read in the papers . . .

Everybody reads newspapers. But why do you want only me to change? Why don't you change yourself? Is not everybody required to change?

Yes. That's correct. Man changes with the situation . . . .

He should know how to change with the situation so that he becomes a better man. It is a quest of life. You must behave as you think. Otherwise your thinking is wrong.

Earlier the impression was you were rigid in certain things.

In what was I rigid, tell me.

You adopted some very stern economic measures?

Which?

The Gold Control Order.
Now, the Gold Control Order was not my creation. The Prime Minister and other people asked me to do it.

But you faced a lot of criticism.
Lot of criticism there will be. That is political. But when I explained it to the people, they accepted it. Wherever I explained it, they agreed with me.

A number of Janata leaders have told me this morning that an Inquiry Commission will be set up to investigate the excesses of Emergency. Excesses were committed and they should be inquired into. But too much talk of this will create a scare. Don't you agree?
It is not a question of any personal matter. There are typical examples of corruption. They will be inquired into. He stated matter-of-factly.

Politicians as well as officials?
Against all. Whoever is concerned.

What kind of commission? An ombudsman?
Depends on what comes. First, the evidence. Then the records.

Will you call for them?
There are certain instances where it (corruption) has been there.

Would you use the vigilance or anti-corruption departments?
I won't use these departments against any person particularly. Not in the manner in which they have been used.

This means you are planning to set up independent commissions?
That's bound to be. There can be a separate commission for everything. It cannot be an Ombudsman. After all it has to be done quickly. And why is it to be done? It is to be done in order, that in future nobody indulges in this kind of thing.

Will these be corrective as well as preventive measures?
Yes. To prevent future occurrences. These will be corrective measures only for the future and not out of vindictiveness. Nothing like that.

Are you giving an assurance to the nation?
Yes. We'll dishonour ourselves if we are vindictive. That's all I can say.

That is what the whole country expects of you. This will remove the fear of witch-hunting.
No witch-hunting. Absolutely no witch-hunting.

While he talked he was totally sure of taking over the reins of power. It was a matter of hours.

His son Kanti Desai received visitors with a broad smile and saw to it that everybody was comfortable. Kantibhai made his presence felt.

What kind of government, I wondered was Morarjibhai mentally conceiving? He surely will avoid the awesome mistakes his predecessor committed—ostentation, arrogance, misuse of power which were the bane of the vanquished regime.

What kind of government . . .

No ostentation. There must be simplicity. No misuse of government transport. Not in elections at all. We will make that a rule. The rule that nobody can use government means for personal purposes.

Even if the party pays?

If the party pays, then all parties should be allowed to pay.

Would you have a similar policy about AIR and the news media?

Definitely. All India Radio will be made independent. Autonomous.

And Samachar?

Samachar will go.

How?

It will remain as one of the agencies, autonomous. There will also be other agencies. Agencies competing against each other.

Will you float your own agency?

No. We won't. We will allow people to float agencies if they want.

No government interference at all?

Government will not interfere. The Managing Director will go if he is an IAS.

But you surely will permit a newsman as Managing Director?

They must have their own.

Will you remove all controls over Samachar?

Completely. There should be no government control. There should be an elected Press Council.

Will there be a new Board for Samachar?

This Board will go. They will have their own. Let them do what they like.

What about their finances?

They will have to find it themselves. The government can only help them as they did before. But it will help all news agencies. There will be no favouritism to any section of the Press.

What will be your attitude if some papers become critical of you?

They should be.

But you punished Times of India?

No. I did not do it. That's where you are wrong. You read my replies in the Press about this. I have said that *Times of India* was dealt with not because of its critical attitude but because it lapsed into yellow journalism like personal abuses.

Now, who will decide what is yellow journalism?

The Press Council. Once the matter is with the Press Council. I'll not interfere.

What will be your advertisement policy?

It is the government's business to decide to whom advertisements should be given. But the government will not discriminate. It should not. It can make a policy that those who advocate violence will not get it. Those who advocate communalism will not get it. Those who are against democracy will not get it. Yellow journalism will not get it.

Who will decide these things? I asked him.

Is there any difference of opinion about yellow journalism? It means you become personally abusive to people. And if that is what one indulges in then it is yellow journalism.

Criticism of policy should be permitted, I said.

Yes, even the severest critics of policies and actions must be encouraged. The criticism may even be wrong, completely wrong. What does it matter?

It certainly will help create a healthy atmosphere, I assured him.

This will make the Press responsible. The Press becomes responsible when you give it complete freedom. If it is irresponsible the matter can be referred to the Press Council.

Will this Council be elected?

Yes. By the Press men. By journalists themselves. They will have their own chairman. No chairman will be nominated by the government. Had I been oppressive, Karanjia (*Blitz* Editor) would not have escaped. Is not it a typical example?

We began the long interview with an argument. I had asked whether as a popularly elected leader would he endeavour to avoid concentration of power, arrogance and vindictiveness. The Congress was trounced by the people because of these abominable defects and human weaknesses.

He would not agree to my calling him "leader of the nation."

I'm not yet elected leader of the nation, therefore, I cannot accept that, he said.

But you are the leader of the Janata Party?

Not even of the Janata Party. I'm only its Chairman. The leader is yet to be elected. I talk to you as Chairman of the Party. We have been fighting these human weaknesses. We will not allow this to overtake us at any time. Moreover, we will have to educate people to be fearless. Once fear sets in, no government is able to function. The people have to be fearless to throw it out."

You mean your government will recognise the supremacy of the people's power.

Well, the people's power is Supreme. There is no question of recognising it. Democracy means everybody must have his freedom and that must be guaranteed and nobody should take it away at any time.

I understand from your talk with Yashwantraoji in the plane that you encountered a lot of fear in your constituency?

Yes. I was referring to the fears that she would not allow us to function. She would again put us in jail. I personally had no fear.

Yes, you are fearless, what about the others?

The fear was instilled by the government and you have seen the reaction. Wherever the (sterilisation) operations were largest, there they revolted completely. Not so much in the South nor in Gujarat. Solanki had to function better because there was the Morcha tradition.

What is the reason for the Congress victories in the South?

It is difficult for me to say. But I do not think there was this kind of operations.

The Chief ministers were more careful, you mean?

No. The Chief ministers were more effective there.

Were they effective in implementing their programmes?

No. In winning elections. In Hyderabad, he (Chief minister Vengala Rao) had purchased all the newspapers.

You mean he controlled the mass media?

Completely. He purchased it . . .

When he said this, he was not bitter but firm.

The leadership of the nation, has come to you after a long struggle and it is natural that you have dreams to fulfil?

I have no dreams.

Current, 26.03.1977.
pp. (1 + 2)

Storm brewing in Janata

A storm is brewing in ruling Janata. Though our story (CURRENT FEB. 25) "Morarji-Charan Poised for Clash" was promptly denied by the Prime Minister, a visit to Delhi further confirmed our apprehensions.

The gulf between Morarji Desai and Choudhury Charan Singh has widened. It has become unbridgeable.

Battle lines have been drawn. Junior Janata leaders are watching the quick pace of polarisation with bated breath. The process of realignment in the Party is shaping up. Congressmen of all hues and varieties in the Janata have thrown their weight behind Morarjibhai.

Though the dominant group in Jana Sangh is in a quandary it has definitely moved towards the Prime Minister. Concerted efforts are being made to isolate Charan Singh. Some senior Cabinet ministers have even suggested to Morarjibhai to either take away his portfolio or drop him from the Cabinet. He has not yet made up his mind, but he is definitely keen to clip the Home minister's political wings.

Jagjivan Ram's frontal attack on Charan Singh has dismayed responsible Janata leaders. He has not only called his adversary a "Kulak" but also attempted to tear Charan Singh's economic theories into smithereens. Ram's belligerence has incensed the Home minister's followers and shaken the Janata.

I found Charan Singh disturbed—rather grave.

You do not look your usual self, I prodded.

He was glum. Then he stared at the painting of Swamy Dayanand hanging on the wall in front of him and came out in almost inaudible voice: "My mind is ill at ease."

There was a vague smile on his weather-beaten face. Again he went into deep thought. He was reluctant for a formal interview and a public debate. The matter may better be discussed in the highest forum of the Party.

But suddenly he brightened up and settled down for a long recorded conversation. I asked him straight away about the attack on him. He began calmly:

Those who never put up a struggle against the Congress and who were enjoying the fruits of power till the very last, have no right to claim to have constituted the Janata. Is it they who conceived the idea of a National alternative or formed the Janata?

You have been 'accused' of being a congressmen and using the same policies.
I have not been following the same policies and the whole country knows it. In 1959 I had opposed Nehru and told him that his policies were wrong.
Economic policies?
Yes, economic policies, cooperative farming, state trading in food grains and such matters. I opposed all these Nehru policies. He could not execute them.
How do you explain the charge of your being a spokesman of the "Kulak" lobby?
It is a term of opprobrium. It was originally used for the landlords and gradually it became a term of abuse.

Well, I want to raise these and several other issues in the party. I would not like to descend to the level of "these people." They charge us that we have seized the levers of power in the Party. It is they who are the real party 'constructors' and we are the outsiders. Look at this. This is what I want to blast.

The future of the Janata is very much clouded in the wake of its defeat in the recent Assembly elections in the South and the imminent threat from Indira Gandhi in the North too.
It is not due to any fault of the people that the Janata lost in the South. It is due to the failure of the Janata itself. There was no organisation. Even at the state level it was set up hardly 15 days before the nomination. There was no organisation at the district levels at all.

If we cannot reach the people through our organisation and the people are not able to understand our policies then who is at fault? It is largely due to the failure of the executive here in Delhi.

The other reason was the induction of too many Congress candidates. These were the very congressmen who were lambasted a few days before they were nominated.

These congressmen were responsible for the Emergency and for all that happened during that dark period. The Janata was born out of the travail of the people during Emergency. If you set up those very people who were responsible for the Emergency as the Janata candidates then the people had a right to ask: "What do you mean?"

You had been telling us that these congressmen were not honest, that most of them were corrupt, that they tried to erode democracy. And now you are imposing the same people on us.

These congressmen sponsored by the Janata had a bad reputation in their constituencies. That is why the Janata lost. For example, in Andhra, out of 260 candidates put up by the Janata, 120 were these congressmen. All of them except 8 lost.

The Janata had no candidates and it was forced to fall back on these congressmen.

There was no organisation. There was a great demand for me in Andhra and Karnataka for addressing meetings. But not from the Janata Party. The demand was from the farmer's organisations. These organisations are very good in the south. But I said that if a public meeting is held, it should be under Janata auspices. Then alone will I come. Farmer's organisations are not political parties and they include all kinds of political opinions. So I refused to go.

Had the Party units been set up a few months earlier in every district, the result would have been different.

There was another important reason for the defeat of the Janata. Some Janata leaders told the people that there was no difference in the policies of their party and that of the Congress.

In fact they went to the extent of saying: "It is the Nehru policies alone which can solve the people's problems. An attempt was made to blur out the difference between the Janata and the Congress, people began to say that the contests were actually between the three Congresses: Reddy Congress, Indira Congress and Janata Congress.

Do you attach any significance to the Indira charisma and her popularity in the south.

She sobbed and wept at every meeting. In a public meeting in Maharashtra she made three points: I have been late to the meeting because the Janata government did not allow me a seat in the train. In our tradition—in our villages and towns if a rich man comes from outside, the Sarpanch invites him to dinner and the important people of that village.

But when American President Carter and the Shah of Iran came to Delhi "I was not invited to the dinner." And then she wept and added so I had dinner with my Harijan brothers. I would prefer to dine with the poor than go to Rashtrapati Bhavan banquets.

Then she said: "I have not been given a home and somehow I have to make both ends meet." And the people shouted "Hum Rupya Denge," and some women began to take off their ornaments. She then cried: "No, do not do this" and then went away in a helicopter. She enacted this "tamasha" at almost every meeting.

Yet the people voted for her. This phenomenon has to be analysed.
The Choudhury kept silent. Perhaps he did not want to answer the question. I suggested that the Janata defeat may also be due to the non-implementation of the policies.

Does your party have the will to implement these policies?
How can I condemn myself.

Choudhury Saheb, what do you think of the Indira threat now?
There is no threat. She is a spent force.

She has built popular support all over the country. The masses seem to be moving towards her.
No she may be going around. People do not have such short memories.

Do you think she will ever come back to power?
No, never.

If she launches a civil disobedience movement against your government, how will you face it?
We will face it as such movements have been faced till now.

Will you deal with it as a law and order situation?
Yes.

Will you then use draconian measures to suppress her movement?
If somebody creates disorder, whosoever he may be, political, non-political, Janata, Congress, any party, secessionists, rebels, spies, everybody will be dealt with in the same way.

She tried to suppress the JP movement by draconian methods and you criticised it.
We will not use the same methods.

If she launches a JP-type movement all over the country how will you contain it? Will you face it politically or . . .
Normal laws, politically and legally also.

Some people in your party and outside are talking of a Third Political Force.
The so-called Third Force cannot emerge, unless the Janata breaks, and the Janata is not going to break.

If some Janata leaders try to break it?
They will themselves be broken. They do not know what it takes to form a party—perseverance, hard work, identification with the masses and integrity. All these qualities are rare in any organisation, in any individual.

People who were enjoying power by quirk of fortune are enjoying power even today. They think it is very easy to form a party. They are enjoying the fruits of sacrifice and labour of others.

The differences in your party have become deep, and the idea of a Third Force is gaining ground. It means all ex-congressmen, some Socialists and some liberal Jana Sangh in the Janata Party. The Second Force will be Indira Gandhi and the Third Force you and the Jana Sangh.

Why Jana Sangh and myself.

Because you have been aligned with them.

No. I have not been aligned. There is no question of alignment with the Jana Sangh or any other group.

But your two groups were functioning together?

How? Only we have been the two biggest groups. We have naturally co-ordinated. There is no question of alignment or realignment. I am close to the Socialists and others also.

You appear to be the main target.

Why?

Because you have been too honest and too good. Your detractors blame you, perhaps unfairly, as anti-Harijan and anti-minority.

The accusation is being labelled against me by my own friends for political reasons. Anyone who says that I am anti-Harijan and anti-Muslim is dishonest.

I have done more for Harijans than most of these political leaders. How can I be anti-Harijan. I took a Harijan boy as a cook in 1932 when I was in Ghaziabad. When I was in Lucknow there too my cook was a Harijan. I am anti-caste. I have always campaigned for the demolition of the caste system.

Our caste system is based on birth, and caste is rooted in marriage. A caste can be defined only as a group of persons who inter-marry amongst themselves.

I wrote a long letter in 1954 to Nehru in which I suggested that he should amend the constitution to the effect that after a certain date only, those young men would be recruited to gazetted services and also permitted to enter the legislatures who married or were prepared to marry outside their caste.

In 1967 when I headed the SVD Ministry in UP. I wanted to enact a legislation on the above lines. But my cabinet colleagues went against me. But I did take the decision to abolish the caste names carried by educational institutions.

The Zamindari Abolition and Land Reform Act of 1951 in UP has been considered as the greatest achievement of the state government in the field of agrarian reforms. According to this act, millions of tenants and sub-tenants were made owners and thousands who had been evicted were restored their rights.

Under this act every resident of a village was made owner of his house including the site and appurtenances and including the trees and wells. This provision largely benefited the Harijans.

For the first time during my Chief ministership in 1967 I appointed a Scheduled Caste person as member of the Public Services Commission. The BKD manifesto contains a clause under which 20 per cent of the unskilled jobs in factories in public and private sectors shall be reserved for Scheduled Caste.

How do you plan to abolish the caste system now?
By inter-caste marriage as I said earlier.

Do you want to follow the same pattern for the legislators also?
Yes. After a particular date anyone who seeks to be a legislator should give evidence that he has risen above caste considerations. And the evidence is based only on inter-caste marriages.

Man consists of three major things: Head, Heart and Hands. Head means the brains. Hand means physical health. Heart is the most important because it is the seat of sympathies, antipathies, love and hate.

All these are important but perhaps heart is more important. That is why we say that a man is 'Tangdil' or a man has narrow sympathies. So the quality of the heart is that you should have broad sympathies, the broadness of the heart. It is the caste which narrows the sympathies of man. A man who is not able to rise above his family or caste is very narrow-minded.

Would you like a Brahmin to marry a Harijan?
Where is the harm. What is wrong in that?

When would you like this to be done.
If I had my way I would like this to be done tomorrow.

But the reservation for 26 per cent backward classes in service in Bihar has already raised a storm.
This too stems from the caste business. I fully support Karpoori Thakur in his endeavours to abolish the caste system. During my Chief ministership, I did not allow any Harijan to be ejected from the land holdings, whether he was a sub-tenant or a trespasser. In no other state it

happened. But it was done in UP, in a state where 27.5 per cent were Harijans. Has anything like this happened anywhere in the country?

What about Muslims?

Muslims? Well I do not think Muslim masses are to be blamed for anything at present. Whatever is being done is being done for political motives. The BKD was formed in 1967 and two years later there was a mid-term poll in UP. Out of the 99 elected on BKD tickets, 11 were Muslims whereas out of the 210 who won from the Congress 13 were Muslims. In 1974 we had 14 Muslim MPs in the Lok Sabha. All the 9 Muslim MPs who won from UP in 1977 belonged to the BLD.

People ask me about Urdu. I have no objection to Urdu. I will gladly accept it if the majority of the people accept it. But I cannot make a promise which will alienate the Hindu majority. Then I will not get a majority and I will not be able to do anything.

The charge is that you said something against Urdu in a Press interview.

It was like you are interviewing me now. The interviewer showed me one part and not the second. He perhaps forgot to show me the other part.

So, you are not anti-Urdu?

No, no. I use more Urdu words than most public men.

Do you speak Persian too?

Yes. I use many Persian words too.

Your close association with the RSS and the Jana Sangh may be one of the reasons of this antipathy.

What a thing to say. Everybody knows my attitude towards the RSS.

Did you ever suggest that the RSS should not be permitted to join the Janata Party?

Yes.

Do you still insist?

What is the use of saying that now when the Prime Minister has already said that there is no harm in it.

Do you think the RSS is a sectarian organisation?

Why use harsh words. Everybody knows about my attitudes about the RSS. I was opposed to the entry of the RSS into the Janata if they engaged themselves in political activities.

I understand the basic issues. You seem to be facing tough resistance because of your priorities. Your suggestion for allocation of 40 per cent national revenue to the rural sector has apparently raised eyebrows.

It is a muddle. They say it was 35 to 37 per cent in the Congress regime and now it is being raised to 40 per cent. Many of us like myself however thought that it was a substantial raise. We also thought that they were making it 40 per cent from 20 per cent.

Whatever be the investment on power only 12 per cent or so should be considered the investment on agriculture. The electricity consumed on tubewells should not be counted as expenditure on agriculture. But more than two-thirds of the power that is generated goes towards heavy industry, that cannot be, but in urban areas? About 20 per cent is spent on traction. In some zones for Railway trains too.

Only 12 per cent goes to agriculture. As for fertilisers the entire allocation should be counted under industry. The decision was taken by the Planning Commission 20 years ago. Their argument is that because fertilisers are utilised in agriculture the power allocation for them should be counted in the category of rural sector. Then cotton and jute production should also be counted with industry.

What is their main objection?
Their main objection is that this does not give the correct picture in the urban sector.

How do you plan to break this huge accumulation of wealth?
There is a solution but someone should be prepared to accept it. The Janata is not willing to accept it. Things which can be manufactured by small-scale and cottage industries need not be manufactured by big industries. No medium or large enterprise should be allowed in the field where goods can be produced by the cottage or small-scale industry.

What about the existing large industries? What will happen to them?
My suggestion is that they should export their goods. They should not sell their products in the country. They are mostly consumer products. This is also applicable to textiles. In any case they cannot compete in the world market and thus they would have to shut down automatically.

That will mcreate tremendous labour problems?
That labour would be absorbed in small-scale and cottage industries.

Current, 25.03.1978.
pp. (1 + 2 + 3)

Charan: myths and realities

Charan Singh, the fifth Prime Minister of India, is a man of parts. The general impression is that of a village pumpkin, muzhik, a casteist, the Jat supremo.

The people in his state know him and his politics rather intimately. He has been loved and hated, adulated and despised. Beyond the borders of UP people have vague ideas of him. He has done little to demolish the image.

The Leftist branded him a Kulak, the Rightist described him as a half-backed Gandhian, the intelligentsia treated him with contempt and the industrialists condemn him as a rustic with antediluvian ideas.

Since the formation of Janata, the arrogant 'Sarvochch' took him as an uncouth power-hungry Jat, Jagjivan Ram looked down on him as a Harijan-baiter and Chandra Shekhar thought of him as a religious bigot disguised as a Gandhian. In the Janata which he ultimately demolished he was more feared and suspected than loved and respected.

Charan Singh's India has been confined to UP alone: After his ascendancy at the centre his political borders extended to other northern states. He is little known in the South and if the people down the Satpuras known him at all, it is as a Hindi protagonist.

In the East, the Bengalis care less for him, and in Gujarat he has come to be known through his association with Chimanbhai Patel and the lesser known R.K. Amin.

This is the awesome picture of a man who now heads the largest democracy of the world.

But is it a true picture? Is it the image of a real Charan Singh?

The Charan Singh known to his associates, comrades and friends is entirely a different person. Though he alone can refurbish his distorted profile painted over the years, it will be interesting to know him as he is.

I too had queer ideas of him. I had not met him before he came to the centre. We met a week after he became the Home minister.

He began with eyes half closed, almost in an inaudible voice: "If you have come to meet a Jat leader, a reactionary, a Kulak and a bigot then this meeting is not necessary. We will be wasting each other's time. But if you have come to meet the destroyer of an authoritarian regime and the builder of a new democratic path then you are most welcome."

I was taken aback by his frankness. The meeting lasted hardly ten minutes. The next day his secretary rang-up suggesting whether I would like to meet Choudhary Saheb again in the evening.

Our next meeting lasted nearly two hours. It was a formal interview-cum-conversation. At the end of the meeting *Choudhary Saheb* introduced me to his wife, the great *Choudhrain,* who wields immense influence on him and some of the members of his family.

He came out of his room to see me off. As I stepped into my car he put his hands on my shoulder and said: 'From today, you are a member of this family. I am a strict vegetarian but I will be glad to offer you *gur, chana,* home made *laddus* and *chhach.* I cannot afford the luxuries of good food. I come from a poor family. I don't drink. I don't smoke. I don't chew *pan.* All my dependents are in service and my whole property and that of my wife can be packed into one trunk. The one thing I value in life is honesty and sincerity towards my friends.

"Political or personal friends?" I asked.

"Personal. Politics is just a game. In politics, friendship and enmity has no values. Friendship can be brittle and enmity transient."

That day, during those two hours, Charan Singh spoke a great deal on his economic and social concept. He is not an economist but his approach to our economic problems is that of a man deeply committed to the well being of his countrymen. Whatever knowledge of our economic problems he has, it is from his understanding of Gandhism plus his own approach.

"The question is not only to solve the unemployment problem but to prevent the growth of unemployment. Industrialisation has not and will not solve the problem of unemployment. We have to go to the root cause. Unemployment grows in the villages. It spreads like a cancer towards the cities. The battle against unemployment, has, therefore, to be fought in the villages. The Capitalist view is to have more industries, to absorb the unemployed. It is wrong—it is wrong. Industrialisation can never solve the problem of unemployment. It can only be solved if our villages are made self contained and self sufficient."

Charan Singh can talk of the various economic issues and problems for hours. He can quote facts and figures like an economist. He is always working on one or the other book expressing his views on the problems.

I must have met him dozens of times for hours together and more often than not he would pull out a file containing type scripts of one or two chapters of his book and ask me to read pages after pages.

His picture of a thoroughbred politician deeply involved in the game of power politics changes when one comes to know of him. He is a politician. And he is absolutely justified in thinking that if he has to implement his ideas he cannot do that without having the required power.

The Choudhary hates to travel. He is perhaps the least travelled top politician. But he loves to meet people. All kinds of people, make friends, denigrate the detractors and demolish the enemies.

Though he is an Arya Samaji he believes in the stars, in tantra and has a soft corner for *Sadhus, Gurus* and *Sanyasis.*

He is basically a peasant—a landless peasant. The peasants of Western UP and especially the *Jats* are known for their toughness and frankness. He is tough as well as frank.

He cannot tolerate insults and he will make the friends with his worst enemy if it suits his 'purpose'.

Morarji and he could have pulled on well for some more time had Morarji not treated him contemptuously. In his famous letter of resignation he accused Morarji of treating him as a *chaprasi.*

In private conversation he express his opinion with brutal frankness about politicians in his and other parties. He is awfully well-informed about the personal lives of most of the political leaders in the country and if you enjoy his confidence he would not mince words in describing their ugly aspects.

He is soft-spoken, he speaks in chaste Urdu and would avoid to speak in English if he could. Recently he discarded furniture from his room where he receives visitors. There is a wall to wall *duree* in the room with no carpet. He sits on the floor and all his visitors, most of whom are clad either in *dhoti* or *pyjama,* also join him on the floor.

The *khadi* he wears is not of fine variety. At home he is dressed in the most casual manner and puts the cap on only when he goes out on an important visit. He is used to the walking stick which he fondly calls *danda.* Often he is found searching it from one room to another because his stick has no fixed place and the children in the house often hide it behind the doors. At times of crisis and tension, he finds relaxation in playing cards with the members of his family.

The *Chaudhrain*, short and plump and in her late sixties, is a typical village lady who receives visitors and talks to them while her husband is busy with some visitors. Apparently she does not interfere much in his day to day politicking but wields considerable influence over her husband. Clad in rough white *khadi saree* she manages the household on a shoe-string budget.

There is no doubt about the honesty and integrity of this family. There is also no doubt about the Choudhary's egalitarian approach. His secularism needs no proof. His BLD has the largest number of Muslim MPs and the Harijans and the weaker sections of UP still remember him for his radical land reforms. His anti-Harijan image is, in fact, painted by the upper castes of his home state.

Speaking about the Jats, he told me a day before he was asked to form his government: "In western UP there are hardly two per cent *jats*. In the rest of the state the animal known as *jat* is not found at all. It is a blasphemy to brand me a *jat* leader."

Charan Singh depends a great deal on his friends and associates for sharing his burden. Once he trusts somebody he does it fully.

His greatest asset is his mass base in North India and the whole country will be his constituency if he succeeds in implementing his 'radical' ideas in the rural India.

He knows one thing that Indian democracy has to be *kisan* based. He does not give much thought to the ten per cent urbanites who do not have more than a nuisance value.

Current, 04.08.1979.
pp. (5 + 8)

B. Janata Leaders and ministers: Many Voices

George Fernandes: arrogance destroyed Congress

The Baroda Dynamite Case will remain a mystery unless it is specifically unravelled by George Fernandes. During our interview I pressed him hard to take the country into confidence but he preferred to remain silent.

Wearing a white Mundu and Kurta, he insisted he wished to remain a commoner and didn't want to grow into a "minister". Now the time had come when he should also look after his family and especially his little son Sushanto who was with his mother Leila in the U.S.

"I spoke to him yesterday on the long-distance telephone after 22 months. He said 'Hai' and spoke to me in Americanese. Look what has happened to us, my son. Son of George Fernandes speaking Americanese. When I saw him last he was 17 months old. I brought him up in Hindi."

When I called on George at his ITI Jorbagh flat, over 100 people were waiting to see him. It was Sunday morning and he didn't have time to take bath or shave or even to wash his face. After I entered the room, he immediately bolted the door, looked relieved and said: "Let us have a quick breakfast."

He had no proper secretariat or even a secretary unassuming Simply-dressed Ravi Nair was "functioning" as his secretary. An expelled student. Ravi has a police record "half-a-mile long."

I heard Ravi telling people on the telephone: "No. This is wrong. Politically this is not in the interest of our Party." So Ravi was more a political aide than a secretary.

Let us start with inquiries and commissions into excesses. My apprehension is if care is not taken and restraint shown, it is likely to lead to vindictiveness and witch-hunting. The guilty must be punished but an atmosphere of fear should not be created. Your fight against fear should continue.

I entirely agree with you. There will be no question of seeking revenge. We shall not be revengeful, we shall not be vindictive. But justice must be done. The laws of the land wherever they have been broken for personal aggrandisement, for feathering one's own nest, or to settle scores with people, or such other excesses where the constitution or all those things we held sacred were defiled and defied.

Should there be judicial commissions?

Why judicial commissions? Why not allow the law to take its own course. For instance, a certain family in this city was arrested and sent to Tihar Jail, their home broken up. They were beaten up and all this was done because some young men had a score to settle with that family. I believe the Indian Penal Code should take its course.

You want to apply normal laws for all these crimes? You rule out judicial or special commissions?

Well, special commissions and judicial commissions are necessary in a certain situation. For example let us take the constitution.

Mutilated it?

Even 'defiled' is not the word. She just decided she will declare Emergency, arrest everybody. She decided everything that night and next morning at six she woke up everybody and said, we are now going to have an Emergency.

If you want to punish the ex-Prime Minister, on this issue, what course will you have to adopt? A Parliamentary Committee, a judicial committee or what?

Well, I think there has not been any crystallisation on this point as to how one goes about it. There are a number of complaints, there are a number of charges.

Against her?

Yes, for instance, I have charges against her. I have charges that she protected the smugglers.

How?

Yes, I accuse her of having protected the smugglers. From 1970 we have exchanged 100 letters. Mrs. Gandhi and Mr. George Fernandes have exchanged 100 letters on the issue of smugglers.

Where are those letters? Do you have the copies?

Very much. They burgled my house twice to get copies of those letters, to get my files.

Did it happen during Emergency?

Yes, my house in Delhi was burgled twice. But those letters are lying . . . they were fools to think they would be lying in my house.

Now if you keep writing to the Prime Minister of India giving specific cases of smugglers pointing out that this is what is happening and if the Prime Minister of this country refuses to do anything for seven long years and then suddenly brings the *COFEPOSA* or MISA or something or the other and puts them in, what is the conclusion? You come and report to me that my Secretary or someone or the other is in league with foreign power and for seven years I do nothing about it. What is the conclusion that you could draw?

That you have been protecting . . .

That I have been protecting the man. Therefore I have charges. Take the Nagarwala thing also. How can you say that was a fair trial that Nagarwala got . . .

I am not convinced about it . . .

Then, it has to be investigated. Modalities and the norms, these are matters of detail.

On principles you have taken a decision?

Yes.

What is your concept of Janata Socialism? Will it be accepted by the party?

Our manifesto has by and large spelt out the programmes which we are going to implement. When one talks of what kind of socialism, that's a question which has a long-term implication. I would confine myself to the short-term programmes which flow from certain socialist and democratic concepts to which we are committed. There has been some kind of discussion on the Gandhian framework within which we need to operate.

Is a consensus evolving in favour of Gandhian socialism?

Yes, because it was discussed after we started with the Janata Party idea in 1974, much before Emergency, Remember in 1974 we had a meeting here in Delhi of opposition leaders, Jayaprakashji presided over it. At that time a programme committee was set up. Madhu Limaye was the man. An outline, or rather a framework, was drawn.

While socialism is a much larger concept, some people try to simplify it by saying 'No exploitation of man by man.' They also say no exploitation of nation by nation. I would confine myself at the moment to the short-term programmes which we would like to implement.

Can't you have both short-term and long-term programmes?

No. I am concerned with the short-term. What is it that we are going to do in this country in the next five years? Now you don't have to define it as socialism or non-socialism.

The important thing is can you implement it?

Yes, thirty years after independence when you don't have drinking water in half of India's villages, then providing drinking water to the people is socialism. Your emphasis on heavy industry on the one hand, concentration of all your investments in the urban areas, putting money on capital intensive industry has created a situation where there is massive unemployment.

We have first to shift the emphasis from heavy to small-scale industry, from small-scale to cottage industry, from urban to the rural areas, and provide employment. Create situations where it generates employment very fast. To me that is socialism for the present. Not where there is ostentation, in five-star hotels, where a bed costs you perhaps Rs. 200 a night.

Rs. 500 a night. You are outdated in this.

Yes, since I do not live in such places, I do not know. You should know better. So in a country this kind of ostentatious living ultimately affects the common man.

The industrial executives, the company bosses stay there. Ultimately the common man pays for it out of his pocket. It is linked with our price index. Doing away with this kind of ostentation, bringing about simplicity in our behaviour, in our conduct, our living . . . to me this is socialism.

Do you mean to do away with the-five star hotels too?
Well, I suppose those five-star hotels which are there, cannot be done away with. But personally I would oppose construction of these hotels. We don't need them in this country.

How would you accommodate the foreign tourists?
Well, foreign tourists who want to come to this country should be given the minimal comforts without having to go in for the type of luxury that you are today putting up because our problem is money. We have no resources. Our priorities have been wrong. You know what went wrong during the last thirty years, your priorities were totally wrong. Therefore, to me a five-star hotel is not a priority.

George, I want you to clarify, you are opposed to five-star hotels in the private sector or the public sector?
I would oppose it in both the sectors. We don't need them in this country. People in this country know the conditions in which we have to operate.

Will it not affect the tourist industry?
Well, tourism has to be encouraged upto a point. Not at the cost of the nation's economy. We are not operating in a system whose parameters are not being changed, the Janata Party in the ultimate analysis is trying to operate in the same system. It is the same establishment. Therefore, it is not possible for me to talk about such radical programmes like not having tourists coming to this country for the next ten years. I am not interested in tourists coming to this country.

Why are you not interested?
Personally I am not, the government has its own policy. I have said over the years, let us close the frontiers for 10 years. Let us decide our priorities and let us build. Tourists will come when there is something really happening in this country. Tourists will keep coming. But if somebody tells me you put Rs. 10 or 20 crore a year in building five-star hotels because tourists will come and we will get some foreign exchange and if this is not going to provide drinking water to half the villages in this country, then to me it is lopsided.

I entirely agree with you that providing drinking water to half the villages in India is more important than promoting tourism, but we can have a balanced view.
Yes, that is right.

That puts the matter very clear that your priorities are to remove poverty instead of building five-star hotels.

Yes.

We had discussed socialism in the past in detail including Dr. Lohia's concept with which I agreed with you. You know, he (Dr. Lohia) was totally against ostentation, against the establishment guiding the intelligentsia. He also opposed casteism, communalism, all the evils in the society. And he said "this is my brand of socialism." Is the Janata party victory therefore, a realisation of Dr. Lohia's dreams?

The Doctor simplified everything. But his thinking and his vision cannot be simplified.

He tackled the various contradictions in our society, the caste and class contradictions, the urban and rural contradiction, the man-woman contradictions, the rich and the poor contradictions within the nations and between the nations contradictions. He tackled all these problems and had a certain approach. So when we discuss the Lohia concept of socialism, we will have to take the total, as he called them the seven revolutions, the Sapt Kranti. We will have to talk about all of it when we meet next. This is certainly not the occasion because the Janata Party is certainly not the party of Lohia's dreams or his ideology. He had his ideology.

The Janata Party has accepted the Gandhian framework and as I said we have certain short-term perspectives, programmatic perspective which we would like to implement.

But I recall the Doctor telling us, let the opposition parties be first united then we will decide that . . .

That is where I was coming to the tactical line of his position. The doctor had a certain ideological perspective. He was a socialist. He was also a tactician. He was the architect of the 1967 Congress defeat in 9 states in the country. The Congress also lost its majority for all purpose, but for the CPI.

The DMK too?

Yes, the DMK also. That was a short, tactical line that he adopted. Now, if he were alive he would have welcomed the creation of a Janata Party also.

Yes, the doctor would have been happy.

There is no doubt about it. Because when the SVD governments, because of different organisational set-ups, each one operating within the framework of its own discipline, did not really click, as we expected them to click, then the only alternative before us was to create a more homogenous platform. And Lohia, in my opinion, tactically would have gone along with the formation of the Janata Party.

Will you be able to prevent the SVD experience, the units falling apart and quarrelling amongst themselves?

No, because I think we have learnt from the SVD experience. Now we have a party with one discipline. The formal launching of the party is on May 1, but the party has been formed. We contested the elections as Janata, we are operating as one party in Parliament, we operated under one discipline during elections. We had no problems.

I think the most important problem will be inner party democracy. In some of your units the concept of inner party democracy is different. In fact all the major units, the Congress-O, the Jan Sangh, the BLD, the SSP, have different concepts of inner party democracy. How will you evolve a collective formula of inner party democracy?

There are two factors. One is the experience which we have gone through in the last 20 months particularly and also the earlier experience must make people realise that if inner party democracy is dead, your whole concept of democracy dies. First it has to be inside the party; if you are not democratic within your own party, you cannot be democratic in the running of the affairs of the people. So with our commitment for democratic functioning inside the country we will have to make a beginning inside the party. I am certain that everyone of us is conscious of the fact that only by observing inner party democracy will we be able to make democracy real and lasting. I consider this as the most important factor.

Don't you think this process is likely to cause some tension within the party? Misunderstandings?

No, for the simple reason that we have gone through this real crucible of suffering. I think people have learnt their lessons. After all one couldn't have imagined a situation where these four parties in the normal course would have come together. But they come together within two months.

I do not want to make it very personal, but I think Morarjibhai's concept of inner party democracy is different. He is rather rigid.

No, I do not think so. I have seen Morarjibhai very closely in the last few years. But during the last 20 months, of course, we were not together. But in these two weeks since we got on to the exercise of forming the government and earlier also, I found Morarjibhai a completely different man. The man that you and I know. I think in fact I have been fighting with Morarjibhai since 1950.

Yes, nobody has fought more against him than you.
But he is a different man.

You have completely forgotten those things.
Not only forgotten, but I have developed tremendous admiration for that man. The thing that really brought it about was that fast of his. At that time, I wrote an article. I don't know if you remember reading it.

I remember, I have read it.
In this article I said it was a spiritual experience seeing this man at the age of 80 holding onto a principle, risking his life, and going on a fast. And to me it was a very deep spiritual experience which completely wiped off all the bitterness that I had for him.

Now you have no bitterness towards him.
It ended the day Morarjibhai launched his fast, in April, 1975. And from then on I have a different relationship with him.

George, how do you propose to balance the two extremist elements in the Janata, the RSS and the socialist youth. The socialists have a very militant youth. We have seen them in BHEL and various other campuses. You might have reconciled at the leadership level but what about the grassroot level, the district and the taluka level?
I think there is a misconception about the RSS also. I haven't been very closely associated with any RSS leaders. I do not know the RSS functioning. But in prison a large number of my colleagues were with the RSS. In Karnataka, Bhopal, Ambala, Rohtak and in Uttar Pradesh. And what they have now been telling me about the way the RSS and the socialist youth and for that matter even the RSS and Jamiat-e-Islami people lived . . .

They were put together in jail.
Yes, they spent 20 months together.

You mean that Indira Gandhi brought them together?
Yes, and apart from the various misconceptions about them being removed, they have been so much exposed to each other.

The Jamiat-e-Islami and the RSS?
Yes, and the Socialists and the RSS and just about everyone of us have been so much exposed to each other and they have discovered by and large that there is very little that divided us and there is a lot that unites us.

New ideology is one thing. And if the Janata Party in its short-term projects prefers the Gandhian concepts, I think we shall be able to evolve a certain ideological concept where it would not be necessary for us to talk in terms of RSS . . .

This is very interesting. You mean the RSS, the Jamiat-e-Islami, the SSP, the Cong-O and the CPM are making an effort to evolve a new concept of socialism, democracy and parliamentary system?

Well, I would not say a new Parliamentary system is being evolved. The parliamentary system is the same.

But this parliamentary system was completely debauched, ruined?

Yes, but what was debauched is now being cleansed and all that we are trying to do is restore the equilibrium that was lost. We are not yet trying to break away from the systems as it existed. We all took the oath by the constitution. We are all going through the same exercise . . .

In the pre-Emergency days the Jamiat-e-Islami and the RSS for the past 30 years, had no place in our political system. They were castigated, they were stigmatised. They were taken as anti-socialists and anti-national. But in the new situation they have become a very respectable force. Isn't it?

I would put it slightly differently. The RSS became a kind of whipping boy for the last several years for the Congress party, in order to keep the Muslim masses with it. Anything happened, they blamed the RSS for it. For instance, take the Hindu-Muslim riot question. It was always easy to blame the RSS and get away with it. After all the government had the means of publicity and propaganda.

But you remember there was a report in the late 1960s.

We, the socialists, had to go through this exercise. We were called people with a negative programme. The refrain always was that this party was opposed to the Nehru family. As though the Nehru family was something so sacrosanct that saying that someone is corrupt, that someone's policies are wrong is immediately considered as an attack on the Nehru family. And we went through this. So it was very easy to damn the socialists.

You must have heard Mrs. Gandhi in Bombay. You might have covered her meetings. She used to dispose off the four parties. Congress-O, *Yeh to buddhe logon ki party hai. Yeh sab log hamare sath the, ab sab yeh lalachi hain. Jana Sanghi yeh to Mussalman virodhi sampradayik hain aur in logon ke pas koi niti nahin hai. Socialiston ke pas na koi niti hai na karyakram hai. Sivai mere khandhan ko gali dena. Aur yeh logon ko kuch nahin ata hai. Aur voh ek aur party, (BLD)* Uttar Pradesh *tak nimit hai aur unko kursi ke sivai aur kuch ata nahin hai.*

So in these eight sentences Mrs. Gandhi used to dispose off all the parties. This is what her father also did. Of course at that time we did not have the Congress-O but whatever we had he also disposed it off like this.

Now you talk of programmes. Was the ruling party ever prepared for a national debate on programmes? Has there ever been a debate on programmes between any parties in this country?

Therefore all that is now happening is that we are restoring the equilibrium. We are not trying to evolve a new parliamentary system. You know the Jana Sangh was committed to the abrogation of Article 370 in Kashmir. Five days ago in the Lok Sabha Atal Behari Vajpayee intervening in the debate made a statement that there is no question of abrogating Article 370.

And we should accept this change. Let's take the elections in Bhopal. What is the Muslim vote in Bhopal. Eighty thousand out of 6 lakhs. Arif Beg belonging to the Jana Sangh won by a margin of a lakh and a half against Shankar Dayal Sharma.

The voting pattern had also changed. The Janata wave has shattered the old patterns. It has completely demolished the caste, communal and regional considerations.

Yes, this is an achievement.

Now we move onto your relations with the CFD. Do you think they will ultimately merge or remain separate?

I would consider it rather premature to give any final opinion on this question. There is an urge on both the sides to come together. We are operating as one parliamentary party and as far as I can see, there is a perfect understanding between all of us on every issue.

In my views the Congress was thrown out of power because of arrogance, ostentation and total disregard to people's miseries and problems. Finally it became repressive. How do you propose to prevent the repetition of these things in the Janata?

By being just the opposite of what the Congress was. I would like my party and all of us, from the highest to the smallest of our workers to be humble. In the place of arrogance, we shall have to have humility.

You should also prevent ostentation. You have seen the Congress ostentations.

Yes, so where there was ostentation there should be simplicity.

I want to ask you a question every friend of yours in Bombay is asking. It is not my question: Will you continue to be a rebel, a trade unionist, a firebrand socialist, a friend of the underdog and a vocal critic of the evils of the establishment? Or as a taxi driver in Bombay told me, "Our George has become a minister." This is a people's question I am asking you.

I cannot be anything but what you asked me whether I would be.

A rebel?

Yes.

A trade unionist?

Yes.

Then how can you remain a minister? This is a conflict. I know you are facing this conflict. You seem to be in a miserable position.

Yes. I am. But now that I am there, I also try to make a good job of my responsibility.

Current, 16.04.1977.
pp. (10 + 11 + 13 + 19)
and
Current, 23.04.1977.
p. (6)

I'm against witch-hunting—Jagjivan Ram

Janata Party stalwart Atal Behari Vajpayee once commented in remorse the Congress is too large to be defeated. If at all it can be defeated, only congressmen themselves can do it.

The Goliath was, at least, felled. The David turned out to be Jagjivan Ram, an outstanding congressman with deep roots in the organisation.

The Janata would have been reduced to a farce had he not timed his exit and fired the first salvo against fear. 'Democracy versus Dictatorship' suddenly became a movement with tremendous depth and intensity.

He has been so much and so long in power that the lust for more power had become meaningless for him. He took the stern action to denude those who sought to institutionalise one-person rule.

When I called on him last Tuesday morning for a formal interview, he was standing in his spacious lawn acknowledging the greetings of thousands of admirers.

People were dancing and beating drums. The melody of the Shehnai filled the air.

He took no time in extricating himself from the crowd to sit with me in his modest drawing-room.

The Janata leaders, I said, are talking about enquiries into excesses committed during Emergency. I know you support this demand but I hope you will prevent witch-hunting.

Well. I am always against witch-hunting but, during the election, Congress leaders promised to go into the question of excesses and punish the guilty officials. I had asked then: why only the officials?"

Politicians also?

Politicians who gave directions to the officers either expressly or impliedly should be brought to book. Responsibility will have to be explained.

Does this include Indira Gandhi also?

Well, so far as the acts of commission and omission by Sanjay are concerned. I maintain I do not hold him responsible for that.

You mean there would be a Commission of Enquiry against her?

It need not necessarily mean a Commission of Enquiry. But the responsibility will certainly have to be explained. How is it that a person who has no locus standi either in the government or in the Congress was permitted to perform certain works or give directions?

Do you propose to have a Commission for this?

Well, as I said all these questions will have to be carefully considered.

As I understand you, you won't permit vindictiveness?

Of course, in political life there should be no vindictiveness.

Particularly against individuals?

Yes. Unless they are found guilty. Then the law should take its course.

I began the interview by saying that he was the real architect of the popular verdict against personalised rule and monopolisation of power. The country would remain indebted to him for its intellectual emancipation. He certainly ranked next to Gandhiji as a destroyer of fear.

He is always smiling and one never knows from his expression whether he is pleasing himself or others. The *Babuji smile* has always been a pet topic among central Hall gossip-mongers. But one thing is sure, no leader in the Congress government had been as accessible as he.

The secret of his survival has been his humility. Despite enormous power, he never permitted arrogance to cast its shadow on him. In this hour of supreme glory, he paid personal attention to all who came to greet him.

But he is certainly aware of the sudden, unexpected and unprecedented greater love and affection people are showing him.

"Well, there has been great popular support for the stand I took," he began. There was something like a popular upsurge throughout the country. The support we received from the people has been truly magnificent. Now, people have expectations from us. And our government will have to take care to see that promises are kept, programmes are implemented. This is the only way to maintain the tempo, the only method to receive people's support continuously.

My fear is people's expectations have risen too high and I hope the Janata and CFD will be able to rise to these expectations.

I'm sure, the government will be able to liquidate large-scale unemployment and ensure that the masses get the bare necessities of life. If genuine efforts are made in this direction, then the day is not too distant to realise our desires.

Will you continue the private and the public sector policy of the Congress?

Well, I do not see any government in this country being anything but socialist. There is no alternative to socialism.

Would you like the kind of discipline under Emergency to continue or let the working class and the employees revert to the pre-Emergency situation?

No. I hope the working class, the government employees and ordinary citizens will appreciate that everyone in a democracy has responsibility. Rights flow from responsibility. Everyone should be aware of his responsibility and carry it out faithfully. This applies to all classes of people and all citizens.

You mean you will not permit any laxity?

There should not be any laxity because the nation will go to pieces. It will be bad if there is no discipline and the people are not aware of their responsibilities.

There are suggestions for rapprochement between you and the Congress now that the elements you've been opposed to have been eliminated.

There is no question of a rapprochement at present. The whole question is how to resurrect the Congress and restore democracy in the Congress which has practically disappeared. The whims and wishes of certain individuals were carried out, irrespective of whether they violated the rules and regulations of the Party and its constitution. There is little hope for the survival of the Congress unless inner-party democracy is restored.

Will you invite congressmen to join you?

I have already done that but I would not invite any person individually. I have appealed to them and if they wish to join, they are welcome.

You have promised to remove all Draconian measures and amend the constitution accordingly. Will you also unchain the news media, radio and TV. I mean from government control?

I can only say that the status quo ante will be restored.

That means the government will continue to control radio and TV.

I have not applied my mind to this particular question. We will have to think whether they should be with the government or converted into a corporation or made into a limited company.

And Samachar?

From the very beginning I was not much in favour of unification of all the agencies and lumping them in one agency under the aegis of the government.

Justifying the lifting of the ban on the extremist communal and sectarian organisations, he said people should know that there is no alternative to secularism. For those who do not believe in secularism, the law will have to take its own course.

As I talked to him a large number of people waiting outside attempted to gatecrash-Atal Behari Vajpayee, giant-killer Chandravati and some industrialists, who only recently had organised Indira Gandhi's election campaign, were also waiting to speak to him.

I'll have an in-depth interview with you after you assume leadership of the nation and get settled. I said, But before I leave I'd want to know if you envisage any change in the foreign policy.

No. It has no defects. Our aim is non-alignment and friendship with all countries.

That means Nehru's tradition will continue?

Yes. It has to. It is very rational.

The Indo-Soviet Friendship Treaty?

I believe in friendship with all countries. The Indo-Soviet Treaty should certainly continue but we should have similar treaties with other countries too.

Are you aiming to improve our relations with the United states?

We will make all efforts to improve our relations with the US and other countries.

Current, 02.04.1977.
pp. (11 + 13 + 18)

Indira will be arrested on criminal charges—Charan Singh

Charan Singh has struck terror among public men guilty of social and economic crimes.

Whether he will succeed in this crusade and be ultimately be able to book and punish the 'criminals' only the future can tell.

He is determined and relentless.

After two long sittings with him last week, I got the impression that no political force in his Party or outside will succeed in deterring him from throwing his net far and wide. Neither Indira Gandhi nor her top political associates will he spared.

His integrity and honesty has been unquestioned. So far he has received unstinted cooperation from senior party colleagues. Prime Minister Morarji Desai, who was initially reluctant to adopt such stringent measures, has finally agreed that the "guilty must be punished "irrespective of their political or social stature."

Charan Singh is a man of few words. He is straight forward and knows what he is aiming at.

The raids on Nandini Satpathy's properties have proved that his war against corruption transcends political affiliations.

The demand for the arrest of Indira Gandhi has been made by a number of important members of your party. EMS Namboodiripad also has asked for her prosecution. You too seem to be in favour of her arrest. But there is an impression that you apprehend her arrest may add to her popularity and lend to new kind of polarization.

No, no there is no question of apprehension or fear. Not at all. If she is arrested it would be not because of her political views or because she took any risk in the national interest or because of her ideology or because she was prepared to suffer for the sake of the people—nothing of the kind. Politicians arrested for these reasons ultimately emerge as heroes. Not criminals.

You want to arrest her on criminal grounds?

What else?

What crime has she committed?

I won't disclose the offence now. But it will be an offence under the present law.

The Criminal Procedure Code?

Criminal Procedure Code is a procedure. It is not a substantive law. There are so many acts.

Will you use one of those Acts?
Yes. The IPC, Prevention of Corruption Act, etc.

It seems she is fearing arrest within a week or so. She told an American journalist she was about to be arrested.
I also read it in the papers.

How soon will she be arrested?
I can't say. I can't say it she will be arrested at all.

Is there a difference of opinion between you and Morarjibhai on the issue of arresting Indira Gandhi.
No.

There used to be but now I think you have persuaded him.
There was none earlier also.

Does Morarjibhai agree that she should be punished?
Yes. If she is found guilty. He agrees with me.

I understand you have collected a lot of evidence against her?
Investigations are going on not only against her but others guilty of wrong doings in the Congress.

Does your list include important ex-ministers.
Yes, it does.

I hope you arrest them on criminal grounds and not for political reasons.
No. I assure you. It will not be on a political basis.

Don't you think such large-scale arrests will create a scare in the country?
Why? People will celebrate another Diwali.

If they are arrested?
Yes.

As I was telling you yesterday, these arrests may lead to a sense of unity amongst congressmen. Fear of arrest may even throw them on Indira Gandhi's lap.
No. It is not a fact. Only those who feel that they are really guilty will bond themselves together. I hope all are not guilty.

You mean the guilty will unite and stand behind her?
Yes, the guilty will unite.

You seem to be forcing the Congress into a split. This time the guilty and innocent will split.

They'll form another party.

By guilty you mean the people with ill-gotten money?
Yes. The Congress was in power. It used its power to collect funds to the extent of hundreds of crores. Not crores, hundreds of crores.

When you say hundreds of crores, do you have proof?
Yes, I have. For hundreds of crores. I have information in respect of other hundreds of crores. It is estimated at Rs. 600 crore.

How do you know?
Responsible people are talking about it.

It is nearly Rs. 900 crore. We have documents for Rs. 350 crore.

There is a view that raids on Congress Party offices are malafide and that in all fairness the Janata offices too should be raided. There should not be discrimination between parties.
It is not the people who say it. It is only congressmen and Ayub Syed who say it.

I'm not here as a congressman. I am talking to you as an Editor.
Everybody is satisfied in the country. The raids have revealed the truth.

Will you take similar action if you come to know that some members of the Janata have collected funds in the same manner?
It is not a question of collection. The question is the diversion of these funds for personal ends. That is the charge.

But if you come to know of misuse of funds by certain Janata Party members . . .
I will bring it to the notice of my Party's national executive.

Would you take executive action against them as you did in the case of the Punjab Congress?
It is the scale of an operation of an act which makes the difference. For example, you and I enter the railway compartment at the same time and being stronger you push me aside. By law it is an offence but shall I file a complaint?

For such matters complaints are not filed and people are not fined. So if there is a minor complaint, raids and searches would not take place.

Can I draw your attention to P.C. Sen's allegation against D.N. Lahiri? Sen has charged him with misappropriating over Rs. 10 lakh.
I have not received any complaint from Sen. Moreover as Bengal Party Chairman it is for him to make a complaint.

People are full of appreciation for the bold steps you are taking. They

are fully with you in your fight against corruption and illegal gratification. But do you feel you will succeed in your crusade?
The future alone will show.

Are you getting total cooperation from the bureaucracy and the investigative authorities?
So far as the investigative authorities are concerned, I'm getting full cooperation. No complaints. They're very efficient.

What about Party support? I think some of the steps you have taken have created tension in the Janata.
I don't think so.

Are you confident of your Party's full cooperation?
Yes. And if there is any dissenting voice it will keep quiet.

But I understand the raids on Nandini Satpathy's house have created tension in the Party. It is believed it is a result of the intensified faction-fighting and Nandini is a target.
One hundred and seven Janata Party MLAs hold an opinion against this lady. They have given in writing that she should be turned out of the party.

Turning out is a different thing but searches are rather serious.
They were done on the basis of evidence. The Congress government had set up a fact-finding Committee. The searches were made on the basis of its report.

Will it have repercussions in the party?
What about the people? It is the people who matter.

If you come to know of other cases in the Janata Party would you take similar action?
When she resigned from the Chief ministership, the Congress ministry told the police to start this and got an inquiry instituted. Judge P.R. Das was asked to look into it, though a regular Inquiry Commission was not appointed. On the basis of his findings the searches started.

The general impression is that it is a reflection of the fight between her and Biju Patnaik, a sort of personal vendetta.
What will you say: "because I had ordered raids on congressmen it is a fight between me and Indira? It gives a bad colour.

There were allegations against Biju Patnaik too?
Yes. The Khanna Commission said he committed some improprieties.

No serious allegations?
No corruption. On the basis of the Khanna Report Lal Bahadur Shastri

appointed another committee with Chagla as its member. Its report said that what he did was not wrong but the way he did things created suspicion. He adopted wrong methods.

Commissions of Inquiry have been instituted against certain Chief ministers and ex-Chief ministers. What about the Lokpal?

Lokpal is nothing but a standing Commission of inquiry. At the moment we have separate Commissions for each case. The Lokpal's findings will be placed before Parliament. Chief ministers will also come within its purview. Its findings about Chief ministers will also be placed before Parliament. Exposure of misdeeds of a politician is the greatest punishment awarded to him and if it is a criminal offence, cases will be filed in a court of law.

In Maharashtra, Lok Ayukta has given its report against two ministers. But the Chief minister has refused to take action against them.

In that case, the Chief minister can be hauled up for abetment. Not for the commission of a crime by himself but for abetting in the crimes of his colleagues. His case can be sent up to the Lokpal.

President's Rule seems to be imminent in the four Congress held states before the Assembly elections.

Elections will be held after six months.

But do you propose to have President's Rule before that or will you permit elections under Congress rule?

You're talking of the future. As of today there is no proposal for taking over.

What action will you take if the Grover Commission gives its report against the Urs Ministry?

We will consider what we should do.

Dismiss the Ministry?

Can't say.

Is the anti-defection Bill being delayed because of differences in the Janata Party?

No. The differences are between the Janata on the one side and the Congress on the other.

Then what is the delay?

No delay. But we cannot do everything at one time.

Will the Bill be introduced in the next session?

I hope so.

The Shah Commission is facing the gigantic task of sifting the grain from the chaff. There are reports that it does not have enough staff.
Who told you this? We have given it 32 investigation officers.

Are you satisfied with its pace and functioning.
Yes. Certainly.

You recently suggested that certain provisions for anticipatory bail should be removed. How soon will they be removed?
All I can say is that there is no such anticipatory bail provision in any other country. We will introduce a Criminal Law Amendment Bill, a Cr. P.C. Amendment Bill. I'm bringing the proposal before the cabinet. It is for the cabinet to decide.

Do you agree with the RSS leaders' suggestion that their organisation should be kept separate from the Party?
Leave it. It is a complicated question.

But some people in your Party are deeply concerned. It is a raging controversy.
The Prime Minister has already made a statement. That ends the matter.

Do you agree with the Prime Minister?
How can I differ from him.

Current, 17.09.1977.
pp. (1 + 2)

Return of Indira

The sudden return of Indira to active politics has caused a flutter in the country. Once again she is trying to manipulate her way into power.

But this time it will not be a bed of roses. It will be an uphill task for her. She will have to swim against the national mood. No party or responsible individual is in favour of her return.

The Janata is vehemently opposed to her. In her own party a big chunk of the leadership has arranged itself to block her way. Her dinner diplomacy was a flop and her presence at last week's Working Committee meeting was taken as an attempt at stooping to conquer. This is not enough. She will have to crawl before she can climb.

Whether it is hate or apathy, the Indira Factor haunts the rulers and the ruled, government and opposition.

Last week we spoke to her arch detractors and Congress leaders. Their attitude has stiffened. In a forthright conversation lasting two hours, Home minister Charan Singh made it explicit that he'll show no mercy to her and would take all the legal steps to punish her and her son.

Can she return if she apologises?
No. There is no question of apology. Apology cannot wash her sins away.

What do you propose to do against her politically?
To defeat her in every election.

There's an impression that her re-emergence is keeping the Janata together.
No. This is wrong.

Do you agree with us that she is a liar?
Yes. I made this charge against her in almost every speech made during the election and also after. In no country does a Prime Minister make a false statement but she has never made a true statement.

Janata Chairman Chandra Shekhar was less harsh, more polite—rather diplomatic. Or was he trying to be magnanimous? He did not think her return to politics would pose a threat to our democratic system. In a free society he thought, there cannot be a ban on any individual from entering political activity.

It is for the people to judge whether they accept her, he said. They have already rejected her. If she wants to try again, she is free to do so.

This is one view. JP feels she must first apologise. Do you agree?
I don't know. Again how can I ask an individual to apologise? I can only say that people would not like to repeat the old mistakes.

Do you still consider her a threat to democracy?
No. If as Prime Minister she could not remain a threat to democracy I see no reason why she should now become so powerful. You are giving her too much importance. I don't.

Has the fear of her re-emergence kept the Janata United?
I don't agree with this and if the Janata Party depends on this fear, it is not going to last. It will have to survive on its own merit. The 'fear' cannot be an enduring factor. The Janata Party will die or survive on its own deeds or misdeeds.

Her expulsion from the Congress it is assumed, will break the Janata.
Had it been so, the Congress would have taken this step much earlier. Indira Gandhi herself would have suggested the course.

Is it true she is the only stumbling block to the return of some former congressmen to the parent body from the Janata?
I do not think Congress can be rebuilt only by expelling her. It is true that she has been the main factor for its disaster. How can others absolve themselves of their responsibility? What were they, including Ayub Syed, doing when she indulged in all these activities? I was a congressman. I never supported her.

Hemavati Nandan Bahuguna thought it was 'certain shared values' and not fear of Indira which kept the Janata together: "There is nothing like fear. Fear disappeared the day Babu Jagjivan Ram and a small man like me came out of the Congress. Nobody can put her back into power. The people of India have rejected her.

Will lot of people from the Janata be tempted to return to the Congress fold if she is expelled?
This is not correct. When the Congress entered coma, or she put the Congress in coma, at that point no congressman had been left with any sensitivity. Men like me were completely disillusioned by the party as a whole. Not by its principles but by its functioning. She eliminated people one by one. Everytime she eliminated someone, the rest thought it was not they, why bother?

Does her return pose any threat in any way to the Janata?
Nobody defeated Indira Gandhi. She defeated herself. Let me be frank. The Janata cannot be defeated by her. Our danger is that our functioning will either keep us or throw us out.

The situation can go from bad to worse in five years.
Therefore, you think we'll extend the period by imposing Emergency?

It may be too early to judge but she has begun to draw crowds.
What crowds? People go to see what she looks like after defeat.

Out of curiosity?
Yeah, Yeah. That she was our Prime Minister, let us see how she looks now, she is the first living ex-Prime Minister!

Has she any chance of returning?
I don't think she is subject to any such consideration. To us what is more important is our economy, our administration and our organisational capabilities. They are more than taxing. So why bother about her.

As a former colleague, do you think she is a habitual liar?
I don't want to use strong words. A politician has his or her idiom. The idiom is sometimes capable of two meanings.

You're being diplomatic. I want a straight answer.
It is rather difficult. All that I can say is that she lacks courage to own up her faults. It should not be equated with telling lies.
In the BBC interview, she said things about Sanjay which were not correct.
That's why, I am saying she lacks courage to own her mistakes. It is not like Mahatma Gandhi saying I have committed a Himalayan blunder.

Opposition leader Yeshwantrao Chavan is a believer in the aphorism "Discretion is the better part of valour." His smile remains as enigmatic as ever.

As opposition leader your duty is to replace the Ruling Party and come into power?
I would put it this way. The duty of the opposition Party is to project itself as an alternative government.
Excellent. It means, if the Janata government collapses, you become Prime Minister?
Theoretically, Yes.
Will you be able to fight the cult of personality and establish collective leadership?
I'm confident of it. Collective leadership means the party has created certain institutional instruments for implementing policies. It does not mean a group of people or a caucus.

Current, 13.08.1977.
pp. (1 + 21)

Indira factor haunts Delhi

The national debate on the Indira Factor launched by Current has assumed tremendous political significance.

Our readers have reacted sharply in favour as well as against Indira Gandhi's return to active politics. They have shown an astounding involvement in what happened to her. We have received bouquets and brickbats on our branding her a liar.

Last week, national leaders of the stature of Charan Singh, Chandra Shekhar, Bahuguna and Chavan agreed with us that she has outlived her political utility. She will be a positive menace to our democratic framework if she once again gatecrashes into national life.

This week we highlight the views of the country's two most astute politicians : Babu Jagjivan Ram, architect of the Janata Wave and Nanaji Deshmukh, powerful spokesman of the Jan Sangh-BLD combine.

Raj Narain, who finally exploded the Indira myth by defeating her has also expressed views in his inimitable style.

Congress President Brahmananda Reddy, too, agrees with us that she is basically a manipulator and not a democrat in the true sense of the word.

The Indira factor thus haunts Delhi, the Janata stalwarts and the vanquished Congress warriors.

She has somehow once again emerged as the single most important factor in the game of power politics.

Jagjivan Ram, who annihilated the despotic Indira Empire with one stroke and gave a shot in the Janata arm, remains a determined and articulate detractor of the former Prime Minister. We asked him:

How do you rate her chance for a comeback?
In a democratic set up nothing is ruled out. In other countries too when people calculated that a particular leader had no chance at all, he tried to come back and did come back. So nobody can say that she will not return. What response she will get from the people will depend on how she will conduct herself in future. If she follows the same style. I will say perhaps she will have no chance.

If she changes her mood of functioning, perhaps she will get a response from some more people. But that depends on how the Janata Party functions.

But if the Janata fails in rising to the expectations of the people . . .
If the Janata Party fails, as the Congress did, in fulfilling the pledges made in the manifesto. I will not say that Indira Gandhi will succeed in her come back, but the country will be faced with a situation which one shudders to think of.

You mean if she comes back?
No, if the Janata Party fails, Indira Gandhi may not come back, but the situation which will be created in the country is what one shudders to think of.

Do you share the views that if she is removed from the Party a number of congressmen who had joined the Janata will return to the parent body?
I don't think so. It was expected at one time that a large number of congressmen would join the Janata Party and with that expectation and

also to meet the challenge of the CFD the Janata Party reversed its decision and opened its doors to all people.

Encouraged defections?

I will not use the word 'Defections', but they opened their doors to all people. But after they opened the door it was not very attractive.

The main reason for your leaving the Congress was not ideological differences. You objected to her style of functioning. If she goes out of the Congress, there is no reason why you should not go back?

Well, one will have to see how it shapes. And then after having left the Congress and joining the Janata why should I leave it again.

That seems to be the national pattern. People think if you could time the JAG-Bomb, then you could do it again!

That I can do only when I feel that the nation demands it.

Coming back to Indira, I think she is trying to capture the Congress Party.

Well, she may capture a part of it.

Which means the Congress will split?

I think so.

Is the split imminent?

I'll not say imminent. It all depends on how she conducts herself within the party.

As her former colleague do you think she is prone to telling lies?

I will not discuss that.

Nanaji Deshmukh clenches his strong jaws and firmly declares : "She will not come back."

Do you agree with JP that she may have a chance to return if she apologises to the people?

I differ with JP. After committing the wrongs, apology will not change reality.

I don't think she will apologise.

I agree with you. It is not her nature. She is altogether a reactionary woman. She reacts. She has nothing positive in her. Only those who do not have any positive thing in them, turn into dictators.

What will you do if she comes back as the head of the Congress?

She cannot be and she will not be. That is my calculation.

Another hypothetical proposition. How would you react if she becomes the leader of the opposition in Parliament?

This proposition I refuse to accept, because the people in the Congress are fed up with her dictatorial trends. She never consulted anybody. So a person having self-respect will never accept Indira Gandhi as leader.

You seem to be giving credit to many congressmen for self-respect!

People have a natural sense of self-respect. Most times it is subdued, but not forever. They are realising their folly. People have been employed to boost up her image again. It is not spontaneous. It is not natural. She cannot tolerate anybody else. She can only think of herself.

Do you agree with us that she has been lying?

Definitely, we were the main targets of her lies. She is still telling lies about the Jan Sangh. She has raised the bogey that the Jan Sangh will capture the Janata Party. This is not the fact. The Jan Sangh has merged completely. We have no identity, nor any memory as such. Now we are dedicated to the cause of the Janata Party.

There is a feeling that some prominent Janata members might return to the Congress if she is expelled?

You see it is alright for congressmen to organise the party well. We want a strong opposition. They will have a better chance to reorganise the party if they expel this Indira Gandhi and get rid of her leadership. But it is not possible. Congressmen have always thought of some particular leader and never of an ideal or programme. They should not only leave Indira Gandhi but this psychology of dependence on the individual. Removing Indira Gandhi won't do, they must have an ideal also.

Congress president Brahmananda Reddy, who we thought was a puppet in the hands of his former mentor, has proved us wrong. He is not the spineless, gutless fellow we thought he was.

As the head of a battered political party, he has decided to assert his positions and ignore Indira Gandhi's a claim of hereditary leadership.

Do you agree with JP's view that she should first apologise and then re-enter active politics?

I do not want to get into what JP has said. But certainly it is in the Gandhian tradition that if we commit a mistake and if we feel it so, we express our regrets. For the excesses and misuse during Emergency, I have expressed my regrets.

Wouldn't you advise her to express regret?

If a statement like that helps the Congress she must consider it.

Do you think these dinners and counter-dinners will lead to another split?

Normal get-togethers are not bad, but dinners like these with a motivation and for a purpose are not good. They are not desirable in the interests of the unity and discipline of the Party.

The most urgent need is to get back to our democratic fold, establish collective leadership, infuse confidence in our Party members and regain credibility amongst the people about our efficacy in solving problems. The Congress has a much greater role to play in the future.

Do you think, Indira's ways of functioning has created tension in the Party?

Yes. And these kind of activities are not desirable.

Is it because of this attitude that you boycotted the dinner?

Yes.

As the Party President cannot you issue directives to prevent a repetition of the dinner episode?

I don't believe in directives but I do believe in the voice of our congressmen prevailing over such things. This has proved effective.

Some people have started a signature campaign ostensibly at her behest?

If this is part of our democratic functioning, I don't mind. But the move is motivated. It is to pressurise me. I shall certainly fight back.

Will you take action against this move?

We want no disruption. If there are any forces for disrupting our unity, we'll certainly take exception to it.

Does she expect you to call on her every time she wants to discuss things? As Congress president you are not expected to run from house to house!

Yes. The Working Committee is the forum.

You have got to assert yourself as Congress President?

Certainly.

Raj Narain sat cross-legged on his swivel chair with his walking stick lying on the table. His ministerial room in Nirman Bhavan was over crowded with comrades, admirers and officials.

Shru Keejiye, he said (please start). I said I want a proper interview. "Yes, yes." he said, "it will be a proper interview." I looked around to indicate the difference between a proper press interview and a public meeting but 'Netaji', as he is fondly called by admirers and officials, started addressing the gathering before I could finish my first question.

I wanted to ask whether he and his party were afraid of Indira's return to politics.

The interview was obviously in Hindi:

Raj Narain: Indira Gandhi has never been in politics. She knows nothing about politics. But she definitely is a diplomat, she knows diplomacy. Politics is sacred like religion. *Rajneethi* and *dharmaneethi* are entwined. Only one having faith in truth can be a politician. He who believes in falsehood adopts diplomacy.

But she is ruled for 11 years?
You think by ruling the country she can become a politician?

Do you agree with JP's apologise-and-return statement?
Please ask this question to JP. I can't answer for him. Congress is an aged party, Janata is a young party. When an aged man fails he breaks. The child stumbles and gets up and learns to walk. This is the difference between the two. Congressmen made a mistake by not listening to Gandhiji and dissolving the party after independence.

But your treatment to JP is exactly the same. JP says the same things of Janata as Gandhiji said of the Congress.
The Janata gives due importance to his statements.

There's a view that Janata will break if she's expelled?
The Janata is not concerned about her relations with the Congress. The Janata won't break.

What I mean is that many former congressmen who are in the Janata now will be tempted to return because she has been the main cause of their discomfiture.
I am not concerned whether they will return. I want to tell you that the Janata has come to stay. It is made up of a number of parties and groups who have agreed to forget their past.

It is said the people of Rae Bareli who defeated Indira, also defeated your nominees in the assembly elections. Their defeat is construed as your personal defeat and humiliation.
People who don't know Rae Bareli talk like this. It was Janata Party people who defeated the Janata Party. They became over enthusiastic and over a dozen candidates contested from each constituency on the Janata banner. Even the total votes polled by them was more than that of the Congress votes.

Now she is planning to go to Rae Bareli and her presence will definitely affect your position.
Let her go. The more she stays there, the greater would be her unpopularity.

(He suddenly switches over to English) Indira Gandhi actually was virtually defeated in 1971; but by hook or by crook, due to official interference, she managed everything.

Do you agree that she tells lies?

Yes. I do. It is mentioned in the Allahabad High Court judgement. Justice Sinha has pointed out at three places about the false statement she gave.

Current, 20.08.1977.
pp. (1 + 10 + 11)

Jagjivan Ram says: Indira is the real target

Babu Jagjivan Ram, the Janata leader and the Prime Minister in awaiting, is absolutely confident of a landslide victory at the polls. The split in the party has done good to him. Now he is the Janata's unquestioned leader.

The Janata has not left anything to chance and has assured the nation that in case it wins a majority Babuji will be its choice for the Prime ministership. The question of his being in two minds and of looking around, he assured me, does not arise.

I found him completely relaxed. His successful visit to Punjab had given him a shot in the arm and he felt that when he starts his whirlwind tour of the country he would attract huge crowds.

During an hour long interview he made it abundantly clear that caretaker Prime Minister Charan Singh is out of the race. The real battle at the hustings will be fought between him and Indira Gandhi. The choice is clear and it is up to the people of India to decide.

Babuji made several controversial points clear.

He has no understanding with her and the possibility of his joining that party is absolutely ruled out. He has never met her after the break in 1977.

She offered him caretaker Prime ministership with two conditions which he turned down.

Authoritarianism poses a greater danger to democracy and talk of communalism in his party is just a bogey.

The consequences will be disastrous if the elections are postponed. Devraj Urs will be wiser if he maintains his Karnataka Congress.

For the first time the people have a clear cut choice to elect their Prime

Minister. There are three contenders in the field. How do you visualise the situation?
Well, the people will have to make a choice not only on the basis of the individuals but the policies and programmes of the parties.

So far the individuals are concerned you, Indira Gandhi and Chaudhary Charan Singh are very well known to the people. The choice is limited. Your party has already declared that in case of a Janata victory you will be the Prime Minister. The Lok Dal is unanimous on the choice of Chaudhary Charan Singh and of course Indira Gandhi is there as a formidable candidate. The parties have made their choice now. The people will have to make their choice.
I agree with you. Therefore the people will have to choose between the three.

Babuji, how do you propose to project your new image to the people?
The people of this country know me. They also know that I know a little bit of administration.

You know too much of it.
Yes, people know that whatever I have handled I have done it successfully. People also know that if I become the Prime Minister I will also handle it successfully.

But the people also know that Indira Gandhi too was a successful Prime Minister except for some time when things went out of her control.
Well, everything will have to be taken collectively.

Are there basic ideological and political differences between the Janata and the Janata-S, the new Lok-Dal, or is it merely a clash of personalities?
I don't think there are many fundamental differences. The whole thing was one of personalities and the ambitions of one person.

One or two persons?
I think it was the ambition of one person only.

It was not only one or two but three persons. When the question of leadership arose in your party you were immediately challenged by Chandra Shekhar. In fact in your party about half a dozen people aspired for the leadership.
The situation was created by the ambition of one person. After that many people developed ambitions.

Is it not a fact that immediately after the formation of the Janata many people aspired for the Prime ministership and staked the claim? Chaudhary Charan Singh was not alone.

Not to that extent.

Also, Morarjibhai's determination to stick to the chair by hook or crook vitiated the atmosphere.

Well, I would not like to comment on that.

You think it was merely a clash of personalities?

I think it was.

There are rumours that the mid-term poll may be postponed on the excuse of drought. Do you apprehend such an eventuality?

When the President dissolved the Lok Sabha the drought was already there and he was aware of the situation. Having called for the elections there is no constitutional scope for the postponement. The election will have to be called before the third week of January. I don't see there is any ground for postponement.

But there are persistent rumours that the elections will be postponed.

I don't think so. The constitution has to be observed and the elections will have to be held.

Who will observe the constitution? The President or the caretaker Prime Minister?

No, the President.

But if the Prime Minister and his Council of ministers advise the President that the situation is not conducive for elections and the government and its machinery will be busy in drought relief work, the elections may be postponed.

We will see to it that the constitution is observed.

You have said several times that the President did not observe the constitution. What is the guarantee that he will not repeat the performance?

Then a different situation may develop in this country and the people will not like it.

What kind of a situation you expect?

Well, people will have to decide whether the country should be governed by the constitution or by the whims of an individual.

In 1971 the main slogan was Garibi Hatao; and you have been very much a part of it. In 1977 Indira Hatao was the national cry and once again you were on the forefront. Whom are you going to Hatao this time?

The question was put to me whether Emergency will be the main slogan of our election campaign. I said no. The main plank of the Janata Party will be the economic programme, something in general terms and something specific which will have to be implemented in the course of five years. Of course, the emphasis will be on the rule of law, on the independence of the judiciary. Defections will also be our main slogan.

Will you again try to bring the anti-defection Bill? Last time you failed. It was opposed by some prominent members of your own party.
You know how it was done and who did it. Those who opposed are now out of the party and in the other camp.

The question about Hatao remains unanswered.
Your question is whether our slogan will again be *Indira Hatao.*

Or Charan Singh Hatao?
Naturally our effort will be to defeat both of them.

To you who is the greater menace, Indira Gandhi or Charan Singh?
I think in this battle Charan Singh does not count much.

So your main battle will be against Indira Gandhi.
Yes, definitely it will be against her.

Your main slogan will be Indira Hatao though she is not yet in power.
The question of *Hatao*-ing anybody does not arise and specially the question of Charan Singh does not arise. Even in villages the people are very much against defections.

This has been proved in the case of Chand Ram. He defected to become the Chief minister of Haryana and now he is nowhere.
Correct. Even the Harijans don't support him or may have some kind of an understanding with Indira Gandhi. In fact Charan Singh has given public credence to the rumours. Well, he must have something to tide over his frustration. In fact there is no secret understanding between Indira Gandhi and myself. We have never met after I left the Congress except on ceremonial occasions or some marriage parties. The only persons who met me are Kamlapati Tripathi and Stephen in the presence of Chandra Shekhar. That meeting was not a secret, that was merely to exchange ideas. There is no secret understanding whatsoever.

The meeting between Sanjay Gandhi and your close associate D.N. Tiwari at a very crucial moment created a lot of misunderstanding.
That was at that time. Tiwari never consulted me.

Was Sanjay invited by Tiwari for political settlement?
That I don't know. I know that Dwarkanath did not invite Sanjay, he went to his house on his own.

The misunderstanding was because both of them met while the issue of

Prime ministership was hanging fire and that they did negotiate certain political things. Do you know what transpired between them?
No, there were no negotiations.

Did Dwarkanathji offer some political solution to Sanjay? Did Sanjay make some offer to you through him?
No, there was no offer. I think there was some political talk. He was trying to find out if there was any possibility of our people joining Indira Gandhi.

She has said that she did not sabotage your chance of becoming the Prime Minister. Did she offer you the Prime ministership?
Yes, she did. She wanted me to be the caretaker Prime Minister which I refuse. Well, she was a party to the dissolution of the Lok Sabha and the President says that her advice to him was one of the reasons for holding elections.

You think she was genuine in her offer to you?
Well, there was no reasons to question her genuineness. When Kamlapati Tripathi met me he put two conditions that I become the caretaker Prime Minister and I will not include any member of the Jana Sangh in the Cabinet and after two or three months I will call for the dissolution of the House and mid-term polls. I did not accept the conditions.

Did they also put conditions about the special courts or withdrawing of cases?
No. There was nothing like this. No other conditions.

Is there any possibility of a meaningful dialogue between you and Devraj Urs? You and Devraj Urs had developed a close affinity and he had gone to the extent of disclosing that he will be happy if you become the Prime Minister.
Yes, he has been very close to me, but I don't know why he has entered the Congress. I don't know why he has decided to be an undertaker President. Where is the Congress? Take for example Maharashtra, West Bengal and Madhya Pradesh. Almost all the Congress leaders there have joined the Congress-I. The combination between the Congress-S and the then Janata-S and the prominent Congress leaders joining the cabinet has practically meant the annihilation of the Congress. Where is the Congress now? It will be wiser for Urs even now to maintain the Karnataka Congress.

Or join the Janata?
Of course, he would be welcome.

Were there any political negotiations between you and him?

No, but he publicly invited me to join the Congress and also came to see me before he became the Congress President. Many of the old congressmen when they are in Delhi come and meet me. When he came to see me last I asked him why he joined the Congress and told him that it would have been better for him to maintain the Karnataka Congress.

Had he followed your advice, he would have become a regional party and he would have been isolated in national affairs.

No, I don't think so. He would not have been isolated. Is MGR isolated in national affairs? He is playing an important role and even regional parties have their men in the Parliament and from that angle they do contribute to national affairs. So to assume that the regional parties will be isolated from national affairs is not correct.

Is your alliance with the AIADMK final?

Yes, the alliance is final. There are no conditions from either side.

Why MGR decided to throw his lot with you and not with Indira Gandhi?

Because Indira Gandhi preferred the DMK.

Which is the major threat to the country communalism or authoritarianism?

I think both are bad but authoritarianism is very bad for democracy.

How do you analyse or interpret the word authoritarianism.

Authoritarianism means one person tries to control the whole party or the whole government. One person's supremacy and the concentration of powers is authoritarianism.

With you and other leaders in the Congress, how one person was permitted to concentrate all the powers? What happened to the democratic tradition of the Congress?

The whole thing boils down to the period of Emergency.

Was it not there before Emergency?

Well, may be in some little way.

Why did you permit it?

Why go to that chapter now? Let us not talk of that.

Indira Gandhi has remarkably recovered her ground in the last six months. What are the contributing factors for her resurrection?

I personally feel that her recovery, started from the point she was arrested and released. From then it went on gathering momentum.

Another turning point was yet another stupid action—her expulsion from the Lok Sabha. It added to her popularity.

It did. Moreover, she has a very well-knit organisation which no other party has.

It is different from her increasing mass popularity.

Well, she has always been attracting crowds.

Babuji, what are the basic differences between you two? Recently, she told me that you had been constantly conspiring against her while a member of her Cabinet and that your aim was to become the Prime Minister.

It is wrong. I never conspired to oust her. If she has told you that I have been plotting against her, she is not correct.

What is the fact?

If she is honest, she will admit that I gave her full loyalty.

Did you apprehend that in case of yours and the Janata Party's defeat, you will be liquidated?

Yes. I feared that.

You and Bahuguna have much in common. Is there any possibility of your coming together again?

Well, our personal relations are very good.

I am talking of your political relations.

Let me hope that after all the changes in the Janata constitution and the RSS attitude, he may change his mind, see his way and return to the Janata.

Despite your differences neither of you have spoken against each other.

I have not said a word against him.

He too has not uttered a word against you. Has this kept the door open?

As an exponent of Nehruism how do you feel in the company of Nehru-haters?

I have spoken on Nehruism on several occasions but it was not the Jana Sanghis who objected to my praise of Nehru, but it was Charan Singh who took strong exception. If you remember my speech at Mumbai's Nehru centre, after the speech it was Charan Singh who kicked up a row. I have not so far heard any Jana Sanghi attacking Nehru.

Charan Singh has promised to give one acre of land and a cow to every landless labourer. Will you also make such spectacular promises?

I hope he starts from his own Meerut district of distributing cow and land to every Kisan.

Is it possible?

I cannot think of such a promise but I will certainly think that every family should be provided with a house site in rural as well as urban areas and it is not only the landless people, but there are Brahmin families which do not have houses to live. They may be having a house acquired in their great-grand-father's time. Now the family has grown and it too needs house sites.

Some people have attempted to turn democracy into castocracy. You are undoubtedly above all these considerations but how do you plan to break these caste barriers.

I have always felt that casteism is no less dangerous than communalism and we have to fight both the evils.

Organised casteism raised its ugly head in Bihar and UP during the Janata regime. People like Karpoori Thakur feed casteist feelings to serve their selfish ends. Your party is to a very large extent responsible for giving political sanctity to casteism.

Not exactly. Casteism is a part of Indian society but in the last few years it is accentuated not because of Janata policies but some leaders have been playing upon the caste factor. The backward classes are not a homogenous element. They may combine on certain issues and demands but I don't think they will remain united during the elections.

Will you expose the casteist leaders during your election campaign?

I have always attacked casteism. It has done the greatest harm to the country.

But I am sure that the Janata leaders will succumb to caste pressure while distributing tickets.

In some cases. But not as a matter of policy.

Though you have a Leftist image, the Left has left you. Is it because the Jana Sangh is the main constituent of the Janata?

That is what they say. But I wonder why for more than three years when they have been with us they ignored the Jana Sangh factor. They were in alliance with us and they were with the Jana Sangh. I wonder whether it is a question of communalism alone or they are guided by some other political considerations.

Whether you agree or not the Jana Sangh has become a bone of contention and you will have to work very hard to change the image of your party.

I do not agree with you. The Janata is a secular party and it believes in the creed of socialism and democracy. Every Janata member has to sign a pledge accepting secularism as our policy. Communalism is a mere bogey.

I ask the detractors to give a single instance where the Janata Party took steps which went against the minorities.

Have you, during your two and a half year association with the Jana Sangh in the Janata, found any communal or chauvinistic pressures?

No, not. So far the government is concerned, I have not noticed anything. The way Atal Behari Vajpayee approached the problem of Pakistan, Bangladesh and the Arab countries—well, one cannot say that one who believed in communalism would have done that.

The Janata broke down mainly on the issue of dual membership. Is the issue settled in your party permanently?

Some positive steps have been taken to satisfy the critics of the dual membership. One is the change in the constitution of our party: no person who is a member of any organisation which believes in the establishment of a theocratic state—Hindu or Islamic can become member of the Janata.

Some discussion is going on about the RSS concept, Hindu Rastra too.

Yes, I had a discussion with Deoras and he is thinking of changing Hindu Rashtra into Bharat Rashtra.

Will it solve the problem?

It should. It makes a fundamental difference. It makes a lot of difference to say that the Hindus are a nation and that Indians are a nation.

In some of the states the minority votes are crucial and with your association with the Jana Sangh it will be difficult for you to explain your position.

I do not think so. We will assure the minorities that there won't be any discrimination against them on any ground and all citizens will enjoy equal rights. All protection will be provided to them and this announcement will be made by the leaders of erstwhile Jana Sangh.

I understand your party is planning to give them greater representation in public life.

Yes, we are. I have already asked our party units in Bihar and the UP to give adequate representation to the minorities at the time of the selection of candidates.

Is that enough?

I do not have to prove my bonafides to the minorities. They know I stand for them. The only thing is that whether I will be able to make, the Jana Sangh also see the situation as it is in our country. Everybody has to realise that with its multi-lingual and multi-religious character, India cannot be anything but a democracy based on secularism.

Are you sure the Jana Sangh will realise this?
The Jana Sangh must realise this. There is no other way out of it. You know. Deoras has recently stated that the RSS should not encourage the legislatures to participate in its Shakas. The RSS is in a process to liberate its action.

The CFD's 31-point programme appears to have been drafted by you. It reflects your thinking.
I have not yet seen it.

As a champion of the weaker sections and minorities what possible and acceptable suggestions you can put forward to solve the problems?
The whole thing is a matter of confidence. Unfortunately, we have lived together for centuries as two societies. We will have to come closure to each other socially and culturally though politically there was no distinction between the two communities.

Why not three societies—the Harijans?
Yes, our society is divided into compartments. Unfortunately, the Harijans have adopted the evils of the Hindu society. The integration of these three societies on progressive lines is a long-term progress.

Despite defence minister Subramaniam's clarification ruling out any irregularity in the Jaguar deal, Raj Narain has been repeating his charge of kick-offs and of slush money.
How can I help it? This was discussed in Parliament. I made it quite clear that there was nothing wrong in the deal and that everything was cleared at the official level on both sides and that no private parties were involved. Besides that Subramaniam, who does not belong to my party, has also stated clearly that the deal was in the national interest.

But Raj Narain has threatened to make it the main issue in the elections.
Well, in that case I leave it to the people of the country.

Current, 13.10.1979.
pp. (10 + 11)

Bahuguna: my ordeal is over
A question of survival

Hemvati Nandan Bahuguna was left with only one choice—to join Indira Gandhi in the epic electoral battle. Apparently the development was dramatic but the meeting between Her and Him was a culmination of long and sustained negotiations.

For both of them it was a question of survival. Despite her swelling popularity she was not confident of securing an absolute majority. Bahuguna too was aware that his mass appeal will not get him more than 10 seats.

Politics is a game of survival; ideologies and principles are a mere camouflage. But in the case of Bahuguna certain ideological postures were inevitable. Indira Gandhi too has been overwhelmed and is conscious of the fact that she has the following but not the talent. She has the men but not the men with experience. If she gains majority and becomes Prime Minister she alone cannot run the country. She needs people who can deliver the goods. She thought Bahuguna was one of them.

When the larger national interests are at stake personal animosities and petty quarrels have to be kept aside.

She knew victory was within her reach. But to sustain it could be a problem. Perhaps she is more aware than anybody else in her camp that she is surrounded by sycophants. Bahuguna has the courage. He had crossed swords with her. He also had the fortitude of subjugating his personal interests for greater national cause.

The meeting between Indira Gandhi and Bahuguna should be looked in this perspective.

Myself and Mahavir Adhikari met Bahuguna a few hours after this historic meeting. He was perplexed, withdrawn and overwhelmed. She took him by storm. The whole Nehru clan along with dozens of jan nissaries (people willing to sacrifice) descended on his 5 Sunehri Bagh bungalow.

We again met him the next day soon after he finished parleys with Indira Gandhi at her residence.

By going back to Indira Gandhi you have done nothing new, it was expected, though it looks strange. You belong to the Congress. You are really a dyed-in-the-wool Congress traditionalist. While in the Janata you could not emotionally delink yourself from the Congress nor could you disown the Congress ideology. Your going back to Indira Gandhi is considered a historical necessity, but while in that camp will you be able to improve on the situation?

First of all let us understand that my going back to her or her coming back to me is of no significance. The question is whether this meeting of minds will be able to give a direction to the country.

It was a short though painful and torturous break. If you recall you carried my interview in *Current* in the last week of February 1977. I had said that till the last moment I have been trying to save the Congress and Indira Gandhi from the situation. I forecast the doom. Unfortunately my warnings were ignored. But I continued to be loyal to those values. Today I am happy that there is realisation in that camp.

What did you mean by the Gandhi-Nehru frame of politics?

A forward looking society based on equality of opportunity, irrespective of caste, religion, sex, etc. It visualises a society egalitarian in character and not explosive in its economic endeavour. It also visualises the full development of human personality. It means and represents a value system.

Gandhi thought of self sufficiency from the village level itself. Nehru translated this concept into self sufficiency for India. Gandhi talked of self reliance and Nehru achieved it or wanted India to achieve it, by basing its entire thrust on development in science and technology. Gandhi thought of a human society in which all religions would have equal respect and Nehru worked and devoted his whole life for establishing a secular society. As Nehru put it, secularism did not mean irreligiousness but meant equal respect for all religions.

The Gandhi-Nehru framework represents the real ethos of the Indian society because even in the largest of its religion, Hinduism, there is place for different minds and different worships. There is place for different social relationships and there is place for the opposites.

There is a very interesting development. During the last five or six months two names are being very often mentioned. Charan Singh is exclusively for Gandhi and Gandhism. You have said that all those people who believe in Nehru's philosophy should come together. Recently, Indira Gandhi has also started mentioning about Nehru. This is an ideological turmoil we are passing through. In again coming to Gandhism and Nehruism you are trying to create a consensus between Gandhi and Nehru. You want to bring them together. But some people will be trying to separate the two. The leftists, the socialists and the progressives have been emphasising more on Jawaharlal Nehru.

Gandhi is the seed, Nehru is the plant, Gandhi is the thought, Nehru is the voice, Gandhi is an idea, Nehru is the moulder who gave practical shape to that idea.

That was a concept presented by Jawaharlal Nehru to suit the struggle for freedom all over the world. But why do you interfere with the basics of socialism? Do you think socialism needs any props?

Mankind, in its long march, has never found the last word of wisdom in any area. But Nehru talked of socialism as he integrated the dignity of the individual with the concept of economic liberation of all the toiling masses accepting a democratic parliamentary system which he worked hard to preserve, protect and promote.

I want you to comment further on the synthesis of Gandhi and Nehru which you are trying to bring about in the present context.

I feel that Gandhi was a servant of humanity when he talked of India and the Indian people. He was merely trying to liberate the one which was closest to him, his sights were fixed very high. When I said Gandhi was the soul and Nehru was the voice, when I said Gandhi was the seed and Nehru the plant, I was trying to say that Nehru tried to carry forward the whole idea. The personality of Nehru, the belief of Nehru, the whole conceptual frame of Nehru—social, economic and political—is a gift of the compassion of the human approach, Gandhi had developed this outlook of life of which Nehru was the messenger. It was integrated in one word called Gandhi.

Perhaps you looked to the support and co-operation of Indira Gandhi and did not look to the support of the Communist Parties of India, because you thought whatever socialist doctrine of ideology these parties are offering is perhaps inadequate.

I am sorry, I am sorry Mr. Adhikari's question is loaded. I must at the outset say that the Indian Communist Party has over the years, changed a great deal. They have been acclimatised for the new socio-economic development the world over. The Communist movement is no more what it was the 1920s. Even the international Communist movement has changed itself. It has had its own impact on the Indian Communist movement.

I have great respect for the Communist Party of India but I am sorry to say that somehow or the other in the present context its approach is negative. I am talking of the limited scope, I am not commenting on the whole economic, social and political framework it represents. I have my doubts on many grounds. But the question is that of the current political stance that it has developed like anti-congressism and anti-Indiraism. This anti-Congressism left bitter fruits with Communists and anti-Indiraism will also have them with bitter fruits.

What do you suggest now? That they should change this policy of anti-Indiraism?

I personally feel that there is nothing permanent in politics. Even Marx talked anti-this anti-that, Marx had thesis and anti-thesis and then synthesis.

The value of a socialist thought or ethos depends on first a thesis, then an anti-thesis.

When the Communist Party thinks that the recognition of Kampuchea is not that important as defeating Indira Gandhi in India. I feel that they are, if I may say so, trying to skip a very important factor. India cannot build a society within its boundaries, without having effects, or being affected, by developments beyond our borders.

Now, Kampuchea is so close to us. It is so important, politically very important. But the still more important question is what type of a society the Communist want to build. The Pol Pot type of society? A society in which, out of seven million people, three million have been exterminated? Children have been killed because they thought they will not respond to a particular type of political rule.

I do not think the Indian Communist Party believes that way. Moreover, if you do not stand by the right type of direction in the Kampuchea situation, you may really be failing in discharging your historical duties to remove the distortion of politics in the whole south-east Asia. Therefore, India is deeply interested and the whole socialist movement is deeply interested in this. If the image of the socialist movement is carved in the Pol Pot pattern, I think people will run away from the socialist movement, and to that extent, therefore, condemnation of the Pol Pot regime, regardless of the substitute, is a must.

You have been emphasising on your 31-point programme, that "whoever agreed to my 31-point programme I am ready to cooperate with him." You were rejected by Charan Singh and the Janata and others. Indira Gandhi appears to have accepted your programme, and that has paved the way for co-operation between you and her. She also had a 20-point programme. What do you think is the basic difference or the common points programme? And how these two programmes will be integrated with the merger of the CFD and the Congress-I?

Mr. Editor, you are going far beyond the situation as exists on the day we are meeting. The question is that those who rejected the 31-point programme did not reject me. They rejected the future of India, they rejected a value system. It is not a question of being rejected or accepted. I am hardly in the bargain myself. So far as Indira Gandhi is concerned, it appears she agrees that the 31-point programme is based on the ethos of the struggle for freedom. There are common points like implementation of land reforms, strengthening of the non-alignment movement, the question of the minorities and the language policy. There are a number of other common points. But the 20-point programme did not touch on the foreign policy. It was obviously basically a very small package. Well, the package that I have given is wider in concept which includes several items of the 20-point programme.

That was basically motivated by the Garibi Hatao programme?

I am sorry to say it was a sort of a sop, a sort of a healing touch on the situation arising out of Emergency. But I am very sorry to say that the 20-point programme came essentially in the wake of Emergency. Therefore, I do not mean to say that it was dishonest, or that it was not motivated by higher ideals but obviously this 31-point programme and the 20-point programme both grew out of the basic value system of ethos of the struggle for freedom.

We have failed miserably. I am not the one who refuses to see the blind spots. In spite of the Congress rule over the years, in Bihar, till date we do not have the record of rights. What land reform can we do in Bihar with all the 20-point programme? How could Indira Gandhi achieve land reform in Bihar? This was what exactly I was telling the present Prime Minister. "Mr. Prime Minister," I said, "If you want to do something right now (land reform is a concurrent subject), do something about setting right the record of rights in Bihar. After all I told a gentleman yesterday, a person from the press, that the record of right is actually the land I sow."

What is the record of rights?

Ise khata khatoni kahte hain hindi main kahi nahin hai idher. This means the record of rights in Bihar is quite a misnomer, totally a misnomer. Therefore there are people who are having *benami* holdings who have land of about 1000 acres till date.

But it is not the Congress alone which is guilty. I do accept responsibility as a congressman. We could have done it during Jawaharlal's time. But did the SVD government take any steps during 1967 in that direction? Did they take even one single step towards land settlement which is quite a complicated question? They will have to start field by field, crop by crop, there will have to be a major operation of land settlement and it is bound to take five to six years. It is a monumental work, but the point is that anybody who wants to bring in land reforms shall have to start it with full force.

Good land reforms have been done in Karnataka. What is being done there is that the surplus land found above ceiling has been distributed to the people. They are the occupiers of that land. Now occupation is alright. I occupy my Sunehari Bagh residence but I am not the owner of this house.

These people who have been given the land have the title of an occupier. What I was arguing with the Prime Minister is to immediately have a central Ordinance or to advise the Chief minister to confer the ownership right on them by paying adequate compensation to the owners from whom the land was realised, make use of the provision of compensation as provided in the constitution and relieve these people from the dilemma that 'I am the occupier but not an owner', so that they could take loans against this land or sell it.

It is because of lack of talent or appreciation of these very useful suggestions that you are complaining that the ordinance was brought in.

Well, this is not a question of talent. I must admit one thing. Let me tell you, Charan Singh is one man who is very knowledgeable about land reforms and its various phases and aspects.

More than you?

I must admit that I don't claim any expertise. But I must say that he unfortunately fell in a trance in which he thought that everything is OK.

I want to know what difficulties you will face in case there is CFD-Congress merger—political as well as emotional. What major problems can you envisage? Every congressman wants to know this in UP, Bihar and everywhere.

The majority of the congressmen have welcomed it. The CFD rank and files are also erstwhile congressmen. There is no problem, so we hope, but the whole process is under discussion and we have not yet finalised the conceptual frame of this unity which we want to achieve. Nevertheless, the basic thrust of this whole exercise is (a) to give this country a stable government, (b) to give this country a stable government which will be able to eradicate the communal forces.

What you are calling unity, I would call it coming together of the people who had departed (from the Congress) for a common cause.

And unfortunately, as I said, the politics of negativism has overtaken the whole political psyche of the country. Therefore, we want to take a positive direction of building a new type of order. Those 31-points, if you look at them and if you look at the manifesto, will clearly demarcate the lines as what is going to happen to the small industries, the cottage industries, the artisans, the rural folks, the landless labourers, the students, the teachers and so on.

My dealing with the multinationals, with the development in the oil and natural gas sector, my approach to the public sector and to foreign relations have all been consist with the basic Congress ideology. We had some deviations. I will give you an example. Indira Gandhi nationalised the banks. It was a great act in fulfilment of the Karachi Congress Resolution. But what happened to the nationalised banks? Let me tell you very frankly that they have not carried out the policies of the government. For example, it was decided something in 1971 that the total loaning done by the banking system in particular area should have a differential interest rate to the people whose needs were small. The differential interest scheme was opposed by the bankers first by saying that we will be losing money and so on. Then a Credit Guarantee Corporation was created to safeguard the money.

Seven crore of rupees should have been given as loans during the last three years. But at no point of time did the bankers cross two crore. Why the hell have they not done it? The Janata government came in between. Was any explanation called from any banker? By the time I came to know all these things and collected all the material to blast the banking culture I was out of the government. We have to see that this does not happen.

We will also have to see that the fishermen are not looted by giant firms like Union Carbide or Britannia Biscuits by processing seafood and exporting it. If I had my way I will pick on the fishermen's children, educate them in the best possible schools. Let them have a masters degree in business administration and let them develop a sort of personality in the food processing technology and so on. Let them develop cooperative societies in the fishermen's areas so that the total reward of their labour comes to those people rather than go to middle man.

Similarly we are exporting meat. The Kirloskars are doing it from Bombay. Why cannot the butchers and other form cooperative societies and do it for themselves?

I must tell you. I have a total concept. I just cannot say in a few minutes time. But I will give you another example. Now whom have you selected as Principal of our art school? Do you have people from Gujarat or people from Tirunelvelli or the Kanyakumari areas? Or the master craftsmen from Jaipur? The educated boys should be taken as advisers there. The whole concept should be that we should pick up boys from these areas and draw them into it and let them develop. My point is that a new culture shall be born out of the ashes which we see around us today.

After your meeting with Indira Gandhi, Janata leader Piloo Mody commented that you have been led into a slaughter house. Do you apprehend yet another uncertainty?

I have acted with malice toward none, with faith in the destiny of the people and with courage of my conviction. I have nothing to fear, nothing to gain, nothing to lose. The people can see the forces of disintegration, the forces that are now challenging the economy and the political disorder.

You had a series of talks before the merger. What is the gist. Did you discuss the strategy of the campaign?

No, not yet.

Is it too early?

Not so. No, it is not at all early. It is rather becoming late. But I am saying nothing for the while except one thing. Let us regenerate ourselves with all honesty and purpose to build the India of Gandhi's and Nehru's dreams.

And that's why you have joined Indira Gandhi?

That is my expectation, that is my hope, that is my effort.

I am asking a controversial question. Everybody wants to know it. Sanjay Gandhi seems to be enthusiastic about the new development. Is it a temporary phase or a long-range political strategy?

I have no comments.

Well, he came to your house.

Well, why do you want to say this? You see after all, Mrs. Gandhi was kind enough to come. And along with her came Rajiv. The whole family came. The point is that you forget her elder son. Why do you always remember the younger one.

Because the younger one plays crucial role in politics.

I do not know. I do not really know, what role he is playing right now. But it is not my concern. I have nothing to do with that. So, no comments to make. Rajiv came, Sonia came, so did Sanjay.

Did you talk to Sanjay?

No, there was no reason to talk, except to say hello, you are welcome, I didn't talk alone, Mrs. Gandhi and Kamlapathiji were in this room.

But I understand it is mostly political strategy that was discussed, in what way the thrust is to be made.

How can one say anything as to what will really happen? In a war you know you can have a common control, a common message, a common strategy and a common thrust.

You want to fight the elections on a war footing?
No. The battle of the ballot is not that important, it is the battle for the regeneration of Gandhism and Nehruism.

Do you think these elections will be more important than the last one?
Well, the last elections lost its importance because it was a deteriorating type of happening. One could see the end in its very birth.

Was it a kind of aberration.
Not aberration exactly. It was the result of an aberration. This time common ideas, common ideals, common purpose and a basic thrust towards them is the real objective. The future will be most challenging. The post-election period will be more challenging than the elections themselves.

The whole point is, I must tell you the rest of my life I cannot remain a silent spectator. I propose to let my views be known candidly, positively, categorically and strive towards them. I hope that in the new dispensatich there is enough place for discipline.

Discipline?
Yes, discipline. I want to develop that type of attitude in the functioning, in my political functioning, in which opinions are freely expressed and ideas consistently advanced.

The people are emotionally involved in the whole political process. This time they will be voting for individuals. The union between you and Indira Gandhi may lead to the expectation that in future the thrust towards socialism and economic growth will be greater—both of you have emphasised on that.
It is only a question of executing our wishes. And the better the executors, the better the results, the goals. Wiping every tear from every eye was the dream of Gandhi and Nehru.

But the bureaucracy may come in your way.
Well, I must say bureaucracy never came in the way. It is the incapacity of ministers that came in the way. The bureaucracy is like an Arabian horse. If you know how to ride, it will take you to your destination. If you do not know how to ride, it will throw you off.

Current, 24.11.1979
pp. (1 + 2 + 8 + 9 + 10)

and

Current, 01.12.1979
p. (5).

C. Two Years of Janata Rule

A visit to Jayaprakash Narayan

Loknayak Jayaprakash Narayan is a sad man. His weak, inaudible voice trembles when he speaks about his disappointments.

One gets the feeling that he has lost hope in the Janata government. He stares into space. He is physically weak and cannot walk without the assistance of two people. He is mentally alert but anguish is writ large on his sad face.

When I went to see him last week there were hardly any visitors, a bunch of boys were playing on the dirty uneven 'road' facing his Kadam Kuan house.

His secretary told me "No formal interview but you can chat with him." We spent 45 minutes. Twice I attempted to get up to go and both times he asked me to stay on.

We discussed the performance of the Janata government at the centre, the initial signs of some central ministers succumbing to the lure of money, the tensions and squabbles among top Janata leaders.

To my surprise he was extremely well-informed about goings-on in Delhi, though almost every top Janata leader has tended to ignore him. They have confined themselves to paying him courtesy visits whenever they come to Patna.

Is there any ray of hope? Most of his visitors come to him with long political tales of woe. He listens to them patiently, utters a few words weighed with disappointment, and then stares into the vacuum.

At one point during our conversation he called his lean pale, shabbily dressed secretary, Sachidanand: "Please prepare clippings of my speeches in which promises were made to the people and assurances were given to the country."

What will you do with them. I asked him? Will you once again go to the people? Will you launch yet another movement?

"Unfortunately my health does not permit me. I am very weak. But I have full faith in the people of this country. They will not tolerate injustice, corruption and the people of this country will never forgive us if we go back on our promises."

Will, you warn the Janata leaders? This government is a non-performing government. It is no government at all. "Yes, I will not keep silent. I have given them one year. After that I will come out. I will speak. I will not tolerate anything which violates our basic principles."

The Loknayak, the father of the Janata revolution, the destroyer of an autocratic regime, the hope of millions is a sad man.

A visit to him leaves one sadder still.

Current, 25.02.1978.
p. (5)

Total revolution Bihar-style: Chief minister Karpoori Thakur

Bihar Chief minister Karpoori Thakur can be easily taken for a coolie on a railway platform, a newspaper vendor in the market, a vagabond in a metropolis like Bombay.

That is Karpoori's exterior. But he is perhaps one of the finest, most dedicated and committed politicians in the unwieldy and characterless crowd which goes under the august name of the Janata Party.

I met him for the first time in his Patna office and was taken aback by his modesty and simplicity. Though in public life from his childhood, Karpoori remains penniless.

His father Gokul Thakur is still the local barber in his home town. In a state like Bihar where almost every politician is known for the amount of wealth he has amassed or the tag of corruption he carries or the charges of nepotism and casteism affixed on his forehead like a tilak, Karpoori stands out like a gazelle in a pathless desert.

He spoke in Hindi in his typical Bihari accent and quoted facts and figures like a seasoned mathematician. During the two hours we spent together a huge crowd of party members and favour-seekers waited outside.

Karpoori's only dream is to realise JP's total revolution. This he wants to do by turning Bihar's villages into 'kranti grams' and 'sampoorn kranti grams'.

He has plans, ideals and dreams. He also has the sincerity and will to carry forward his programme.

But will he succeed in his mass-oriented ambitions? Nothing has changed in Bihar. The same politicians with casteist intrigues, the same lethargic bureaucrats with no properly organised party machine, dominate the scene. The picture is bleak and frustrating. Karpoori alone remains a ray of hope. He is an idealist and deeply involved politician.

"I will fight against corruption tooth and nail and smash casteism into pieces. I have told the people of Bihar to be fearless and come straight to me if they even suspect any of my ministers or officers of corruption. If I am convinced of the suspicion I will first remove the man concerned and then order an inquiry. To the young men and women of Bihar my offer is that they will get Rs. 15,000 cash and a government job if they make an intercaste or interreligious marriage.

"Total revolution has to be total and the social, economic, political and culture scene has to be transformed. Bihar has to change. If it does not it will be my failure. People will lose faith in me, in JP and in everything good and decent associated with us."

Like a general Karpoori wants to fight his battle with the help of 'Armies'. From October 11 this year he will declare hundreds of villages in his state 'kranti grams' and 'sampoorn kranti grams'.

His Bhoomi Senas and Sinchai Senas will take over the backward and poverty-ridden state.

Could you tell us what actual progress has been made in Bihar in the last seven months?

The promises we made to the people have almost all been kept. We are working now on what is left to be done. We have freed all the Nexalites. All political cases between March 18, 1974 and April 1977 have been withdrawn. Extremists against whom there were serious charges have been released on bail.

Since JP's birthday last, October 11, five lakh high school students have been given full fee concessions. 22 lakh primary school children have been provided free books. College education for women will be free from next October 11.

From April 1 this year no more revenue will be collected from poor farmers. This will benefit about 85 per cent of them. Farmers who have 2 to 3 hectares in Chhota Nagpur will not have to pay any land revenue. Twenty-five per cent of them in that area will benefit.

Landless labourers and poor farmers owning up to 2 hectares of land will get Rs. 10 each towards membership to cooperative land committees. Under this scheme 39 per cent of the landless will gain as will 49 per cent of those with small holdings.

A three-year plan for adult education for illiterates between 15 and 35 years is to be launched. The Adult Education Board is working on the scheme and it will go into effect on October 2.

Within 5 years 10 lakh tubewells will be commissioned all over the state which will irrigate about 30 lakh acres. This project will be supervised by the *Sinchai Senas*, and funded by nationalised banks.

A scheme to generate massive employment, the first of its kind in the state, is underway. Our war on casteism begins with my colleagues who will be encouraged to make intercaste marriages for their sons and daughters.

Three instances of young men marrying outside their caste have come to our notice and they have been duly paid Rs. 15,000 each and government jobs found for them, under our war on caste plan.

For elderly people, above 60 years, we propose to pay a pension of Rs. 60 a month. Officers from BDO to commissioners will be able to apply for this pension plan.

Agriculture and industry are being boosted. We invite industrialists from other parts of the country to set up units in the state, small, big or tiny as they think fit. We promise them attractive terms and state finance.

We intend to start several small employment schemes which will go a long way towards eradicating poverty and backwardness. Here irrigation and agriculture will head the list. It is our intention to be self-reliant in electricity in the next ten years.

There is no shortage of water, coal and minerals in this state. Our daily requirements are 1,011 megawatts. Of this we presently get 735 megawatts. This includes what we generate and what we get from UP and Orissa. In our next plan we will earmark Rs. 106 crore for electricity generation. Two new power houses will be ready in the next three years in Muzaffarpur and Tenughat.

We have asked the centre to permit us to import gas turbines. Quite soon we shall begin other electricity schemes at Kahalgaon, Kattihar and Koelkaro. These three stations will produce 3,000, 60 and 200 megawatts respectively.

We have placed special emphasis on cottage industries and wiping out unemployment.

Several stories have appeared in the press about tortures of Harijans, rape and burnings and looting of the backward classes. What are you doing to stop this?

District Collectors and police officers are fully responsible for this. They have been asked to take extra measures to protect these weaker sections. Four top police officers have been suspended in Belchhi.

Land and jobs are being given to Harijans in Dharampur and Patrahat. Five thousand in cash, land and jobs have been given in compensation to the dependents of the deceased. We have created a separate Harijan Cell also. The firearms of those who have threatened Harijans in the villages have been confiscated.

We will be providing houses for Harijans under a new scheme called *Ghar-banakar-do* within the next five years.

Is it true that the government here is run by bureaucrats and not by elected Janata politicians?

Of course, some of the ministers are new. They are still learning their jobs. There are quarrels sometimes with their officers. The guilty officers have been punished. And naturally if we ever find a minister at fault he will be immediately replaced.

What have you done to usher in JP's total revolution in his home state?

Besides what I have already described. I do meet JP sometimes for his advice and guidance. I think he is happy with us.

You have promulgated an ordinance against goondaism. What is the guarantee that this would not be used against the political opponents?

It will absolutely not be used in that way. But, if opposition parties take part in any *goondaism,* then the law will apply to them as well. I assure you it will not be used against the workers and leaders of any political party for any other reason. It is necessary to keep law and order and will be used only against *goondas.* There has been a marked fall in crime in recent months. The law and order position is good and will remain so.

It is said that most of your cabinet colleagues are corrupt and have violated the code of conduct laid down for Janata ministers. What are you doing about this?

I have no information whatever about this. If I were to get a reliable complaint about bribery and other illegal transactions I would not hesitate in punishing the erring minister.

But I have received no such complaint so far. I am watching carefully the tussle between senior and junior ministers in the Industries and Irrigation Ministries. I have also called for strict discipline in the Education and Animal Husbandry Ministries. The situation is under control. My instructions to follow the code of conduct rigidly went out to my ministers long ago. Otherwise they will have to think of something else.

What is the future of Congress, the two parties in this state?

I need an opposition party. But in Bihar both Congress parties are dead. They are infested with casteism. We don't trust this woman, Indira Gandhi at all. She can do something anti-social at any time or get someone to do it for her.

What are you doing to eradicate corruption?

After coming to power seven months ago the Janata government organised a vigilance cell. Fifty-five notorious and corrupt officers have been arrested to far. They include a number of police and senior civil service officers. Former CM, Jagannath Misra's house was raided following charges of corruption against him and we have seized some important papers from there. Five lakh rupees of unaccounted money, jewellery and incriminating documents were also found at the residence of Jagdish Pandey, an official in Jalpat Division. He is the brother-in-law of Kedar Pandey a former chief minister and also closely related to Bindeshwari Dube a former Congress minister.

Did you realise that only seven officers were ever arrested in 30 years of Congress *Raj*!

Do you have any plans for the youth of this state?

Every young person above 18 will be enfranchised for Gram Panchayat elections, this will be the first time this has happened in the country. Village panchayat and district board elections are going to be held—after twenty years—in May or June this year.

We will provide books, clothes and food at subsidised rates for students. Another scheme we have in mind is to vocationalise education to a greater extent. Elections to all students unions, senates and syndicates of colleges and universities have been completed.

Education will be changed radically along the lines of JP's ideas, in the near future.

Will you comment on the elections in five states this month.

Janata party will definitely win in the southern states.

In Maharashtra our prospects are quite bright.

Current, 25.02.1978.
pp. (12 + 13 + 15)

'They thrive on crisis—I don't' : Chandra Shekhar

The Janata President Chandra Shekhar has emerged uninjured in the war of attrition launched by his arch foe Chaudhary Charan Singh. His position was shaky and there was an impression that he took the Party problems rather casually. But the fighter in him came out when he was dragged into the arena.

"I am not a dictator, but I will not let the Party break", he blurted at a senior Cabinet minister who asked him to be more lenient towards his detractors. "Not if discipline is not maintained. Not at the cost of the very existence of the Party. It is not an attack on Chandra Shekhar. As an individual I am a very small man. But as President of the Party I will have to act. The integrity of the head of the organisation has been challenged. I will not compromise."

The minister raised his voice. Chandra Shekhar was louder. "Power has gone into the head of some of your ministers. Do not forget the people are watching you and your performance," and he banged the telephone.

This was Chandra Shekhar in action. But the next moment the little hut, which he occupies in the corner of his residence, rent with laughter. Like Jawaharlal Nehru he knows how to blow hot and cold. But the laughter, unlike Nehru's is unmodulated. It has the peasants roughness.

While he is the centre of the storm blowing over the Janata, he remains unruffled. As the head of an unruly, unorganised, unwieldy Party he has been mastering an acumen to deal with each ticklish and thorny issue in his own down-to-earth manner. He plays the game with the cards close to his chest and can be irritatingly evasive if he wants to be.

"Let us discuss something meaningful, something constructive. No, not the rally and all that mudslinging going on" he suggested as we settled down to a long conversation. He would not reply to any of the controversial issues because "we have many in the party who can take care of controversy. They thrive on crisis I do not."

You have a reputation of fighting your political battles on ideological issues. At least in the Congress Party you invariably raised ideological matters. But as the Janata President you have hardly spoken on serious problems facing the country. The quarrels amongst Janata leaders have degenerated into clashes of personalities. Why don't you stop this rot and say enough or quit the party.

No. I cannot quit the party because it is against my habit. I am least interested in these quarrels. I have been observing enough restrain during the whole controversy though I have been the main centre of these attacks. I have not been in the habit of shirking away from responsibilities.

But how long you will tolerate this tamasha.

I will not tolerate this any more. I am doing the best possible that can be done in the present situation. I cannot expect *EL Dorado* at the moment.

I am not talking of EL Dorado but one and a half years is too long a period for a Party not to come out of a mess. As the Head of the Party you are expected to act in certain directions.

Why are you so impatient. You never showed this impatience when we were together in the Congress.

It is not a question of my personal impatience but the people feel that the whole thing is disgusting. For the last so many months newspaper headlines speak of nothing but your quarrels. This kind of thing did not happen during the Congress rule.

The Congress was an organisation with a long history eighty years to be exact. In 1971, I had told the Congress leaders to address themselves to the basic problems of the people and stop slogan mongering.

The Congress failed to deliver goods and that's why it was thrown out and that's why your party came into power.

The people endured the long Congress rule. Why do you think that 15 months are enough for my Party.

The Congress failed because it was slow, it grew sluggish and flabby and then collapsed but the people expected better and quicker performance from your Party and the government.

I agree with you. If the Janata Party too fails in its performance, the people will not tolerate it. I have been warning my colleagues.

But why should the Janata fail?

It will not fail. Who said it will fail?

What measures you have adopted to see that it does not fail?

Unfortunately, for friends like you politics centered around certain individuals. I never thought on these lines. I neither care for individuals nor blame them. The Janata is the expression of the aspirations of our people. If it does not come to their expectations, it will go the Congress way. Why should one shed tears about it? But I can assure you that as the head of the Party I shall try to make it an instrument capable of fulfilling the aspirations of our people.

While you are busy in your inner-party quarrels, the country is passing through a gloomy phase of demoralisation and despondency. If your quarrels continue unabated the people will ultimately lose faith in your party and also in democracy.

I am not so pessimistic about the people's mood. In March 1977 many of us thought on similar lines and almost lost hopes in their capacity to understand the situation in its proper perspective.

The people are definitely watching us. But some of our intellectuals ignore their capacity to understand the situation. They think that illiterate masses lack basic understanding to assess the depth of the problem. Mahatma Gandhi was correct when he said that our people are illiterate but not ignorant. They will give their judgement when the time comes.

That means you are waiting for the peoples judgement. We are more involved in highlighting petty quarrels.

No I am not waiting for the peoples judgement. They are making the judgement everyday. There are certain jaundiced-eyes which cannot see. What can I do?

What are the basic differences between you and Chaudhary Charan Singh. Why there is a sudden demand for your replacement.

I really do not know. When we discussed the economic policy resolution we agreed on most of the points. The only issue which I can visualise is my view concerning the role of Jawaharlal Nehru in the economic development of the country. I never made a secret of that. I don't think that can be the bone of contention.

The Charan Singh group's complaint is that the Janata is dominated by the Nehruties and that there should be a radical departure from this line of thinking—it should be towards Gandhism.

I think there are no basic differences between Gandhism and Nehruism in the economic field. There are certain parameters under which we have to function. A country of our size cannot depend on foreign sources for basic materials and if we have to develop we must produce cement, steel, fertilizers, etc., etc. Their argument is that we should pay more attention to agriculture. There is some validity in this point but we cannot have modern agriculture without steel and fertilisers.

I have always said that Nehru purposely opted for big industries in certain sectors. There is no going back from this. Anybody who is interested in the rapid development of the country cannot ignore heavy industries in certain sectors.

It does not mean that you give secondary importance to cottage and small industries.

No. I don't. But they cannot develop without heavy industries. Our small scale could grow in last 30 years because we had established a base.

Chaudhary Charan Singh's argument is that products which can be produced in cottage industries should not be taken up by big industries or multinationals.

I fully agree with him. Even in the 1969 I spoke about it.

Then where are the differences?

I do not know. You better address this question to those who have made our economic policy a bone of contention.

Has your party adopted certain concrete steps to break the hold of monopolies and multinationals in the one and a half year. I am asking you this question because you have been constantly campaigning against the concentration of wealth.

No I do not think any concrete steps have been taken to break the monopolies. That is true. But I do not think that there were any concrete suggestions from the campaigner of the cottage industries to the government in this regard. I will extend all support if such steps are taken.

In practice the Janata government is as much for the monopolies as the Congress. In this one and a half year over 100 licences have been given to monopoly houses. Particularly some of the licences in the core sector should have gone to the Public Sector.

That is true. But many of those against monopolies are also against the core sector. Suppose if they say we should not go in for big industries, so you cannot go in for core sector also, and unwittingly these people are supporting the monopolies. But we should remember one thing that heavy investment can only go to either the public or the private sector.

So mixed economy has to continue.

My point is that we have heavy industries they can be either in public or private sector. Those who are basically against heavy industries in public sector are supporting the monopolies.

Though the Janata is composed of various ideological groups, the fight amongst its leaders appears to be a clash of personalities or for gaining more power. The country has yet to witness some kind of an ideological thrust.

This has been our misfortune. The question has been dominating my mind for over a decade. In 1969, I pleaded for a "socialist advance" but again the whole matter was brought around an individual. Even at that time ideological questions were raised, but the whole politics was dominated by individual considerations. Even today unfortunately this trend persists.

We expect at least from you to have a breakthrough.

I have been pleading for this kind of politics for the last so many years and even in an interview which I gave you some time back I raised this issue. I had then told you that the question is not that what type of ideological dialogue we require but the machinery and the organisation necessary to implement our accepted policies.

There are certain policies which have been accepted at the national level and we should create an atmosphere to unite ourselves for the implementation of these programmes. But I think neither the politicians nor the press are interested in such issues.

Politicians are more responsible. It is they who have made a mess.

I don't know who is more responsible, yes may be politicians are more responsible. They seem to be involved in highlighting petty quarrels.

Between you and Charan Singh—is it really a fight between rural and urban India. He says that the Janata is dominated by a capitalist lobby.

In a parliamentary democracy the party President has a role to play and quite significant, but if the Home minister says that the party has been dominated by the capitalist, I would say it is the administrative machinery. And there the key was in the hands of the Home minister.

In what way?

The capitalist domination is precluded in our constitution, in our law. He should have initiated action against these capitalists, I want to know one instance when the Home minister, who is so much worried about the capitalist domination, took even one step against them.

He could take only penal measures not the policy steps.

Capitalist dominance itself is a criminal act. Capitalists dominating a political party attracts the penal laws. Why he did not take any action against them? He should have at least brought this matter in the cabinet, because he was second to the Prime Minister.

Neither the Prime Minister nor the Home minister brought any such proposal either in the Party or the Cabinet. If you remember I had told you in the last interviews that I was against the capitalist domination of any kind. But I cannot present papers to the Cabinet on this issue. If you recall, a committee for the purpose was appointed under the Chairmanship of Charan Singh but that committee has not met so far. I reminded him more than once about the committee's report. Nothing has happened so far. But the fact is that some people do not own their responsibilities and indulge in mud-slinging.

Are you sure the Janata will emerge as a more cohesive body after the organisational elections. What will be its class character.
I do not know but I hope that it will become a more cohesive organisation. This is my expectation. The class character of a political party is determined by the policies it pursues. Ultimately a political party is judged by its economic and social performances.

Certain economic classes have gone against you. For instance the industrialists are not happy with your Party and the poor have been won over by Indira Gandhi. The Janata is left with its middle class base and pockets of influence among the peasants.
It is a sweeping impression. The money bags do not determine the political cause of life. I do not bother about them. About the poor classes, I do not think they have lost all hopes with the Janata.

The future is very short. Only three and a half years are left with you.
I know my problems. I am also aware of the instrument of self-survival. That makes people do things that they don't like to do. The Congress adopted certain progressive and radical measures in 1969-70. Not because of conviction but because of a certain situation.

I was expecting that after the removal of Chaudhary Charan Singh and Raj Narain your Party and the government will announce certain very drastic and progressive measures to capture the imagination of the people and to divert their attention from the petty squabbles.
Yes. I agree with you, I don't use those adjectives but I agree that we should do something to channelise the people's energy in constructive and purposeful activities. We should have mass-oriented programmes— to involve the youth and all sections of the people.

Are you taking some steps in this direction.
We are proposing to take.

Do you agree with the view that after the ascendancy of the Janata casteism has raised its ugly head and the Janata politics has become caste-oriented.
I don't think so. The 1977 elections broke the caste barriers.

But after that we have been hearing nothing but caste alliances in various Janata dominated states.
Ayub *Saheb* where are you? You are talking of the bungalows of New

Delhi. Their attitude does not determine the fate of the 600 million people in the country.

The RSS has finally stayed away from the Janata. The impression is that it runs a government.

I do not agree with you. My experience as party President is totally different. The RSS has been claiming that it is a cultural organisation and has nothing to do with politics. But some time friends in my own party level charge against the RSS of indulging in politics but I have not found any such manipulations.

Do you think RSS is really a cultural organisation.

What I think about the RSS I do not want to tell you. It is for its leaders to make their position clear. I would like all sections of the population to join Janata and the doors of the party are open to RSS also but it is for them to decide. I cannot force my full cooperation on any of them.

There is an impression that the government is being run by bureaucrats. Most of your new and inexperienced ministers are overawed by the bureaucrats.

There has been a tendency to accuse bureaucracy for all our failures. In the past, when we were in the Congress many of our failings were explained in the name of bureaucracy and we advocated the idea of a committed bureaucracy. That was just another way of introducing totalitarianism or authoritarianism in this country.

Our bureaucracy can achieve great things provided, we, at the helm of affairs are clear and categorical in our policy decisions. I don't say that they are infallible creatures but they are as good citizens as we are. Moreover they have to discharge certain responsibilities in a given situation and atmosphere. Given the direction, precise decision and clear thinking by the policy makers, I don't see any reason why bureaucracy should not make headway.

These very things are lacking in the government.

This has been lacking in all the governments, not only in the present government.

This government is more ineffective and inefficient.

I really do not know but if that impression is there. I am very sorry about that. You should try to dispel that impression.

Why should I try?

Well, we should try, I should try.

You have ministers who cannot assert politically on the bureaucracy. They are totally inexperienced.

May be. I can't speak about the government.

If your government has not so far found any concrete basis to prosecute and convict Indira Gandhi, why go on raising the bogey of her arrest.

We have not raised any bogey.

Morarjibhai has said that if enough evidence is found "we will arrest her, we will prosecute her".

I also say that if there is some evidence against her she should not go scot-free. This is what I have been maintaining from the very beginning. But the people have not given us power to arrest her or any individual in violation of the law.

Chaudhary Charan Singh wanted MISA to be used against her.

I am against this suggestion. No individual should be singled out for the use of MISA. Our commitment is that MISA will not be used in this country for political purposes.

So far no valid reasons have been found by your government to arrest her.

You better direct this question to the Home minister.

You have no Home minister at the moment.

The Prime Minister is there. He should reply to the question.

Some people are seriously discussing unity amongst all congressmen minus Indira Gandhi. Do you think it is a feasible proposition.

I don't know.

A section in the Janata apprehend that congressmen in the Janata are consolidating their position.

What do you mean by congressmen? Congress was also not a cohesive force. Ayub, as you know, we have enough various groups. It is no use talking in terms of congressmen in this context.

The Janata has failed to involve the youth in the implementation of your policies.

Yes. I agree with you. The youth remain uninvolved. Our whole emphasis has been about the involvement of certain individuals. We are not bothered about the involvement of our people. Our newspaper headlines highlight the personalities and personal clashes. But when I make a statement appealing to all political parties, academicians, professors, doctors, trade unionists, students and youth that let us join hands on certain fundamental issue, then I get only one line and *Current* completely ignores it. I know you will give my picture with Charan Singh if I say something against him. I do not know what we are going to gain by this. It might help you to sell your paper, it might be good for me to get publicity but it is not good for the future of this country.

If all of you stop issuing controversial statements, we too will cooperate with you.
Yes, I beg of you to switch over from this 'individualism' and try to mobilise public opinion in favour of solving national problems. If my appeal works, let us begin with you then I shall try with other friends also.

Is there any possibility of the emergence of a Third Force.
I do not believe in Third Force or First Force. I believe in People's Force and it can be mobilised by agreeing to certain fundamentals of our national policies. Let us keep aside the ideological considerations.

Is it because of this that in this one and a half years you have not talked of socialism. The word socialism is missing from your pronouncements.
It is not missing. Socialism was being announced every day on All India Radio during two years of Emergency. What happened. Did socialism come?

Socialism should not become 'repulsive' because Indira Gandhi had misused it.
No, not repulsive. But just using socialism as a slogan is meaningless. Socialism should be reflected in our behaviour, in our attitude, in our actions.

Current, 15.07.1978.
pp. (1 + 5 + 6)
and
Current, 22.07.1978.
p. (9)

Janata must answer: who set Aligarh on fire

Belchi was the beginning. There will be more Belchis and more Aligarhs if the reins of power remains in the hands of Morarji Desai.

He is a curse on the nation and a threat to parliamentary democracy. The man asks the simple hill folks—the Mizos and the Nagas—to pray for his long life and strength so he may continue to rule. He has no right to perpetrate his misrule on the 600 million people of this country.

Morarji must go, if greater holocausts have to be avoided. He has totally failed to realise the single factor of our democratic pattern that the Harijans and the minorities constitute the most decisive and formidable vote bank?

The Janata could not have come to power had these two powerful sections not overwhelmingly supported it.

Aligarh is not only a victim of communal carnage. It is a writing on the wall. The Janata lost the Harijans in Belchi and offered them on a silver platter to Indira Gandhi. Now the Muslims too have been gifted to her.

Even this ignominious turn in the Janata fortunes did not open Morarji's eyes. Millions of Harijans constitute to live under the shadow of death and persecution.

His government has recorded over 500 cases of unparalleled brutalities on these hapless people in the Janata dominated states. Can Morarji rule without the Harijans?

And can he govern this country without the minorities.

Over 300 communal riots have been reported under his nose since he acquired power. Aligarh is not a city. It has been a symbol of Muslim renaissance. And any damage to its traditions, to its citizens amounts to a nail in the coffin of secularism. Aligarh can make and unmake the fortunes of the rulers. With this communal carnage, the fate of the Janata has been sealed. No Muslim worth his name will ever dream of supporting it.

From Belchi to Aligarh is a sordid story of insanity, barbarity and bloodshed. The 'bunch of impotent people' who unfortunately occupy the GADDI in Delhi suffer from a death-wish. Within no time, they have shattered the enormous goodwill and confidence the people bestowed on them.

Our worry is not the Janata. For sooner it is pushed into the sea the better for the country. But this party is like the retreating army which follows the scorched earth policy. Its most unpardonable crime is that it has given away the Harijans and the minorities to the Lady who least deserves their support.

Remember, the Muslims were the worst sufferers of her Emergency rule. They do not love her. And if they attach themselves to her apron strings, it is due to the sheer hatred of the Janata and its RSS 'Goons' whose hands are smeared with the blood of the dead of Aligarh.

To whom Aligarh should look at? To Chandra Shekhar, who has suppressed and then misquoted the report of his own representatives in which the accusing finger was pointed at the RSS? Who can doubt his faith in secularism? Yet in his scheme of things a few communal riots like in Aligarh can be ignored if Jana Sangh can promote his designs to attain power.

Though the Janata, the Indira Congress and CPM leaders, who visited Aligarh, have squarely blamed the RSS for fanning the communal flames, none of the Janata stalwarts have the courage to call a spade a spade, such is the power equation.

Only Madhu Limaye and Raj Narain have shown the guts to focalise the real problem.

The lust for power should not blind the Janata Socialists and secularists to ignore the vital factor that people are not mere pawns on their chessboard.

Current, 18.11.1978.
p. (1).

The bloody road: Belchi to Bajitpur

Bajitpur is not merely a village razed to ground. It is a sordid story of continuous *zulom,* rape and murder of a people whom Gandhiji decreed as the 'Children of God'.

Which God? Whose God? Where is that God? Is the God of Gandhi dead? Is the God of the Harijans dead? If he is alive, if he can see and if he can protect, punish and retribute, then why Bajitpur? Why Belchi? There will be more Bajitpurs and more Belchis and the 'God' cannot save them, so far he has not saved them.

Gandhiji was an unflinching believer in God, I am not. Bajitpur has put the medieval marauders to shame. With what face can we brand

Chengis Khan and Nadir Shah the barbarians.

The crime committed in Bajitpur is enough to hang our heads in shame. If Chief minister Karpoori Thakur has been left with any democratic decency, he should quit, go to Bajitpur as an ordinary citizen, wipe out the tears from the faces of the raped women and tortured men and build a new Bajitpur. If he shrinks from his duty he will have no moral right to rule the state. Is his socialist ethics and Gandhian morality only skin-deep, or is he too consumed by his lust for power.

Bajitpur is a few kilometers away from Samastipur, his town and political 'fortress'. The tragedy of Bajitpur happened on the eve of election while he was assuring the Harijans a 'golden era', a life full of prosperity and security.

His voice was not heared by young, pregnant Manju who was being raped in the midst of the village. Over a dozen Harijan women were also being mass raped by armed *goondas* who had raided the village to 'punish' the Harijans because they had asked the rapacious landlord to return their land.

The entire village was ransacked within minutes by 400 armed men. The police knew about their plans and took no preventive steps. It reached Bajitpur 24 hours after the reign of terror. The area Superintendent of Police R.R. Verma has not ruled out the possibility of connivance of the local police.

Yes, the police, the bureaucracy and the 'politicians' are the real culprits. So long as they feel that they are the 'real Children of God' and not the Harijans, the *zulm* will continue. One Jagjivan Ram at the top or a few Harijans as *chaprasis* cannot prevent the repetition of Bajitpur.

Bajitpur can be undone only by a revolution left unfinished by Gandhi and Nehru because they too belonged to a certain economic and social order. It can be a bloodless revolution if our police, army, bureaucracy and legislatures are thrown open to Harijans. At least fifty per cent of them should be accommodated to these key positions.

But it will not happen. This kind of economic and social change are never peaceful.

Bajitpur and Belchi will therefore be repeated every now and then. They cannot be stopped. Only a revolution can stop them and that 'revolution' cannot happen. It is not in our soil.

Current, 02.12.1978
p. (2)

From Gandhi samadhi to its own samadhi

The 28-month old uneasy truce in the Janata has finally been exploded. The founder-fathers of this novel conglomeration in the national political scene, who came into power after taking oath at the Gandhi Samadhi, have ultimately fallen apart. In the beginning it was mere birth pangs, then the 'teething troubles' and now suddenly, the dying declarations.

It all began as a personality clash. The three giants of the Janata—Morarji Desai, Babu Jagjivan Ram and Chaudhari Charan Singh were finding it difficult to pull on together from the very beginning. Added to their own egos was another disastrous element—Kanti Desai, the Prime Minister's son. Charan and his closest disciple Raj Narain, who was often described as the court jester and the joker, had to finally quit the government at the 'request' of Morarji Desai.

Though an unhappy man still, Charan returned to the Cabinet last January with a 'promotion' as Deputy Prime Minister. Raj remained outside, but was still loyal to his *Chaudhary Saheb*. He said that he will fight the authoritarian rule of Morarji Desai from outside while his mentor will do it from inside.

At that time actually many 'hawks' in his BLD were against Charan Singh rejoining the Cabinet. At the Kisan Rally held on December 23 last year, there were even demands that Charan and his follower should come out of the Janata itself. But Charan could carry the day and preferred to return to the Cabinet saying that he will act at the 'appropriate time'.

It was a little after this and the Aligarh communal riots that followed, the RSS element and the Jana Sangh's dual membership issue cropped up. Raj Narain came out openly against the Jana Sanghis in the Janata and pledged to fight the RSS tooth and nail. Logically enough, he began the fight from his home state, Uttar Pradesh.

The Jana Sangh also did not take it lying down. The BLD-Jana Sangh war carried on by Raj Narain had the first casuality in UP where the Ram Naresh Yadav government was toppled.

Raj Narain continued his relentless crusade against the RSS and the Jana Sangh in turn tried to topple the BLD governments one by one. Bihar's Karpoori Thakur was the next victim of this factional fight and the last straw came last month when, amid high dissident activity, Haryana's Devi Lal, a Charan protege, was asked to seek a vote of confidence by the 'partisan' Janata Parliamentary Board. Dissident activity was intense in the neighbouring Jana Sangh-ruled Rajasthan, too, but the

Board ordered that Chief minister Bhairon Singh Shekhawat need not face the ordeal.

Charan Singh was still keeping quiet and waiting for the 'appropriate time' to come but the 'hawks' in the BLD camp were getting impatient at Charan's 'patience'. The discontent, which began with the ouster of Ram Naresh Yadav had reached the flash point. After all the calculated moves by the Jana Sangh the 'militant' followers of Charan Singh didn't see any reason why it should still continue in the Janata and moreover, why should Charan Singh continue in the Cabinet co-existing with avowed Jana Sanghis?

With Charan keeping his options 'close to his chest' again, the BLD was virtually on the brink. The state leaders of the group—Devi Lal in Haryana, Karpoori Thakur in Bihar, Ram Naresh Yadav in UP, Kumbharam Arya in Rajasthan and Chimanbhai Patel in Gujarat—were on the warpath. In some places they even set up rebel parallel committees. At the Kisan Sammelan Working Committee held on June 21 and 22, a majority of the state leaders wanted that the BLD should sit as a separate party in this session of Parliament. But, ultimately, they again succumbed to the Charan pressure and it was left to him to choose the right time for revolt.

The final parting of ways came two days later when Devi Lal was asked to seek a fresh vote of confidence from the state Janata Legislature Party. Raj Narain decided to quit the Janata and lead the revolt against the 'corrupt' Morarji rule. At a meeting organised by the Devi Lal supporters in Rohtak he declared that the Morarji government cannot last for more than a month and that he will topple it before September.

At a meeting held just three days before the beginning of the monsoon session of Parliament, it was decided that Raj Narain, alongwith 10 or 15 MPs will sit separately. The meeting was attended, among others, by Raj Narain, Karpoori Thakur, Devi Lal, S.N. Mishra and H.N. Bahuguna. At that meeting, Raj also threatened to expose Morarji further by raising the Kanti and Balasubramaniam issue.

'Bala' was a close 'business' partner of Kanti and had easy access to No. 1. Safdarjang Road, where the father and the son and their unholy rackets were going on. He had even accompanied (unreported of course) the Prime Minister and his son on many foreign tours.

Bala's houses in Delhi and Madras were raided on June 4 when Morarji was on his East European tour. It is said that Charan did it to embarrass

Morarji under pressure from the 'hawks'. Bala came out openly indicting Charan Singh. But at the same time he publicly exposed Kanti and Morarji too by narrating his connections with the Prime Minister's family. Before more damage could be done, he was allowed to escape to Frankfurt. This was yet another stick Raj got to beat Morarji with.

An exasperated Karpoori Thakur and Devi Lal came to the rescue of Raj Narain. The trio began the signature campaign and by Monday when the session began he had already collected the signatures of 10 MPs of the Party, all ready to quit. Three of these MPs were from Haryana while the rest were all former Socialists owing allegiance to Raj Narain.

On July 11, fourteen more MPs quit reducing the strength of the ruling party from 301 in the beginning to 274. The Congress, which became the main opposition in the Lok Sabha after the split in the Indira Congress, moved a no-confidence motion against the Morarji government. Despite a last-minute appeal by Party President Chandra Shekhar "not to disturb the stability of the organisation," the revolt continued. This fast-paced development in the party gave a new dimension to Y.B. Chavan's no-confidence motion.

At one stage Charan was said to have opposed the idea of revolt. He presumably was feeling that he has not been able to consolidate his position in the Janata and wanted to carry out the 'coup' sometime in November and just before the Gujarat elections. He was sure that the Morarji gang will lap up all the party tickets there which could be used for the final parting of ways.

But by Wednesday last more than 50 MPs had joined Raj Narain and Charan was left with no other option. He finally agreed with the 'toppling game' initiated by the hawks.

By mid-week last the Janata had been reduced to a minority with a total strength of 255. Raj Narain went and met President Sanjiva Reddy and claimed that he will be able to form the government. He, however, did not specify how he can do it. He also requested the President not to dissolve the Parliament even if Morarji, who is in minority, advises him to do. Meanwhile, the debate on the Chavan motion had started.

Just as the BLD faction was split in the beginning between the hawks and doves, Jagjivan Ram's CFD was also split. It had actually begun when the Yadav government was ousted in UP when Jagjivan Ram supported a Jana Sangh nominee for the Chief ministership and Bahuguna opposing it. In Bihar again, Bahuguna wanted Karpoori to continue but Ram helped Ramsunder Das to become the Chief minister. Bahuguna, with his Muslim base, was increasingly finding it difficult to co-exist with the Jana Sangh and the RSS. This had brought him closer to Charan Singh and the one-time rivals of UP had joined hands.

By the week-end Raj Narain had claimed that over 70 MPs were with him. This had reduced the strength of the ruling party to 239. Two MPs had already joined the Congress. Bahuguna with nine MPs and Biju Patnaik with another nine also quit the party. Ram was still firm on backing Morarji and had called a meeting of his MPs to make them toe his line.

Raj Narain was, meanwhile, in regular touch with like-minded forces inside and outside Janata. He had talks with Congress leader Y.B. Chavan, CPI leader Bhupesh Gupta, Marxist leader P. Ramamurthy, H.N. Bahuguna, Madhu Limaye and the Akalis. Raj Narain's first choice was for mid-term polls in Haryana and Bihar with an eye on the Gujarat elections. When this effort failed and after the virtual revolt in the state groups, he was finding it difficult to work within the framework of the party.

Another major development that gave rise to the hope of a third force was the Bangalore convention called by Karnataka Chief minister Devraj Urs. Interestingly, Raj Narain's emissaries Karpoori Thakur and Rabi Ray were camping in Bangalore for five days before, during and after the convention.

On Saturday, the Janata Parliamentary Board finally asked Morarji Desai to step down and save the Janata from disintegrating but Morarji, adamant as usual, gave a firm 'no'. George Fernandes, who was the main defender of the government against the no-confidence motion, was compelled to take the initiative for asking Morarji to step down. "I will put it more strongly the next day", he said and did it—by resigning from the Cabinet along with his socialist colleagues Purushottam Lal Kaushik.

Charan Singh also was becoming more aware that with the Jana Sangh in command he will never be able to achieve his life-term ambition of becoming the Prime Minister. He has also been all along seeking support from the Congress, the Marxists, the Akalis and from a section of the Janata MPs.

Raj Narain had predicted that Morarji will fall before September. The end came too soon for him. As *Current* had written earlier, he is a born fighter. Once he takes up a crusade he does not look at the faces. He fought and finished Indira Gandhi. Now, his victim is Morarji Desai. And in the present fight he even did not hesitate to revolt against his mentor Charan Singh. It was he who gave the lead to topple Morarji. The victory is his and the day belongs to him.

Current, 21.07.1979.
pp. (10 + 11)

The tragedy of being JP

'Is andhere mein ek hi prakash, Jayaprakash, Jayaprakash,' 'Lok Nayak Zindabad,' and *'Doosra Mahatma Gandhi Amar Rehe',* these slogans have become an echo of the past JP is not dead, he is alive, but is that life politically worth living?

Perhaps no leader in this country has been fooled, ignored, insulted and rejected in such a short period by so many of his 'admirers' as this recluse in forlorn Kadam Kuan. The road in front to his house remains as dirty, unpaved and deserted as it ever was. No change has come in the life of the urchins who swarm the filth-ridden alley.

This is a road to despondency, it reflects the general atmosphere of gloom in the country. The road ends nowhere.

He is no more a *Lok Nayak* nor a *Mahatma*. He is once again reduced into a simple JP which he actually was. The Janata 'stalwarts' call on him reluctantly, casually or when they plan to use him as a pawn in their vicious power game.

JP lost his lustre and aroma the day the Janata got power. It was nothing unusual. It had to be that. It happened with Gandhi too. But what has shocked his 'disciples' and benumbed him is the challenge to his moral right to guide and advise the ruling party and the government.

Morarji Desai and JP have never seen eye to eye in their long political life. The two belong to two different schools and have their own set of political and 'moral' values. JP talks of 'consensus' while Morarji has floated the theory of 'prerogative' and has questioned his 'right' to intervene in the party and the government affairs.

'He is not even an ordinary member of the Janata'. Morarji, who could have been conveniently consigned to the waste paper basket had it not been for JP, had told the startled JPites soon after he was installed in power.

During my last meeting, when I told him that JP was hurt at his imperious manners, Morarjibhai retorted: 'Why should I go to him. Who is he? What has he done? He has always been a failure. If he thinks I depend on him and rush to Patna to seek his advice he is expecting too much from me. It is a blasphemy to call him the second Mahatma.'

One may or may not agree with Morarji's views about JP's moral authority to guide him and his party. But the fact is that his has been an inglorious story of failures. All his *Dans—Gramdan, Bhoodan, Jivandan, Bodhidan, Sampatidan*—have proved a flight of his imagination, a colossal failure, a pathetic record of waste of human efforts. The *Sarvodaya* is as dead as dodo . . .

The 'Total Revolution' too crash landed the moment its followers realised the 'virtues' of power. Though he may be called the creator of the Janata, it is in fact the people's contribution. In sheer desperation they forced the warring *ghattacks* to mould themselves into one 'party'. JP was merely an instrument in giving shape to the patch-work. It was a historic need and he only acted as a wise man to fulfil it.

His utility as an 'instrument' is over and sooner he realises it the better it will be for him and his 'disciples'.

Current, 20.01.1979
pp. (2)

3

Return of Indira Gandhi

A. Indira confronts government suppression

Indira rises again

For the first time in its eventful history the country stands divided. The south, with pristine pride in its ancient culture and heritage, has embraced the "discarded dictator," "Indira Amma."

It has taken unusual and exceptional courage and enthusiasm to install her back to power.

Only less than a year ago the north rejected her in a massive sweep; within a year the south has crowned her with glorious victory.

India is one, its people are one. Yes we are witnessing an unprecedented spectacle of parallel politics. No democratic force in this country can now prevent her from consolidating the land beyond Sehadris to attain her burning ambition.

She has risen from the lush green fields of the south to avenge her abject defeat in the north.

Her spectacular rise is a warning to the Janata. It is also a grim challenge from the people to the rulers in Delhi.

There is still time for them to show guts and courage in ushering in the much expected social and economic changes.

The people's mood is changing. They will not compromise short of a revolution.

The victory of Indira has once again proved that it is the poor and the down-trodden, the backward and the discriminated against, who constitute the bulk of the population, make and unmake democracy.

It is with their help she will march forward and plunge the country into a new kind of politics—politics of confrontation.

She has already eliminated with one stroke the spineless Reddy Congress.

The Reddy congressmen will now rush to her with supersonic speed leaving "Opposition Leader" Yashwantrao Balwantrao Chavan in the lurch.

He should immediately resign if he has a sense of dignity and before he is reduced into a scare-crow.

She is poised to emerge as the real powerful, strident opposition leader.

Soon she may be in Parliament. And once she is in Parliament the ruling party will be faced with a crisis of the first magnitude.

Despite humiliations, arrests, exposures, commissions, stones and black flags, she has been succeeding in remoulding the most powerful vote bank Nehru built—the *Harijans,* the Muslims and the weaker sections. They are switching their loyalty to her.

This will be her real strength and as they gather around her the sands will slip from under Janata feet.

But the Janata should complete the five-year mandate given to it by the people. If not in its own interest, at least in the interest of democracy. Its collapse will certainly shake peoples' faith in the viability of a democratic parliamentary system.

The future of democracy is, therefore, inextricably linked with the survival of the Janata.

Indira has no faith in democracy. She has all through been justifying the Emergency and its "gains". She has divine faith in the cult of personality. She has refused to distinguish between truth and untruth and has been lying all through.

A day before the assembly elections, she told a Bombay daily that during her regime Sanjay Gandhi had "not interfered in any administrative or political affairs."

Asked whether her son would also stage a comeback along with her, she replied curtly: "Sanjay has already said that he was out of politics and nobody in our family is in the habit of telling lies."

This is Indira. Yet the Janata has not been able to deal with her. Is it because its leaders have been telling greater and more lies?

The Janata's performance is poor. It is dismal. The intrigues, the infightings, and squabbles amongst its leaders have generated widespread disgust amongst people.

It is group-ridden. It has failed to emerge as a single, cohesive political party with a will and determination to govern the country.

The gap between its promises and performances has been widening. No collective and concrete steps have so far been taken by it to fight the devils of poverty, unemployment and hunger.

Restoration of democracy is not enough. And it is time they stop claiming that it is they who restored democracy and freedom.

It was the people of India who struck a deadly blow to authoritarianism. The Janata leaders were merely the beneficiaries of their upsurge against an autocratic, dynastic rule.

No sooner had the Janata leaders perched themselves in the seats of power in the name of Gandhiji, than they started apeing their predecessors.

As congressmen forgot and ignored Gandhi soon after they assumed power, so did the Janata leaders with Jayaprakash Narayan. The architect of the "Janata Revolution" is a sad, disappointed and thoroughly disillusioned recluse.

The Janata ministers wallow in luxury, ostentation. Some of them have been frequenting Europe more often than their constituencies.

The Janata leaders adopted the same reprehensible tactics in the just finished assembly elections as congressmen had been doing. No funds were raised from the people this time. Unaccounted black money flowed from Janata coffers.

They engineered a shameless process of the politics of defections. They opened the party's doors to all hues of opportunists and careerists. Not only this, these ignoble defectors sought to become the people's voice. But the valiant South taught them a lesson. They were discarded like old shoes.

A professor of Banglore University who voted against the party replied to my query in Khalil Gibran's words: "He brings disaster upon its nation, who never sows a seed or lays a brick or weaves a garment, but makes politics his occupation."

He added, the Janata leaders have made commissions their preoccupation.

The grandiose Shah Commission has dragged its feet far too long. It has outlived its utility. Once she emerges as the real, effective Opposition leader the Shah Commission will lose its relevance. Before the catastrophe occurs it should voluntarily fold itself up. The Grover Commission is already a mockery. The return of Devraj Urs to power has blown it into smithereens.

If the government has at all any tangible evidence or even a prima facie case against the guilty men of the Emergency, then they should be handed over to our courts of law.

The people have chastised them by defeating them and if they are criminals the Courts should take care of them, it is not worth otherwise spending crores on these Commissions.

The only effective way to forestall the re-emergence of Indira Gandhi is to fight against poverty and hunger. If her victory has knocked any sense into Janata heads they should sink all their differences, emerge as a powerful, democratic party, expedite the social and economic revolution which they have promised.

The destiny of Indira is in the hands of the poor. Unless the Janata identifies its cause with them it will be swept off the scene.

Current, 04.03.1978.
pp. (1 + 2)

Indira's *Agni Pariksha*

The Janata rulers in Delhi are gripped with fear. The rulers appear awestricken. Uncertainty is writ large on their pale, long-drawn faces. Not that they are cowards nor are they a bunch of 'impotent people' as an enraged Charan Singh once branded them. But they are not themselves. They have definitely lost the will to survive. They are like a pricked balloon.

Indira Gandhi's decision to comeback from Chikmagalur has panicked them to such an extent that they have lost coherence. They stare in a vacuum, merely to relapse into silence. This is no exaggeration.

I met and spoke to a number of the Janata leaders. I was horrified at the pathetic picture they present. The game is over. They have lost the battle even before it began.

She will rise from Chikmagalur like a Phoenix. She is determined to win this battle for power and indications are that she will.

The mood of the nation is changing. It is not that she has suddenly become a darling of the people. It is the Janata leaders who have turned out to be villains. They know she has not changed. Her style of functioning remains the same. The caucus, which promoted her authoritarian rule, is intact. She has not abandoned any of its members. In this agonising period of her trials and tribulations, she has been brazenly defending Emergency and what she did during that dark period.

Her son, Sanjay Gandhi, perhaps the most hated individual in the history of this country, continues to rule the roost.

She wants once again to take over the country through democratic methods and with popular support. The process will begin from Chikmagalur.

Her national stature will again zoom to uncontrollable proportions once she enters the Parliament. She will be the recognised leader of Opposition with a cabinet rank, salary and perks. There is no voice of dissent in the well-organised party.

Her first target in Parliament, will not be the Janata, but the other Congress with its 54 members. The pro-Indira faction in this Congress dominates over the pro-Janata group. With her ingenious methods, she will accelerate the process of disintegration of this Congress.

At least 40 Congress MPs will gradually switch their loyalties to her leaving the hardcore Chavan rump to stew in its own juice.

She will launch a frontal attack on the Janata only after consolidating her position in both the Houses. The Janata is not made up of angels or Sadhus. The ruling Party's ship is loaded with *ayarams* and *gayarams* who will jump onto her bandwagon the moment they realise that the ship is about to sink.

And sink it will. She will pressurise the Janata leaders to withdraw the criminal cases against her and most of her colleagues. She will force them to confine the Shah Commission report to the archives. Though she is a poor parliamentarian, she will undoubtedly turn the Parliament into a stage to dramatise the situation.

Her victory from Chikmagalur will, in a way, vindicate her stand on Emergency and it will be exceedingly embarrassing for the Janata government to prosecute her later. The Janata leaders will, also, soon realise that she will be much more powerful behind the bars than in the Parliament. Her 'Punishment for the criminal acts' is now nothing more than of academic importance.

The horror of horrors is that some of the 'chickens' among the Janata leaders have already started thinking of the punishment she will give them when she gains supreme control.

This is not a fancy of imagination. This is writing on the wall. The Janata is a gone case. A Party, which has been preoccupied in saving itself from disintegration, cannot govern the country. If Prime Minister's primary concern has been to save his chair by putting one *ghatak* against the other, he is incapable of seeing beyond his nose. He is vindictive and authoritarian.

Indira Gandhi, the people have 'unfortunately' begun to realise, despite her defects, was an effective and efficient ruler. This feeling is growing.

It will gradually snowball into a national mood and then envelope the country as a wave.

Indira Gandhi rides well on the crest of such waves. The wave will begin from Chikmagalur and by the time it reaches Delhi it may turn into a tornado.

It is the fear of this possible tornado which has struck terror in the hearts of the Janata rulers.

Current, 14.10.1978.
pp. (1 + 19).

Indira launches her election campaign
The Nation must survive

The atmosphere at 12, Wellingdon Crescent, is as though she is the virtual Prime Minister of the country. The people who surround her, ex-minister, ex-MPs and senior party colleagues, give the impression that the taking over the reins of the government is matter of time.

The number of visitors to her is far greater than to any other leader in Delhi, the hush-hush atmosphere reflects her powerful personality and the security arrangements are much more elaborate than even at the caretaker Prime Minister's house. Her schedule of engagements is much more jam-packed than when she ruled the country.

When we met for a two hour long sitting, Indira Gandhi was totally relaxed. The two and a half year witch-hunting, commissions, enquiries, threats of physical and political elimination and arrests have left not a shred of rancour. She has aged, but her determination to survive is steeled. There is a twitch in her left eye which might be the result of the nerve-wrecking life she is leading.

But she is relaxed. She answered my questions without once betraying her emotions, in a straight, matter-of-fact, simple language. The question-answer session could have continued longer as she appeared to be in a mood to communicate her views. We had moved from her drawing room to the dining room and then to the verandah at the back of the house to avoid noise. But the crowd outside the house had swelled. It was getting impatient to have her darshan.

It is felt that the mid-term poll is in fact a battle for the Prime Ministership. For the first time the people have a clear choice of electing their future leader. How do you envisage the outcome?

I never prophesy about elections. But the people have seen the performance of all the three. Charan Singh is not a newcomer, I mean, he may be a caretaker Prime Minister, but he has been in government for two and a half years.

And Babuji?

Babuji has also been in the government for a long time including the two and a half years. Both of them have whole-heartedly co-operated with the RSS. They never spoke about any atrocities or anything until I spoke up, whether it was about Belchi or Jamshedpur.

Yes. It is significant. It's a fact that neither of them bothered to condemn these atrocities.

And Bahuguna too. He also kept silent.

No. I do not agree with you here. He is the only man in the Janata who has been speaking and expressing his anxiety.

May be at a later stage, not at the beginning.

Whenever there were riots he wanted to speak and visit the affected areas. I remember Morarjibhai prevented him from going to Aligarh when the riots broke out there a year ago. As a Cabinet minister he could not have defied his Prime Minister. He is the one man who has been exposing the communal forces. But my question remains unanswered—the choice between the three.

Let the people decide.

During the Janata rule the social and secular fabric of the country was sought to be destroyed. Will you be able to undo it if you come to power?

Firstly, the elections are going to be pretty tough, so anybody can say who will come to power. Naturally our efforts will be to restore it because that is the very foundation on which the country stands. If that is weakened, the country itself is weakened. We will have to spend all of our energy to bring the country back on the path of true secularism, by which I mean not just between Hindus and Muslims, but you know. I mean this caste war which is going on.

The very concept has to be restored.

Yes. That is true. Everybody in India should get equal opportunity. That is in the Constitution.

How you will be able to undo the caste barriers? They have become fortified, especially in Bihar and U.P.

But one can't say how. It is just a matter of how you feel, how you pursue a particular situation. It has to be undone by meeting people and creating a particular atmosphere.

But you may face tough times, particularly in Bihar, if you decide to demolish these caste barriers. It may lead to agitations and violence.

The point is that we too have given reservations in Congress ruled states without creating caste animosities. It was done in a way that people thought justice was being done to them. But in Bihar it was done in such a manner that certain people were made to feel that it was at their cost. They were made to feel that the caste reservations were going to harm them and despite the damage being done, the backward classes have really not gained except in theory.

The reservations in services have definitely benefited them.

No. I have been told that practically nothing has happened.

The time factor was also there. As they started implementing their schemes the government fell. There was total confusion in Bihar after Karpoori's fall.

No, no. The caste reservations were there for quite some time. But they were done in such a complicated way that what was given by one hand was taken away by the other. Something like that. I don't remember the details now.

Will you make the caste reservations one of the major issues in your election campaign?

No. Our major point will be that unless there is stability in the country, none of them will be benefited, they may be *Harijans,* forwards or backwards.

You seem to have been justifying Emergency minus its aberrations. And if you win the elections will you consider it as a vindication of your Emergency rule?

(She paused. Closed her eyes for a few seconds as though recalling the immediate past. Then began in an inaudible voice).

Well, It will not only be the vindication of Emergency rule. But it is only fair to acknowledge that a large number of people were much happy under Emergency, especially in North India.

Emergency, as I have often said, was a very special medicine, for a very special situation which is not going to be repeated. And therefore there is no need for such a medicine to be given again. But the major thing is that there were some people who suffered and we have apologised. It will not happen again. But can you forget the 20-point programme or the voluntary discipline? We didn't impose it, it just came on its own, everybody felt that it was a situation in which we had to work for the country.

But there was fear, and lot of it.

I don't think. And it was certainly not amongst the poor.

It may not have been among the poor in the rural sector.

Neither in the rural nor the urban sectors. It was not there.

It was certainly there. In the cities amongst the organised labour, the middle classes and the intelligentsia.

May be. But later it came because of the propaganda. And a lot of people used our names. They threatened people. Especially about Sanjay they spread rumours, stories and lies. The other day a friend told me that during Emergency he was coming to Delhi from Dehradun by car. His car broke down and somebody gave him a lift. On the way he told his friend. 'You know Sanjay Gandhi has threatened to put me under MISA'. The friend asked him. How and Why? When the two arrived in Delhi, our friend told him 'why don't we just drop in and clarify the matter with Sanjay'.

No no, he said you see, it wasn't Sanjay's fault, it was Dhawan. So he said Dhawan may also be there. Let's go and talk to him. This man said, 'no I don't know if it was Dhawan'. So, I mean, you know how things were working.

Was this man just imagining?

No. He was deliberately spreading the story. There are not one, but hundreds of stories like this and I can give you the names of these people.

This was a very deliberate campaign launched by the RSS. They went on telling people "you will be arrested if you did this or did that". The people naturally got terrified.

How these stories could spread so widely and wildly? The atmosphere of fear had become unbearable.

In fact, it is very difficult to understand, but I will give you one more example of an educated Muslim lady. The Delhi administration started a programme of immunising children against diphtheria, tetanus and tuberculosis. This educated lady rushed to the school and took her children out. A rumour had been spread that children were being sterilised. Now this lady tells me that she did not know what happened to her, how she believed such a rumour.

I know, I happened to be in Delhi that day.

So you remember that. This is how they created fear by propaganda.

I agree with you that the RSS has succeeded in sabotaging most of your programmes during Emergency. But it happened because of the closed atmosphere.

You see, I have met people who have told me that they were paid to travel up and down the trains and sit in pan shop and coffee shops just to spread rumours.

It happened because newspapers were not used to contradict. The censorship. It was too much. But I will discuss the censorship issue later. I want to discuss with you your future plans. You recently said that your programme will be to implement the 20 points. What about the five points of the Youth Congress? The Gauhati session had adopted these five points as an addition to the 20 points.

The five points are part of the government programme. They are not of the Youth Congress except that the Youth Congress suggested that they be taken up vigorously. The Youth Congress wanted to work purely on constructive programmes, and not political. Moreover, they wanted to do something in which they could be personally involved—for instance, the dowry. It's for the young people to decide that they will not take the dowry. And that they will create an anti-dowry movement for they will plant trees and things like that.

In the 20 point, most of the items had to do with the government. Private individuals cannot do them, whether it is bonded labour, minimum wages, or land reforms.

Do not you think that nasbandi did the maximum damage?

You mean family planning? That was part of the government programme, wasn't it?

You see, the Youth Congress boys became over enthusiastic and sought to implement it vigorously.

No, no. The Youth Congress did not vigorously implement it. It was the Health Ministry which put out the programme of motivation and quota system. This led to misuse. They were supposed to educate the people and persuade them, not force them. And there were cases where people were forced. But they were few. Now they are not finding, I mean, had they found a lot of them, they would have made a hue and cry.

The Janata government did try to give compensation to such cases.

But how many cases they found?

Few, very few.

That is what I am saying. But at that time they made such a hue and cry as if everybody had been sterilised.

Will you again pursue the family planning programme vigorously if you come to your?
It is being pursued even now by this government.

Not vigorously. It's being done half heartedly.
But they are doing it. Wherever there is a good in it's being done especially in the industrial areas.

What I am asking is will your government pursue the family planning programme as vigorously as it did during Emergency?
You cannot have healthy population unless the parents are able to look after the children and give them their due as citizens. We have never regarded family planning as purely population control but as a wider programme of healthier family.

Yes. The family has to be planned.
Yes, but there should not be any force or coercion in it.

Let's come out of the Emergency era. I want to ask you about the din and dust raised by the recent events. Why did you extend support to Chaudhary Charan Singh who never made a secret of his dislike of you and Nehruism, who made desperate attempts to get you convicted and who suggested a Nuremburg type trial for you?
Because we wanted the Janata to go. And there was no other way for it to go.

You supported him as a matter of tactics.
The Janata government had to go, it was as simple as that.

So you supported Charan Singh.
We could not push it out without supporting Charan Singh.

You could have asked for a mid-term poll without doing all this.
We did ask but they didn't agree.
Did Babuji seek your help?
He said no.

You did try to help him.
The point is that we thought that neither of them had any right to form the government, Babuji didn't have the majority, neither did the other gentleman, and we advised the President to hold mid-term poll. But we suggested that he could select Babuji as the interim Prime Minister because he was the leader of the largest group but not as . . . it's I mean, a very small technical point but not as Janata leader.

You mean as consensus Prime Minister?
But he did not accept it. He thought he had the majority.

There is an impression that you put certain conditions especially withdrawing the special courts and certain cases.
No. We didn't. Not at all.

Was your support to Charan Singh also unconditional?
Yes, of course. The 19th night he himself had said our support was unconditional.

But now he is charging you of pressure tactics.
He has also said that I tried to put these conditions when I saw him in the hospital. This is ridiculous. At that time he was not even being sworn in as Home minister later some of our members certainly said that they should withdraw the case, but none of my senior colleagues.

No conditions from you?
Not at all. On the contrary, I specifically mentioned at the party meeting that I didn't expect him to withdraw the cases. But afterwards I said that what we could have hoped for was that we would receive a fair trial. And the sort of pressure which was being brought upon the judiciary, which is continuing today, because the Law minister is constantly seeing the Chief Justice and other Judges.

What will you do of the Shah Commission report and other cases if you come to power?
We will see that.

There are dozens of commissions on you and your son.
Well, we will see. It depends. Well, it's up to Parliament, I don't know.

People have failed to understand your support to the Bihar government and the opposition in UP. Both of them are dominated by the RSS. Why this dual policy? What are the reasons?
Firstly, we are responsible for the removal of Karpoori Thakur because all the major communal riots took place in his time and he did nothing about them. Belchi and Jamshedpur took place in his time. He is the one who started the casteism which is just as bad as communalism and it has divided the minorities too.

Yes, even among the minorities there are backwards and forwards.
Yes, not only this. Even the backwards and forwards had been divided into smaller caste factions, so we thought there is nothing to choose between the two. This person was a *Harijan,* I mean the Chief minister. Secondary, he had removed all his Jana Sangh ministers. So, on that account we supported him. But we don't support him any more.

Now he has lot of Jana Sangh ministers in his Cabinet.
That's why we don't support him any more.

Will your party vote against him?
Yes.

And what about UP? You supported the Opposition in UP.
Yes. UP that just depended upon the situation.

You supported the RSS-dominated opposition against Banarsi Das during the no-confidence motion.
Well, we just do not want any of these governments to continue. We do not see any difference between one or the other.

The exodus. How do you react to this great exodus? There is a rush amongst congressmen to join you on the eve of your victory. What do you call them—'converts', 'defectors' or simply 'returnees'? There is a saying 'Subh ka bhula ghar ko vapas ajai to bhula nahin kehlata'.

What will be their place in the party and the government if you win the elections?
It's difficult to say, it depends on the individual. There are all kinds of them. You see, some stayed out because there were cases against them.

Were they scared?
They thought the cases would go on and the government would pressurise the judiciary if they joined us. And because they were not with us at that time they were spared. They did skip the guilt. This is a fact which one cannot deny.

Otherwise also there was very great harassment some people didn't want to take the risk. And some others were waiting to see which side was going to work out. So there are all kinds and it depends very much on the local situation and as to what position they have.

Why people like Vasantdada Patil, who had nothing to fear, are flocking to you?
They think we have a better future. Also, Y.B. Chavan is very much more an authoritarian and has not allowed them to come up.

Indiraji, this exodus will create problems for you. Your's soon will become an unwieldy party. If you recall, about five years ago you had told me that the main difficulty with the Congress was that it had become flabbly, too big to manage, and it needed trimming.
Yes. I do. But what to do? The situation is so desperate in the country that the main thing is to bring back some kind of sanity and stability.

You can be a little discreet in admitting them. All kinds of people are joining you. You welcome them.

I have welcomed some, not all.

They are coming. They will create tensions. They will establish factions and quarrels will begin. You are buying headache. The faction fights have already begun.

Yes, I admit. They have. It has created tension.

In states too you will face the same problem.

It has created some problems, some tensions, in the states too. But let's see how it is, perhaps with experience we can manage better.

Will it be the same Congress in power with the Socialists, Leftists, Rightists all converging on each other? Will you again try to make the Congress a cadre-based organisation?

These questions are there but the answers are also there. The party has to be mass-based. But it must also have a cadre. Not many people can afford to give full time without any kind of payment. So, there has to be cadres.

Do you want to raise a paid cadre?

Some people are already there. Certain amount of training is also needed about our policies.

Will you again permit the Left and the Right in your party?

How can I prevent it? I can't prevent anything like this. People use these names for their own purposes. And when you have a large party it becomes difficult to control them. The Congress has a very wide range. But why people have accepted socialism? They have accepted this because they have found it is what the people wanted. In my father's time these resolutions were passed in the AICC even though some of the stalwarts were dead against them.

Your father was a much greater democrat than you are. This is what the people feel. You're perhaps more strict. Perhaps you feel an element of strictness is essential.

Of course, you have to be strict.

To keep the nation disciplined?

The most important thing is the nation should survive.

You feel that the problems are more complicated and of greater dimensions than they were during Nehru's time?

Yes, the problems are enormous. Though he laid the foundation, and it was very difficult, at that time there was no opposition as such.

You mean to say there was no organised and strident opposition?
Yes. It was very little opposition compared to what it is now. There were certain individuals and they were not organised in a body.

Current, 29.09.1979.
pp. (1 + 9 + 10 + 11 + 12)

Threat to my life—Indira

Many senior members of her party are deeply concerned at the threat to her life. " It is not a question of my feeling, it is a fact." She suspects that the foreign powers which conspired to overthrow her are still very active and the CIA is one of them. I left her with an impression that she would start a process of national reconciliation if she came to power. She realised the counter-effects of vindictiveness.

She is overwhelmingly aware that even if she gets an absolute majority she will be faced with a much tougher and determined opposition. She may not be the same "authoritarian" as she was during Emergency. But she knows she can ill-afford to be lax. She has seen the Janata being ridiculed for its non-governance and non-performance and she is determined to govern the country if she came to power.

You have been accused of authoritarianism not only by the opposition but also by those who had worked with you for the party and the government for a number of years. Are you really an authoritarian?
On the contrary, I don't think you can find a single person who is as democratic as I am. Somebody puts up a word and everybody uses it without thinking. Mr. Chavan thinks that he was penalised. He was given the topmost Ministries in the government and yet he thinks I punished him.

I am not talking of punishment, I am talking of authoritarianism..
But he is the man who says I am authoritarian.

Your other ex-colleagues too have been charging you with monopolising power and having an authoritarian bent of mind.
People who use this word don't really know it's meaning. The real authoritarian people in this country are Morarji Desai, Chaudhary Charan Singh and Y.B. Chavan.

Was Emergency a mistake?

The question is how you look at. It is only as a result of Emergency that we could take the country out of the economic morass, combat inflation, bring down prices, and raise India to a level from which there could be very rapid economic growth.

Had we not lost the election, the country would have attained commanding heights. It is a strong economic base which is important. It is only with such a base, the backward and the poor can be served.

Your remarks about the freedom of the press have created a lot of controversy. The Fourth Estate fears that it will once again have a raw deal if you become the Prime Minister.

I don't know what Fourth Estate you are talking about.

The newspapers.

Which newspapers? So many newspapers are having a raw deal even today.

What exactly you said at the Bombay Press Club?

There were two questions. First, they asked me about Emergency and the Press and I made it abundantly clear that it will not be repeated—neither censorship nor Emergency. The one chap again asked, so I got a little irritated and I said: Every country puts some curbs on the press in times of war, for instance. Therefore, if you say never, never, it is difficult for me to say.

Are you sure the MISA will not be resurrected.

Frankly, I don't think it was needed even then but the home ministry insisted.

Your Cabinet passed it.

Yes, the Cabinet decided because the Home Ministry insisted. Even at that time I thought that the laws were quite adequate. I don't know whether they were properly drawn or not but as you know, MISA was there even before Emergency.

The pressmen may be wanting an absolute assurance from you.

There won't be any press censorship.

Are you absolutely sure?

Yes.

After 1977 debacle almost all your associates and senior colleagues not only deserted you but also denigrated you publicly. Why did it happen?

Well, they did the same in 1969. Those who had removed me from the party also launched a strong campaign against me.

But in 1977 the bitterness was much greater. Why, so much viciousness was not generated in 1969. The acrimony was not so concentrated. Your cabinet colleagues appeared against you in the commissions. In 1969 people like Atulya Ghosh, C.B. Gupta and Nijalingappa preferred to retire.
No, no they organised into Cong-O.

Why it happened with you alone that most of your colleagues went against you one after the other?
Frankly, they are interested in themselves. With my defeat they thought they would get nothing from me and they may get something by pleasing the Janata.

They didn't join the Janata.
They would have if they had the chance. Now, most of them have joined the Janata-S.

Why did Babuji desert you on the eve of the elections? He had given an unqualified support to Emergency.
Frankly, I don't know. You can tell me why he did so.

He had told me a few days after he left you that you had planned to liquidate him and his family.
I am hearing this for the first time. This is utter nonsense. At that time an American reporter has told me that he had heard that Babuji was being denied a ticket. That too was absolute nonsense. Babuji was a member of the Election Committee. How could a ticket be denied to him? I always accommodated all his people, not just himself. It shows what type of propaganda was at work. He had also said that I had kept a watch on him during Emergency. If that was so I would have known about his secret meetings with Bahuguna. But I did not have a clue till his letter of resignation came.

Then why did he leave.
He thought he could be the Prime Minister.

How, how could he know that you and the Congress Party would lose?
He thought we had grown weaker and he has been constantly in touch with forces opposed to us. He had the same idea in 1971 too, by the way.

Why did Bahuguna leave?
He left because we had removed him from the Chief ministership.

That was a mistake. It was not a good step.
Well, I thought he was destroying the state.

In what way?
His attitude has always been destructive.

But I think he is a competent man.
He is, if he wants to use his competence for the good of something. He gets involved, I mean how is it that he has not been able to make a go with anybody? Even now, he is not happy with Charan Singh.

You went out of your way to protect and promote the Left in the Congress, yet this was the very element which turned against you after your fall. But the Right, whom you tended to ignore, remained loyal to you. Why?
Well, all the time I have been saying that there is no real Left or Right in the Congress.

I think once you patronised the ginger group in the party.
No, I don't remember it. But I must tell you that most of these people say what suits them at the moment. Now I do believe that the government has to be left of centre. I also firmly believe that socialism is the only way for the country of India's size but I don't think socialism has to be what it is in the Soviet Union or in China or even in Sweden. We have to stumble and find our own way.

The carbon copy idea of socialism has been rejected long back. The Indian Left has also realised that ours has to be indigenous socialism.
But there are things which are in common for instance, the commanding heights of the economy have to be in the public sector. They are misused by the private sector and a lot of profiteering is done.

The so-called Left went against me before the elections and not after. The purpose was not to defeat me but to make me weaker so that I would be more dependent on them. This is how their mind worked. So far I was concerned it became an operation over kill. I mean, I had to face the onslaught both from the Right and the Left.

You seemed to have moved quite close to the Left. Was it a matter of tactics or conviction?
They supported my programmes. They supported these programmes more whole-heartedly and it was natural for me to depend on them.

This seems to have antagonised the rightists though they evidently stood by you during and after the elections.
I think they are basically congressmen. Traditional congressmen. They were with the Congress, not with me.

I think D.K. Barooah was a traditional congressmen.
No. He has been in the Congress but he never had a feeling for the Congress. He was there as a member but never closely attached to the Congress.

The inner-party democracy was a major casualty during Emergency. Not only this, but the local party bosses became instruments of oppression. They used MISA more against their political opponents than economic offenders.

The very basis of your question is quite incorrect. In fact, the opposite happened. My first quarrel in the party began when I started fighting against bossism. They ultimately threw me out.

Who was the real boss?

Yeshwantrao Chavan. He is still the boss in Maharashtra.

You are wrong, he is no more the boss. That era is over.

I mean, he may not be that way, but theoretically he is the boss. There was more democracy during my time. Before, during and after Emergency. You think Morarji is not dictatorial. And what was S.K. Patil in Bombay? He did not allow anybody to raise his head. And Atulya Ghosh and C.B. Gupta were the real bosses in Bengal and UP. Though I did not want to drive them all out, I felt the other group, the dissidents, too should not be driven to the wall.

Was not power too much centralised during your time?

No, not at all. It was Chavan who said everything should go through him and if things did not go through him he would say 'Oh! She is not democratic'. But I always consulted him and others too. In Maharashtra everything happened as he wanted. He wanted to remove Naik and then he wanted to remove Shankar Rao Chavan.

During your time, the PCC became rubber stamps.

Not exactly. Things happened because some of the big chaps went out and smaller people came in.

The impression is that you don't like dissidents.

On the contrary, I am the first person who kept dissidents. Chavan was constantly against me, I knew he was working against me, but I kept him in the Cabinet. I knew that Jagjivan Ram was plotting against me but I did not disturb him. Nowhere else this kind of liberty is permitted.

Was it not a mistake? Why did you give them a long rope?

Well, I thought I was strong enough, I could manage them.

It is a Prime Minister's privilege not to keep people in the cabinet with doubtful loyalties.

I know but I just didn't act. My attitude was not one of throwing people out but of tolerating them.

Yes, the MISA, it was terribly misused during Emergency.
A lot of things were misused but they were misused before and now they are being misused by the government. The basic thing is the attitude of the police and the officials.

Though you have been publicly declaring that Emergency will not be brought in, there is a lurking fear in people's mind due to your defence of Emergency.
No, Emergency will not be repeated. It can't be. So many things happened at that time. The Bangladesh war, the global crisis and so many other things had coincided at that moment.

Sanjay Gandhi did play an important role in that context. What will be his role in future? Would you like him to take greater responsibility in the party? He appears to have become more acceptable not only to leaders in your party but also to the leaders in other parties. They have been meeting him and seeking favours from him.
I don't know what his role will be like. It is between him and the people because I don't think it is for me to either encourage or discourage anybody. I certainly should not throw my weight behind him or anybody in that sense. People have to grow up through their own mistakes, their labour and struggle. So it is for him to decide and for the party to decide what they want.

But strange things have been happening. His arch enemies, including Raj Narain, have been meeting him secretly as well as openly and soliciting his support.
Because they have built up an entirely false image of Sanjay. Yes, he met Raj Narain.

Raj Narain meeting him at the peak of a political crisis was a turning point in our politics. Sanjay's acceptability has grown considerably in your party too.
Well, you see the party had mixed feelings. There is a whole group of people which is afraid of the youth surging forward. It is not only Sanjay but they are against all the youth because the youth do want to go faster. They may not be as polite as the older generation.

They are quite tough.
No, not that. The new generation is different everywhere in the world. Life is tougher for them. Many of the older people thought all the time why they should struggle against the Janata. It is the Youth Congress which went headlong and suffered and is suffering.

Do you think the Youth Congress will again play an important role in your Party.

It never interferes with the Congress in any way.

The Youth Congress has played an important role and the Congress always accommodated the youth. Both Valyalar Ravi and Das Munshi were members of the Working Committee as representatives of the Youth Congress. There was no Sanjay at that time.

Our Working Committee has two Youth Congress representatives Ram Chandra Rath and Ram Lingam. The Youth Congress President is an ex-officio member of the CWC.

Do you plan to allocate large number of seats to the Youth?

That depends whether they can win, whether they are wanted and so on.

The Congress was wiped out in the North in 1977 while the South overwhelmingly voted for you. This time the South seems to be changing while the North appears to be in a mood to bring you back to power. Could you explain this phenomenon?

I don't think I can comment. I don't know whether the South is changing. We have recently won elections in Karnataka.

Not after your split with Devraj Urs?

Yes, after that. There were Municipal Taluka and Board elections. We won despite Devraj Urs' efforts.

Your strong base was Karnataka and Andhra Pradesh while Tamil Nadu was also with you. Now the situation has changed drastically.

Let us see what happens in the elections.

Are you confident of winning in Karnataka?

I never speak of elections beforehand but the sort of receptions I have had, the sort of anti-receptions the MLAs who have gone with Urs have had in there constituencies is an indication of how the people feel.

The conflict between you and Devraj Urs remains a mystery. He has been such a strong supporter of yours. He fought shoulder to shoulder with you.

That's wrong. Urs was never with me. He merely used me for winning the elections and immediately afterwards he started speaking against me and even suggested that I should be removed from the party.

Recently he made very critical remarks against you. He has charged that in your camp Sanjay runs the show.

The fact is that he is very ambitious person and he had thought he would not have won the elections without me.

What is wrong with being ambitious? He may have tried to become a national leader or even the Primê Minister..

He was not trying, he thought he had become a national leader.

Did he also try to become the Prime Minister? Did he give you this impression?

Not to me. But this is what he told people in Bangalore. He even suggested to some of his colleagues. 'You take over the Chief ministership after I go to Delhi.'

Do you agree that the North is changing and it is likely to vote for you heavily?

May be. The North has seen the misrule of the Janata, the instability, the disorder and the disruption it brought.

Is this a negative change?

Well, it is negative as well as positive. People are comparing between what was done before and what is being done now.

You had predicted a few months after the ascendancy of the Janata that its rule will not last long and that it might collapse in two years. Was this pronouncement based on your political assessment or on the advice of your astrologers? Do you believe in stars and the tantra?

I don't know enough about stars or *tantra*s to say anything about them. So for the stars are concerned, scientifically people believe the moon does have an effect on some people who are not normal or something like that. It is possible that the other stars too have some effect. But we do not know enough about them. I do not know any astrologer. They may be politicians or bank clerks or anything. I have never consulted anybody nor do I believe in these kind of things.

But you attract a lot of astrologers?

These days they are coming every day.

Do you meet them?

No, not particularly, I meet everybody who comes here, but I do not even talk to them if I know they are going to talk on this subject. I am not bothered about what they say.

It seems you knew the new bunch which came in the name of the Janata would not be able to govern the country?

Yes, by their very composition, I knew. I knew they were thoroughly incompetent. It was partly an analysis and partly an intuition. I mean, when you work for long you develop an intuition.

Are the forces which you believed conspired to oust you from power active again? Will you permit similar 'conspiracies' if you return to power?
It is not in my hands to permit or not to permit. They are very strong and deeply entrenched. As I have said many times they have not been only working against me but also against my father. They have strengthened not only here but all over the world since then. At that time they were rather taken aback by the sudden independence of so many countries and the nonaligned movement and one thing after another came. They were taken aback.

But now they have time to gasp their breath and organise themselves and to use people in this country.

If these people are so destructive why don't you name them, why don't you take the people into confidence, so that the people can be more vigilant about them?
You can't be vigilant because they work through our people.

You can at least name them.
Most of them are these western people.

Is it the CIA?
It's not only the CIA, the CIA certainly has a role to play. The Zionists may also be working. The Americans used all these agents. Besides the CIA, other countries were also active during elections.

Some time back you mentioned about a threat to your life. Do you still feel this danger exists?
It is not a question of my feeling, it is a fact. It is a fact that there are intelligence reports mentioning about this.

Is there a danger to the members of your family also?
Sanjay does face the danger. I don't know about others, this is what we hear.

You have been critical of Janata's favourable attitude towards the multinationals. What will be your policy towards these giants if you come to power?
We do not want these multinationals in this country. Some of these huge multinationals once they come in they spread their tentacles, they get in everything and it is difficult to escape. We know it from the mischief of the International Telephone. The IIT involved itself in too many things everywhere. We have to see that they don't infringe on the Indian interest.

The multinationals in fact grew during your time.
Yes, they were there but they were kept very much under control.

Can't this government keep them under control?
This government is incapable of doing anything.

There is a feeling among the intelligentsia that you ignore the intellectuals and treat the press with contempt.
It is a very peculiar feeling. It was during my regime that intellectuals came back from all over the world and they wrote that for the first time the atmosphere in India is congenial and that they could function and contribute to India's development with a sense of dignity.

The intelligentsia always felt alienated. They remember Pandit Nehru for his close rapport with the intellectuals and people in the field of the arts. Why you could not establish a rapport with this section of society?
They like persons who talk a lot. I am more a doer than a talker. Different things are needed in different times and when your house is burning that is not the moment to describe how it is burning, it is the question of putting out the fire.

Well, I do not know why I am not liked by them. I get along pretty well outside the country.

Why the press has been harsh to you?
Most of the proprietors are against me.

Well, some of the proprietors are close to you.
You know the sort of friendship—these families have friends in all the parties.

The impression is that the poorest and the richest are with you. Isn't it strange.
The rich certainly don't help with money. I can tell you that they may be favouring me in words but not in deeds.

But the middle class remains alienated.
I don't think so. Not particularly in the North.

And the South?
In the South too.

You have been saying that the country's prestige abroad has gone down during the Janata rule. Can you give some specific examples?
It is not a question of giving examples. It is how we play our role in world affairs. For the first time in 30 years, India does not count at all, anywhere in the world.

You also mentioned about the tilt in our non-aligned policy towards the west.

Yes. It is correct but they have been trying to cuddle up with the Soviet Union as well.

And the last question—how many seats you are expecting?
I don't think anybody knows. Let's see what happens.

Current, 06.10.1979.
pp. (1 + 8 + 9 + 10 + 11)

Now that you are the Prime Minister. . .
an open letter to Indira

Dear Indiraji,

Now that you have once again taken reigns of power with a massive mandate from the people of this great country to shape its destiny and, now, when you have attained the commanding heights of a great national leader, we address this open letter to you.

We have been your admirers as well as critics. WE, in our own small way, appreciated your policies and programmes when we thought they were for the good of the country and we criticised you vehemently when we found such a warning necessary in the best interests of the people. We gave up hope in the ability of the Janata rulers to rise to the expectation of the people and take this country forward. They turned out to be a bunch of old cats.

The less said about them the better. Their memory leaves a bad taste in the mouth. That era of despondency, demoralisation and frustration is over. We don't look backward. With you at the helms we have to look forward.

By bringing you back with a sweep the people have reiterated faith in the democratic values and have also asserted their right to reject their elected representatives if they misuse the mandate.

They have also established beyond doubt that they, and not the parties or the leaders, are the supremos. They did it in 1977 by voting you out of power because they lost faith in you. But this week they have once again brought you back with vengeance because they thought they were betrayed and cheated by the leaders who took them for a ride.

They have proved that their love for democracy need not necessarily mean an ineffective government. A strong government can be democratic as well as effective. The much tom-tomed freedom was enjoyed exclusively by a coterie of traders, black-marketeers, smugglers and people with foreign links. This was the freedom, Janata style. But the poor, who constitute the bulk of the population, hardly enjoyed the fruits of this freedom.

In the morass created by the Janata, the people lost their moorings. Their determination to blaze new trails and carry forward the task of national reconstruction was eroded. They yearned for the return of the days when they could contribute their mite under an able and dynamic leadership. They were saddled with an old and decrepit leadership and but for you the country would have drifted aimlessly.

They have reposed their trust in you because you have promised them stability, rule of law and an effective and efficient government.

Their verdict in your favour is deliberate and positive. It was not an ordinary election. It was not a negative action. It was a referendum which they exercised to bring you back fully knowing the consequences. They have voted you back to power because they are against :

Casteism.
Regionalism and communalism.
Political fragmentation.
Opportunism and defections.
Social and economic chaos.

They humble and humiliate those who play with their honour and dignity.

They have given you the mandate because they would like you to:

Demolish the caste barriers.
Eradicate regionalism and communalism.
Foster a sense of political commitment.
Reduce economic disparities, concentration of wealth, bring down prices, launch employment-oriented schemes and provide the people with the bare necessities of life.

The Janata pushed the country to the brink of an economic precipice. The perennial shortage of coal, power, diesel and kerosene has shaken the very foundations of our economy. Normalcy has to be restored on this front.

The steep rise in prices of essential commodities and non-availability of diesel and kerosene have contributed to the defeat of your opponents.

In North India millions of homes are plunged in darkness after sunset. Tractors and diesel engines, which are vital to the rurai economy, are lying idle. The people expect that, with your ascendancy, these problems will soon be solved.

Law and order, as you yourself have been pinpointing, has to be restored. The people have to be given a sense of security.

This election has once again proved that no person can have the exclusive claim of the leadership of a particular community. The Harijans have preferred you over a leader who assumed he would be voted to power with their help and who claimed to have their loyalty. Yet another leader, who sought to divide the country into narrow and vicious caste compartments, has also been discarded. The Harijans, the minorities and the weaker sections have all reposed their faith in you. They will legitimately expect economic and social benefits which they have been denied.

The country was like a rudderless ship. There was total emotional disintegration. There was no sense of direction. There was no sense of attainment because there was none. This nation, which is capable of moving mountains, was reduced into a lump.

It has to be reinfused with faith, desire, adventurism and dynamism for which it has been proud of.

It will be an exaggeration to say that you alone can do it. This is the language of sycophants who will soon surround you. We believe that with the multitude of the people behind you, you can perform miracles.

This time the country has the unique opportunity of having the services of a large number of young people whom you have brought to Parliament. This youth, if properly trained and guided in the art of governance, will be your valuable contribution. The country has to be governed and if you can raise a team of young, able and dedicated leaders it will be another feather in your cap.

These are the national expectations. But if you fall short of them which we hope you will not, then the fury and the ire will inevitably be repeated. Do not forget that the people have learned to assert their sovereignty and supremacy.

They don't expect from you to waste your time and energy in settling scores with your opponents and enemies.

Vindictiveness does not pay. Victimisation boomerangs. The Janata rulers have received their greatest punishment in their defeat. In democracy this is the only kind of punishment.

The nation will not tolerate vindictiveness and vendetta. Commissions and prosecutions too will not yield any result.

No revenge. With unqualified mass approval of your leadership your opponents have been reduced into pigmies and giants don't punish the pigmies. People expect you to usher in an era of reconciliation.

We wish you luck and long life to serve the country with dedication as your father did. Jawaharlal Nehru lives in the heart of every Indian even after 16 years of his death and no power in this country would ever succeed in tarnishing his image. You know the reason why.

Current, 12.01.1980.
pp. (1 + 2)

Renewed mandate: now govern

The world has once again witnessed the resurgence of the democratic spirit of India. In a massive assertion of their collective wisdom the people have voted the Congress-I back to power in the states. They have given an unqualified mandate to Indira Gandhi to guide their destinies.

In the election Sanjay Gandhi has definitely come to the fore. The victory of almost all his candidates reflects the mass approval of his style of functioning and their acceptance of the young man as their new leader.

It is a firm and calculated decision. Now nobody can accuse Sanjay and his men of misusing their position, usurping power or becoming extra-constitutional centres of authority.

What we saw last week was a bloodless revolution. An entirely new class of young men have been given the task of shaping the future of the country.

While the Lok Sabha poll was a national decision to bring Indira Gandhi back to power, the Assembly elections were a reaffirmation of their faith in her leadership and their consent to her resolve to make Sanjay a full fledged politician. The dumb millions of India have emerged as the decisive arbiters.

1. Indira Gandhi is the only leaders who can deliver the goods and provide an efficient and effective administration.
2. The opposition's plan that in a federal system different parties can rule the states is rejected.
3. Now the centre and the states will broadly reflect the will and thinking of the people.
4. People see no danger in giving total power in the hands of one leader. They seem to be convinced that she will not let them down.
5. Last week's mandate was also an expression of enormous faith in her capacity to curb prices, restore law and order, eradicating the black market and solve many an intricate national problem.

6. The people have voted for unitary system. They paid no heed to the rumours floated by the opposition that she was preparing for the presidential form of government by amending the constitution.
7. In the prevailing national mood the opposition parties have lost their relevance. If they want to survive they have to find new modes.
8. Charan Singh on the day of her victory described it 'darkest day in our democratic system'. Their concept of democracy has been rejected.
9. The victory of hundreds of young men with no ideological constraints is a clear indication of the people's preference for 'Action' to 'Isms'.
10. The party leaders in the opposition can ill afford to ignore this factor. They cannot face the onslaught of the Congress-I youth power with ailing, demented, degenerated oldies. For their survival they will have to throw out young and dynamic leaders.
11. People have disapproved the politics of confrontation. The opposition now will have to adopt a positive and constructive approach. In the best national interest it should lend unstinted co-operation to Indira Gandhi's war against poverty. With such a massive mandate of the people hers is no more a party government. It is a government of consensus.
12. The Congress-I's overwhelming success should not be construed as the victory of an individual. It is the reiteration of supremacy of the people's power. No leader is above people.
13. It is a conditional mandate that people have given. The country is crying for economic and social revolution.
14. She could no more find excuses. She has won the political battle. It is the time for the promised war against poverty. The poor will not wait. Failure to act will be disastrous.
15. The implementation of the 20-point programme will now have to be taken up with zeal and dedication.
16. No time can be wasted in ruthlessly carrying out comprehensive land reforms. Poor people's land which has been snatched away by blood thirsty landlords will have to be returned to their rightful owners. Indira Gandhi is expected to see to it that Belchi and Narayanpur are not repeated. And that every Harijan strides his land with his head held high. To the poverty stricken people she symbolises an image of destroyer of social evils. She will have to demolish the social system which sanctifies and perpetuates the oppression of weaker sections.

17. The urban poor, slum dwellers, the homeless look at her as the giver. It is they who have led her through one victory to another and now it is time to expect from her to lead them from one victory to another.
18. India as a nation solidly stands behind her. The world too expects from her a quality of leadership reminiscent of her illustrious father. These expectations are not too much for a person who has gone through hell-fire and emerged uninjured.
19. This is India's finest hour of destiny. People never felt so confident as they do today. Their burning desire for stability, national integrity, communal harmony and economic breakthrough should not remain unfulfilled.
20. The prestige of the country is again attaining new heights in the world. Indira Gandhi enjoys the goodwill of all the friendly countries. It has to be harnessed in the national interest.

Current, 07.06.1980.
pp. (1 + 2).

Where is the government that works?

Indira Gandhi remarked the other day: "I am not weak". This was the most startling statement she made after her return to power. The nation was astounded to hear her say "I am not weak".

Did the negative statement reflect the positive feeling among the masses that she has grown weak? Did she reply to the question: Has she lost the will to rule?

What kind of weakness is this? Moral, political or physical? Morally she remains supreme, has even scaled new heights. The whole country stands behind her like a rock. The elections to the state assemblies have proved her supreme. Physically she may have lost some weight because of her personal tragedy. But politically there should be no reason for her to feel weak. Yet, why does she feel weak? Everything around her is weak, pale and uninspiring.

Look at her cabinet. It is the weakest the country ever had—packed with upstarts, charlatans, buffoons and sycophants.

Her's is no Cabinet. It is a half government. Most of the major ministries are headless. And the few heads are nincompoops.

It is a lacklustre Cabinet. It is not a Cabinet that can rule. It is not a Cabinet that can run a government.

The malady is deeper. The party itself is bereft of talent. In it, only Indira counts. That precisely is her weakness.

Her other weakness is that she has underrated her capacity to rule. The whole country is with her. Why then is she diffident? What is holding her back?

None knows the masses as she does. She also knows that she is the only hope at the moment. If she fails, the people will feel betrayed.

Why then does she not act? Why does she have to blame the Janata for the economic and political mess? The people brought her back to set the house in order and not to wail over the misdeeds of her predecessors.

The flame is gone. Her party has lost its elan. Her team is uninspiring. There is no thought, no debate and no involvement. This is in stark contrast to the talent and commitment that marked her previous Cabinets.

The only colourful idea that has emanated from it is Vasant Sathe's colour TV. And she has scotched it. The vaunted 20-point programme and the much tom-tommed five-points are not heard.

This was perhaps inevitable. The man who was bent on implementing them is gone. Others had feared him rather loved him.

The average congressman was psychologically unprepared for such a change. Indira Gandhi knew that the congressmen who stood by her in her tribulations were men of straw. She thought the younger generation that rallied round her son was made of different stuff. But with the son no more. This too has proved an illusion.

The strident Youth Congress leaders who ruled the roost are now in disarray. The Youth Congress has collapsed. It will soon disintegrate.

Those who were hanging on to Sanjay's *kurta* are now desperately in search of a new Neta.

Rajiv Gandhi may not fill the bill. But he can at least save them from total orphanage.

Will he be acceptable to the whole party? Can he carry it with him? Can he be the link between the party and its leader, which is what Sanjay was.

But why does she need another Sanjay Gandhi? Is it always necessary to control the party and the government through an intermediary? Has it become her style of functioning? It was Sanjay yesterday. It is Dhirendra Brahmachari today? And should it be Rajiv tomorrow?

Is it because of this lack of faith in herself that her partymen have been searching for a successor to Sanjay? Is it not an irony that with a massive mandate behind her, her associates are looking for a successor? They are obviously plagued by the thought: After Indira, who?

One of the main reasons of anxiety and nervousness in the Congress rank and file is the total lack of direction on the economic front.

The ruling party has failed to live up to the people's expectations. Things were bad under the Janata, they have become worse.

The anguish and agony have grown since then, yet the masses are bearing it with fortitude and patience. They have not lost hope in Indira's capacity to fulfill her promise. Not that they have lost the will to assert but they are also plagued by the thought: If not Indira, who?

Current, 16.08.1980.
pp. (1 + 2)

Are we heading for a deluge?

Indira Gandhi's decision not to reshuffle or expand her cabinet reveals a significant aspect of our national life. She is absolutely justified in assuming that she has ultimately succeeded in establishing a rule by one party controlled by one person.

More important, the country has willingly opted for it. The acceptance is peaceful and democratic.

The nationwide criticism that she has failed to provide "the government that works", that her cabinet is not complete and what it consists of men of low calibre has not affected in the least Madam Prime Minister's style of functioning.

On the contrary she thinks her ministers are not only competent but also capable of handling several portfolios together.

This imperious self-confidence emanates from a feeling that her massive victory has reduced the party 'stalwarts' to pygmies and made pulp of the 'great' opposition leaders.

From Kashmir to Kanniyakumari and from Kohima to Kutch there is not a single individual who has the moral or political fibre to question her authority.

The country is under her total sway. This is the hard fact. It cannot be denied nor skirted. Let her opponents take note.

To be fair to her, it is not she who has resurrected the obnoxious slogan 'One Nation, One Flag, One Leader'. It is the gift of the people to themselves. It is their free choice.

Never before has the country been so helplessly dependent on one individual. Never before has the fate of a nation hung by a fragile thread held by a weak hand. Never before have the people of this democratic republic gone into such stunned silence after making a choice in such a decisive manner.

Never before has a democratic party so totally and abjectly surrendered its right to a share in power or collective responsibility.

Never before has the voice of dissidence been muted by an iron gavel wrapped in silk.

Yet Indira Gandhi cannot be accused of 'dictatorship' or 'authoritarianism'. The two notorious words have suddenly disappeared from the vocabulary of her critics, not to speak of her own party.

She has assiduously built the party on a unique ideology—unquestioned loyalty to her and her family. Again she cannot be accused of subduing or intimidating the party members into accepting her as their supreme leader. Their's is a voluntary choice.

It may be fatalistic attitude. But she has worked herself to believe: 'after me the deluge'.

She justifiably draws pleasures from the fact that the great Congress '*Netas*' who joined hands with her communal and fascist adversaries to humble her, to humiliate her, have been made to lick the dust. They were small people forced to perform big roles, and now they are returning to her fold in sack cloth and ashes.

Whether it is Karan Singh or Yeshwantrao Chavan, the demoralisation is worth witnessing. Soon Devraj Urs, Bahuguna, Chandrajeet Yadav and many others will find one excuse or other to fall at her feet.

As fish cannot live without water, congressmen gasp without power. And a Sharad Pawar, for instance, is too young to remain in wilderness and he is not cast in the mould of an opposition leader.

Each congressman has a Bhajanlal hidden in him.

Indira's determination not to share power is also intended to show the Youth Congress 'toughs' their place. Some young MPs who claimed close association with Sanjay have been expecting entry to the Council of ministers as a matter of right.

Indira Gandhi, more than anybody else, knows that like the party, the Youth Congress too was a one-man show. She has measured the worth of the Youth Congress MPs—none of them will be able to return to Parliament on his own.

The Youth Congress actually died with Sanjay. For Indira it had a limited utility. She astutely used them for returning to power. The group of young, though boys who rallied round her were not fired by idealism.

Sanjay was their deity. He is no more. Rajiv cannot replace him.

So far Indira Gandhi has not taken any of these young MPs in her government. Not that she has reservations about them, she would like them to climb the hard way, if they can.

These young MPs are rudderless in their own states too. The Chief ministers no more spend their time ingratiating them. They are ignored. The senior leaders are refusing to accommodate them in the organisation.

Sanjay had floated this youth force to fight his two-pronged battle against the RSS and the Naxalites. The RSS has started the plans of reorganisation and rejuvenation on a grand scale while the Naxalites have started regrouping themselves in their traditional pockets.

With the withering away of the Youth Congress the plans for the creation of a second line of leadership have also blown off. The senior leaders are already devalued.

Despite overwhelming majority in Parliament and most state assemblies, there is a pervading sense of insecurity among congressmen. Otherwise the 320 MP legislators would not have rushed to Rajiv as others have already done to implore him to lead them, knowing the fact that he is least interested in stepping into the shoes of his brother.

Rajiv is not a politician but the congressmen in sheer desperation want to turn him into one. It is their way of answering the question that haunts them—After Indira Who?

Current, 20.09.1980.
p. (1)

B. Promises Unfulfilled

Democracy, my foot

Thirty four years after Independence we stand in the midst of a pathless desert of ideological barrenness. We continue to group in the dark, we are not sure of the system which governs us. We are a nation without a destiny.

We have a Parliament, democracy, judiciary and free press. But do we have all these institutions of which we can be proud? Is our democratic system perfect, is our Parliament a dynamic body, an instrument of change? Is our judiciary a paragon of justice and is our press really free? Does it reflect the aspirations of the people?

No system can be perfect. But how imperfect is this system? Can a country of India's size and diversity afford to have adhocism? Can we arrive at a national consensus in evolving a system which can wipe out poverty, ignorance and privation? Or should we submit ourselves to whatever we have inherited—good or bad?

This is an imperfect system and its by-product the parties, the bureaucracy, the judiciary, have not been willingly and universally accepted by the people. They have been tolerated since the people have not been able to decide what other system they can have.

This is an imperfect system. It has definitely failed to make India stronger, better and prosperous. It has failed to provide for full participation of the people in governance.

It has reduced the people into mere tools in the hands of a small group of men who form the ruling elite irrespective of their political or personal affiliations. The people can say 'yes' or 'no' only once in five years, the rest of the time they are helpless spectators.

Can we deny that there are two Indias—the India of the rulers and the India of the ruled? Real democracy does not and should not allow the tyranny of a minority over the majority.

In this country the ruling class has no ideology, no loyalties and no commitments. Its only commitment is to power and the only struggle it has been involved in is how to retain power.

Democracy is meaningless to over 70 per cent of the people who live below the *chapati* belt, who cannot make two ends meet, whose children cannot get milk, medicine and money to buy a pair of *chappal*s.

Democracy is meaningless to millions of Adivasis who still eat roots and leaves to survive. Democracy is not only meaningless, but a curse to those Harijans whose huts are burnt by the *thugs* of the ruling elite, whose land is forcibly taken away and whose daughters are raped in broad daylight.

In this democratic India, thirty-four years after independence, crores of Harijans cannot draw water from a common well and after death they cannot be cremated in community burning *ghat*. They live and die as outcasts.

And what has our great Parliament done to build an India of the common man's dream? How many genuine peasants, workers, Harijans and Adivasis have ever been elected to this so-called custodian of the sham democracy? Will the security guard at the main gate of Parliament permit a common voter to enter the portals of that well-guarded building? Security for whom and from whom?

In this democracy a people's representative who crawls before the voter as a begger suddenly assumes the pompous role of a ruler once he is elected. He demands an air-conditioned bungalow, chauffeur-driven car, air-conditioned railway accommodation, room in a five-star hotel and right sources to live a life beyond means.

Democratic greed has no limits. Once elected by the scum of the earth he gets a ministership, and then the sky is the limit. He vaxes eloquent on the virtue and desirability of more and more five-star hotels—increasing tourism. What about the wretched one in his constituency? What roads, hospital, schools for him? Well, democracy will collapse without foreign exchange. New Delhi must have 16 five-star hotels and half a dozen flyovers. The poor and the hungry can wait. Democracy is a slow process, it needs patience.

There are two democratic ways. One for the poor and the other for the ruling elite. The poor can afford to remain poor but the elite must grow rich. They have no time. One cannot grow rich slowly. They cannot wait for democracy.

Have a look at our ministers and bureaucrats. Yes, why should the bureaucrats deny themselves the maximum benefits of democracy. Have a look at our democratic Chief ministers. They must have a Mercedes, dozens of security guards and a fleet of cars and wireless equipped-jeeps following them. Have a look at our minister's spacious bungalows and then think of the poor Adivasis and Harijans—the cornerstones of democracy. Is it not a big farce? Can it continue? Should it continue? How long will it continue?

This system is a farce. It is a fraud on the people. It must change. And when we say it must change we are not saying something new or very radical or very revolutionary. The founding fathers of this system had doubts about it—Gandhi, Nehru and even Ambedkar who framed the Constitution. They all had realised that if this system failed to remove disparities, perpetuated hunger, fortified the ruling elite and protected the rich, then it will collapse under its own weight.

Ambedkar had forewarned about the doom of the system which he had midwifed:

"How long shall we continue to deny equality in our social and economic life? If we continue to deny it for long, we shall do so only by putting our political democracy in peril. We must remove these contradictions at the earliest possible moment, or else those who suffer from inequality will blow up the structure of this political democracy."

This was his polite way of saying that the poor will not tolerate the rule by the rich for a long time.

Has that time come? Who knows?

Current, 15.08.1981.
pp. (1)

The hungry Republic

We have two important national days—the Independence day and the Republic day. On August 15, the Prime Minister addresses a huge gathering after unfurling the Tricolour and makes a lot of promises about progress and prosperity. On January 26, the President drives in state in a glistening buggy, takes salute from the armed forces and in the night goes on the air to assure the country that the Republic is safe and that 'his' government has been able to do a lot of good things for the people.

The government attaches great significance to these two occasions, and the people in power feel that so long as their bungalows, cars, salaries, perks and 'kick-backs' are safe, the country is safe and the people are happy. The common man, on the other hand, remains a passive spectator for five years and then exercises his right to make or unmake the government in the traditional manner.

He has to choose one representative among the many who solicit his support. Not that he is not aware that the one he voted is no better than the others. Not that he does not know that the one he 'elected' as his nominee is not less dishonest. But he has no alternative and every five years he repeats the performance.

Similarly, every year he listens to the Prime Minister and the President and he knows whatever is promised to him was fake. But he has no alternative. He is a slave to the system. And it is this slavery to the system that is the main cause of his miseries, poverty and gloom.

He knows a vote is not revolt, it can change the government but not the system. No system has ever been changed through a vote. And our Prime Minister, and the President are the creation of this vote.

The futility of the vote is a painful reality. The vote may have ensured our freedom from foreign rule, but has it ensured freedom from hunger? The vote may have slaved many an elitist problem, but has it solved the greatest problem—poverty? Can poverty be removed under the system perpetuated by the vote? And if not, what then is the value of this vote?

The Republic has to live, but can it if its people do not? The Republic is not an abstract idea. It is not a cosmic concept. There is nothing sacrosanct about it. It is the people who make the Republic and not the august Rashtrapati Bhavan or the Rashtrapati flying in his own plane, living in the largest and most luxurious mansion, driven in limousines and taken around in a way as though he is a superhuman being, as though he is not the creation of the vote.

He symbolises the nation and its dignity. Yes he does. But does he also symbolise the nation and its poverty? It is necessary to be independent and to live in a republic, but is it also not necessary to have two meals a day, to have shelter over the head, to have medicine when sick, to send children to school and to have them gainfully employed?

Thirty-two years have passed since this country was declared a Republic. The birth of the Republic must have raised the hopes of the millions. Has the Republic lived up to their hopes? Has it?

No system which cannot provide two square meals a day to its people can hope to survive longer, whether it is a republic or a monarchy. The system must serve the people, not the people the system. The system has failed to serve the people. Long live the Republic.

Current, 30.01.1982.
p. (2)

Can she stop the rot?

The Congress edifice seems to be crumbling. It is time for Indira Gandhi to act—act firmly and decisively in the interest of the country and its democratic structure. Not that the Congress is synonymous with democracy alive, kicking and moving.

The ruling party, its leader knows more than anyone else, is in a bad shape. It has grown too big, too flabby, too unwieldy and too uncontrollable. It is packed with opportunists and time servers. She has not been able to prevent the massive infiltration of anti-social elements who are wreaking havoc with the established traditions of good and clean administration.

The simple truth is that if she cannot run the party, she cannot run the government too. If the faction fights and the dissidence are not brought to an end swiftly at both the Central and state levels, chaos is bound to raise its ugly head. There is total anarchy in most of those very states which were once considered her strongholds.

The party in Andhra is in a shambles. How can it be expected to be a cohesive body when out of 245 MLAs 120 are defectors? Once a defector always a defector, and it was a grave mistake to have encouraged mass defections. It leads to naked lust for power. And once a defector is denied power, he is on the wings to defect once again.

Things have to be controlled in Andhra before it is too late, and action has to be taken with telling firmness. It is now an open secret that Chenna Reddy is behind the formation of N.T. Rama Rao's Telugu Desam Party. In fact the simple film idol is a tool in the hands of the young and ambitious Bhaskar Rao, who has been wanting to be the Chief minister after Anjiah's unceremonious sack.

Anjiah, who until his removal was seen worshipping Indira Gandhi's heavily garlanded portrait morning and evening, too has his own designs. He has lost all respect for her; she is no more his Goddess. He has not met her after he ceased to be CM and may soon float his own party.

Dissidence is smouldering in Karnataka with its own share of Bhaskar Raos and Anjiahs. Over 100 MLAs in the ruling party are defectors. Their loyalties to her are skin-deep. Some of these leaders have been secretly hobnobbing with her inveterate foe Devraj Urs. The fierce faction fighting between Gundu Rao, PCC chief Rathod and have-not Bangarappa has sullied her disciplinarian image.

The running battle between Antulay and Bhosale in Maharashtra has paralysed the party and the administration. The Chief minister's writ is confined to his posh Malabar Hill mansion and his image in public is that of a man with a bad character. Sharad Pawar supporters who defected from their leader en masse and joined the ruling party are people with dual loyalty. They would any day cross over with equal swiftness.

The situation in Bihar, U.P., Orissa, Punjab and Haryana is not less disturbing. Faction fight is the order of the day; corruption has gone down to the grassroots level.

The situation, however, has not yet gone beyond her control. As a leader of unquestionable organisational abilities she can still put the house in order. She can indeed create a new party with a sense of direction. What must be done?

First, certain criteria should be evolved for selecting Chief ministers. They should not be handpicked or imposed. People of integrity with comparatively clean image should be given the change to prove their worth. The ruling party has certainly not run out of such men.

Once they are selected, they should be given a chance to control and run the government without interference from the centre. They should work within certain parameters; they must enjoy the respect and confidence of the High Command. Dissidence or factionalism should be put down with a heavy hand.

Second, the PCC chiefs and the Chief ministers should not be allowed to function as rivals but as a team. The PCC chief should not be less equal to the Chief minister. Each state must have its own disciplinary committee, and its verdict should be final.

Third, the party from the AICC downward should be reorganised with fresh elections. At least 50 per cent of the elected members from the DCC to the AICC level must belong to the weaker sections, Harijans, Adivasis and minorities.

Fourth, the Youth Congress should be made a cadre-based organisation with a definite programme. Its place in the AICC should be as important as it was during Sanjay's time. It must be a force dedicated to fight against economic and social evils with the full patronage of the High Command.

Fifth, there should be a moratorium on corruption. The party must have a powerful anti-corruption cell headed by the party president. Reports of corruption against Central and state ministers should be immediately and thoroughly probed. No protection whatsoever should be given to a person found guilty of corruption. He should be expelled from the party and publicly exposed.

Indira Gandhi can control the party and the government and rule the country as long as she is alive if she succeeds in rooting out corruption even half of what prevails.

No society can be and has ever been pure like dew, but a dash of purity does make it worth living. It is not necessary to be as corrupt as most of the men in the ruling party are. The party can raise funds if and when necessary, but raising 'funds' should not be the only purpose of the people in power.

The people have faith in her. They have not lost hope in her, and they know she can act if she wants. What then prevents her?

Current 10.04.1982.
pp. (1 + 22)

Girilal Jain and Ayub Syed discuss Indira Gandhi

The defeat of Indira Gandhi in the two southern states has sent shock waves in the ruling circles. How did it happen? Why did it happen? The question mark is writ large on the face of every congressman. They have the answer. But they dare not face it.

Girilal Jain, Editor, Times of India and Ayub Syed discuss in depth the how and why of it.

Ayub Syed: We are passing through an interesting phase. Indira Gandhi appeared to be invincible a year ago and it seemed the country stood by her. But in the last six months the situation has begun to change. I would not say as yet that there is an anti-Indira wave, but wherever I go in the country I find well-meaning people getting utterly disillusioned with her performance, especially in the Congress ruled states. Her post Janata slogan that she would give the country 'a government that works' has boomeranged.

My anxiety is that if a leader of her stature cannot fulfil her promises, who else can. I don't find any other leader in the country who can take an integrated view of India's needs—from Kashmir to Kerala and from Assam to Gujarat. This is disturbing, because our hopes of an economic and social revolution under her leadership have been dashed.

Girilal Jain: I agree with what you say in fact, during my editorship for over five years. I have supported Indira Gandhi in the belief that she is irreplaceable at least for the time being. But it seems to me that to an extent we have to distinguish between her and the party she leads. I do not wish to go into the reasons for the decay of the Congress party. We can discuss this question separately, but I have no doubt that it is facing an irreversible decline.

I am not at all surprised by the miserable performance of the Congress governments in the states. As a friend of Indira Gandhi herself put it to me, not long ago, 'the people selected to head governments are either corrupt Chief ministers who can somehow manage to keep the party with them or incompetent but relatively honest Chief ministers who cannot keep the party with them and, therefore, face dissidence and revolt.'

But the question now is whether the people will any longer make this distinction between her and the party. You will remember that the people did make such a distinction in 1967 when they gave the Congress party a majority, even if a small one, in the Lok Sabha, but defeated it in all north Indian states. From 1967 to 1969 you could move from Simla to Calcutta without going through any Congress-run state.

Ayub: In my view she is directly responsible for what the Chief ministers have been doing in the states. For instance Antulay, Gundu Rao, and so on. None of them was elected by the legislative parties. They are all her nominees.

Giri: There can be no doubt that Indira Gandhi must accept responsibility for the poor performance and the misdeeds of the Congress Chief ministers. But I am not personally convinced that if the choice had been left to the legislative parties, the result would have been very different.

That apart, Indira Gandhi has taken on herself responsibilities which she is in no position to discharge. She has no machinery whereby she can keep an eye on the performance of Chief ministers on a day-to-day basis. Our structure is such that while Chief ministers can blame her for denying them the necessary freedom to perform well, they in fact enjoy enormous power. Antulay is a case in point. He could do almost anything he liked in Maharashtra. All that he had to do was to profess loyalty to Indira Gandhi and her sons, first Sanjay and then Rajiv.

Ayub: I am not worried about the emergence of regionalism because this is an outcome of the lopsided policies followed by the centre. What worries me is the impending disintegration of the Congress. A country of India's diversity has to have more than one political party with a national outlook. No opposition party, including BJP, Janata and Communist, has succeeded in establishing a national ethos. Their range, depth and width is confined to certain pockets.

The Congress is the only party with roots in every city and every village of the country, and it is in the doldrums. Its collapse is bound to have an immensely adverse impact on the democratic process. And even the Parliamentary system may receive a severe jolt. There is still time for Indira Gandhi to put her house in order, but she seems to have lost the elan.

Giri: We have to wait and see if she has still the will and the capacity to convince the people that she is in earnest. Right now the people do not seem to think that she is keen to stop the disintegration of the Congress.

It is self-evident that we do not have any other truly national party. That is why we have this upsurge of local, religious and regional sentiments, as witnessed in Assam, in Punjab among the Akalis, in Andhra, and to some extent even in Karnataka.

Ayub: I am afraid if the Congress disintegrates Indira Gandhi will also disintegrate with it. She has completely identified herself with the Congress.

Giri: The Indian political system is undergoing rapid transformation. It can be said with a measure of certainty that its shape is going to be very different from the Congress-dominated system, which we have been used to for the past 35 years. Whether this will be good or bad for the country it is too early to say. We should not rush to conclusions.

The Congress party under Nehru was able to cater to the regional sentiment and at the same time preserve its national character. Under Indira Gandhi this has clearly not been possible. Her opponents hold her mainly responsible for this failure of the Congress. I take the view that she has wilfully narrowed her own choice. Even so, we must admit that she also reflects the reality on the ground.

The people want several things—national unity, regional and religious identities, and a moral political order which is also representative. It is not possible to say whether these demands can be and are likely to be reconciled in one system or whether we are once again moving towards confusion and even chaos.

By temperament, I am an optimist and I believe things will work out in the end, though the process may take as long as a decade or even two.

The critical battle is going to be fought in the Hindi-speaking states. Right now, we cannot even name the final contestants. If some organisation emerges as the spokesmen of the Hindi-speaking people, then the prospect for the country may not be dismal. But if such a party does not emerge, we may be in for trouble.

Ayub: I am not a pessimist either. But I feel that one of the reasons for the present mess is the total concentration of power in one individual. The power structure built by Jawaharlal Nehru and also sustained by Indira Gandhi for some years has evaporated. Both the government and the ruling party are controlled by one person. This is something physically impossible. A country of 700 million people cannot be controlled and governed by one individual. The situation has degenerated to such an extent that even if she wants to delegate powers she cannot do it.

Most of her partymen whom she has picked up for inclusion in her cabinet and for appointment as Chief ministers are of poor quality, besides the fact that they have no commitment. I think her one big mistake was to make loyalty the only test for promotion. Loyalty is necessary, but it cannot be a synonym for sycophancy. The result is that competence, efficiency and integrity among party leaders are not considered necessary at all.

Giri: There cannot be any question that Indira Gandhi has approached problems since she returned to office in 1980 in a haphazard manner. I have written any number of articles to make the point that it is wholly unjust for her to discriminate between the so-called original faithfuls in her party and the so-called late-comers. In this process, talent and integrity have obviously been sacrificed at the altar of professed loyalty. Mind you, this loyalty has not been genuine. People have professed loyalty to her in order to be allowed to feather their own nests.

Having said this, I may add that the party is in such a bad shape that it is irrelevant to talk of concentration of power in one person. Indira Gandhi is in a sense a victim of the so-called concentration of power because all the blame for the failures of other Congress leaders finally come to her. In another sense she has become a kind of idol to which one offers flowers in the expectation of an immediate reward.

The issues in our age are also too complex to admit of that kind of concentration of power. Even dictators like Hitler, Stalin had colleagues who felt free to give them honest advice. Indira Gandhi no longer has such colleagues. You can imagine the result. What we have witnessed in her case is not concentration of power except in a very superficial sense, we have witnessed the virtual abdication of power in the deeper sense decisions are taken on an adhoc basis or out of considerations which are improper. It is the case of an inverted pyramid with the person who is supposed to be standing at the top being crushed under it. That is what has been happening to Indira Gandhi.

Ayub : I think she is, in a way, justified in emphasising loyalty in the party in view of her bitter experience in 1977-80 when almost all her advisers betrayed her. But she has extended the same test to bureaucrats and judges and to the cabinet. That is clearly wrong.

Giri: The trouble is institutions including the Cabinet have been devalued. Some adventurers with some right connections use her name and order ministers and bureaucrats to do whatever they like. You will agree that this is not concentration of power but abuse of power.

You must have read Andre Malraux's Anti Memoirs in which he has written at length on his discussions with Jawaharlal Nehru. Nehru had an obsession to build and sustain institutions because his reading of India's history had convicted him that the country has suffered grievously for want of stable institutions and there can be no doubt that a similar lack of a strong institutional framework would be responsible for even more serious troubles in the future. We are now living in a world which is far more cruel than at any time in the past.

Ayub : I am worried about the most important institution which has been devalued—the Congress party. It has not had internal elections for the past 13 years, the Working Committee and the parliamentary board seldom meet, the AICC session is hardly held. In the past these were important forums where important decisions used to be discussed by the people who felt involved in the affairs of the party. But today I feel that whatever happens to Indira Gandhi the party will disintegrate, and that will greatly hurt the country.

Giri: You hold Indira Gandhi directly, personally and entirely responsible for the decay of the party. I have seen the process of decay in the Congress commence in Nehru's time. The process was not so visible because stalwarts thrown up by the freedom struggle continued to dominate the political scene at the centre as well as in most of the states. The split in 1969 accelerated the process. The second split in 1978 almost completed the process.

I am afraid I am one of those people who believe that it is not possible to revive and renew the Congress party. Yet it is possible for Indira Gandhi to pick up honest candidates and get them elected. They may in course of time form what in effect will be a new party even if they continue to call themselves by the old name. This is a crisis situation which calls for drastic measures.

Ayub: In a democratic system the most important element is the political organisation. As it happens Indira Gandhi has no reason to go out of her party in search of men of integrity and ability. A whole lot of them exist in the Congress. Only they have been ignored and pushed aside.

Giri: I have no difficulty in accepting your proposition. There are such men in the party, and even if they are not there then they should be brought in if we are to escape a dangerous political vacuum. In fact, such a vacuum has already arisen.

Ayub: I think 32 years are enough for a system to justify itself. As we see the situation, the promises made on the eve of independence have not been fulfilled. I don't agree that our system has failed. The people have repeatedly asserted themselves in favour of democratic norms. They are conscious that there is no alternative to the system founded by the Congress leaders on the eve of the independence. From 1952 onwards it has been the victory of the principles of socialism, secularism and democracy.

Now, it seems the people have greater faith in the tenets than the leaders. They have endorsed the Congress party's economic policies, especially since the Avadi resolution. The one reason for disillusionment is that the

Congress leaders, including Indira Gandhi, have made half-hearted efforts to implement these policies.

A major thrust of these policies has been to remove disparities and inequalities, but it is a fact that the rich have grown richer and the poor poorer. The weaker sections remain weak, the lot of the Harijans has never been worse, while the minorities continue to suffer from a feeling of insecurity. I think Indira Gandhi, instead of considering their problems from a social and human angle, has reduced them to a personalised affair.

Her post-1969 policy has been to demolish, one after the other, the leaders of these communities. She sought to become herself the leader of the weaker sections, Muslims and Harijans. There is nothing wrong in this. But how much can one person do? During Nehru's time there were people in the party who reflected the feeling of these sections of society and he was able to understand their problems. The policy of maintaining vote banks may not prove useful any more. Poverty has no religion or caste.

Giri: I agree that parliamentary democracy is best suited to our needs. I also agree with you that there is a consensus on certain broad principles such as secularism, socialism and parliamentary democracy which the Congress has so for embodied.

You and I are agreed that the Congress is in a very bad shape and that the chances of reviving it are not bright. So in a sense we have to look beyond the Congress in spite of our involvement with it for many, many years. I ceased to be a member of the party some two decade ago. You are still a member and very much involved in it. But regardless of our personal predisposition in favour of the party, we are left with no choice but to look beyond it. When I make the attempt. I see no individual or party on the horizon ready to take the place of the grand old party. That is the meaning of the crisis of which we speak these days.

Developments in Andhra and Karnataka have only confirmed our worst fears. They cannot have come as a surprise to anyone who has been witnessing the drift of events carefully.

Ayub: Talking of Andhra and Karnataka, if I could assess the situation correctly, it was the revolt by the poor of all beliefs against the khadi-clad nouveau riche. It was definitely a revolt against corruption and arrogance. It is strange that Indira Gandhi continues to deny corruption amongst her partymen. But it is a universal belief that most of her partymen have amassed wealth. The rot can be stemmed if she curbs corruption with an iron hand. But then charity should begin at home.

Giri: To use the phrase which George Fernandes popularised, many post-1969 Congress luminaries have become used to a five-star culture. This is an affront not only to the poor, but also to the middle-classes who cannot afford to go to these places for lunches and dinners. There can be no question that this has been a major factor for the loss of support of the Congress.

Ayub: I met N.T. Rama Rao the day after his victory. I asked him what was the major cause for his victory. He said it was a victory against corruption. He did not attribute his success to any regional sentiment. A similar view was expressed by Ramakrishna Hegde in Bangalore. These two Chief ministers believe that they would be able to remove corruption, and if they succeed, their position will be unassailable in those states.

If the Congress party goes out of power in Maharashtra, Gujarat or Bihar, it will again be a vote against corruption and inefficiency. If Indira Gandhi is not in a position to get rid of her corrupt colleagues and launch a war against corruption, she cannot save the Congress party from disintegration.

Girl: I do not have much to add to what you have said except that when a region gains political expression as Andhra has in N.T. Rama Rao's Telugu Desam, then that instrument somehow digs in and strengthens itself. So whatever be the causes which have led to the defeat of the Congress in the two southern states, we are in fact now face to face with regional parties which will be guided broadly by their perceptions or the interest of the people of the states rather than of the country as a whole.

Ayub: One more thing that has been worrying me—Indira Gandhi's use of religion to meet her political ends. I should not call it religion; it is superstition and obscurantism. *Tantriks, sadhus, sanyasis, fakirs, brahmcharis,* godmen have been having a field day. I cannot convince myself that the daughter of Nehru can take recourse to these most unscientific and irrational acts.

Her liking for them increases during elections. It looks odd that in the morning she advises an impressive assemblage of Indian scientists in Tirupati to endeavour to create a scientific temper and a rationalistic approach, and soon after that she rushes to every shrine, *mutt* and *dargha* in the area. I am irreligious, but I respect all religions and I think religion is much more than racketeerism enacted by the fake *gurus*.

Giri: I would not like to answer this question. Indira Gandhi's beliefs and practices are her personal affair. If as you say, she has tried to use religion for political purposes, she has not been particularly successful.

Ayub: In the midst of elections in Karnataka and Andhra she visited a place where the two Shankaracharyas from Andhra and Karnataka addressed a large gathering. They asked the people to strengthen her hands.

Giri: I will take the view that the two Shankaracharyas genuinely believe that she is the best bet for the country.

Ayub: I think 1983 will be the year of turmoil, instability and economic stagnation. I do not want to sound like a prophet of doom. But I do not see any ray of hope. The whole thing has gone topsy turvy. The priorities are wrong. The Asiad was an achievement, but at what cost? And was it not a wrong priority?

The festival of India was yet another waste of time, money and energy, and it too was a wrong priority. The forthcoming nonaligned and Commonwealth conferences are also exercises in futility. The colossal waste of time and money is unpardonable. The more she indulges in these kinds of acts, the farther will she be from reality.

Giri: I do not agree with this approach. A great nation like India expresses herself in many ways. Asiad was one such expression. So was the festival of India in London and so will be the two conferences. When a political order gets into trouble, it cannot follow that the nation begins to have a low opinion of itself.

India is potentially a great economic, military and cultural power. She should send out waves of ideas to other nations. As for the prospect of a difficult 1983, I agree with you. Indeed, I will add that we are going to have a difficult period so long as a new political order not emerge.

Current, 29.01.1983.
pp. (17 + 18 + 27)

Politics takes to the street

Confrontation, Violence, hangs overhead like thick, dark clouds threatening to burst any moment. As the elections draw nearer the threat to law and order, peace and security is becoming more ominous.

The meeting of the National Integration Council, held after a lapse of four years, ought to have normally soothed ruffled tempers and set the pace for regional and national harmony. But it witnessed a slanging match between the opposition and the Prime Minister—in fact it widened the chasm.

The events are inexorably leading to a situation reminiscent of the pre-Emergency days. It seems to suit the ruling as well as the opposition parties. Both unfortunately have assumed that an atmosphere of confrontation is necessary for a greater involvement of the masses in the 'democratic process' and that the battle of the ballot has to be fought with no holds barred.

The fact is that both the Congress and the opposition parties stand exposed. They have lost credibility. The people laugh at them, at their gimmicks, at their hypocrisy, at their double standards, at their lack of values and at their lust for power and pelf. Politicians as a class have lost their honour. They are held in contempt, and rightly so.

The NIC meeting was turned into a rehearsal for the impending battle. The Prime Minister's sermon that she was opposed to violence and that she would not permit the breakdown of law and order was pooh poohed by all the non-Congress Chief ministers and opposition leaders.

Karnataka's Ramakrishna Hegde accused her of devaluing politics, reducing democracy to a farce and fomenting violence. Looking into her face, the diminutive, bearded chief remarked:

"You are directly responsible for these ills. National integration does not mean only communal harmony. It is not possible to believe that the Prime Minister, who is also the Congress president, cannot exercise her authority on her party functionaries who have been spearheading violence not only in my state but also in Kashmir and Bengal and would soon do it in Andhra."

He is convinced that the Congress is behind Rajkumar Fans Association, and having failed to dislodge him through horse-trading it has planned to create a law and order situation.

Kashmir's Farooq Abdullah took over from Hegde to tell the Prime Minister that his life was in danger and pleaded with her to advice her followers to call off the agitation because "it is widening the gulf between different communities" and great damage is being done to the process of national integration.

"I am being branded anti-national. Can anyone provide a shred of evidence to prove the charge," he asked.

The whole country is witnessing the despicable ding-dong battle between Farooq and his Congress rivals. They are after his scalp and he knows it.

The 'value' of a National Conference MLA has gone up to Rs. 20 lakh but nobody dare defect. "The people will lynch him. I have shown great restraint. I now say, enough is enough. I appeal to the Prime Minister to restore sanity to her partymen in Kashmir."

Farooq is hitting back not only with words but by deeds as well. He got half a dozen Congress agitators shot down, his followers burnt Indira

Gandhi's effigy in Srinagar's *Badshah Chowk* with a huge crowd clapping and dancing. The atmosphere in the valley is surcharged with violence and his unrestrained utterances are adding fuel to the fire.

He flew to Delhi for the NIC meeting after unleashing a virulent attack on the Congress. He called them "thieves and liars," and threatened : "I shall ask my soldiers to make the Congress behave and if I am killed thousands and lakhs of Farooq Abdullahs would spring up from every drop of my blood."

The Congress is getting ready for a similar confrontation in Communist dominated Bengal. Violence is in Bengali blood. A spark can ignite flames.

Last week the Congress held the first rehearsal in a quick sharp act of lawlessness. It erupted following the arrest of youth leaders Priya Ranjan Das Munshi, and Somen Mitra on the charge of stoning Farooq's car at Calcutta Airport.

The intensity of the sudden violence took the Jyoti Basu government by surprise. Basu blamed the "Congress gangsters" for the violence and the police for their laxity in controlling the situation. He warned the Congress "toughs" to stay off the streets, or else he would call his party cadres to retaliate.

The agitation was immediately withdrawn on the orders of the Congress High Command, but the state Congress has decided to launch a fortnight's mass movement from January 30 to "save democracy, save Bengal."

Basu is not Hegde or Farooq. BPCC chief Ananda Gopal Mukherjee has charged him of "precipitating a serious situation which might lead to a civil war."

In Andhra the atmosphere of confrontation may not be that easily created as the ruling Telugu Desam truly rules the roost. Its chief NT Rama Rao's popularity has gone to the roots. Yet, the Pradesh Congress has drawn elaborate plans to whip up a 'mass' movement.

And Punjab might overshadow the Congress-opposition confrontation in these states if the '*Khalistanis*' seriously decide to implement their threat to 'do or die' and set up a 'parallel government'.

The Akali Dal youth influenced by their extremist leader Sant Bhindranwale have already declared the Congress their Enemy No. 1. Thousands of Sikh youth are kept in readiness to lead the 'morcha' to its logical end—realisation of a Punjab with Sikhs as rulers.

Punjab has as much potential for violence as Bengal. The Akali action is scheduled to begin after Republic Day.

Bombay's Bal Thackeray has been sharpening his claws. After a smooth and fruitful flirtation with the Congress, the Shiv Sena lion has come out of its den to roar. He has threatened to stall the entry of Indira Gandhi and President Zail Singh into Bombay if the Karnataka-Maharashtra boundary dispute was not solved in a month.

"The endurance of Marathi-speaking people is fast approaching breaking point and it will find its expression in violence on this issue," he threatens.

The multilingual city of Bombay, which has been bereft of violence for quite some time, was stunned to hear. Thackeray speak: "The Sena will resort to its own methods, which will not be democratic. The Sainiks should arm themselves with swords, pistols, revolvers and sten-guns to fight for justice."

The Conclavists are marching in the same direction. Led by Chandra Shekhar they have decided to start a mass movement from the middle of Fabruary to 'highlight' the people's problems. He fears Indira Gandhi is once again pushing the country towards Emergency.

"All over the country there is great concern over the manner in which Indira Gandhi is making persistent efforts to disrupt and destabilise non-Congress governments in the states. Farooq is her special target."

The Janata chief would personally lead the mass agitation against her with the support of the Left parties, and "in every town and city we will raise our powerful voice of protest and make it clear that 1984 is not 1975 and that we will not permit her to carry out her diabolical design."

The National Democratic Alliance is not lagging behind. Both Charan Singh and Vajpayee will jointly tour the country to explain the 'charge sheet' which they have prepared to the masses and expose "Indira Gandhi's acts of omission and commission."

All this is high-level confrontation. The masses have had enough of it. If the opposition has the strength, the credibility and the acceptance it should wait for the D-day, and Indira Gandhi too should instruct her party-men to have patience and wait for the ballot box to decide the future of their party.

Current, 28.01.1984.
pp. (1 + 3)

C. Rajiv as Political Successor

Amethi will vote for 'Izzat'

Amethi: It's a cake-walk. Rajiv Gandhi exudes confidence as he campaigns with aplomb from village to village in the scorching sun. His speeches are short, his manner is simple, his approach straight, and he speaks no politics.

It's a smooth election. No emotions, very little slogan-shouting, few banners and buntings, and no posters except that of Indira Gandhi with her powerful hand raised high. I did not find any poster bearing Rajiv's picture in the constituency.

Party functionaries are not encouraged to build the personality cult and a distinction is made between sycophants and genuine workers. Racketeers and professional 'electioneers' have been kept out.

It's a neat and clean campaign. Rajiv very politely turned down offers from his partymen—Union minister, Chief ministers, state ministers and known wheeler-dealers, to visit Amethi and help him in the campaign.

Most of them had thought it an excellent opportunity to go close to him, but their entry into Amethi is totally banned. Strict vigil is kept on party leaders on 'unofficial' tours of the area. The Sanjay men too are conspicuous by their absence except Sanjay Singh, the MLA from Amethi.

The Youth Congress had planned to make it its own election and put up a grand show, but Rajiv thought nobody should be allowed to take the credit for his victory except himself and of course Indira Gandhi, the supreme vote-catcher. Only youth Congress Chief Gulam Nabi Azad could manage to convince Rajiv of his utility. He toured parts of the constituency.

Rajiv who visited Amethi for the first time—on the day of his nomination—and knew very little of its economic and political problems, lost no time in chalking out his campaign. He placed his cousin Arun Nehru, MP from adjoining Rae Bareli, in charge of it. UP minister Veer Bahadur Singh was asked to assist. The planning had, in fact, begun much before Rajiv had filed his papers, and Arun Nehru had told his confidants that Rajiv would definitely contest from Amethi.

The constituency is divided into about 50 sectors and each sector is placed under the charge of a trusted party worker. The control office at Goriaganj receives information from all over the constituency and young men manning it act in consultation with Arun and Singh. Rajiv's tour programmes are set by Arun and the local MLA concerned.

Some of Rajiv's close friends including Shivenbahdur Singh, a young Lok Sabha member from MP, and Dhruv Sahani, a budding industrialist from Delhi, are there to lend a helping hand or just to be with him.

"I am not a politician, nor have I any political ambitions. I am here because I just could not be away while my friend is engaged in his first political battle," Sahani says puffing his expensive cigarette.

The absence of hordes of congressmen who would have lent colour to the campaign had they been allowed to enter Amethi has made all the difference. The heat too has taken away the election heat. Rajiv addresses small gatherings in the mornings and evenings. He is accompanied by half a dozen local workers and the MLA in whose constituency he is conducting his campaign. The crowds vary from five hundred to one thousand including children.

I heard one such speech. Hearing him once it is not necessary to hear him again because he talks of no major issues. He knows that the electorate wants to be assured that projects started by Sanjay and promises made by him during the last election will be fulfilled. Rajiv speaks slowly and selects his words carefully with no jargon. He begins :

"*Matao, behno aur bhaiyo*—you had elected Sanjay with a huge majority and given him your love and affection. He is no more. I am contesting for the Lok Sabha from here primarily because of the overwhelming desire of the people of Amethi.

"It is indeed a very backward area. The nearby Rae Bareli has progressed but not Amethi. That is why Sanjay had decided to represent it in the Lok Sabha and devote his life and time for its development. Now the responsibility has fallen on my shoulders.

"The developmental work had started here in 1976. Construction of roads had begun. A big industrial complex was planned in Jagdishpur, an IIT college was to come up and many more things were to come up. But in 1977 the government changed and the Janata stopped all those schemes.

"These projects were launched by Sanjay not for himself but for you. The water from the canal would have benefited you, electricity would have brought light in your homes and factories, and young boys and girls would have gone to college and the factories would have brought prosperity to your area.

"Why did the Janata stop all these development programme? It was an act against you. They may talk big, but you should know it was they who put a spoke in the wheel of progress.

"Now they will again come to you. They will make promises. But you should remember what they had said earlier and what they did later. They just talk. It is easy to talk, but difficult to perform. They will come to you. You should listen to them, treat them nicely, give them a cup of tea, but the answer to their gimmick should be made by you on June 14 through your vote. You should teach them a lesson in such a forceful manner that they dare not come to you after June 14 (clapping).

"All the projects started by Sanjay will be fulfilled. It is the promise of the district Congress and it is our promise. But the government alone cannot bring prosperity unless you also contribute. The government can give water to your fields, but you will have to work on them.

"As your representative, it will be my duty to get your demands met by the government. But as you know, there are lots of projects and the government does not have enough financial resources to meet them. So you should not expect too much from the government. Yes I can assure you that we will make the maximum efforts to come up to your expectations.

"Your vote is very precious. You have earned it after a hard struggle. Each one of you—rich, poor, peasant and worker—has one vote and you should use it judiciously. On June 14 you should come out in your full strength and cast your vote. It is said there will be a Congress wave that day. You should turn it into a tornado. Thank you."

His main rival Sharad Yadav, who began his campaign here, is a firebrand socialist who was the first Janata candidate to win the 1977 election from Jabalpur. Now he is a Lok Dal nominee. He tours round the constituency and gathers crowds. But Yadav uses all the socialist jargon in his armory and makes long winded, vociferous speeches attacking "dynastic rule" and giving warnings of a disaster if his opponent was elected.

He is abusive, and Rajiv's militant workers, specially Sanjay Singh's young team of Thakurs had to be restrained from retaliating. Rajiv feels the Lok Dal workers want to provoke his followers and involve them in violent clashes. "I have advised my workers not to lose their temper, not to be tempted and pay Yadav in his own coin," Rajiv says emphatically.

The Amethi electorate places itself in a special category. In the 1980 poll they voted the "future Prime Minister:", and when he died Kunwar Anwar Ali Khan said: "We lost our pride. We felt like orphans. All our hopes were dashed to the ground and we did not know whom to go to. Now this young man has come to make our dream come true. And we must thank Indiraji for this magnanimous gesture. Which mother would offer her other and the only surviving son for the sake of the people of Amethi, please tell me."

The sturdy Rajput Muslim breaks down. "When Sanjay died," he continues, "each of us thought a death had taken place in our own home. There was darkness all around. But now this young man has come. We hope there will be light once again."

The privileged Amethians who are nobody's slaves—they have defeated Sanjay in 1977—have somehow got in their mind that by voting Rajiv they are electing the "future Prime Minister". "We are a spoiled lot", a young tea shop owner in Jayes, said with a big grin, "we may be poor but we have a sense of pride. If the people of Rae Bareli can elect or defeat Indira Gandhi, we too can make or unmake the future of the ruling party."

"Is it because you sell more tea that more visitors will come?" a bus conductor interjected mischievously.

"No. No. We care two hoots for money. It is the people in the cities who bother about money. Richness does not necessarily bring happiness. What ultimately counts is the sense of pride. It is *izzat* and not wealth. Tell me which other area will be able to boast that Rajiv belongs to it?"

It is '*izzat*' and not politics or ideology. It is development and not caste. It is in fact competition with the 'very well' developed Rae Bareli.

People in Taloi, an Assembly segment who generally favour non-congressmen appear this time determined to outdo other assembly segments of Rajiv's Parliamentary constituency because of an "unusual promise". Rajiv have been saying in his speeches that he would launch his development schemes from the area which gives him the highest number of votes. The competition is on in other areas as well.

The educated youth as well as the illiterate farm hand have pinned their hopes on Rajiv's victory. The proposed industrial estate in Jagdishpur is expected to change the economic face of Amethi. The suggested fertiliser plant may not come, but a unit of Hindustan Aeronautics has been assured. Bharat Electricals has been in the process of finalising plans to put up a huge complex and a big paper mill too may come up.

In private group meetings Rajiv assures people that he would avoid involvement in national issues and give most of his time to the development of his constituency. "Amethi first" will be his motto, because the nation will judge his success or failure from his work in his constituency. He does believe in "hard work" and some kind of productive activity. His constituents are sure he will succeed because of his unique position.

His modesty and simplicity has endeared him to his constituents. They believe power has been chasing him and he has sacrificed his personal and family life by agreeing to enter public life.

"His victory is as sure as the rising of the sun the next morning but our effort is to send him to Parliament with a massive mandate", Jagdish Parshad Shukla, a Gauriganj school teacher remarked enthusiastically.

It will be mistake to pass judgements on Rajiv at this stage. He has just entered public life. How he will shape his political career or what will be his performance in Parliament is yet to be seen. In fact, he is justifiably unsure of himself. He was not cut for the role thrust upon him.

Born in a family of traditional politicians, he had a distinct dislike for the run of the mill politicians. This is perhaps the one reason why he has kept out the young and tough Sanjay men, and heavily bends on his own friends none of whom has been in politics. His idea is that politics should not be left to politicians alone.

He is indeed a family man. He definitely shuns pomp. His wife, Sonia, and children Rahul and Priyanka, flew in a commercial flight from Delhi to Lucknow. No VIP front seat for her. At Palam, Sonia checked in herself, relaxed in the passengers' lounge and passed through the security hazards.

At the Lucknow airport, Rajiv was there to receive her. He had driven with a personal friend in a private white Ambassador. He did not rush to the tarmac as the plane landed but waited in the passengers' lounge.

The people at the airport treated him and his family in the routine manner. No running about or the usual excitement. He hugged his wife and kissed her on the forehead publicly and nobody even noticed it. The airport officials treated him as any other visitor to the airport, and his wife any other passenger travelling with them. Sonia and children had flown to Lucknow to spend the weekend with him.

He avoids publicity. He would prefer not to meet the news-hounds and he will not be unhappy if his name does not appear in the newspapers. Not that he dislikes the Fourth Estate. It is his shyness. Also, he does not have much to say because there is nothing much to add to what his mother says. He does not want to be presumptuous or loud-mouthed.

"I do not want it to be a formal interview, not with you at least. Let us talk", he suggested when I asked him for an interview. There may be questions which he may not like to answer and it should not be assumed that he is the paragon of wisdom and that he has solutions for all the problems.

The interview was brief as he did not want to commit himself to controversial issues on the eve of the elections. But he promised a long chat after the poll.

In his first interview after entering politics, Rajiv Gandhi gives a glimpse of his mind. His advice to young MPS popularly known as Sanjay-men is, "Work hard, don't run after position." He himself has not fixed his eyes on any position either.

His reply to the most important question in the minds of the people.

Would you like to take some responsible position in the party, say the General Secretaryship?
Really, I don't know. How can I say, I'm so new in politics and the party. I cannot say anything now . . .

You became a member of the party only last week.
Yes, this is how it happened. I'm in the midst of an election. How can I think of anything, least of all the General Secretaryship of the party?

What about this younger group in Parliament which Sanjay had built? They appear quite frustrated, leaderless and rudderless. They feel they have been ignored completely. What will you do about them?
They appear quite happy. I have met a number of them—about 40 to 50. I don't think they are feeling too unhappy.

There is a feeling among them that after Sanjay's death they have been dumped and now it seems that they are looking up to you for leadership. Their loyalty to the Prime Minister remains beyond question. Will you take them under your wings?
I will help them whenever they come to me with specific issues or problems in their constituencies. I shall certainly help them.

Here I feel very strongly that nobody should be after office and run after positions. It is a question of work and hard work. You don't have to be a secretary or a president of some party unit, but the concentration has to be on work.

What are the major issues in Amethi?
The only issue at the moment is development. A lot of work was started in Amethi in 1976. It was stopped. It started again in 1980. Now we must see the fact that Amethi has got left behind. It is a very backward constituency. Effort is needed to bring it to the level of other districts of UP.

In this area people compare Amethi with Rae Bareli. They are aware that it being the Prime Minister's constituency a lot of attention was paid to it while the adjoining areas remained backward.
We should not forget that two assembly constituencies of Amethi fall in the Rae Bareli district. A lot is being done for Amethi too. For instance the whole area will be 100 per cent irrigated in a year or so.

Electricity is already 100 per cent, that is every village has electricity. But the complication is that co-ordination is needed among various government departments and the bottlenecks have to be removed. In this typical case, the Electricity Board has to do the wiring from the poles to the houses.

There was a suggestion for a big fertiliser plant in Amethi during Sanjay's time. I'm told it is being put off.
Yes, it was there. But now there is fresh thinking on it. It is said that the plant might cause pollution. But we shall compensate in other ways. We are trying to do a lot of things. I'll work in a particular village and try to understand its problems and think of solution—solutions such as solar heater and *gobar* gas.

Do you want to build a model village?
Not exactly a model village. But I would like to carry out certain experiments.

Do you plan to build a house in Amethi and stay there for longer periods?
I don't think I shall build a house, but I shall certainly nurse my constituency by visiting it very often.

You would like to develop a kind of emotional attachment to this area.
Not only that, but there has to be a working understanding of the people and their problems.

After all, you have decided to enter politics. What was the compelling factor?
The most compelling factor was that one generally looks at the situation and does not feel very happy. I did not want to sit and look at it. I thought: why should I not try and do something?

Were you not very much impressed by the pleas by Chief minister and ministers imploring you to join active politics?
That was there. But it was not that much. The most important thing was that you see something and you feel it could be better.

Personal conviction?
No, it was only a question of doing something. I have to see whether I would be able to do what I want to do.

In Parliament would you specialise in certain subjects?
No. I'll stick to Amethi at the moment.

But as a member of Parliament you would not be able to avoid certain issues. I understand you have been working on changing the archaic income-tax, sales-tax and other headaches in the world of finance?

I'm really not an expert in that. I will leave it to the people who are really qualified to grapple with the problem. The maximum I shall do is to have some study or discussion groups. I think it is basically a question of reducing road-blocks.

So many bureaucratic bottlenecks come in our way. They hamper progress. There are unnecessary controls over the functioning of the government. I call them obstructionists. Something will have to be done about them.

As a member of Parliament you would like to . . .

Arrey bhai, abhi kahan member of Parliament? *Abhi to* election *shuru hi hua hai. Dekhen kya hota hai* (How am I a member of Parliament? The election has just begun. Let us see what happens)—and he laughs heartily.

Current, 06.06.1981.
pp. (1 + 3)

Left turn for Congress again

An influential section in the ruling party is seriously thinking of reviving the 'Kumaramangalam Spirit' of the late 1960s which had boosted the sagging image of the Parliament. Hundreds of ex-Communists and leftists had joined the ruling party at Indira Gandhi's call to build a socialist society and implement her *Garibi Hatao* slogan.

But less than six years later, the Congress lost its ideological moorings with the rise of Sanjay Gandhi who began to weed out the left elements from the party with the ruthlessness of a Chanakya. The left got disillusioned with Indira Gandhi during and after Emergency. 1980 was Sanjay's year, and had he lived, he would have completed the right-turn.

The situation has changed. The visit of Congress general secretary Rajiv Gandhi to the Soviet Union and the kind of reception he was given there has opened new vistas of a broad understanding between the ruling party and the progressive and left elements in the country. Rajiv has no ideological hang-ups, but he is aware that a vast majority of the country's youth and the intelligentsia tilt towards the left. The sharp decline in the influence of the BJP and other rightist forces is an unmistakable indication of the new mood of the people, specially in the north.

The Soviet Union continues to be viewed by the country's progressives as the pillar of anti-imperialism and a staunch supporter of the democratic regimes in the Third World.

That Rajiv decided to pay his first independent political visit to the Soviet Union is of immense significance. His post-visit utterances will influence the thinking of thousands of his partymen and will also enable the leftists to make an assessment of this young man who occupies the second position in the ruling hierarchy.

In the Soviet assessment Indira Gandhi can serve the cause of Indo-Soviet relations much more effectively than the Communists of all hues and varieties and that her successor Rajiv Gandhi too can be a 'continuer' of the Nehru legacy.

He had extensive discussions with a number of Soviet ideologues including Komsomol boss V.M. Mishin. As head of the Soviet Youth organisation he is a weighty member of the politburo. A few days ago Indian Youth Congress chief Tariq Anwar too was Mishin's guest. Plans have been discussed of close co-operation between the IYC and Komsomol.

Interestingly Rajiv's visit to Moscow was preceded by a long meeting between Pranab Mukherjee and the communist party general secretary Rajeshwara Rao. They discussed the ways and means of paying the way for 'friendly collaboration' between the two parties.

Like the Congress, the CPI is divided. A section in the ruling party is undoubtedly scared of the party's tilt towards the left, while the pro-CPM faction in the CPI is opposed to any 'alliance' with the Indira Congress.

There is no possibility of CPI-CPM unity despite EMS Namboodiripad's visit to China and Jyoti Basu's current jaunt to Moscow. The CPI would definitely split on the issue of building a left image for the Indira Congress.

It did so three years ago when its founder, Comrade Shripad Amrut Dange, proclaimed Indira Gandhi as the paragon of progressivism, was expelled from his own party and floated a pro-Indira Communist party. But Dange failed to carry the left with him.

The party managers in the Congress have Rajiv's future in mind and they would like him to grow with a left image. They fear that Indira Gandhi has acquired the image of a pro-Hindu-superstitious, temple-going and godmen-worshipping woman. This may have endeared her to the masses, but has alienated the liberal and secular intelligentsia and those schooled in the Nehruvian way of life.

The hardcore left will not touch her with a pair of tongs, but the CPI and pro-Moscow elements will not hesitate to join hands with her if she snubs the chauvinist and pro-RSS Hindus. Her present stance, they fear, will antagonise the minorities, especially the Muslims and the Harijans.

Having humbled the BJP in its dens of Delhi and Jammu, she will now be amenable to a left stance. It will pay her in the long run, especially in states like Bengal and Kerala where the CPM is deeply entrenched.

A left image can do tremendous good to Rajiv, who at the moment has no image of any kind except that he is a 'good cultured' young man. Leftist scribes such as Mohit Sen and Nikhil Chakravarty are excellent image-builders and formidable slogan mongers.

The young men around Rajiv and the not so young do feel that he needs some kind of an image. He seems to be more acceptable to the left than Sanjay ever was, and a leftist magic wand is necessary to make him acceptable to the masses, who invariably get moved with socialist and leftist slogans.

The perceptible tilt to the left will be discernible after Rajiv returns from the Soviet Union. Reports from Moscow suggest that he is impressed by the Soviet leaders sincerity of purpose and their commitment to the continuation of the Nehru legacy—in other words, Rajiv as the next Prime Minister.

The Mohit Sen group, which is in a minority in the CPI, will undoubtedly press for a broad understanding with the ruling party—the kind of understanding that existed in the early 1970s. It is likely that the Rajeshwara Rao faction may also revise its stand after it is briefed by the Soviet leaders about their impression of Rajiv.

Such a move is inevitable. If Rajiv has to be acceptable to the people, he will have to be—to use a cliche—left of centre.

In a democratic set-up such as ours, a person aspiring to be at the helm of affairs has no choice but to be anti-Right. By nature and upbringing and tradition he cannot align himself with the chauvinists of any brand, while the hardcore left will never accept him.

The future strategy of the ruling party will be Rajiv-oriented because it has accepted him as the undisputed leader after Indira Gandhi. If 1980 was the year of Sanjay, 1985 will be the year of Rajiv. Let there be no mistake about it.

Current, 16.07.1983.
pp. (1 + 3)

Sycophants' manifesto
Congress on wrong key

"Like the morning sun you have risen. Congress, strong and people based as it is, will not fail to secure your future.

"We have nothing to claim from you now. You are our leader and honoured guest, the grave responsibility of maintaining the units and integrity of our society, civilisation and our country is yours. We pray you will succeed . . .

"Let Mahatmaji's humility, Jawaharlalji's foresight, Firoz Gandhi's progressive ideas and Smt. Indira Gandhi's right and courageous leadership qualities, coupled with the love of our countrymen, all combine to mould you into a true leader of the people.

"You pilot of the new age let success come your way and let you be the guiding star of the future . . .

"Do not misunderstand this to be an act of flattery. This is the first occasion when you will be present in a plenary session."

The excerpts alongside are from an advertisement issue in the national dailies by the publicity committee of the Indian National Congress on the eve of the 77th Plenary Session. The object of adulation is none other than Rajiv Gandhi.

With his ascendancy a new era of sycophancy has dawned, a new class of flatterers has emerged on the horizon. It has placed into insignificance the professional flatterers of ancient Persia.

Rajiv is undoubtedly a much respected and admired young man. He had entered politics under great pressure, and one of his own conditions was that he would not tolerate sycophancy. He must have blushed after seeing the ad, or was it published with his consent? If it was done with his knowledge, then grim days are ahead for the Congress, the country and the people. An organisation like the Congress should not be reduced into a doormat of a family.

At least Rajiv with his modern outlook should not permit a disaster. He must resist the temptation of being placed on the pedestal along with Gandhi and Nehru. There is no dearth of flatterers. They are available in legions. His mentor should not permit this young, sincere, well meaning man to be sucked into the system which is fast replacing the one so assiduously built by Gandhi and Nehru.

In a widely distributed leaflet signed by a number of young men including industrialist Salim Shervani, they compared him with the Polestar.

"The Poleastar's place in the universe is fixed. From a fixed position it gives a sense of direction to the universe. Mr. Rajiv Gandhi's leadership has also emerged like a Polestar and will be a perpetual source of strength for the organisation. He has provided us with a strong, dynamic, realistic leadership as per the aspirations of the countrymen. Fortuitously he has got a friend and a guide in the person of Mrs. Indira Gandhi."

The leaflet, widely distributed at the Plenary ended by adding: "Our sense of duty prompts us to propose Rajiv Gandhi's name for the next Congress President."

The situation may soon go beyond redemption. At the Plenary a group of flatterers from UP demanded that the "time has come when he should replace" his mother as President of the party. The demand was raised in all seriousness though knowing fully well that, for all practical purposes, he is the de facto chief of the august organisation. Another group in the party may demand that he be made Prime Minister in his mother's lifetime.

At the Plenary more people were 'eager' to meet him than the party President. They repeatedly showered praise on him in their orations. Poor working president Kamlapati Tripathi who set next to Indira Gandhi was not mentioned even once.

On his arrival at the Calcutta airport he was totally ignored by the volunteers who were after some Central ministers arriving by the same flight. In the plane, Tripathi was in the economy class while all the ministers and Chief ministers travelling with him were in the executive Class. And none bothered to turn his back and greet him. These are ominous portents.

At the Plenary it was Rajiv all the way. The session was undoubtedly held to proclaim him, as Priya Ranjan Das Munshi remarked, "the leader and hope of the nation." Rajiv does not appear to be confrontationist. He is soft spoken and mild-mannered, yet he has been advised to take on two most formidable leaders Jyoti Basu and Farooq Abdullah. Both enjoy a certain amount of popularity in the country, and both are known for their patriotism, dynamism and forthrightness.

Though Rajiv had helped in the drafting of the political resolution which clearly indicated a shift to the left of centre and sought to revive the 1969 spirit, his speeches stunned the Marxists and their sympathisers in the Congress.

Some leftists are still left in the party despite repeated 'purges', and a number of delegates from UP, Bihar and Kerala had come with the view of talking to him on the desirability of 'be friending' the Left.

Kerala's Antony would want the CPI to be an ally in the next election at least in his state, while men from the two populous northern states thought of making common cause with the left against the revivalist forces and specially the Lok Dal-BJP combine.

All these hopes were shattered when he launched a scathing attack on the Marxists and particularly Jyoti Basu. It became clear that he would go in for pitched battles with the Marxists in the next battle of the ballot and that he wouldn't bother if the CPI is pushed into the lap of the Marxists.

The Marxists handed over Calcutta to the Congress for the Plenary and did whatever they could to make it a trouble free session. They even wrote off the Rs. 17 lakh dues to the government left by Siddharth Shankar Ray on account of the last Congress session held in the city some 10 years ago. Jyoti Basu cancelled all his programmes to remain in the city and laid a red carpet to receive Indira Gandhi at the airport and presented her with a bouquet of red roses.

But the very next day, Rajiv attacked the Marxists saying that the West Bengal government had been 'squandering money on non-development plans.' Basu reacted sharply and told reporters "Rajiv is still a novice in politics and needs to learn a lot more before commenting on such things. How did he know that the Left Front government was squandering money? Could be specify a single instance? If he is so well informed, why does he not tell us how to prepare a budget?" He added, "It is very like Rajiv to make such statements because expenditure on education is a waste of money for the Congress."

From then on it was a slanging match between him and the Marxists, and the political resolution going soft on the Left lost its relevance. Bengal Congress activists including Ghani Khan and Das Munshi played a crucial role in pressurising him to take the Marxist bull by its horns.

Addressing the packed Netaji Stadium the next day he did real sabre-rattling, much to the delight of the Bengal delegates and other anti-left factions. He had asked his aides to compile facts and figures on the Left front government's 'squandermania' for his major speech.

Loudspeakers blared half an hour before the speech announcing the "epoch-making event". He came well-prepared, spoke in chaste Hindi and in a clear and firm tone, raising his modulated voice whenever needed.

"Jyoti Basu wants me to learn economics. Now, I want to tell him something about economics." Then he reeled out figures like a don. The Marxist government, which was to mobilise Rs. 455 crore on its own during the last five years, had managed to mobilise only 90 crore.

Under the Gadgil formula, the state was to receive Rs. 900 crore from the centre during the period. It received the same amount in four years. It had again overdrawn from the Reserve Bank of India to the tune of Rs. 340 crore and was still having a deficit of Rs. 150 crore.

The other states had resorted to overdrafts to increase their plan size but West Bengal had done the same to complete its previous year's plan.

While other states were utilising the loans from LIC, the Marxist government did not apply for these loans, nor have they proposed setting up any industrial units during the three financial years from 1981 onwards. Now it has asked for only Rs. 25 lakh after the "Congress ministers and MPs raised a hue and cry."

Maharashtra and UP had applied for LIC loans to the tune of Rs. 66 crore and Rs. 54 crore for water supply projects, but Jyoti Basu sought only Rs. 1.27 crore. These Marxists do not apply for loans and fail to spend whatever they get, but "cry to heaven that the centre is doing nothing for them."

The state's power-generating capacity has dropped to 740 MW against an installed capacity of 1840 MW. It received 95 per cent funds released by the Industrial Reconstruction Corporation for running sick units. "But how can that assistance be worth anything if the CITU unions force units to close down and there is no power to run the operational ones?" West Bengal spent only 17 paise of every rupee on plan programmes. The rest, I believe, is being distributed among the cadres."

In this state, he said in a raised voice, one has to be a Marxist sympathiser to get any work done, and a card-holder to get a job. Bengali culture is under attack and history is being twisted. Tagore has no place in the text-books. The Marxists have killed over a 1,000 congressmen since they came to power. Who would invest here as there is no power and the government is keen to close industries by encouraging adventurous unionism? "I presume that except at this Plenary venue, power is available nowhere else in the state".

Once again Rajiv raised his voice: "The days of the Marxists are numbered. It is evident from the recent by-election results".

Rajiv's was a virulent attack and he was cheered lustily after the 50 minute oration. Ghani Khan clapped and jumped like a baboon with sheer joy. Bengal congressmen had not expected such militancy from the young leader, it was a clarion call to them to get ready for the hustings.

Ghani Khan who aspires to lead the next non-Marxist government in the state once again shouted at the top of his voice: "If I had the power I would throw this Marxist government in the Bay of Bengal." This government had no moral values; they arrested me and treated me like a common criminal.

His followers led by Somen Mitra went wild when he said the only aim of the Marxists was to "annihilate" the Congress, but "they cannot destroy the Indira Philosophy."

By Bengali standards Ghani Khan lacks finesse and his boorish manners do not appeal to the Bhadralok. But in the eyes of the High Command he is the man of Bengal's destiny'. It is he who can 'liberate' Bengal from the Marxists. The prominence given to him at the Plenary was in contrast to the devaluation of his arch-rival Pranab Mukherjee.

The Marxists reeled under the attack but they finally pushed their prized tongue-lasher, Finance minister Ashok Mitra. "He is an ex-pilot. What does he know of economics? He had better learn more of economics, history and geography from his mother before pronouncing verdicts."

Ashok Mitra then pulled out figures to prove Rajiv wrong on each point. "The centre of which Rajiv talks as though it is his personal property is virtually run on the subsidies given by the states. Let Rajiv know that out of a total expenditure of Rs. 3,404 crore in 1982–83, Rs. 1,313 crore accounted for loan repayments to the centre, while Rs. 1,431 crore was spent on the on-plan sector and Rs. 659 crore on the plan sector.

"And let Rajiv know that the centre received from West Bengal as much as Rs. 6,052 crore under various heads. Of this, only Rs. 1,533 crore has been returned to the state government in different ways, while the huge balance is still lying at Delhi. This is exploitation. Much of the outstanding loans payable to the centre—now Rs. 6,500 crore, is the result of accumulation over the last 35 years, which include the Congress regimes too."

He challenged Rajiv's right to "lecture us about the propriety of expenditure". And "I am not willing to be hustled about by an outsider. And Rajiv should know that 'his' centre has printed currency notes for Rs. 10,000 crore in the last three years to meet its deficit financing needs, and "it does not befit him who spends Rs. 40 crore on a pleasure trip to Goa during CHOGM to blame us for non-plan expenditure."

Talking of licences, he added that there was hardly any licence issued by the centre to the industrialists "for which the ruling party did not demand a cut". Why should Rajiv Gandhi consider an expenditure of Rs. 250 crore on primary education in a year as wasteful? He should also know that while the Maharashtra Chief minister drew a sumptuary allowance of Rs. 7 lakh, the West Bengal Chief minister spent only Rs. 4,200 a year.

While Rajiv was engaged in a duel with the Marxists, Indira Gandhi breathed fire and brimstone against Kashmir's young Chief minister Farooq Abdullah. Rajiv had earlier pronounced him "worse than the Marxists", his mother accused him of indulging in anti-national activities. It appeared to be a well thought of tirade against the former friend of Rajiv who went from one *guli* to another begging votes for his party's victory in the last Delhi Corporation and Metropolitan elections.

The same Farooq was now under attack because he refused to be defeated by the Congress in the Kashmir Assembly election. What he was doing, she said, was "exceedingly unfortunate." Houses of many congressmen have been razed to the ground, rations were denied to Congress workers and their sympathisers.

The police are partisan and are behaving in a most deplorable manner, anti-national elements are having a field day, and those who look towards Delhi for help are being asked to leave the state "as if Jammu and Kashmir is not a part of India".

The attack was followed by yet another tirade against Farooq at the press conference on the eve of the session. Press reporters were taken aback at her virulence against the Chief minister. They got the impression that he may be dismissed soon after she reaches Delhi. What actual steps is she contemplating against him, she was asked by a shocked newsman. "How do you conclude that I will disclose them", was the straight answer.

Farooq and Basu were deliberately chosen as the main targets of attack since neither Karnataka's Ramakrishna Hegde nor Andhra's NTR were even mentioned either by her or any of the senior Congress leaders. MGR, of course, is a prized acquisition and an ally though AIADMK is as regionalist as NTR's Telugu Desam. But political yardsticks have their own way of measuring who is what.

The Plenary was undoubtedly aimed at the 1985 election. The future of the Congress is once again in danger. Indira Gandhi cannot afford to lose the country once again. The partymen who flocked from all over the country betrayed nervousness, specially the ones from UP and Bihar.

The south is lost though not irretrievably, but the north seems to be slipping. Both the steps at the Plenary were wrong—they reflected a death wish. If Rajiv or Indira Gandhi has to fight against the Right—Charan Singh, Vajpayee, beef tallow and Ekatmata—then the left will have to be involved in the battle. The Congress is no more in a position to face a two-pronged attack. That will be fatal.

And the attacks on Farooq without rhym or reason are fast antagonising Muslims. In UP and Bihar it is the Muslims voter who will tilt the balance. The more Farooq is attacked the greater is his acceptability and popularity among not only Muslims but a very large section of Hindus too. How has he become anti-national overnight? Even Indira Gandhi who brands him anti-national does not believe in what she says.

Rajiv's full blast against the Left has harmed him in a way. The Right will never support him and his national acceptability will receive server jolts if the Left decides to reject him.

The leftists, he and she both should know, are the most effective drum beaters. They were her drum beaters during the worst days of her political career, and had they not stood by her she might not have survived the Syndicate.

Rajiv needs the Left more than the Left needs him.

Current, 07.01.1984.
pp. (1 + 3 + 21)

No wave

"I am not going to be the donkey this time to carry the entire burden of campaigning. The responsibility of winning the election rests fairly and squarely on your shoulders."—Indira Gandhi

This stern warning from the tallest leader of the party sent shivers down the spines of the 3,000 MPs and MLAs gathered at the airconditioned, spacious, thickly carpeted, plush auditorium of the Asiad Village. One wished India was made of villages like this. The congressmen, most of whom visited the dreamland for the first time, were indeed overawed by the majesty and the opulence.

This was the venue of the three-day computerised *mela*, the first of its kind, to assess the performance and mood of the party legislators about to be thrown into a fresh battle of the ballot. And that was the danger signal held forth by history's most indefatigable wave-maker.

Perhaps no one knows the pulse of the nation as intensely as she does, and she has realised much before time that the crucial battle will not be made of waves. It will be a no-wave election, and each one will have to mind his own fences.

It is a chilling idea for an average congressmen who has been thriving as a 'parasite'. It was Nehru to begin with and his daughter for almost two decades. And was it to be said that 1980 was the Sanjay year and that 1985 will not be the Rajiv year? Today's congressman is made of brittle fibre. It may not withstand the tides of time.

The well-fed, well-dressed, over-conscious legislators were in a sombre mood. They could perhaps see the writing on the wall. Unlike the Bombay AICC session and the Calcutta plenary this meeting demonstrably bore the mark of Rajiv Gandhi, his no nonsense style, his desire to modernise the party and his efforts to inject a sense of accountability among the legislators. Though he is one of the many General Secretaries of the party, Congress do not have to be told who is who. He is heard with the attention and awe a person in power evokes. He speaks softly but firmly and would not let anybody fool around, and he doesn't suffer fools.

Everybody was provided with an opportunity to "let off steam", and now factionalism has to end. Demands and grievances can be directly communicated to the leadership, and one "should not read them in the press. The media should not be used to settle scores with one another at least until the elections," otherwise extremely serious action would be taken.

The partymen also knew that now it is an Indira-Rajiv party and that they will have to make an addition to their vocabulary. Though sycophancy was at a low key, perhaps due to widespread public revulsion, chiefs of the zonal committees who reported the gist of the 'interviews' did repeatedly eulogise Indira Gandhi without failing to 'Rajivji'.

Sanjay Gandhi, who single handedly re-created the post-1977 party, was not mentioned even once. Who can know better than congressmen where their bread is buttered? They seem to be in such a hurry to accept Rajiv as leader that the huge portrait of Indira Gandhi which adorned the stage made her look much older with all her hair painted white with only a thin black streak.

Rajiv perhaps knows about the undercurrent of resentment among a number of senior congressmen in the centre and in the states against him and his team of young, methodical, non-political people who manages the show from behind. They talk in whispers and some of them ridicule his 'unusual' methods. He said that the interviewing of very senior people by some juniors was disliked, and assured that this would not happen in future.

The whole thing has been an exercise in futility, a senior Cabinet minister remarked, laughing at the "new school boy" methods. "I know, most of the MPs and MLAs have told lies in the interviews, but the 'data' will be fed to the computers and they will churn out white lies, and we will go to the polls with computerised lies as our major plank."

Rajiv must have come to know about these derisive remarks, and quick was his reaction. The massive information collected at the legislators' conclave, he retorted, "is not going into a machine, but in the minds of the people."

Cynicism apart, for the first time an attempt has been made to bring in professional management techniques in a party which could easily be called a huge 'organised' crowd. Rajiv's team is busy formulating an election arithmetic with an in-depth study of each Assembly and Lok Sabha constituency.

The conclave was an exercise in preparing a socio-economic profile of these constituencies and also to put the legislators to a 'severe test' in assessing their performance. The proforma given to them was based on 18 questions which could be taken as lie detectors. And that something more than the facetious profession of loyalty was required was obviously the main idea.

The 366 MPs and 2,400 MLAs had earlier submitted reports after 'touring' their constituencies in a mass contact programme, with the implementation of the 20-point programme as the sheet-anchor. They were interviewed by five zonal committees.

Headed by Pranab Mukherjee for the south, Buta Singh for the east, Narasimha Rao for central India and the north, Vishwanath Pratap Singh for the west and Shiv Shankar for the crucial Hindi heartland of UP and Bihar, these committees were constituted by party President Indira Gandhi soon after the Calcutta session to look into the "organisation and political situation" in these zones with special attention to the implementation of the 20-point programme.

The whole exercise was organised with military-like precision. Each legislator was given a coloured card which carried the number of his or her constituency, the time of interview and the room where it was to take place. Each zone was given a different colour. As the legislators answered the 18-question proforma in their respective language, clerks went on writing down these answers.

Ten members of the Rajya Sabha were associated with each zonal committees. The Chief ministers and the PCC chiefs were present when legislators from their states were interviewed. Rajiv was interviewed by

Shiv Shankar. The claims of the MPs will not be cross-checked with the reports of the MLAs from their constituencies.

The AICC secretariat and the Rajiv boys have made over 600 files with scientifically processed data on the caste complex, opposition strength, working of 20-point programme, past record of the legislator and his predecessor, economic and social problems, etc., in each constituency.

Most MLAs did complain about how they have been ignored by the local and union ministers whenever they visited their constituencies, about the district administration refusing to 'co-operate' with them, poor implementation of the 20-point programme, rampant factionalism, widespread misappropriation of funds and the inactivity of the DCC and the PCC. They also talked about corruption at every level.

Corruption which has seeped to the lowest of the political and administrative level was least talked about in the open session of the conclave. It was either taken for granted or the leadership did not wish to stir the hornet's nest. How and why most ministers in the states and at the centre suddenly began to wallow in wealth has not been explained either by the ministers or by the leadership, and some of the senior Union ministers and Chief ministers have been able to successfully hide their opulence.

The Indira-Rajiv team rarely talks about it, and one wonders whether it is aware that corruption will undoubtedly be a major issue during elections. The 20-point programme has been a victim of corruption, and it goes without saying that the whole party will soon bear the brunt of this.

Nothing, virtually nothing, moves without greasing the palms of the concerned people. People are facing the hydra-headed monster of nepotism, corruption and skyrocketing prices. The ruling party has deliberately turned its face away from these issues of the deepest concern to the people. It has become so sensitive, that even well-intentioned criticism of these monstrosities results in instant enmity. Indira Gandhi went out of her way to defend her ministers who have been leading five-star lives.

It was pointed out by a local english Daily that despite general secretary G.K. Moopanar's circular asking for austerity from partymen in power, during the conclave a number of ministers and Chief ministers did stay in five-star hotels. The paper gave their names and suite numbers.

She was irked at the expose. She denied that anyone of these ministers was staying in such hotels. She said her party did not believe in five-star culture but in five-star performance. There was loud applause, and the loudest was from those ministers who had driven from their five star suites straight to the venue.

It seemed she had made inquiries from them after reading the newspaper report, but they denied the news. It means they lied to their 'supreme' leader and if they lie about such a 'trifling' matter, wouldn't they be lying to her about the wealth they have amassed and about the 'implementation of the much tom-tommed 20-point programme?'

It is not immoral to have the luxury of a five-star hotel, they are meant for providing comfort to those who can pay. But the question is, can a Chief minister or an ordinary state minister afford to stay in such opulence on his own?

One Chief minister, who had publicly confessed a few years before he assumed the august office that he was so poor that he did not have enough money to complete the construction of his very modest house in his very small village, did stay in the capital's most expensive hotel and he was seen by hundreds of congressmen driving in and out in a gleaming imported car. It is said his domineering wife dons diamond studded 'paazebs'.

Can he explain the sources of his 'wealth', and if not would his party leader ask him whether he made all that money through "fair means"? And if not, should he be allowed to stay where he is? This man will soon go and tell the people of his state, 70 per cent of whom not only live below the *chapati*-belt but a large number of them subsist on roots and leaves, to strengthen the hands of his leader.

Corruption will be and can be a major issue, and if a great leader like Indira Gandhi cannot fight against it in her own party, who would? The Asiad Village exercise will indeed help Rajiv to steamline his party, but not the people that make it up. A well-oiled disciplined party is desirable, but if it is packed with people whose diamond-studded wives flaunt their ill-gotten wealth at the starving millions, then that party is not worth its name. It may have led a glorious past. It cannot have a glorious future.

Current, 17.03.1984.
pp. (1 + 21)

Stunned nation looks up to Rajiv

The nation was least prepared. That Indira Gandhi, the apple of their eye, would be gunned down by her own security men was something they just could not imagine. They were horrified, benumbed.

The entire globe trembled with a shock-wave. History has seldom witnessed so outrageous, so heinous a crime. The apostle of secularism was felled by the bullets of religious fanatics.

The first task of Prime Minister Rajiv Gandhi is to dig out the conspiracy, identify the forces behind the assassins and wipe them out once and for all. The country's intelligence and security's intelligence and security system has undoubtedly fallen into the hands of its enemies, and unless it is completely purged, there will be more tragedies. This needs draconian operation, ruthless action. It has to be now or never.

The Sikh extremists in India and abroad make no secret of their wish to wipe out the whole Nehru family, also President Zail Singh on whose orders the army has stormed the Golden Temple. The liquidation of one of the assassins on the spot could well be an attempt to destroy the evidence of the conspiracy to destabilise India.

The enemy within and abroad appears determined to throw this country of 700 million struggling people into turmoil, to browbeat them and subdue them. That is the writing on the wall.

The wound will take time to heal. The loss of Indira Gandhi will haunt the people for years to come, and her absence will be felt at all times of crisis. Like her father, she was made of unique fibre. Like her father, she was totally committed to the concept of secularism. And because of this faith of the Nehru family the country has narrowly escaped a communal holocaust.

The cause of secularism for which she made the supreme sacrifice should be upheld by her successor. Preserving the unity of the country and pulling the starving, dumb millions up by their bootstraps which were her major preoccupations, should find the highest priority with the party which has miraculously survived its worst shock.

It was her party, created by her single-handedly in the midst of political storms. The whole country was her constituency and she knew that few in her party had the vision to look at India as an integrated whole, and that the country would go to pieces if her successor were made of lesser stuff, that it could be held together, despite the religious, regional, linguistic and emotional diversities, only by a person who is above all these pulls and counter-pulls.

We had criticised her for various lapses of her government, and we will preserve our independent approach towards her successor too. But we are convinced that had Rajiv been unprepared to take over the ruling party and the reins of office, the country would have been in turmoil.

The party is made up of small, very small men. The writ of none of them goes beyond their posh bungalows along the tree-lined roads of New Delhi. None of them has a base, nor mass appeal or the aura that can endear them to the people.

Only Rajiv, and none else, could have filled the void immediately, though he will take time to grow, to mature, to attain commanding heights, to infuse his countrymen with confidence and prove his mettle.

The smooth transfer of leadership within hours of her assassination is a great tribute to her total command over her party in the absence. That the party was psychologically prepared to accept Rajiv as her successor was never in doubt. In the past three years he had travelled extensively, met thousands of people, addressed vast crowds.

He was virtually the party chief. He had reduced the burden of his mother by taking the onerous task of putting the party in shape, modernising it, and keeping it well-oiled to face the battle of the hustings.

The real Rajiv was born the day his mother attained martyrdom. He was without a shadow. He was his own. The millions who saw him on television for three days with his thin, tight lips, moistless eyes, his pointed Nehru nose, his determined forehead, were convinced of Indira Gandhi's right choice. At forty he looked exactly forty, and whenever he looked up he seemed to be telling his mother, "I will not let you down, come what may."

This was a new Rajiv Gandhi, the legatee of a glorious heritage, a true son of a rich soil. Seeing him on TV, standing near Indira Gandhi's body, viewers felt secure, assured. The country, they felt, was safe, its destiny in good hands.

In those three days he won the heart of India, and no doubt he will win its democratic soul also. With his election the nation heaved a sigh of relief. They also saw the faction-ridden ruling party exhibiting a rare show of discipline and loyalty on the issue of selecting their beloved leader's successor.

It was a changeover that ensured continuity. Congressmen refused to play the opposition's game. They did not go in for an interim Prime Minister and they reduced the opposition to a laughing-stock.

It was these very opposition leaders who were unable to elect a leader democratically after their victory in 1977 and were forced to hand over the selection of their new Prime Minister to two individuals, Jayaprakash Narayan and Acharya Kirpalani. Neither Morarji nor Charan Singh were elected by their parliamentary party.

Charan Singh who led a delegation of opposition leaders to President Zail Singh questioning the method of making Rajiv Prime Minister had himself been 'nominated' by President Sanjiva Reddy on the assurance of Indira Gandhi that her party would not oppose his heading the government. Charan Singh never faced Parliament during his short and turbulent tenure as Prime Minister. This much for the opposition's talk of conventions and precedents.

Firmly in the saddle with the full backing of his party and the enthusiastic endorsement of the people, Rajiv's first task is to console the nation. The anger of the Sikh terrorists, the Akalis and, unfortunately, the Sikh community as a whole will have to be controlled. He has already made it clear that the entire community should not be held responsible for the dastardly act of a few mad men.

The Sikhs in the country are passing through a period of immense agony, a sense of insecurity has gripped them. Their alienation can do incalculable harm to the country. They must be reassured, and brought back into the national mainstream. Failure to do this would negate the noble cause for which Indira Gandhi sacrificed herself.

Rajiv has lost his mother, and the nation has lost its most loved, leader. Yet Rajiv will have to rise to new heights to heal the wounds. Punjab is crying for a political solution and it is his sacred responsibility to inject sanity and win the Sikhs over to the secular concept. That would be the first feather in his cap, and he will be crowned with glory.

There is no doubt that like his mother he too will visit the Golden Temple and by this single act of magnanimity win the hearts of Sikhs and put the extremists to shame.

He has time to prepare the country to accept him as the leader through the popular democratic process. There is no doubt that he will hold elections, and on schedule. That will add another feather to his cap. And an election of this magnitude, soon after taking over the reins of office, will gave a shot in the arm to parliamentary democracy, his position will become unassailable.

He will then have enough time to prove his administrative worth and his ability to justify his party's choice as Indira Gandhi's successor. His first political act of not making drastic changes in the Cabinet reflects his concern for continuity, though he deserves a better and more efficient council.

Indira Gandhi had retained some deadwood and many more inefficient men in her government due to her consideration not to let down the loyalists. It is mainly because of this that the government that works she had promised the people did not work much.

Rajiv will have to give the country a government that works and a government which is more poor-oriented. He will have to reinvigorate his image of Mr. Clean and he will have to seek out people with a better image, maturity and experience.

For the first time the country is in the hands of a very young man. It can be a turning point in its destiny. Rajiv should not fail. And the entire nation should stand solidly behind him to see to it that he does not fail.

Current, 10.11.1984
pp. (1 + 3)

4

Rajiv Gandhi Inherits the Mantle of the Congress

A. Indira Wins Election for Rajiv

It will be Congress all the way

Two waves are sweeping across the country. One is a tidal wave of sympathy and admiration for Rajiv Gandhi. The other, less visible but equally potential, is that of despondency, disillusionment about the opposition. The feeling is that in the post-Indira period the survival of parliamentary democracy depends more on the performance of the opposition than on the electoral fortunes of the ruling party.

Though Rajiv is the Prime Minister and leader of the party, it will undoubtedly be Indira's election once again. The ruling party will be justifiably projecting her as the *Rashtra Mata* with the emotion catching slogan, *Indiraji ki antim ichcha, boond, boond se desh ki raksha.*

The slogan cannot be questioned even by her most inveterate enemies. Her martyrdom is fresh in mind. One can imagine the soul-stirring impact with millions of people shouting the slogan in one voice. Elections are after all won mostly on slogans. *Garibi Hatao* and the 'government that works' after all had their effect.

And Rajiv will also be there with his crystal-like image : *Rajiv Gandhi ka sandesh, ek rahe yeh Bharat desh.* And the ruling party whiz kids have not ignored the minorities, *Har ek dharam ka ho samman, par sabse bada hai Hindustan.*

The ruling party has the means and the machinery to carry the slogans to the remotest corners of the country. The television with its coverage of almost half of the population of the country will play a role so far unthought of.

The young men in position and power are overwhelmed by the idea that Indira Gandhi is more popular, powerful and omnipresent than she was before her assassination. Political, religious, regional and caste barriers have crumbled under the emotional avalanche. The Congress which was on the way out couldn't have dreamt of such a fabulous windfall.

Delhi is a window on the national trends and one can literally feel the sweet smell of victory. The Left as well as the Right is morally torn apart. In both the Communist parties strong factions are militating to lend support to the young Prime Minister. And the RSS stalwart Nanaji Deshmukh has let the cat out of the bag by extending his unqualified blessings to BJP's uncompromising critics.

It will not be short of a landslide for Rajiv—more than the 1971 post-Bangladesh and still more than the post-Janata victories. In the two historic polls the warrior that Indira Gandhi was had to fight every inch of her way to establish her superiority. In this election the battle seems to have been won before it is joined.

The people appear determined to vote the Congress back to power with a vengeance. No seat is safe for the opposition and no seat is unsafe for the Congress. The one-time aspirants to the *gaddi* Charan Singh and Atal Behari Vajpayee, Bahuguna and Chandra Shekhar, and a whole lot of them are scampering about in search of safe seats.

The expectation is anywhere between 350 to 375 seats for the Congress, and it does not seem to be wide of the mark. The mood is such. It is an awesome yet not a random figure. One can only ask whether this kind of mind-boggling victory is in the basic interest of democracy itself. Can a system like ours afford the total slaughter of the opposition?

But what has the opposition done to deserve the people's affection, sympathy, support or vote? It has already been in total disarray. The death of Indira Gandhi has further divided it. It is left with no issue. Its main target has gone and with it has vanished its raison d'etre.

It has very little to say or project against Rajiv or his band of functionaries. Its slogan that the polls will be a battle between the rich and the poor or a fight against dynasty has lost its magnetism, lustre, credibility.

It is the poor from the slums and the landless labourers from the fields who will vote for Rajiv. It is as the duly elected leader of the party that he will be seeking the mandate of the masses. Let them defeat him if they want to destroy a dynasty.

Rajiv has become the central figure of national politics. He has no rivals in the party. He has given the impression of being a status quoist, a traditionalist. The cabinet is in tact, the party hierarchy is more or less in tact, with the only major inclusion of cousin Arun Nehru as the new boss, the bureaucrats who served his mother more or less remain at the helm.

The smooth succession is a tribute to the departed leader and evokes confidence in her successor. Imagine what would have happened if one of those buffoons were in power! The fear that the Congress was 'I' and that it will dismember once she is removed from the scene has had no basis.

At the moment Rajiv and his young team is in full control of the government and the party. President Zail Singh is quiet. Gone are the days when he used to invite Indira Gandhi to the Rashtrapati Bhavan for 'active' consultations and he had his own views on certain burning issues. He has assured Rajiv of his full support though the inclusion of Darbara Singh in the Parliamentary Board has obviously piqued him.

Rajiv's problems of governance and management of the party will crop up only after the elections. The dissidents, the factionalists and the aspirants for chairs will lie low because the party rank and file is in no mood to allow anybody to challenge his authority.

He appears to have given up the idea of injecting the Congress Parliamentary party with 'fresh' blood, an euphemism for 'Rajivites'. Before he became Prime Minister he had planned to bring in his chosen and trusted followers. Now every member irrespective of his group affiliations is expected to be with him and follow him, no questions asked.

He is aware that a section in the party is not happy with the elevation of Arun Nehru. Certain congressmen from UP are squirming under the impact. He carried a lot of weight and power with Rajiv, but in an unofficial capacity so far. Now as the most important General Secretary his authority cannot be questioned though the post does not seem to have added any more power than what he was enjoying.

People close to him feel that he is more accessible, more amenable and more responsive to the feelings of the rank and file. The tragedy has changed him for the better. He has been putting in almost 18 hours a day to organise the party and the election machinery.

Other general secretaries feel that at this critical moment Rajiv does need a close associate who is in tune with his thinking and can ensure smooth co-ordination between the Prime Minister and the party. Moreover, no congressman can deny the fact that the Congress as it is today is the creation of the Nehru family and it has to be guided by one of its members if it has to survive.

The victory at the hustings with such a streamroller majority will undoubtedly lead to another election. The opposition governments in Karnataka, Andhra, Bengal and Kashmir will fall under the impact of a total opposition rout. Reports reaching the capital clearly indicate that the Congress will sweep Karnataka, that the ground will be cut from under NTR's feet in Andhra, that Jyoti Basu's Left Front will crumble, and that in Kashmir Farooq Abdullah and brother-in-law Gul Shah will eliminate each other to the advantage of the Congress.

The centre in that case will be left with no choice but to order fresh polls for the Assemblies. The Congress Chief ministers will not be left behind in taking advantage and Rajiv to go in for Assembly elections all over the country.

The writing on the wall is: it is going to be the Congress all the way. Who said India is not a congressland?

Current, 24.11.1984.
pp. (1 + 3)

Rajiv wave in Hindi heartland

Lucknow: This Hindi heartland has taken Indira Gandhi's assassination as a personal loss, and Rajiv succeeding her as a personal honour. Last week I witnessed an unusual sight at the city's Hazratganj Park when PCC chief Vishwanath Pratap Singh asked a huge crowd "Do you want Rajiv to serve the nation as Prime Minister after the election."

Rajiv was sitting on a 15-foot high rostrum to address his first public meeting in Lucknow after he became Prime Minister. The crowd, nearly two lakhs, went delirious and raised its hands without exception. "We accept your magnanimous gesture with thanks," Singh said, and requested "beloved young and dynamic Prime Minister Rajiv Gandhi to address you."

Uttar Pradesh is unmistakably in the grip of a Rajiv wave. To begin with it was a sympathy wave, but as Rajiv began his electioneering from one city to another and from town to village to most parts of the Indo-Gangetic belt, he won million of hearts with his sonorous well-modulated voice and touching references to his mother.

Had the tragedy not occurred, most seasoned political observers believe, the Congress would have been routed at least in UP. The situation has changed dramatically, and it will not be surprising if the Congress bags more than 60 out of the 85 seats. It will be a landslide, ensuring a large majority for the party in Parliament.

This state is the battleground of titans, but the Rajiv wave has made the earth shake under their feet. So formidable is the pressure that opposition stalwarts like Charan Singh, Bahuguna, Chandra Shekhar, Charanjit Yadav, Menaka Gandhi and hordes of other mini-leaders have been pinned down to their constituencies.

The people of UP have somehow assumed that they are the kernel of India that is Bharat, and that it is their sacred duty to preserve its unity and integrity. Indira Gandhi's last speech in Orissa that she would defend the unity of the country with the last drop of her blood is broadcast over loudspeakers in every village and town, and people genuinely believe that only Rajiv can save the country from anti-national forces' which is seen as a euphemism for the opposition—the Abdullahs, the Bahugunas, the NTRs.

The Congress is undoubtedly concentrating on UP. It is a virtual blitzkrieg. Millions of posters, banners, bunting, audio and video cassettes and films portraying Indira as Mother India and Rajiv as the new messiah have flooded the region. The visuals are dazzling and the publicity is mind-boggling. At least 2,000 jeeps and an equal number of cars are seen running across the state. They have taken the opposition citadels by storm.

It is by all means an unequal battle. In Rae Bareli the DMKP candidate Savita Ambedkar who is opposing Arun Nehru has only one jeep, and that too is often found on the roadside with a young *Harijan* boy carrying out repairs. The Congress general secretary, on the other hand, has over 100 jeeps at his command and thousands of workers.

Rajiv's strength is also due to the total disarray in the opposition ranks and multicornered fights in every constituency except Amethi, where the opposition has not put up any candidate against the chief rival Maneka Gandhi.

Though each constituency is important for the ruling party the real election is somehow being fought in the few VVIP ones Amethi, Rae Bareli, Allahabad are the places where power and prestige is at stake. Amethi, of course, is the constituency one has to visit to see how a modern campaign can be organised with terrific audio-visual impact.

Until October 31, it was generally felt that Maneka would give a tough fight to Rajiv, but the situation has dramatically changed. Now Rajiv is not a mere MP, he is the Prime Minister, and the people of Amethi would hate to lose the opportunity of being the constituents of the VVIP.

The entire constituency gives the appearance of a vast cinema hall in which two lucidly made video cassettes are shown to the voters. One is Amethi ka Sooraj, a 20 minutes glossy which shows Rajiv as the new symbol of hope. It is a masterpiece of cinematography and captures the young leader nursing Amethi tenderly like a gardener at one place the sun is shown rising from behind a tree with tricolours fluttering in the fresh morning breeze, and Rajiv appearing on the horizon, driving his jeep in spotless *khadi kurta* and *pyjama* and wearing imported glasses. The soothing voice of the commentator is that of friend Amitabh Bachchan. The impact is dazzling.

Another video cassette Ma, an intimate narration by Indira Gandhi of Rajiv's life and his likes and dislikes. Indira Gandhi comes out as a master narrator with all the charm she could command. In this Amitabh is the interviewer.

Wife Sonia is in charge of their most well-organised campaign the country has witnessed. The constituency is divided into zones from the village to the district level, with one man in charge of each zone which is monitored daily at the end of the day. Hundreds of jeeps run across the narrow roads, carrying slogan shouting activists. Indira Gandhi's and Rajiv's posters are everywhere, with hardly any space left out.

Despite this onslaught, Maneka's determined supporters are holding the fort with grit and doggedness. I could hardly see any of her posters or banners. Occasionally the eye falls on a lone bicycle hanging on a pole, or a little green and white flag struggling to assert its identity in a jungle of Congress flags.

But in each Assembly segment I found a well-organised group of young men, most Muslims and those belonging to backward communities, canvassing for her. In Jayes, a predominantly Muslim Assembly seat, the local MLA assured me of 100 per cent support to Rajiv. As I walked out, his young son came out and whispered in my ears: *"Janab* whatever you have been told is a tissue of lies. Jayes is 50-50. I know most of youth would vote for Maneka, you take it from me."

A family of two Muslim Rajas is divided. While Akhtar Husain of Mohana is for Rajiv, his brother Azhar Husain of Inhona, a few miles away, holds the fort for Maneka. As Rajiv was addressing a massive rally at Jagdishpur, the industrial complex where over Rs. 1000 crores are being invested, Jagdishpur, I asked an old bared Muslim peasant whom he would vote. "I will vote Menaka, he shouted. I know you are a CID, and you can report to Rajiv. I am not afraid." The group around him looked at him with admiration.

As I was driving down from Jagdishpur to Goriaganj. Sonia's headquarters, I met a group of about 50 young men on cycles with Maneka flags flying on their handles. "Why do you support her," I asked them.

"We are against *atankwadi,*" they shouted in one voice. "We are prepared to face bullets and go to jail, but we will not surrender to this naked show of money power and muscle power."

Democracy has indeed taken roots, and Amethi is not an island. In the constituency running parallel to Amethi, cousin Arun Nehru is facing Jagdish Narain Mishra of the Sanjay Manch and Savita Ambedkar of DMKP. Both are non-candidates, financially as well as politically. Though Arun Nehru has to put in some extra efforts to make himself acceptable to local Congress workers, he will certainly win with a large margin.

"We had committed a sin by voting out Indira in 1977. It will not be repeated any more whoever is the Congress candidate." In Rae Bareli it will be victory of the Congress and not the candidate, say most of the Congress workers, he will certainly win with a large margin.

Arun Nehru is taking no chances. He has parked himself in the constituency, and does an 18 hour campaign visiting the remotest hamlets everyday. His wife, who is equally involved in the campaign, appears to be more popular with the voters.

Her simplicity and charming manners are a feather in Arun Nehru's starched Gandhi cap which he has been wearing to the surprise of his friends. "You look funny in the cap." A smiling Rajiv remarked when he first saw him. "It is the cap of the boss," Nehru paid back, the two sharing the laughter.

His rival Jagdish Mishra indulges in personal attack on Nehru. He says Arun is surrounded by the most undesirable elements in the area including Dhunni Singh, a notorious Thakur goon. "Do you want to hand over the fate of Rae Bareli to a pack of *goonda*s," he asks. But neither he nor Savita have much to say against either the Congress or Arun Nehru.

Where Rae Bareli ends, Allahabad begins. The city of the Nehrus, Saprus, Katjus and the Jhas is witnessing an epic battle between an actor who is learning politics and a politician who is outdoing him in acting.

Allahabad is the political capital of UP, its people take to politics like ducks to water. They smell politics like alcohol and they are always tipsy with the dizzying influence.

The hipster-hero of several celluloid battles in which he invariably reduces the toughs to pulp has perhaps chosen a wrong battlefield. He is no match to Hemavati Nandan Bahuguna, the lord of the political state. A spell-binding speaker, he captivates his audience with his gimmics, acrobatics and oratory. The crowds he gathers on the confluence of the holy rivers are not less impressive than the ones Amitabh collects.

The only difference is Bahuguna's listeners are a powerful political lot made up of the voting age groups while Amitabh's crowd is that of admirers who see him for the first time in flesh and blood, and most of them are under-age. The super star hardly knows the A, B, C of politics.

The Allahabadis are having a whale of time. Amitabh is not alone: his prize-winning charming wife Jaya Bhaduri too is on the roads, addressing small groups of urchins and well-groomed ladies in clubs and drawing rooms.

But local congressmen who claim to have produced a Nehru and a Shastri and an Indira are not pleased with the idea of swallowing an actor. In his election camp at the spacious bungalow of Advocate Khar, I met a number of senior Congress leaders putting on long faces. They are reluctant to canvas for Amitabh.

Bahuguna knows the constituency inch by inch, and its people in the thousands by name, and also the names of their fathers. "Allahabad is my home, my breeding ground, my past and future is part of its soil, and Allahabad as I know it will not disown me. But it is a stage for the actor from Bombay, and he will pack up and fly back to his celluloid world if he loses, and would never show his face if he wins, and it is a big if," the master tactician remarks with a grin.

He is in his elements. I have seen him fight many a battle, but in the present one he is at his deadliest. He knows that if he loses Allahabad his career and his politics ends with a big thud, and if he wins the ruling party will have a big thorn in its flesh.

"I am only a fortnight old in politics and I have staked my future for the sake of friends. I had never thought of entering Parliament but the day Indiraji was shot and Rajiv became Prime Minister I decided to stand by him, not only as a friend but as a politician"—Amitabh spells his 'ideology'.

Bahuguna is as sure of his victory as he is about the sun rising, though Amitabh has been assured of a landslide win by his newly found political *chamcha*s. "The political wisdom of the people of Allahabad is on test, and my victory will be that of the politically conscious people of this historic city," adds the veteran leader, who has thinned and aged after by by-pass surgery he underwent last year.

Amethi and Allahabad are so much on the minds of the people that Baghpat, from where Charan Singh and Raj Narain are trying to eliminate each other, takes the back stage. Raj Narain with his flowing beard and a green scarf tightly tied round his head, bounces from one village to the other like an actor in comic opera.

He talks in parables from Ramayana, which goes down well with his rural audience. He had projected himself as Hanuman to Charan Singh when the two were in power. Now he says: "Just as Ram went from Ayodhya to Lanka to fight Ravan, so also I have come from Kashi to Baghpat to take on this Ravan"—that is Charan Singh.

"Charan Singh is a dacoit who snatches away your votes, defeat him with all your might, you sons of Baghpat," he shouts at a corner meeting in the stronghold of the Choudhary, and he is heard in pindrop silence.

Something unusual. It needs guts to denigrate the Jat lion in his own den. Raj Narain may or may not win, but he will certainly tarnish the DMKP supremo's image.

A number of people in this area feel that Raj Narain is a Congress agent, but on cutting into the backward class votes to help Congress candidate Mahesh Chandra Sharma win. And the Choudhary may be defeated if the electorate decided to get rid of both the opportunists.

The apprehension is that Baghpat might witness a lot of violence this time. A number of known criminals have taken to politics. They enjoy the local leaders patronage, and some of them have shown the temerity to aspire for the law makers' role in Parliament.

Two most notorious criminals are locked in a fierce battle from Gorakhpur. Hari Shankar Tiwari with 50 criminal cases pending against him in various courts has filed his nomination as an independent. He is in jail as an NSA detenu.

His rival is Virendra Pratap Sahi a Sanjay Manch nominee. Sahi has 40 criminal cases against him. Both surrendered to the District Magistrate a day before the nominations and both are lodged in the Agra central Jail. Their gun-toting supporters have taken over Gorakhpur by storm and the Congress and other candidates have vanished in the heat and dust they have raised. The worst sufferers are the voters.

Tiwaris and Sahis are not an aberration. Criminalisation of politics in UP and Bihar is such an ominous development that, if not prevented or controlled in time, the Lok Sabha will be packed with them in future.

Current, 22.12.1984.
pp. (1 + 3 + 5)

Congress banks on caste banks: Bihar

Patna: Bihar is like Salvador Dali's masterpieces. Its caste pattern is like his surrealist puzzle. As it need a Dali to understand Dali, one has to be Bihari to fathom the caste complications in this hapless state wallowing in abject poverty.

The poor and the rich, the illiterate and the intelligentsia, all suffer from this plague. While 95 per cent of the people are in the category of poor, the rich can be counted on the fingers.

There are very few rich, and they are politicians, with a few exceptions. The major chunk of the benefits of parliamentary democracy has been cornered by the pot-bellied, neatly-dressed-in-*khaddar* politicians, irrespective of party affiliations.

Feudalism, feudal habits and feudal culture are intact. The caste barriers cannot simply be broken so long as the present political system prevails, and one has to submit to it.

This election too is being fought with caste as the only yardstick. The Congress, the DMKP, the Janata, the CPI and the CPM are all incurable victims of this malady.

The state is divided into forward and backward communities on official basis. Brahmins, Rajputs, Kayasthas and the Bhumihars are the main forward castes. Yadavs, Kurmis, Koeris, Mallahs and Dhanuks are the main backward communities. The Banias fall in the middle category, while the Harijans, Scheduied Castes and the Scheduled Tribes are placed in an entirely separate category.

The backwards are nearly 60 per cent. The Yadavs among them are predominant, while Muslims are about 18 per cent, but they are divided into forwards and backwards. The Ansaris the weavers—are backwards, and the Syeds are forwards.

All these castes and communities are further divided into nearly 200 sub-communities and each one of them is determined to maintain its caste origin. Talk to any politician, he begins with a hair-splitting analysis of the caste pattern in a particular constituency and then reaches a conclusion about the prospects of a candidate.

A senior retired civil servant at general Sinha's election office in Patna was visibly agitated on the "Shabby, insulting attitude of the Congress towards the *Kayasthas*. Not a single *Kayastha* has been given a Lok Sabha ticket by the ruling party, and do you know the reason?"

I said no. "Because the *Kayasthas* produced Jayaprakash Narayan." Was he a *Kayastha,* I asked. "Yes, very much so, and we are proud of him," he added, in the hearing distance of the much-decorated General who is contesting as an independent supported by the BJP from the city.

The *Kayasthas* are the white-collared core of Bihar and all other castes are wary of them and their ability to corner a large chunk of the competitive jobs. The General may or may not win, but he is sure to get "hundred per cent *Kayastha* votes."

The editor of a city english Daily maintains a file with a neatly-typed castewise list of candidates belonging to all parties. Eight seats have gone to Brahmins, five to Bhumihars, five to Muslims, he went on reeling the list from memory.

The Congress is in a comfortable position despite its sins of omission and commission mainly due to the total disarray in the opposition ranks. Had there been a straight contest the ruling party would have come a cropper. There is the 'sympathy wave' in the urban areas, but it is felt more among the constituents of the Congress vote banks—Muslims, Harijans and Brahmins. These vote banks are almost intact, and because of the cohesion the Congress is expecting to win at least 35 out of the 54 seats. In the 1980 elections, it had won 30. The improvement, if it happens, will therefore be marginal.

Muslims are the backbone of the Congress base. In almost every constituency their voters number anywhere between one to three lakh, and in north Bihar the figure is much higher. In 1977, they voted against the congressmen enbloc, and the party lost all the seats. But in this election they seem to be preparing to vote overwhelmingly for the Congress.

Only the CPI has been making some inroads in certain pockets. Of all the parties the CPI has apparently improved its position. In the last election it won six seats and this time it hopes to bag at least ten. It has put up 16 candidates and is supporting eight more belonging to other Left parties including Marxist stormy petrel A.K. Roy from the coal belt of Dhanbad.

Most of the Left parties are concentrating their effort in the tribal belt and in strong Muslim pockets. The Left is more articulate and well-organised all over the state, and it seems it will soon emerge as a formidable challenge to the ruling party.

Patna city, perhaps the filthiest in the country, with over 35,000 cycle rickshaw pullers, a large number of them in tatters, suffering from tuberculosis, and other lung diseases, is largely with the Communists, and their candidate Ram Avatar Shastri, a diminutive ex-journalist living in a middle class two-room apartment, cannot be rivalled either by the General or his Congress rival Thakur, who is a new comer to politics.

The General will loss his battle in the lanes and bylanes of Patna which respects him but would not send him to Parliament. The mild mannered General begins by saying "even if I lose, I would be happy that I fought for some values." His main support comes from city Kayasthas and the BJP activists.

The Communists are tarnishing his image with the CIA brush. "Yes, I did meet the American Ambassador, he had asked for an appointment and I did not refuse. But I have sent a seven-page resume of my talk with him to the defence minister. Look I have been in charge of military intelligence for a number of years, and I knew how to deal with these foreign diplomats. Those who question my integrity are traitors."

The general ostensibly lacks resources and also good copy writers. A shabbily-produced hand bill in English begins with "Lt. General Sinha was the first and only Bihari General in our army till his premature retirement from the army."

Former Chief minister and now DMKP leader Karpoori Thakur appears to be the major casualty of the mess created by the opposition parties when he switched his support to the *jat* supremo Chaudhary Charan Singh, a large number of Lok Dal deserted him and formed their own Lok Dal. Once a fiery Socialist and a formidable challenge to the Congress, now he is a mere shadow of his past. He has staked his claim from his home constituency Samastipur.

He is facing three backward class leaders—Ramdeo Raj of the Congress, former Patna High Court Judge and Lok Dal man R.P. Mandal and a BJP man, besides a Sanjay Manch contender. The aging backward class leader is fighting with his back to the wall, and it will be surprising if he is routed by the Congress. If that happens it will be the ruling party's most prized trophy.

His predecessor in office and the AICC general secretary Abdul Ghafoor, who is trying his luck from Siwan is in a comfortable position with over a dozen candidates from all conceivable parties opposing him.

His formidable rival is Khurshid Jahan, widow of Mohammad Yusuf who held the seat for Congress from 1962 to 1980, conceding it to the Janata only in 1977. She will divide the Muslim votes but Gafoor is a darling of the Thakur who are likely to vote for him en bloc.

The opposition could have done better had it agreed to a direct contest with seat adjustment. Less than half of Bihar has been with the Congress and the rest has always voted against it. In this election the strength of the ruling party is the multicornered contests.

While it has fielded candidates in all the 54 constituencies, the DMKP is in the fray in 28 constituencies, the Janata in 31, the BJP in 33 and the Left parties in 24, with smaller factions like the Sanjay Manch and the Jharkhand adding to the mess in the opposition camp. If the Congress gets more than what it got in 1980, it will be entirely due to the rift in the opposition.

"We would have won more than 30 seats," says Chief minister Chandra Shekhar Singh, "had wrong men not been given tickets in over a dozen constituencies." He ruefully remarks that he had been over-ruled by a Bihar leader who has the ears of the High Command which agreed to his nominees. It appears AICC treasurer Sitaram Kesari and former Chief minister Jagannath Mishra have had their way in placing a number of their nominees over his head. He is sore about Mishra running a parallel party and a parallel government in the state. Singh feels he will never be effective in holding the state if he is not permitted to have his way.

But Mishra appears to have more resources and men at his command than the PCC and he is more active on the election front than the Chief minister. He has been out of Patna touring the remotest corners of the state, boosting the morale of his nominees. His daily tour programme appears on the front pages of the newspapers just like Rajiv Gandhi's.

Mishra draws huge crowds of Muslims, Brahmins and Harijans. Most of his detractors in the Congress concede that the Congress couldn't have hoped for 15 seats had not Mishra kept the Congress vote bank intact, specially the Muslims and the Harijans.

The High Command is aware of this fact, and that is why his "independent activities" are not stopped. A unique but disturbing feature in this election, which is found in Bihar and parts of UP, is the open entry of the toughs and the Mafia leaders. Every party with the exception of the CPI has its own tough, antisocial and mafia bosses. Some of them are nominees of these parties though in the field as independents.

These gangsters operate on caste lines like their political patrons. West Champaran, Dhanbad, Begusarai, Bettia, Rohtas and Bhojpur are infested by them, and almost every candidate has his army of toughs.

In Jagjivan Ram's constituency of Sasaram it is the goons who will influence the fortunes of the contestants. Dhanbad is the stronghold of dozens of Al Capones and all the parties without exception will solicit their support.

The Bihar Assembly has several MLAs with criminal records, and one Bahadur Singh who represents Jagdishpur, a National Security Act detenue, tightly controls the Buxar, Bikramganj and Arrah region.

As I was talking to a senior minister at his residence, his secretary sent in a slip. The minister suddenly got up and asked his secretary to send the visitor in immediately. In walked a hefty man dressed in silk kurta and *churidars.* After he left, I asked the nervous minister who he was. Well, he is an influential MLA, he controls several gangs in the area, and murders and killings are his hobby.

Bihar abounds in social, economic and political criminals. The proverbial long arm of the law does not reach them. Such is the powerful patronage they enjoy. Democracy of which we are so proud is a farce in Bihar, and it needs only a Bihar to promote, preserve, deify this farce.

Current, 22.12.1984.
pp. (1 + 5)

Sympathy wave—Karnataka

Bangalore: It will be a neat, direct fight in this caste-ridden state. The Janata and the Congress are locked in a fierce battle, with Indira Gandhi as the dominant factor.

The Congress camp, which had lost hopes of regaining power, is now on the offensive. Its leaders have had a new birth with the death of their leaders. Her assassination has boosted their morale.

Most leaders whom I met appeared determined to turn the tragedy to political advantage, with the first shock over. They are exultant. The sympathy wave, they assert, is sweeping not only Karnataka but the whole south.

"We will get back to power everywhere," they shout with boisterous confidence. KPCC boss K.H. Patil begins his conversation with "we will win all the 28 seats thanks to the sympathy wave and also to the single impressive wave." What is this impressive wave? "This has been unleashed by Rajivji. He has impressed the whole nation, and I call it the impressive wave," he comes out with a grin.

Former Chief minister Gundu Rao is again in his elements. The announcement of elections has once again placed him in the centre of power politics. In the last one month he has been in constant demand from Rajiv Gandhi and Arun Nehru, and it seems he will be rehabilitated soon.

He is jubilant over the prospects of the Janata losing the battle of the hustings. "I say, please listen to me, I must say, and you must believe me, that we will win all the 28 seats."

Patil and Gundu Rao, once bitter adversaries, have now teamed up. The battle for the Lok Sabha has been already won, the voters are impatiently waiting for the D-Day.

"On December 30 Ramakrishna Hegde will drive down to Raj Bhavan to tender his resignation, and the sordid Janata game will be over, thank God," Gundu Rao remarks loudly, and the faces of over a dozen legislators in his drawing room brighten up with hope.

But both Patil and Gundu Rao are not members of the Assembly and neither of them will be in a position of stake his claim for the *gaddi.* Their plan is to ask for immediate dissolution of the Assembly and fresh elections. Congress Assembly leader Veerappa Moily, who has been isolated in the power game, does not agree with them.

"Why dissolution", he asks, "I will insist on being called upon to form the government as leader of the second largest party." But he will be in a minority, no doubt. "Oh no, not at all," he is sure of winning over at least 30 MLAs from the opposite camp within a day. His only fear is that he may be challenged by Bangarappa who joined the Congress two weeks ago with the blessings of Rajiv Gandhi. In the Moily-Bangarappa tussle the Patil-Gundu Rao combine will throw its weight behind Bangarappa on the understanding that he will accommodate their men in the Council of ministers. That he will do. He is also sure that in the event of a Janata rout his erstwhile Kranti Ranga MLAs will flock back to him. This is post-Lok Sabha election scenario lurking in the minds of the Congress leaders.

In the Janata camp diminutive, taciturn Ramakrishna Hegde is unperturbed. He exudes confidence, but he is not exultant. He is more realistic, less adventurous. A hard-headed, consummate tight-rope walker he is concentrating only on those seats that the thinks can be won with some effort.

At the moment his party does not have a single seat in the Lok Sabha from this state, and "whatever we win will be a gain. Each seat we win will be a loss to the Congress, and I am confident of winning at least 14 seats, which means the Congress will lose as many."

He seems to have succeeded in papering over the factional fights especially between Deve Gowda and S.R. Bommai, the two powerful Vokkaliga and Lingayat caste leaders. Gowda is the state party chief while Bommai is Finance minister. Hegde has accommodated the nominees of both of them. They are contented. And he is heading a cohesive team, determined to fight back the Congress onslaught.

"While the Congress plank is the dead Indira asking for votes, our plus point is our leader, Ramakrishna Hedge," Gowda assures me. He does not make any secret of his hold on his Vokkaliga followers and his effort to exploit voters on caste basis. In a lengthy constituency-wise analysis, he breaks the voters in caste fragments and names their leaders who will help his party win their votes.

Like a mathematician, he counts how many voters belong to which caste in each constituency, and his figures are accurate. He seems to know the caste pattern like the lines of his palm. According to his calculations his party will bag "not less than 16 seats." He is not bothered about the four seats left out for the BJP or the two for the Communists. "Let them win or lose, how does it affect us?"

The fact is that Ramakrishna Hegde is the single biggest asset of the Janata Party. He has made a considerable impression on educated youth and large numbers of urban voters with his style of functioning. Suave and mild mannered, he does not hurt his opponents and does not pamper his supporters. He has been in power for over two years, yet not even his Congress opponents have been able to level any charges of corruption, nepotism or high-handedness against him.

Though he has not been able to rule effectively, the administration is less corrupt and the bureaucracy is more responsive to popular urges. This is no mean achievement for a man heading a government of a party which depends on its erratic BJP and Communist allies for maintaining a majority.

"I go to the people with clean hands and a cleaner conscience. I will tell them I will not stay in power for a day more if they did not want me, but then I should not be blamed for the miseries that will be wrought on them by my Congress successors. Kannadigas are a literate lot and they are politically conscious, and I am sure they will not let me down," he comes out in soft unruffled voice.

He praises Indira Gandhi for her exceptional qualities of leadership and decries her assassination, but wonders at congressmen's jubilation over the prospects of victory "as a parting gift." He is not overawed by the sympathy wave. "It is not a sympathy wave, certainly not. If at all, it is just a sympathy factor and the overjoyous congressmen should not forget that it is sympathy for Indira Gandhi and the brutal way she was done to death, not for the discredited congressmen."

"The people will soon begin to question the congressmen who are exploiting the dead leader, and they will ask, if they could not save her how can they save the nation. We will effectively counter this sympathy racket. We are not worried about this factor."

Hegde wants to make Karnataka the testing ground for the political consciousness of the voters. Both the Congress and the Janata appear to be fully prepared with money and muscle power. Neither complains of dearth of resources. And both have fairly well-oiled election machinery. Their workers in thousands are fanning out of the 28 constituencies with confidence.

Unlike in the north, there is no acrimony, and there is no danger of any breakdown of law and order. Politicians on both the sides are more articulate and civil than their counterparts in UP and Bihar. There is a marked sense of decency and decorum, no invectives and abuses.

The fair assessment is that the Janata will win around 10 to 12 seats. Hegde's difficulties will begin after the elections. He has fielded six of his cabinet ministers. If they win, they might possibly opt out of their Assembly seats which would mean six supporters less for the Hedge government in the Assembly and six by-elections. If they lose, he will forfeit the moral authority to continue as Chief minister. Some of the ministers are bound to lose. "I will cross the bridge when we come to it," he says. "At the moment my job is to win, and win as many seats as possible."

He has brought George Fernandes to contest from Bangalore North against railway minister Jaffer Sharief. It will be the most prestigious battle in the state, and it is a touch and go situation. George is a classic fighter, and will surely put Sharief on the defensive.

The other city seat too is a Janata fortress, and its candidate V.S. Krishna Iyer, a minister, is popular. He is opposed by controversial economist Prof. Venkatagiri Gowda of the Congress. Both the camps are talking confidently of winning the two seats, but Bangaloreans generally seem to favour the Janata. There is not much of a caste factor in these highly urbanised constituencies.

Mysore city too is likely to witness an epic battle with the son of the former Maharaja, Srikanta Datta Wodiyar, taking up cudgels for the Congress. He has not been in politics and his nomination was a last-minute recommendation from Gundu Rao. The young *Maharaja* is fatter than his fat father. With his nearly 200 kilos he can hardly walk and does not know the ABC of politics. But he is likely to cash in on his family name. He is opposed by Janata stalwart P. Vishwanath, till recently mayor of Mysore. The Janata is hopeful of defeating the obese Maharaja.

The Janata is excessively dominated by Lingayats and Vokkaliggas, with the Harijans, backwards and the minorities, particularly Muslim, having little say in its affairs. It has fielded only one Muslim, Abdul Nazir Sab, from Dharawar South. He is pitted against Azeez Sait, a Janata minister who left Hegde only recently and joined the Congress. Both are exuding confidence. The constituency has a fairly large number of Muslim voters, but Nazir Sab is depending on pro-Janata Lingayats. The constituency, however, falls within the influence of PCC chief K.H. Patil, who is a Lingayat.

Current, 08.12.1984.
pp. (1 + 3)

Give him a chance

It is not merely a wish. It is a decision of millions who cast their votes in a massive exercise of faith in democracy. With the ballot in the tiny box they have also placed their hopes, expectations in that young man.

He has promised them unity, integrity, stability, a clean and effective government. His appeal to avenge the assassination of his mother by voting her party back to power has gone down deeply in the conscience of the electorate.

Call it a sympathy wave or Rajiv charisma, the Congress is poised to smash all its previous records—a two-thirds majority with booty of over 350 seats. A dazzling performance by a party which was about to be wiped out. Nothing short of miracle by a man who has been in power for hardly a month and in politics for less than three years.

Our 'unbelievable' prediction is not a shot in the dark. It is based on calculations, assessments and analysis from all over the country filed by our reporters. The mood of the nation is for a single-party government at the centre.

In the last one month I have travelled from one corner of the country to another, met thousands of people of all castes, creeds, communities and hues, in villages and in towns, in fields and in factories. I heard one single wish: give him a chance.

The Indian voter is aware of his democratic rights, his vision is clear, his involvement in the safety and integrity of the nation goes deep down into his conscience, he sets certain values for the parties and their leaders. It is what collective wisdom is made of.

I was told by men on the road, in the huts and in the fields that he is their choice because; he belongs to no caste, no religion, no region, no faction. He is fresh. His record is clean. He is young. He is sincere, he means business. Give him a chance.

It was a unique election. It was fought in a void. It was fought in a totally de-ideologised atmosphere. The picture would have been entirely different were Indira Gandhi leading the campaign. Her assassination benumbed the people. They suddenly woke up to the fact that a powerful leader like her could be killed in a jiffy by her own security guards, that the tragedy was part of a heinous plot to dismember the country, and that it was a sacred duty of each one of them to protect its sovereignty.

The sympathy wave took a positive turn with the succession of her son and the Congress, breathing its last, suddenly got a shot in the arm. It showed remarkable will to survive, bounced back to a new life. It began to speak, to act.

Rajiv infused it with new hope and soon everybody in the party was dwarfed by him. The Rajiv wave took over from the sympathy wave. He strode the country like a colossus, a charismatic leader in the making, a man of destiny. The charge of dynastic rule was gone with the wind.

The election which has just ended was an event packed with hopes and expectations. The youth for the first time found a young man in tune with their aspirations and with a modern and scientific outlook. The aged ones took him like a son with a tradition and a heritage. The women saw in him a protector and a person who would understand their problems.

The toiling masses genuinely believed he would relieve them of their economic and social burdens. The urban elite and the intelligentsia thought he is too liberal to encroach upon their set pattern of life. And the industrialists, large, medium and small, expect him to usher in a period of technological breakthrough with fewer restrictions on their growth.

But Rajiv will sweep back to power for many more reasons:

First, the Congress remains the only national party with a single leader, with nobody to question his authority. It is a well-knit and well-oiled organisation with its cadre entrenched in each and every village and town. Its resources and manpower cannot be matched by any other party. Despite factions and groups, it functions under a central command. The word High Command reassures people of a powerful group of men who take no time in putting the party machinery in order.

No party is credited with such a cohesive, superior organ. When it comes to the battle of the hustings, no other party or all the parties put together can equal it in its thrust and single-mindedness in winning elections. Above all, the Congress is a party, others are groups based on regional, communal and casteist appeals.

Two, with the bitter experience of 1977 the people do not wish to have the luxury of another nightmare. The opposition leader, with the exception of the Marxists, have lost credibility. They are taken as bunch of buffoons and an untrustworthy pack of hungry power grabbers. It is because of the personal ambitions that the opposition parties have failed to throw up new, fresh faces who could generate the people's trust.

The conclaves and unity efforts for the last three years were keenly watched by the people with sympathy and hope. After all, the country does have a solid chunk of 40 per cent opposition votes at any given time with about 10 per cent on the periphery. The opposition leaders with their selfish and cheap antics dashed the hopes of the traditional anti-Congress voters and most of them have undoubtedly switched over to the ruling party out of sheer frustration and in utter disgust.

Third, as if the opposition's failure to put up a united fight was not enough to demoralise its followers, the talk of a coalition government panicked them out of their wits. Coalition is a dirty word. It has become synonymous with horse-trading floor-crossing and rank opportunism.

Coalition in the popular mind means chaos. And no Indian in his senses would want chaos, at least at the centre. Rajiv's dig that how these people can function in a government at the centre unitedly while they could not come to terms on how to grab power had its impact.

The multi-cornered contests will help the Congress to improve the percentage of votes and also to bag some of the seats it had lost with slender margins. A divided opposition facing a united Congress will be the main cause of their disaster.

Fourth, as in 1980, the 1984 vote is also a positive verdict of the electorate. In the last election it was the people's intense desire to humiliate the warring opposition parties and bring back Indira Gandhi. In this election too the vote against the opposition will be a protest vote. A protest against its leaders short-sighted, selfish, over-ambitious antics. Each one of them imagined himself to be the next Prime Minister, and the people thought none deserved the coveted honour.

Fifth, since they decided to sink separately, Rajiv took them by the horn one by one. In Andhra he attacked the Telugu Desam and regionalism, in Karnataka he exposed the misdeeds of the Janata when it was in power at the centre, in the north he came down heavily on the communal role of the BJP, the casteist approach of the DMKP, and in Bengal he accused the Marxists for supporting Akali separatism. As a whole he beat them with the stick of Anandpur Saheb resolution. It became a rat in the opposition's collective throat, which was on the defensive all the time.

Neither Rajiv nor the opposition raised any basic economic or social issues. He nearly succeeded in likening the Anandpur Saheb resolution to the one passed by the Muslim League which ultimately led to the creation of Pakistan.

The dreaded idea of having Khalistan as a buffer state between India and Pakistan undoubtedly alienated a big chunk of the voters.

Rajiv, they thought, should be given a chance to save the country.

Current, 29.12.1984.
p. (1)

B. Rajiv as Prime Minister

Will this government work?
Rajiv rides a wave of hope

It is a victory written in blood. A victory of this Himalayan proportions strikes fear, it is awesome. It makes men small and the victor carries tons of load on his head. Yet, it was victory the nation desired. The election has established the supremacy of the people over their leaders.

Rajiv Gandhi, the architect of this mind-boggling achievement, will now have to find ways and means to unload this enormous responsibility in bits and pieces. He has assured the people that the trust reposed in him will be justified in action. The promises will be kept and the march towards progress will continue with vigour and zeal.

Having given the massive mandate, the nation will sleep with its eyes open. It will not be taken for granted. Each step of the man of destiny will be judged, evaluated and assessed by the watchful electorate. There should not be any mistaking about it, that the people are determined to act as judge and jury. The new rulers can therefore ill-afford to rest on their oars.

This is neither a sermon nor an advice, but the articulation of the expectations of the people. This paper has wished for and predicted a landslide victory for the Congress soon after Rajiv decided to seek the popular verdict. We were never off the mark.

We had predicted a two-thirds majority, in fact over 375 seats, at a time when the opposition was banding about the idea of a coalition, almost all the newspapers and journals were in no mood to concede more than 300 seats. Even Congress leaders had failed to gauge the popular mood, and none of them in his wildest dreams could think of the bagful of 400.

In 1980 also we were one of the two papers in the country to predict a massive victory for Indira Gandhi, the other was Surya, then edited by Maneka Gandhi. In 1977, too, we had front paged the inevitable rout of the Congress a weak after the elections were announced. None of these predictions came out of a computer. They were based on political calculations and were arrived at by judging the nation's mind.

The new and young men at the helm of affairs are expected to be humble, with their ears close to the ground. At this finest hour in the 100 year history of the Congress and of its dynamic leaders we make bold to say that the electorate will never forgive them if they failed to fulfill the promise and attain the goals set by them. No excuses will be tolerated.

The opposition is virtually slaughtered. There is slender hope of its rejuvenation in the near future. Its leader are totally discredited and their followers are thoroughly demoralised. There was a time when Indira Gandhi used to blame the opposition for all kinds of failures of her government but in the new situation nobody has been left to put the blame on. This is a unique opportunity for Rajiv and he has to grab it. The euphoria and the jubilation will soon be over. Soon the people will be in a somber mood, especially the youth, the poor, the downtrodden, who have made the Congress what it is today. The fact is that this ancient country is made up of young people. Some 87 per cent of them are in the 40-year age group and 78 per cent of them constitute the 35 year age-group, both men and women.

Rajiv did succeed in establishing a wavelength with this youthful section of the population. It is this segment that is for rapid progress and modernisation, for a breakthrough in science and technology. It has been given a vision of new India as Nehru had done in the early stages of our freedom.

It is these people who have shattered the communal, sectarian, casteist and regional barriers at Rajiv's behest. It is a dream come true, and it is a dream which he has been enjoined to preserve. The talk of a Hindu backlash is hogwash and the sooner the ghost is buried the better.

The hope and the wish is that he will succeed. He is no ideologue. The Left and the Right do not bug him. He did not once mention the word 'socialism' in his election speeches, nor did he criticise any opposition party because of its ideological stance. He knows the era of ideology is over not only in India but even in countries like Russia and China.

He is development-oriented. He plans to unshackle the economy from its traditional trappings, give a thrust to the industry, revolutionise rural India by providing it with the benefits of new and scientific techniques, remove unemployment by creating new job opportunities, give a direction to the educated youth in self-employment and free the vast women populace from its ante diluvian shackles.

A dreamer that he appears, he has now the power to translate the vision into reality. There is no ambiguity about it in his mind. This is the impression left on my mind from the talks I had with him from time to time.

Yet, the people are realistic enough not to expect a sudden miracle from him. What they expect from them is:

1. Settle the Punjab tangle as amicably as possible and soon. It has to be the first priority. The Sikhs cannot for long remain an alienated 'sect', and the nation will remain weak until they are brought back into the national mainstream. Imagine there will be only one Sikh in this Lok Sabha and he too elected from Rajasthan. Let Rajiv pay his first visit to the Golden Temple.
2. Assam is a dormant volcano. He will have to apply his mind to bringing this crucial border state back to the national ethos. Though there is peace at the moment it might shatter any time. His next visit should be to Gauhati. The people dealing with the situation there neither have the vision nor the stature to grapple with the running sore.
3. Curb the menace of corruption and begin the crusade from the top. No use catching a peon or a constable for a pittance of a bribe. The big sharks will have to be caught first, and Rajiv alone can do this without fear or favour. This is what he has promised repeatedly.

   His fight against the monster of corruption will probably be the toughest. What set-up or machinery he will create to take this bull by the horns is not yet known but some of his young colleagues with impeccable record are at it.
4. Provide the country with a government that works. The government largely means the bureaucracy. Its traditional approach, its unconcern for the problems of the country, its lethargy, its anti-people outlook, its self-centred attitude, its habit to create road blocks in the way to progress are not a new phenomenon. Both Nehru and Indira Gandhi had to face this stone wall. They often complained publicly about this bureaucratic anachronism, but could hardly do anything to mend it.

   Rajiv has promised an effective government. It goes without saying that he too will not succeed if he cannot overhaul this leviathan, change its concept of functioning and give it a new orientation. It is an enormous task, but it will have to be achieved if he has to give a government that works.

5. Poverty: Sixty per cent of the people live under the *chapati* belt. These have-nots turned his success into a colossal triumph. He is mandated to remove poverty. The slogan of *Garibi Hatao* which his mother launched in 1971 will now have to be resurrected. The unity and integrity of the country will remain fragile if half the population continue to find it difficult to make two ends meet. It is a tall order indeed, yet not unattainable.

If he has to meet these goals, largely if not fully, during the mandated period, he has no alternative short of launching a new revolution, the kind of which the world has not witnessed. Traditional methods following the beaten paths will lead to a disaster our recent history has not known.

The country has seen him as decent, cultured, liberal with a glorious family tradition. He has to emerge as a doer. Nothing short of a revolution will satiate the people's thirst. And with 400 seats in the Lok Sabha, what more effective instrument does he need?

Current, 05.01.1985.
pp. (1 + 3)

A budget of rising hopes: quantum jump

Finance minister Vishvanath Pratap Singh is an unassuming, modest man and in no way betrays his royal lineage. He is more at home with poets, litterateurs, metaphysicians and of course journalists. His latest love is Computerji.

As I enter his spacious room in the North Block I see him engrossed with the computer installed a few minutes earlier. He is the first minister to have a computer installed in his office, and he means to use it as often as he can. The wind is blowing over Delhi's head and it seems very soon the electronic revolution will have it's impact.

He is a politician with a rare quality—honesty. It is difficult to be honest these days, and former Chief minister of UP and now Finance minister, he prefers to live in his modest flat in a South Delhi colony. The flat is so small that he leaves home latest by 7.30 in the morning for his office and goes back late in the evening. He receives all his visitors in the office though the list does not include more than half a dozen.

He was first reluctant to give the interview—so close to the budget—but he agreed when I assured him not to ask any embarrassing questions. The interview continued for over two hours.

Massive mandate means massive expectations. And next to the Prime Minister it is the Finance minister who has to bear the brunt of fulfilling these expectations. How do you see the prospect?
Massive mandate does mean massive expectations. But I do not feel that the Finance minister is next to the Prime Minister. Next to the Prime Minister are all the ministers. People's expectations are on various issues and all of us have to exert ourselves to fulfill them. Rajiv is very candid about things, and specific. Under his leadership the government is giving results. The anti-defection bill is just one of the examples.

Secondly, he is looking into the future towards a modern India. And he is thinking of quantum jumps, not slow process—especially in selected areas. Thirdly, he has tried to inculcate values into public life. When he speaks of a clean government or a clean public life, he is referring to many more things than merely financial matters. Of course, clean administration and clean public life do have economic implications. It is the general thrust that matters. Then, we have also to take into account the constraints.

You mean paucity of resources.
Yes, both rupee resources and foreign exchange.

India's standing in the international financial markets is very high. We had earlier plans to tap these markets, but little has come out of them. Would you go in for substantial commercial borrowings in the world markets? Possibly this is one sure source of augmenting our resources.
True our standing in the world markets is very good. We have, for instance, floated some bonds in the UK. They sold very well. We could tap the European markets also. But there is a limit to borrowings, because ultimately it depends on the capacity to repay.

But we have the capacity to repay.
We have. But we should not go in for reckless borrowing. I mean we should be cautious.

Then there is this IMF loan.
From the IMF loan, we have taken the amount we wanted.

Will you start repaying from next year.
We well start repaying it. And we will manage our finances well on that account. At the same time we should not lose sight of the limiting factor.

The real answer, if we are not to get caught in a debt trap, is a massive effort to increase our exports.

About rupee resources, there is a feeling that our non-plan expenditure is becoming far too much, leaving less and less for development.

Non-plan expenditure does not mean unnecessary expenditure. Previously, our revenues used to meet the non-plan expenditure and even leave some balance for the plan. But now, revenue expenditure just about balances the non-plan expenditure or sometimes falls short. So the plan has to rest on borrowed money.

Now, borrowed money is at a cost. We have to pay interest to the extent of 8 to 10 per cent. If the return on the money is lower than this, then we are in trouble. So we have to be very careful about how we distribute the resources. For this we have to be careful in ordering our priorities. That is the way to beat the resource constraint, making careful selection of growth points.

Now, we are talking especially the Prime Minister and you, of entering into 21st century. Do you want to take the entire country into the 21st century or only a part of it? India is simultaneously in various stages of development. We have the computer, and we have the bullock cart. We have islands of riches in a sea of extreme poverty, consumerism side by side with scarcities.

Technology is for the benefit of all. Our concept of technological revolution will encompass all the sectors, all the areas.

So you are planning a comprehensive technological revolution.

Now, as the Prime Minister has perceived quite clearly, there was a challenge in space technology. We took the challenge and our scientists have shown results. Similarly in the field of atomic energy. This proves what the Prime Minister has said many times, that the fourth standard boy who sat under a tree and read with no roof over his head grows up—and one day one Rakesh Sharma goes and orbits the earth. This is what India has achieved. What you may call from the bullock cart to . . . the computer.

Yes, it is the same boy, coming and achieving these results.

The Prime Minister has talked about importing the best technology.

If I have understood the Prime Minister correctly, he feels that in certain areas we have to go in for the best straightaway, not in stages, because even as we progress in stages, world developments will overtake us and keep us continuously obsolescent.

That means borrowing foreign technology on a massive scale.

Not necessarily on a massive scale, but on a selective basis. In the final analysis, what is important is that the technology that we import has to get absorbed and we have to regenerate it on our own. Then it would not be like a postage stamp struck on a paper, but like a skin-graft, it becomes our own and grows on its own, from then on.

How are you going to reconcile modern technology with the appalling conditions particularly in our villages. A majority of the villages lack even the most basic needs like drinking water, electricity, roads. And we suddenly talk of a very high technology. Does not it smack of elitist thinking, technology for the benefit of the elitist classes.

You see, in the villages, especially in agriculture, even putting fertiliser to use was initially considered a foreign idea, hybrid seeds were unknown. Now, they have taken to it in a big way. You can see modern satellite antennas even in the villages today. So it is not true that our village people are not ready to adapt themselves to modern methods, new technology. With the right approach you will find that they readily respond.

Talking of fertilisers, their use as also the use of several other facilities is encouraged by giving substantial subsidies. Fertiliser subsidy alone is said to amount Rs. 3,000–4,000 crore. The Prime Minister has hinted that these subsidies will have to go. But what is the alternative if agriculture is not to suffer.

We will have to have a hard look at the problem.

Industry too is favoured with some subsidies—rebates and duty drawbacks to make imported inputs available at international prices and exports competitive. There is a feeling that a general reduction in excise duties would be a more efficient and less cumbersome way to encourage exports. It would also perhaps reduce excise evasion. What are your views on the subject?

This is a question I am not going to answer now.

Governments all over the world have been resorting more and more to a value added tax (VAT) system which makes excise evasion difficult. Do not you think it would be worth while for us to study the various available VAT models and formulate our own VAT system?

We are studying this. There are certain problems, because in our accounting system, everyone does not keep accounts systematically. Then, we have concessions on various items. Calculation of value addition becomes complicated. But we have a limited set-off system in some areas.

For instance . . .

For instance, if I have paid a tax on some item, I can show it in my returns. So, apart from these areas, now we have to see the areas where we can introduce the VAT. And whether this system, if widely applied, could serve the purpose.

You are studying this question . . . favourably . . .

Yes, favourably. Because this is a system towards which we should go. Not VAT as such but something similar. Not all the countries that have the system have had a favourable experience of VAT. A recent delegation from a South American country told us that their experience of VAT is not good.

It is said that India is the highest-taxed country in the world. What do you have to say about this. Do you agree that tax burden is hindering economic development.

One of the highest tax rates, yes, but if you go by the effective tax, we cannot be called the highest-taxed country.

But you have done your best to tax the people. And the taxes are not forthcoming.

We'll, after a point, increasing the rate of tax is counter-productive.

Which is more important, increasing the tax rate, or collecting more.

There are two things. Higher rate of tax does not necessarily mean higher realisation. You can have lower tax rates, then more people can afford to pay.

This is what you are going to do, right.

I did not say that. I am not going to answer this question.

Lower rates bring a more spontaneous payment of taxes. And less corruption and less tension.

Perhaps. But you are taking me to sensitive areas.

Now, the tax-collecting machinery has become one of the biggest dens of corruption. The threat of raids and often actual raids with little justification are used by the taxmen to amass wealth. Innocent people are harassed and the guilty can buy peace. Don't you think the assault on corruption must start from this end.

It is to start from all ends.

Do you agree that the tax-collecting machinery is corrupt and coercive. And the Finance Ministry is blissfully ignorant about it. For instance, you have ordered raids in Bombay, or Calcutta or Delhi. A multi-millionaire has been raided. He goes and makes peace with the man who has raided him. This happens often.

Wherever there is corruption, whether it is within the machinery or outside, it has to be fought.

My question is whether this kind of raids can really unearth black money, leave alone stop black money generation.

You must have an economic system where there is less impetus for black money generation. At the same time you need some different measures too.

But we have a system that yields black money.

It is not the system alone. The individual is bending the system to suit his purpose.

He is a part of the system.

Yes. But it is both. Even in Hong Kong where there is a 25 per cent income tax rate there is black money.

Are you thinking of changing the system which is generating black money.

You see, there is the individual's greed also along with the system. We will need an imaginative set of fiscal policies as well as deterrent measures.

What is the imaginative set of fiscal policies.

That I can spell out only in a budget.

So you are going to spell out the things in your forthcoming budget.

I cannot say that.

But the Prime Minister is talking about black money.

Under his leadership we will try to implement his ideas.

Anyway, you are very serious about attacking black money and its sources.

Because it distorts the economy.

Now, L.K. Jha favours mobilisation and not confiscation of black money. Confiscation becomes very difficult, because there is Rs. 30,000 crore to Rs. 40,000 crore of black money floating in the market. By confiscation you may at best lay hands on one, or two, or three thousand crore.

All right. I will hear your suggestions.

No. My point is how are going to mop up this Rs. 30,000 crore of black money. Through schemes like bearer bonds, giving some concessions or some incentives.

I will hear your suggestions.

My suggestion is that there should be a national war on black money. People's involvement should be there. I think if the tax structure is simplified—excise, customs and all—half the battle will be won.

But there is a limit to our accusing excise.

What I mean is there will be less corruption. Now, we come to the banks.

These were nationalised to ensure that a few big industrial houses did not corner the public resources. But nationalised banks are proving no better. In fact worse. Bank managers have turned the loaning operation into a lucrative personal enterprise. Kickbacks have become far too common. Look at the Sethia affair and others. And I must congratulate you for having taken very stern step. And this has created a sense of alertness among the bankers. But is it the only solution.
No, that is not the only solution.

Removing a bank manager after he gobbles the money.
I have never spoken of it as a solution, but it is a necessary step that you have to take. Because there has to be an element of constructive responsibility. I mean, a top manager has his supervisory responsibilities. Just passing the buck by saying that someone else did won't do. If there is default in supervision, there is default in his duty.

If the chairman and the manager are themselves indulging in embezzlement.
Then, of course, the sternmost action has to be taken.

That is after the crime committed. Why should not there be a vigilance body within the bank itself which monitors the loaning system.

Today I had a meeting with officials where we discussed the question making use of computer monitoring sickness in an industrial unit in its early stages. That is when the signals should start coming. If you have loaned your money to that unit, you must have the channels to get early indications about the prospects of that money getting into jeopardy. And we have identified some variables for sickness. As soon as they start showing up, remedial action should begin, rather than going on giving money until that industrial unit falls in the lap of the government.

The bank will fall sick too.
We are burdened with a sick unit and a sick bank.

Central Bank is in that predicament. Now if the chairman or the managing director indulges in corruption of this scale, is removal of the man from office sufficient, do not you have to penalise him too, file a criminal case against him.
Wherever there is evidence on record, we shall.

In the case of central Bank and Punjab National Bank, are you thinking of filing criminal case against these people. I think there was a news item that the ministry is thinking of that.
What is the next question.

You parry questions so easily. O.K. Estate duty and wealth tax collection are very poor, the cost of collection is said to be as high as the recovery. Would it not be worthwhile to scrap these levies. That would reduce the incentive to make black money.
I am too near the budget.

As elusive as black money is smuggling. Punitive measures have proved to be awfully inadequate. Do you have any plans to attack the problem at the root.
We will have to do both. Take economic measures as well as punitive measures.

The biggest smuggled item is gold.
It is the price differential that induces smuggling.

So how do you plan to face it.
The simplest economic solution is to remove the price differential. But the question of exchange rates is involved. Secondly, there are structural problems in our economy itself. Now, the tax structure is said to be one. But even that is not the whole thing. High cost of production is also one. When there are smaller units, the cost of production is high. Now that is not a part of the tax structure. So there are so many factors. It is not an easy problem. But you know in which direction to move. You know you will have to take economic measures as well as punitive measures.

There is considerable demand for gold in the country, especially in the rural areas. And smuggled gold to the tune of Rs. 10,000 to Rs. 12,000 crore is coming in every year. Why cannot we import gold instead of letting the smugglers infest the market. We can officially import gold and sell it to the people at the same price.
And thereafter what do we do with our gold.

We don't have much gold. The government doesn't have much gold.
No. That much foreign exchange we need for our ONGC drills, for our fertiliser. Where do we get the money for all that?

All right. But it is even otherwise going away. The gold price goes in foreign exchange. It does not go into Indian currency.
Yes, it is. But now it will go from the official kitty—that is the matter.

Then, what is the solution.
It only means that foreign exchange is being generated outside the country and it is being paid. Previously silver used to go out in lieu of what was smuggled in. Now the international price of silver has equalised, so that is not of use.

With all these difficulties, finance minister you have to apply your mind very seriously to the problem of smuggling.
I know. The problem is that you can deal with one factor, but there are many factors. In the treatment of a patient you just say bring down the blood pressure, and a quack doctor can do it. But the kidney might collapse. You don't treat the economy like that.

Are you thinking of appointing some kind of a committee or group to make a deep study of this problem.
No. It is a well-analysed matter. There is nothing to study.

So are you going to tackle the problem?
As I said, we have to go in that direction. One is the import route. Another is lower cost of production in the country and more production. Now these are known areas. I can deal with one factor, but there are something . . .

We should do it in the case of computers and other electronic goods. We are aiming at an electronics revolution. We can, but we cannot give up punitive measures. They too are needed.

A protected market dampens technological initiatives, and the system of licencing and control helps a few selected industrialists to acquire and pre-empt capacity. This obviates competition and also perpetuates a shortage economy.
We have to have more and more competition.

Are you giving some incentives towards that end.
Not incentives, change in our policies of licencing, on imports, etc.

I am told you are completely changing your licencing policy.
I think we will have to look into it, because those who get the licences behave like those who get into a railway compartment and then bolt it from within.

What will you do with that.
We will have to liberalise on the licencing side. And we are already following a liberal import policy. There will be both internal and international competition.

Huge investments have gone into the public sector. But the returns are meagre. The PM has talked about sprucing up the public sector undertakings. Are you confident that these undertakings can be made to contribute their due to the national exchequer.
I suppose more than Rs.11,000 crore is locked up in inventory. Even if we reduced it by 15 per cent, Rs, 300 crore of resources will be available.

I am talking of inefficiency in the public sector.

What does efficiency mean? It has to be in terms of various factors. Look at your inventories. Look at your performance. Look at your capacity utilisation. Look at the costs, the realisation. You have to look at the situation in its totality.

Only then can you achieve efficiency. Take capacity utilisation. If adequate power is made available, many of our public sector undertakings would perform better. So it is a complex issue.

What about the sick units in the public sector.

Some could be sick because of certain inefficiencies. These need to be obviated. Some others need modernisation. And the very badly off units will need a rehabilitation plan.

And close down the irretrievably sick. Why don't you hand them over to the private sector.

But who in the private sector will take an irretrievably sick unit?

It depends on the incentives you offer.

I don't think so. They will try to get the better ones. We should not give those to them. If a unit is irretrievably sick, what do you do with it?

But closing down for how long, I am told there are some 135 sick units.

I won't talk in terms of numbers. These studies have not been done. But I think we will have to come to some sort of conclusion.

Let me cite the example of the ITDC. Its hotels division is running in loss since it was formed 25 years ago. All other hotels are making profits, except the ITDC hotels.

I think these areas need to be looked into. Now there are some areas where the government need not enter. If we are short of resources we should stick to the core sector.

There is sickness in the private sector too—the textile industry, for example. The government has taken over a large number of sick units and is nursing them. But the incidence of sickness is increasing. Have you got any plans to tackle this problem. The more you take over, the greater is the sickness in the textile industry.

It is not like that. The greater the sickness the more we take over. But the whole textile industry is not sick.

A big part of it is sick.

No, only a small part. Spinning is not sick. It may have some problem this year. The powerloom sector is not sick. What is sick is the weaving sector of the organised composite mills.

But generally it is made out that the textile industry is sick.

That's what they do. But you see, we have never had queues for buying cloth. The textile mills in Bombay were closed for a long time, still the industry provided clothing to the people.

There was more cloth available in those days.

So the textile industry is healthy enough to cloth the people. There are, of course, some sick units, and there are certain general problems of the textile industry which I don't want to underestimate.

You have been dealing with it as Commerce minister.

One thing is about relative profitability. Textiles was the mother of industry. But new industries have left it behind.

Secondly, its raw material is dependent on rain. Seventy-five per cent of the cotton is in non-irrigated areas. So there is fluctuation, with its attendant problems.

Thirdly, as far as export markets are concerned, there is technological obsolescence. We have to see how the weaving sector of the composite mills can be updated, modernised.

Would you not like the composite mills to become entirely export-oriented and let powerlooms and handlooms feed the domestic market.

Yes. You can have such a mix: Powerloom meeting the domestic demand and the organised sector concentrating on exports and specialised clothes. We are coming up with a new textile policy and for that purpose would be meeting in March.

On the one side we are talking of technological revolution. On the other we are faced with poverty. There is need for serious thinking to ensure that the fruits of development percolate to the lowest levels. This is the gut problem of development.

Yes. There are three problems. One is foreign exchange constraint. That calls for greater exports. That in turn calls for ordering of priorities and better utilisation of capacity. And then income distribution.

The Prime Minister said that within five years there will be an industry in each district. If we succeed in doing this, it will solve the problem of poverty to some extent.

Yes, that is the idea. The benefits will percolate to the lower levels.

But is it possible to establish so many industries in five years.

I think it is possible if we distribute our industries. The non-industrialised areas should be covered.

That should be the policy.

That is the existing policy.

No, no. In the existing policy you are giving units to saturated areas. Bombay is saturated, Bangalore is getting saturated, Hyderabad is getting saturated, yet more industries are coming there.

The argument often is that capital will be under-utilised if the infrastructure is not there, so entrepreneurs are attracted to developed areas. But these are the pangs of development.

Will you in future insist that people who want to start new industries must go to the non-industrial districts.

That in fact is the existing policy. They will be encouraged to go to non-industrial districts.

Is it a policy, or just encouragement?

It is the policy.

Now we have a large number of districts where there are no industries at all. You think in five years new industries will be set up in all these districts. What about the infrastructure—roads, power, water.

Many-a-times when an industry goes to a new area, infrastructure is built up.

That may be true about the sugar industry, but not so about sophisticated industries, synthetic fibre, for example.

When we talk of industry, that includes small and medium industries also, even ancillaries.

Will it be possible to set up these industries in each district in five years.

I think so. I mean, that would be our effort.

Now about prices. What are your plans to keep prices in check? Do you believe in monetary control or fiscal control?

Prices in India depend on so many variables. Weather is one very important variable which is out of control.

Yes.

You see the inflation rate has come down to 5.3 per cent. We have had two consecutive good agriculture crops.

The third is also going to be good.

And we also used imports—edible oil, etc. But there is a limit up to which we can use imports to check prices. We will have to curb money expansion and at the same time have development. It is a difficult assignment. We have to strike a balance. And some element of inflation will have to be taken into account.

I am referring to prices of essential goods—like kerosene oil, sugar, clothes, agricultural products.

We have got buffer stocks and we use them to regulate prices. For instance, we have got enough foodgrains, and it is possible to control foodgrains prices. Now about edible oils, I don't think it is advisable to go on importing such products in order to control their prices.

I think we should allow the price mechanism some free-play so that it boosts indigenous production. For a while this would be a little hard on the consumer but we will be able to get rid of the burden on the foreign exchange reserves.

Are you thinking of giving incentives to this sector.
Yes. I think the Agriculture Ministry has a scheme for it. And then we might think of plantations in some of our island such as Andaman Nicobar.

Current, 09.03.1985.
pp. (1 + 3 + 5)

I have done no wrong

"'He has the smile of child but the brain of a devil.' 'He is the real foreign hand.' 'He is a CIA agent.' 'He is the main destabilising force.' 'He should be expelled from the party before more damage is done to the Prime Minister's image'."

These allegations have been hurled at Vishwanath Pratap Singh not by common goons but in the central Hall of Parliament by senior Congress MPs and ministers.

While the storm blows over his head, he is relaxed, poised, unperturbable. The ex-Defence minister laughs but suddenly withdraws into himself when told his partymen are demanding his expulsion.

"But they cannot snatch the tricolor from my hands. I will continue to hold it. It will continue to fly on my rooftop."

His eyes become misty, a lump in the throat and a long silence. "*Bhai hum ne to yeh sub socha hi nahin tha,*" (I had never thought of it).

How have you been reacting to the massive campaign of calumny against you by your own party men. Are you casting yourself in the role of a Gandhi or a JP.
It was not all by party men.

Yes, your party men, a very large number of them, have been hurling invectives at you.
With some party men we have honest differences of opinion. Basically, I

cannot understand why action against economic offenders or against any agent who is in no way connected with the government can be an embarrassment. In fact, if anything, it would increase the credibility of the government.

And this is precisely what the Prime Minister has endorsed in Parliament. He also said that the policy of taking action against economic offenders will be continued. And also in the defence deal action against the agent will be taken. An attempt will be made to reduce the price in the submarine deal. He also said that the drive against economic offenders that took place in the last two years was unprecedented and he has correctly said that this was not an individual's effort but the government policy.

I have been talking about the hate campaign against you in the party . . . .
I am coming to that because my explanation is very relevant to what you are suggesting. When you speak of the campaign you have to talk of the positive side also. I was implementing the government policy and it got endorsement from the Prime Minister himself on the floor of the House. He also endorsed the inquiry into the defence deal. I think that has been my greatest relief in yesterday's (April 20) debate.

The Prime Minister you think defended you.
No one defends individuals, you see. It is the policy and its implementation which has to be defended. So it was very heartening to listen to the Prime Minister saying strongly that in fact it was government policy I was implementing. I am saying this because the way the question has been framed, answering it alone will not bring out the rest. Yes, some of the things that were said did make me sad but at the same time I am very clear that what I did was right and was in the national interest.

Couldn't these have been said in a proper atmosphere earlier. Why this sudden attack . Don't you think someone instigated them to hurl invectives at you. Some of them are senior MPs.
Why should I ascribe anything to what they said, what they believed, they have a right to their opinions.

In the Cabinet meeting also most of your colleagues opposed you.
Sorry, I can't talk about what happened in the Cabinet meeting.

But that has come out in the newspapers.
Anyway.

In the CPP also and in Parliament too some of the remarks against you were very derogatory.
(Laughs). Okay. I think though I had fought battles outside the party and faced conflicts and went to jail in 1977. So the little bit of criticism was

perhaps . . . I think I had it too smooth for 20 years. The going was good.

For you or for the party.

For me personally because now I have seen myself . . . perhaps this much of seasoning is necessary . . .

Are you trying to be closer to Gandhi . . .

I think you are talking rot.

Why.

I am a very ordinary person.

No. You think, you are an ordinary person but what you have done is rather extraordinary.

Any such talk is sheer nonsense.

What is wrong in feeling closer to Gandhi or JP. They also fought against injustice and corruption.

Why are you comparing me with them. I am very, very ordinary person. I have 101 flaws and defects.

From the behaviourist point of view you are either too naive or very shrewd. This is what they talk in the central Hall.

(A long pause). It is difficult question. (Again a long pause).

It is very difficult to put oneself in a category and evaluate oneself. I devote very little to myself. I devote very little time to self-analysis (Long pause). Maybe a medicore or may be mixture of both.

You are a poet, you love literature, you love the arts, all those fine things of life. You are a sensitive person. But at this juncture, at this turning point in your eventful life, you just cann't dismiss the whole thing by saying 'I am a very simple person.' You have been Chief minister, Commerce, Finance and Defence minister. Simple people do not become such important ministers. They must have some qualities. . .

(Laugh loudly). I think I have been a freak.

You have been Chief minister of UP, the country's largest state, you couldn't have been a freak all the way. You cann't escape by merely saying you have been a freak.

I don't think I fit into the system.

You are saying this after two decades in politics.

You may not love your wife but you have to be a very good husband. (Laughs heartily).

That means you've been husbanding politics.

(Laughs and recites a couplet).

The other day a senior Congress MP remarked that you have the face of a child and the mind of a devil.
(Long silence). I think all of us are a mixture of the child and the devil.

Who has got the better of you—the child or the devil.
No more than it takes the better of any man.

The economic offenders you have been trying to destroy were thought of as devils.
They are indeed destroying the country and with them I will not compromise.

In future also.
Yes.

There are strong indications of a campaign in the Congress leading to your expulsion from the party. For the past three days even ministers have been suggesting your expulsion from the party. You think 'my leader' will come to your rescue.
I am not aware of the campaign. I have already said I will work for the party and will not hold any office (long pause). I cannot say anything more.

Do you know the party is no more in the mood to accept you, to tolerate you despite your protestations of loyalty.
I have said what I had to say about this before. I do not want to repeat any more.

Do you think in case of a very vicious attack on you Rajiv Gandhi will come to your rescue.
(Long long pause). We will cross the bridge when it comes.

From yesterday's Rajya Sabha debate (April 20) it seems you tried to contradict Arun Singh.
No, it is not a fact. Two or three points were being made. That I ordered the inquiry after Fairfax had come. I had to clarify that I have ordered the inquiry on March 1. The inquiry on Fairfax was set up 34 days later on April 4.

The other point made was that the file was lying on my desk for a month. I had to clarify that for 15 days it had gone to the Defence Secretary and then came back to me.

Another point made was that it was an embarrassment to the party and there should have been no publicity. I had clarified that when the agent is of the supplier and not of the government there can be no question of embarrassment to the party. If anything credibility was established by taking action against the agent and also going public to bring it to the notice of the people. I had to explain this. I confined myself within the statement made by Arun Singh. I did not contradict any part of his statement.

It was a clear contradiction of what Arun Singh had said.
No, no, it wasn't. He did say that on March 1. I had passed orders for inquiry. And I had quoted him confirming this statement without contradicting. About making it public, that is a question of opinion.

What piqued Rajiv Gandhi was that you issued the press release without consulting him and that the file reached him around 2 o'clock.
That file was not for approval but for information.

You could at least have told him of the press release.
The government has endorsed my action about the inquiry. About the press release I have given my argument in my statement in Parliament. I think in such a vital matter the country should be taken into confidence. It increases political credibility. The point is there was no embarrassment. How could it be, he is not a government agent but a supplier's agent.

Why is the government feeling embarrassed.
There is no embarrassment. The government is going ahead with the inquiries. The Prime Minister categorically said that we will go ahead with the inquiries. The agent will be punished and the price reduced.

But the Prime Minister was very agitated with the whole thing. He came back to the file again and again.
He was not agitated. He corrected the information that it was not late evening but 1.30 in the afternoon. That is normal.

Did you ever think in your wildest dream of becoming the prime minister of India.
Never. The maximum ambition I had was to become a member of Parliament. Each of the posts I have held so far—whether of Chief minister, Finance minister, Defence minister—is a lifetime ambition fulfilled.

You never thought of becoming Prime Minister.
You cann't force a person to wish what you wish. The only unfulfilled side of my political career is my literary activities. It is not compulsory for me to think these things.

You have been in politics for 20 years.
But I've never got hooked on it. Internally I am not hooked on it. That's why it is a great buffer to me.

But once you become a minister you get very powerful.

That way I did my job. Externally you are involved. Internally these shocks don't matter. Every assignment that came I took seriously.

You are taken as a crusader against corruption. How will you continue?

You said in Lucknow you will continue your crusade against corruption.
By exposures. When you are an MP you can bring it to light. When you are a minister you cann't take action.

But you must be having a lot of information.
But I don't have any proof. I don't have any documents. It belongs to the government.

It is said that you intensified your anti-economic offenders activities with Amitabh Bachchan as your ultimate target.
When the government was formed and declared that it would be fighting economic offenders, as Finance minister I was implementing this. So no individual could be my target. Because you are implementing a policy. And in that, wherever there is evidence, you will have to take action.

Would you have implemented this policy if you had evidence on Amitabh.
We have to go by evidence on record. Let's face it. The government policy is there and it has to be followed. That's it.

You say the Prime Minister and the party should be happy because they wanted you to expose shady deals but the whole thing has boomeranged. You have lost the ministry and they are about to lose the government.
No. It has not boomeranged. I haven't lost my ministry. The Prime Minister has said that all the policies will continue. I don't want to discuss any further about the defence issue.

Why did your drive avoid Amitabh.
The government will be fighting against economic offenders at all costs. As Finance minister I was implementing the government policy. No, individual could be my target, because you are implementing policy. And in the policy wherever there is evidence action will be initiated.

Did you have evidence against Amitabh.
What is there to say in that.

Why don't you say.
(Long pause).

You will have to say.
The network does not have a compilation of all the information that it has.

But you raided so many film actors and actresses, why not Amitabh.

It is not my raid. Look here, I want to make this very clear. The genesis of this question is the concept of a feudal order that I order. That's not true at all. It's not the way with governments. I did not order any investigation because I had to as a minister but because the policy compelled me to do so. It was all done in accordance with the Act passed by Parliament. If I did anything wrong any officer could turn around and say 'Sir, you are wrong.' But that is not what has happened in my case. So I was right. Is it clear now that there is no feudal conception in the order.

When I was Finance minister, one of the members of the central Board of Direct Taxes sent for my tax form from the ITO of Allahabad. There was a Parliament question. Members had asked about the income-tax of all ministers. Poojary said if they wanted it for a particular minister, that could be furnished. They did not want. So the question was over.

As I was saying, one member in CBDT inquired about my arrears. He investigated and showed me that receipts and said that it was all updated. My chartered accountant showed all records. Now I could have told him that he need not have investigated the case because he should have checked on the facts first. But I did not say so. Because I knew it was his job. I never said that the officer was trying to blackmail me, etc. I knew he was bound to do his job and investigate any person however high he or she might be. Here, I'm not a minister. This is not a feudal order.

I agree with you.

Wait, this is very relevant portion here. . . These rights are cast by statutory Acts.

In two years of your Finance ministership almost every film star was raided. Why Amitabh's house was not raided even once. Why is he treated as a sacred cow? I have a right to know this.

You are asking me to dig up finance.

I have a right to know why your department did not take action against Amitabh.

It all depends on what evidence the officers had against him or anybody for that matter.

You mean there was no evidence against Amitabh.

Do not ask for details.

There is a definite opinion in the Congress party that you are a destabilising force in the country.

I feel the country is strong enough to face any destabilising force.

Current, 25.04.1987.

pp. (1 + 5 + 7)

Ten steps for Rajiv

The message from Haryana is loud and clear. Rajiv Gandhi and the ruling echelons are totally alienated from the masses. The elitist policies, the ad hocism, the superficial approach even to the gravest problems, the total lack of direction in the implementation of programmes and policies, the charges of corruption and kickbacks at the highest level have taken their toll.

The political, economic and administrative confusion has grown to unmanageable proportions. The government which Rajiv had promised would move faster is paralysed. The ruling party has collapsed. The morale of the nation has touched the lowest ebb. The promise of taking the country to the 21st Century has turned out to be a hoax.

The tragedy is that the Prime Minister seems oblivious of the impending crisis. The loss of credibility has damaged Rajiv, his party and the government's image. It can be regained only if he decides on a major operation. He can do it if he resolves to:

1. Clear himself of the kickback charges. He should identify the recipients of the slush money, get them arrested and hand them over to a special court constituted with the specific purpose of prosecuting them. The Prime Minstership should not be sacrificed for the sake of unscrupulous friends.
2. Institute a high-level anti-corruption bureau to investigate charges of corruption against his party men in power and hand them over to the special court. He must first sack them from the government and party positions they hold. These people should be thoroughly exposed, if he is sincere in his pronouncements of eradicating corruption. Kickbacks and corruption are now the major issues and he cannot run away from them.
3. Reconstitute his Council of Ministers and induct men of integrity and impeccable image if he has any more left in the party or get them from outside.
4. Revamp the party's policy-making bodies—the Parliamentary Boards and the working committee—and fill them with men of experience and integrity. Let these bodies advise and guide him in running the party and the government.
5. Hand over the party presidentship to a senior congressmen to lessen his burden and allow inner party democracy, freedom of comment and criticism. It can be done only if he liberates himself from the coterie of sycophants.

6. Hold organizational elections without delay despite the odds and obstacles. Rejuvenated AICC, PCCs and DCCs will add tremendous political strength to him as leader of the party.
7. Remove inept and corrupt Chief ministers and their equally inept and corrupt junior colleagues. Restore respectability and functional autonomy which a Chief minister must have.
8. Work out certain definite policies aimed at giving maximum benefits to the poverty-stricken masses. Involve the party functionaries in executing these policies.
9, Give up the life style of Rolls Royce and Mercedes Benz and be more accessible to the common people. The country cannot be governed from a bullet-proof bubble.
10.Use language which does not hurt.

Current, 27.06.1987.
p. (2)

Instrument of change

The system we created 38 years ago is on the verge of collapse. The founders of the Republic had sought to establish an egalitarian society with economic and social equality as the most cherished goal. This group of dedicated, men and women never thought it would ultimately turn into a monster poised to devour the country.

Two Indias have emerged in these 38 years. One of the rich and the super-rich, the other is of the poor and the very poor. These two Indias cannot be united. One of them will have to be destroyed. The very rich and the very poor are like fire and water, they cannot co-exist. Communism is not the only answer though its relevance in certain situations cannot be denied. It has produced fantastic results in China which became a free nation a couple of years later than ours. Had we opted for communism on the eve of our independence, our economic and social problems would undoubtedly have been less.

But we chose a 'softy' kind of socialist path, which suited neither the poor nor the rich. Ours is the only system in which we have created in the name of socialism gigantic disparities. The number of poor has grown larger and the rich smaller. Ours is perhaps the only country where socialism helped the rich to harvest the maximum benefits by its defective application. It did not help the poor.

It's a rich man's system. The poor have no say in it. The government, Parliament, the court—all serve the affluent. A violent effort by an organised group to destroy the system is not likely to succeed. It's too big a country with gigantic problems to be changed, through violence. But a change has to be envisaged, and brought about with no bloodshed. The Constitution and Parliament have enough powers to give a new turn to the situation. Parliament can be an instrument of change provided it is packed with people committed to eradicate poverty.

Is it possible? Is it possible to change the system through Parliament? Can Parliament play the role of an instrument committed for change? Successive British Parliaments did play such roles. Our own Parliament had legislated the abolition of the *zamindari* system and the privy purse. It had also nationalised the banks. But Parliaments that had elected in recent times have been status quoists. We cannot expect them to carry forward the same revolutionary programme. If we have to have a system in which Parliaments have to be the instruments of change, the necessary precaution has to be taken when we elect Parliament. The watch-word should be to ensure that Parliament we elect is committed and capable of changing the system.

How can we ensure this? There has to be systematic political education of the people so that they vote only for those parties whose commitment to the eradication of poverty and destruction of all disparities, is total. Is this possible?

Current, 30.01.1988.
p. (2)

Hang them

What happened in Bihar last week has been happening for a number of years in that hapless region. The brutality of the mayhem sends a shiver down the spine. Children were burnt to death, women were cut into pieces, no body had a head. They were all poor, innocent peasants. It was a caste war in full fury. And as things are in Bihar it may not be the last gory act of human atrocities. The government has so far done nothing, nor has it the will and vision to do anything in future.

India has been in the grip of communal and caste violence since independence and Bihar and Uttar Pradesh have been open, unprotected fields for the marauders. Most of them have gone unpunished. No one has so far been hanged for such acts.

Nehru had dreamt of a casteless, classless India. It was also the destination of our freedom struggle. Ambedkar, who framed the Constitution, had sought to make it a document filled with human values. It was in fact a charter for the emancipation of the country's downtrodden, hungry have-nots. It had sought to break casteist and communal barriers. It had been given by the people to themselves as the symbol of their hopes and aspirations.

Forty years after independence what we witness is an India at its own throat, an India gone haywire, an India flowing with rivers of blood, with marauders annihilating family after innocent family, with arsonists turning fellow beings into human torches, with police running amuck, with law enforcing authorities playing Dracula, with politicians instigating violence, trampling upon Gandhi's and Nehru's dreams.

The ills are the making of the politicians and the remedy lies in whip lashing all those found fueling caste and communal bias, or propaganda. It is the politician who frames the law, who divides people into castes and communities, who thrives on splits and divisions among people. It is the politician who has resisted social and economic reforms. It is such politicians who are the greatest menace to this country. They have to be disciplined, ostracised, outcasted, rejected.

The police and the law enforcement authorities too share the blame but not entirely. A bad policeman or a degenerate bureaucrat cannot survive for a day if he does not enjoy political protection.

The Congress, which promised the people to be an instrument of change, has to take the blame squarely on its shoulders. Nothing prevented it from ushering in a social and economic revolution. Nothing prevented it from shattering the caste and communal barriers. It has had the power and the authority to implement its promises, which it has made in every election manifesto for the past 25 years, with zeal and conviction.

Why has it not carried out the promised agrarian reforms in Bihar and elsewhere? Why has it invariably allied itself with the landlords in these places? The caste war will continue in Bihar and the poverty ridden regions of the north until comprehensive land reforms are carried out and ruthlessly.

Does it have the will, the commitment? Does it actually bother about the poor, the oppressed which make up the skyline of rural India? If it does, it should sack Chief minister Bindeshwari Dube, catch the marauders, try them and hang them in a public square.

Current, 06.06.1987.
p. (2)

Who is anti-national?

Rajiv Gandhi's new 'firman' on nationalism stunned non-Congress Chief ministers who were meeting at a conclave in Calcutta. He insisted, on his way back from Burma, that he would dismiss any state government found to be indulging in anti-national activities, and if its conspiracy to destabilise the country was corroborated by the Home Ministry.

The Home Ministry is made up of pliant *babus* who can be made to prepare any report which suits the man in power. The day Indira Gandhi lost the election, Janata Home minister Choudhary Charan Singh condemned her as traitor and anti-national. He even advocated a Nuremberg-type trial for her. None in the ruling Janata clique condemned the Choudhary's statement and, had the tide not turned against the Janata, he was determined to hang her.

Half of India is being ruled by Chief ministers who do not subscribe to Rajiv Gandhi's policies. And they are within their democratic rights to oppose him and dislodge him from power. The Constitution of India has given them this right. And opposing and changing a Prime Minister in a democratic set-up cannot be synonymous with treachery and anti-nationalism.

The tendency ushered in by Rajiv and some of his senior colleagues is to declare any public figure who is opposed to them as anti-national, a CIA agent. But we have witnessed, in his short term of Prime Ministership, shaking hands with all those whom he branded anti-national.

Not only this, he made them win elections and become Chief ministers. Public memory may be short, but he had denounced Surjit Singh Barnala, Farooq Abdullah, Prafulla Mohanta and Laldenga as anti-national. Has he changed his opinion about them?

His was a disastrous statement. A Prime Minister of a country with such gigantic religious, regional, economic and social disparities is not expected to indulge in this kind of flippancy. Power is transient. He is not expected to rule the country for life, and if he continues to generate this kind of acrimony in national life, he may not be spared by his opponents if they happen to come to power.

The most horrifying part of his statement was that the Home Ministry will certify which Chief minister is patriotic or anti-national. Chief ministers in this country do not come to power through palace coups or intrigues. They, specially those in the opposition, are elected by the majority of the people in their states. His attitude to denigrate them or look at them with contempt may ultimately lead to an anarchic situation in the country. Nationalism is nobody's personal property; the concept should not be misused to browbeat and intimidate those who do not hold similar views.

Current, 26.12.1987.
p. (2)

A constitutional crisis
Giani, refuses to be a robot

The President has not yet finalised his reply to the Cabinet note and resolution asserting the right to withhold information from him. He has asked his constitutional advisers to prepare an exhaustive note adhering to the constitutional provisions. One such expert quotes from the Supreme Court pronouncement in the famous Shamsher Singh case. "The President in India", it said, "is not at all a glorified cipher. . . but actually vested with a pervasive and persuasive role."

The Rajiv government must have felt extremely slighted when the President remarked to a BJP delegation which had asked for details of the arms deals: "If I had fuller information about all this, I would have replied to your criticism and defended my government."

The constitutional crisis and the panic in ruling circles have made people close to the Prime Minister say that the President might resign in sheer desperation. "Not at all", remarks a Rashtrapati Bhavan source. "He is a fighter and he will not run away from his constitutional obligations."

The tussle which began as a clash of personalities has indeed assumed the significance of a first class constitutional crisis. The Giani's letter two weeks ago seeking complete information on the arms deals signed by the Prime Minister in the last two and a half years caused unparallel panic. It compelled the Prime Minister to go in for a series of meetings of the Political Affairs Committee and then of the full Cabinet to consider the wider ramifications of the President's right to seek information.

The President, in his capacity as Supreme Commander of the Armed Forces, had sought full details of all the arms deals including the Westland helicopters, the Hermes aircraft carrier, the German submarines and the Bofors guns. He had also wished to know under what circumstances the Fairfax inquiry was ordered and what its terms and conditions were. He had asked specifically for copies of all the relevant correspondence and telex massages exchanged in connection with these deals.

He had based his right to get the information on Article 78 and said the whole nation was seized of the consequences of these deals. The deals had also caused unusual anxiety in the armed forces because most of their high-ranking personnel were also kept in the dark.

Duties of Prime Minister as respects the furnishing of information to the President, etc.—it shall be the duty of the Prime Minister—

(a) To communicate to the President all decisions of the Council of ministers relating to the administration of the affairs of the Union and proposals for legislators;
(b) To furnish such information relating to the administration of the affairs of the Union and proposals for legislation as the President may call for.

The ten-page reply to the President's letter drafted by the Prime Minister's confidant Gopi Arora was improved by a team of Cabinet ministers including Shiv Shankar, P.V. Narasimha Rao and K.C. Pant. It explained at length the position of the Prime Minister in a parliamentary system and his right to withhold information from the President. The note profusely quoted from the correspondence between President Rajendra Prasad and Jawaharlal Nehru in which Nehru asserted the superiority of the Cabinet and its right to "advise" the President and his constitutional obligation to abide by such advice.

The Cabinet resolution attached to the note tersely told the President that the information given to him by Defence minister K.C. Pant on the arms deals was adequate and the Cabinet was not in a position to furnish him any additional information.

What is understood to have hurt the President is the "attitude of defiance". Also hurtful was the fact that the information he had sought was in the possession of the Defence Secretary and even officers much junior to him in the Prime Minister's office. And it is the President who administers the oath of secrecy to the Prime Minister and his council of ministers. Even the officers and generals who are repositories of this information are appointed by him. How then can he be denied the information he seeks by those who are his appointees?

Moreover the withholding of information by his own Prime Minister clearly means that he does not trust the President. How can a President continue in office even for a minute without enjoying the confidence of his own Prime Minister? How can he command the respect of the armed forces if he is suspect?

Besides the constitutional niceties, sources close to the President point out, any denial of information to the Head of state amounts to denigration of the whole nation and its elected representatives. The Prime Minister, they further point out, is elected from one constituency and then as leader by his party. The President is chosen by both the Houses of Parliament and an electoral college comprising all the state assemblies. While the Prime Minister is the head of the government, the President is the Head of state and upholder of the Constitution.

The President is said to be greatly hurt. He feels that with its totally unconstitutional postures the Rajiv government is hitting at the roots of democracy and denigrating the office of the President. And if this is the Prime Minister's attitude to the Head of state, then in future instead of a human being Rashtrapati Bhavan should have a robot to affix the signature and put the seal. No man with dignity and conscience will agree to be a mere rubber-stamp.

Minutes before the President signed the order to dismiss the Barnala government, a source close to him remarked, the Prime Minister ate the humble pie once again. He recalled that the address prepared by the government to be read by the President at the opening of Parliament's budget session contained laudatory remarks about the Barnala government. The President had objected to these remarks on the ground that the Chief minister of a state should not be singled out for praise in the Presidential address. The Prime Minister had refused to delete the remarks and the President was made to read them out.

Three months later the Prime Minister had to dismiss the Barnala government for its acts of omission and commission. It just showed lack of wisdom, the source remarked in anguish.

Current, 16.05.1987.
p. (1)

Scrap this black bill

***Freedom is in peril defend it with all your might*—Jawaharlal Nehru**

If the governments could be saved by passing BILLS, no government in the world would be dislodged. Had the ACTS could prevent people from rising against the established authority in a democratic manner, Indira Gandhi would not have come back to power. There would not have been any Gandhi or Nehru had ACTS have had their way. To oppose, expose, criticise the government and men who control it is the fundamental right of the people of this country.

No power on earth can usurp it. No man in power can do away with it and hope to survive for long. The soil of this land, soaked in the blood of martyrs, will militate against any such foul deed. One cannot silence 800 million people with the *danda* of a bill. The defamation Bill, if passed, will be the death knell of the government of the day. This is the most reckless act committed by any government in the last forty years.

This obviously is a Bill to preserve, promote and protect corruption at high places, to give a new lease of life to power brokers, fortify graft, institutionalise nepotism. The Bill will be a pernicious weapon in the hands of the authority to silence its critics, to muzzle the voice of dissent, to curb investigative reporting and to allow criminals, the FERA violators and smugglers live a princely life.

An editor and his entire staff including proof-readers can be hauled up in the court if his paper described a smuggler a smuggler and called a thief a thief. As we all know, most politicians are thieves but to brand them as such will be defamation. Frankly speaking the Bill, if made into an act, will turn India into Idi Amin's Uganda. Most of the newspapers will have to close down and the government will have to build new jails to accommodate journalists. Only the politicians and their cohorts in the underworld will be protected by the Bill.

The universal opposition to the Bill has temporarily unnerved the government and it has deferred the decision to introduce it in the Rajya Sabha in the "current session." But Prime Minister Rajiv Gandhi is determined to get it passed in the next session. His decision to form a seven man cabinet committee to make itself available to the Bill's opponents for suggestions is meant to blunt the sharpness of the attacks and also to create confusion among various journalists' organisations and civil liberty bodies.

In fact during his speech at a party functionaries meeting at Delhi he made fun of the eminent opponents of the Bill. "Nobody has sat down to read the Bill and what has happened so far is only "ha ha kar." But he stunned his TV audience all over the country when he said in a firm tone: "We are totally convinced that the Bill is needed. I am myself completely convinced that we are proceeding in the right line." If he were so convinced of the righteousness of his cause, then why did he appoint the cabinet committee and invite suggestions and opinions? Was it not an act of hoodwinking the nation and so blatantly.

This vicious assault on the freedom of the press and on the very basic right of a citizen to know the truth and his fundamental right to information will have to be fought tooth and nail. We will have to invoke the spirit of

Gandhi for preserving our national heritage. The country will no doubt stand like one man behind the media which has done so much in the last three years to expose the misdemeanours of the ruling echelons.

Freedom, as the great Jawaharlal said, is in peril and we must defend it with all our might. The obnoxious bill must be withdrawn completely, unequivocally and unconditionally.

Saturday, 10.09.1988.
p. (2)

Heal thyself, physician

Rajiv Gandhi has failed to gauge the mood of the people. He would otherwise not have called for a national debate on a non-issue like defamation. It has never been a national issue, nor will it ever be. It will be a grave error of judgement if he continues to feel that the people's attention can be diverted from the real problems by raking up phantoms. The withdrawal of the bill was indeed a triumph of democracy and people in power will in future not dare to tamper with what we have inherited from the framers of our Constitution. It is also wrong to assume that he withdrew the bill because he was sensitive to public opinion. No. It is not so. The inexperienced and immature Prime Minister faced a virtual revolt in the rank and file of his party, the intelligentsia and the common people who could understand the dangerous aspects of the legislation. Almost all the Supreme Court judges were against it and had the Bill been made into an Act, the Supreme Court would, at some stage, have most probably struck it down. The situation then would have been irretrievable for the ruling party.

An enormous damage has been done to him as a person and the Congress as a party. He has been losing credibility with each such step. His Prime Ministership is jinxed. Yet, some lost ground can be gained if he implements certain measures that had been promised soon after he assumed power. In fact only one act—a war on corruption—can bring back his lost lustre. He had promised such a war at the Congress Centenary celebrations in Bombay, to purge the party of power brokers and touts. If he did mean what he had said then, it is time he acted on it. He is on a sticky wicket. He was a most admired Mr. Clean. So much mud has been thrown at him since then and so much of it has stuck that it would be a stupendous task to regain what he has lost. Now even members of his close coterie do not call him Mr. Clean. Fortunately, there is still a fairly good number of people among his admirers who believe in his integrity and that most of his friends took him for a ride. His recent interview to a weekly magazine in which he said he cannot have more than one tutor for his children due to financial constraints proved to be a tear jerker. The question is: Is he that hard up? Is he that honest?

What then prevents him from taking the bull of corruption by the horns? Fighting corruption at the national level might be a very hard task but the least he can do is to begin from his party. So far he has not punished a single congressman for corruption despite grave charges against some of them. 'Charity', he had said in Bombay, 'must begin at home'. He should first unmask those partymen suspected to be thriving on graft. He is not unaware of those with a rags-to-riches history. He has agencies at his command which can furnish details and facts of who has amassed ill-gotten wealth, where it is kept, how it is invested and how it can be dug out. He can catch a few top ones who have 'misused' his confidence. He can probe into their lavish lifestyle.

Let Rajiv Gandhi act on this front and he will see people rally behind him. Let him frame a code of conduct for his partymen first, including himself, and he will find the country responding enthusiastically. If he does not do this he may not survive the next battle of hustings. Corruption will be the main issue in the next election with V.P. Singh spearheading the campaign. The people are in a foul mood. The collective show of strength against the BLACK bill was merely a straw in the wind.

Current, 01.10.1988.
p. (2)

Whose Raj will it be?

The 'power to the people' slogan on the eve of the election looks like a gimmick, though the Prime Minister who has worked out several elaborate schemes has not succeeded in convincing the people about its real objectives. He started talking so suddenly and incessantly about 'power to the people' from every platform that even those who believe in his sincerity of purpose have begun taking his words with pinch of salt. His first slogan was about the glamourous 21st century. Then came the era of technology, telecommunication, telemetric and the Sam Pitrodas.

Now and, rightfully so, comes the era of 'power to the people' the

Jawahar Rozgar Yojna, Panchayat Raj and power to the urban local bodies. The constitution amendment in this regard is expected soon. Crores of rupees will flow in the lanes and by lanes of our towns and cities to usher in an urban revolution. New Delhi will directly run the district administration with state governments and chief ministers remaining mute spectators.

What will be the shape of the new amendment is not yet known but the Prime Minister's speech at the Chief ministers' conference left nobody in doubt about the total centralisation of power. The Panchayat Raj Bill will take power to rural India while the Nagarpalika Bill will give power to urban India. Funds for the urban bodies, either direct or through the agency of the state governments, are to be diverted to "carefully-structured urban poverty alleviation programmes which would reach out to the poor and curb the influx of rural needy into towns and cities". But then the Prime Minister admitted that "municipal finances all across the country were in a mess". He is convinced that people can no more be denied their due share in power. "Nothing would be more disastrous", he confessed, than evolving political power to elected members of municipalities without simultaneously devolving fiscal responsibilities on them".

Once again grave mistakes are being made airing the slogan 'power to the people'. The people do have power and can exercise it every five years and make or unmake governments. The kind of power envisaged might land us in trouble, utter chaos and financial bunglings of an unimaginable magnitude.

What will be the role of the state governments, chief ministers and local assemblies? Will New Delhi directly control thousands of panchayats and urban local bodies and, if so, how will it be done? What will happen to the existing civic bodies?

According to official figures, most of them exist only in name. Nearly 40 per cent of these urban bodies have been superseded; most of them because of gross financial mismanagements. Sixty per cent of them have not been functioning for years. A number of these urban local bodies have been clashing regularly with the state governments. More often than not this is the case when opposing political parties are in power. Urban bodies are generally captured by parties opposed to the one in power in the state.

Sometimes local sentiments are so overpowering that people do not care much about the flow of money from the centre. Otherwise why would there be hostile governments in Calcutta, Hyderabad, Madras, Chandigarh, etc? The main contention of opposition chief ministers who boycotted last week's conference was that the financial problems of the local bodies should not be solved by direct central subsidy. There is bound to be unprecedented fiscal chaos in case of allocation and reallocation of funds. The government in Patna is facing such a chaotic condition precisely for this mess. The sudden reallocation of funds of the National Rural Employment Programme and Rural Land Employment Programme to the Jawahar Rozgar Yojna has held up execution of almost all the ongoing schemes. Bihar's Rural Development minister Sushila Kirketa has said "80 per cent of the funds has been diverted to the panchayats under the JRY and 20 per cent are available for completing the ongoing schemes". This is happening in almost every state where the Jawahar Rozgar Yojna is being implemented.

The political pressure of the coming elections is so overpowering that fantastic schemes are being announced by the Prime Minister. In Patna he doled out Rs. 5,700 crore package of central assistance for industrialisation of Bihar "which is very close to my heart". A few hours earlier he had admitted in a seminar that "Bihar's backwardness was due to the fact that funds for development had been going down the drain". Only time will tell what happens to the Rs. 5,700 crore package.

The symptoms are that if the Congress returns to power there would be more centralisation of power.

In that event the chances of a direct confrontation between New Delhi and the districts will unfold a new political scenario.

Current, 15.07.1989.
p. (2)

It's going to be face to face

The election will not only decide who will rule the country but also the fate of Rajiv Gandhi for whom a defeat will prove disastrous. His party may survive such a calamity but he as an individual, may not. Thus it will be a last ditch battle for him. His chief rival, Vishwanath Pratap Singh, has finally attained what looked, a short while ago, an unrealisable dream. The opposition is united and it will face the ruling party in a most exciting battle of hustings in a one-to-one fight.

Rajiv Gandhi goes to the polls with no major economic or emotional issues at stake. The Nagarpalika or the Jawahar Rozgar Yojna cannot generate a wave. And a election under his leadership without a wave could spell disaster, if not doom. He goes to the people with a tarnished image—even his most ardent admirers no more call him Mr. Clean—with soaring prices and with communal frenzy at its peak. It's not a normal situation.

The opposition is united, is in an aggressive mood. It has electorally divided the country according to its pockets of influence and though the CPM continues to criticise the BJP, it does not come face to face with it anywhere in the country. The CPM-BJP ideological skirmish does not necessarily lead to an electoral clash.

The BJP and Janata Dal have come to terms everywhere leaving no room for multi-cornered contests. The BJP knows its limitations and hence does not aspire for absolute power. It might, if the number of its seats goes up to three figures, demand a pound of flesh from the Janata Dal or the National Front. V.P. Singh, despite his shortcomings, is a more effective crowd puller than Rajiv Gandhi. His has been proved to be untarnishable image. Not an iota of dirt has stuck on him.

This election will be the toughest the country has ever witnessed. It will be a door-to-door fight, a fist-to-fist bout, in which the people of India will finally emerge victorious.

Prime Minister Rajiv Gandhi's sudden decision to go to polls took the Congress as well as the opposition stalwarts by surprise. What intrigued the observers was that he took none of his close political associates into confidence. Home minister Buta Singh was as unaware of the decision as the man on the street. President Venkatraman was informed a few hours later and the cabinet approved it in a fraction of a minute.

The heads of the intelligence agencies who had made elaborate arrangements at Palam Airport's technical area for his departure for the CHOGM at Kuala Lumpur were informed on wireless of the cancellation of the trip. The Prime Ministerial baggage which had reached the airport was brought back, our men in Malaysia were informed and External Affairs minister P.V. Narasimha Rao was asked to proceed immediately to Kuala Lumpur.

The central Hall and the capital's less important gossip centres hummed with rumours and speculations. Telephones were abuzz. Several Cabinet ministers and opposition leaders were seen rushing from one VIP bungalow to another. The polls were advanced by almost two months. Why? Who advised him? Did somebody press the panic button? The raging speculations centred on six points:

One: Intelligence reports gathered from all over the country and fed to the computers revealed that the rank and file of the ruling party had begun to feel the sharp decline in the fortunes of the leader.

Two: Some senior leaders including Sharad Pawar, Arjun Singh, Madhavsinh Solanki, Jagannath Mishra, Abdul Ghafoor might form a link a la Syndicate and start searching for a new leader. Nonagenarian Kamalapati Tripathi has been making all kinds of noises against Rajiv's style of functioning and the inept handling of the Bhoomi Masjid issue. Uttar Pradesh is perched on the tip of a communal volcano and any more communal clashes might push the Muslims of the Gangetic belt into the lap of the Janata Dal.

Three: Much more serious exposures on Bofors and the HDW were expected, any day. Reports suggested that some close relatives of the Prime Minister were involved and the most effective way to take the sting out of these scandals was to divert the people's attention.

Four: The President has been 'very unhappy' with the deteriorating political situation and feared a total moral collapse of the nation. He is reported to have advised the Prime Minister to seek a fresh mandate without wasting any more time. He seems to be convinced of the complicity of some of the Prime Minister's close relatives in the kickbacks.

Five: The reports warned of a sweeping feeling among the electorate in favour of opposition unity, and the JD and the BJP were about to succeed in striking seat adjustments all over the north. Efforts to keep them divided had proved futile.

Six: The price situation was not likely to improve and there was a danger of essential commodities vanishing from the market. The spiralling prices have been hitting every middle class, lower middle class and poor people's bellies. The opposition was bound to make it a major poll issue.

Who then advised the Prime Minister to go in for the polls, without delaying it even for a minute? Who pressed the panic button? None of his Cabinet colleagues. Nor any of his whiz kids or the computer boys.

Reportedly the panic button was jointly pressed by Cabinet Secretary T.N. Seshan and his predecessor and now Rajiv's Principal Secretary B.G. Deshmukh. They have been meeting regularly for the past three weeks gathering and sifting intelligence material. Their conclusion was: Polls must be held forthwith.

Before they met him, three more kingpins—Capt. Satish Sharma, R.K. Dhawan and Mani Shanker Iyer—were consulted. They agreed with the powerful duo and approached the Prime Minister even as he was preparing to go for the CHOGM. He accepted the advice. He first informed Sonia Gandhi and then asked Deshmukh to call the Cabinet urgently.

None of the ministers who trooped to 7, Race Course Road had the faintest idea of the momentous decision. Though it came as a bolt from the blue, it was accepted without a murmur.

As the news of the men behind the decision came to be known, it dawned on senior congressmen, that for the first time two top bureaucrats were instrumental in reaching a purely political decision and that the political authority was totally ignored. The Prime Minister had more trust in his bureaucratic eggheads than in the wisdom of his political colleagues.

The ad hocism hurt hundreds of middle level congressmen specially in Karnataka and Punjab. Parliament had extended the President's rule in these two states only a couple of days earlier. The Congress Party is in shambles in both these states and the lumping of the Lok Sabha poll with that of the Vidhan Sabhas will undoubtedly place the local Congress leaders under considerable strain. Karnataka congressmen, among whom the resentment is widespread, had thought they were in a position to give a tough fight to the Janata Dal. But with the Assembly seats hanging round their necks the issues will get mixed.

The decision to hold simultaneous elections to the Assembly has caused widespread tremors in UP too. It has intensified factionalism at the grassroots level and those denied tickets are sure to sabotage the chances of their replacements. UP holds the key to the fortunes of the Congress and it is in this state it faces the danger of losing power.

Most congressmen betray nervousness. Carrying as they are a mountain of sins of omission and commission, they are going to the battlefield half-heartedly. Their leader is under a cloud. His integrity is suspect. He has lost much ground since 1985 when the whole nation had hailed him as a messiah. He was the Mr. Clean who took the country by storm and entered the Lok Sabha with a massive 415 seats, a majority neither his mother nor grandfather could muster. It was a miracle. It had stunned the opposition. It was not only routed, but humiliated when almost all its stalwarts were humbled.

But on the threshold of the most crucial election in the history of their party its leader is perhaps the most maligned man in power.

For the opposition it is a dream come true. Its plans to ultimately achieve the goal of a one-to-one fight is on the verge of realisation. In the opposition ruled states—Bengal, Haryana, Andhra, Tamil Nadu and Kerala—there was no doubt of a one-to-one fight. What is commendable is that the BJP and the Janata Dal, despite ideological and political differences, have reached the final goal in all the Hindi speaking states. In Gujarat, Orissa and Rajasthan, seat adjustment was achieved without much wrangling.

In UP, Bihar, and MP too the Congress will, for the first time, face the horrifying prospect of face-to-face fight. This might spell disaster for the party.

Even if 1984 is taken as the year of its utmost glory, the ruling party had received less than 50 per cent votes in 42 constituencies. A slight change of merely two per cent can be disastrous not only in UP but Bihar too. The calculation is that the shift is more than five per cent. In that case the Congress is not likely to get more than 50 seats out of a total of 139. The situation in Gujarat, Rajasthan and MP is no better.

The damage is bound to be much greater in these states if Kanshi Ram (BSP Leader) succeeds in putting his candidates in "every seat in Hindi belt". Had he not put up his candidate in Allahabad, V.P. Singh's victory margin would have been much slender. Kanshi Ram was number two with nearly 75,000 votes with the Congress trailing behind. His votes come out of the Congress traditional vote bank of Harijans. Kanshi Ram's gain will undoubtedly be the loss of the ruling party. He expects to take away a chunk of 75,000 to 1,00,000 Harijan and backward votes. With him present in each constituency, the Janata Dal expects to be on velvet.

Kanshi Ram, it seems, cannot be bribed or brought over. By fighting this election I am, he says, "paving the way for the next election when I will have enough seats in the Lok Sabha to form government." Five star people may shudder at the thought, but Kanshi Ram as one of the rulers in the near future cannot be ruled out. That's democracy.

And one cannot ignore Syed Shahabuddin in the vicious game of electoral politics. He has emerged as the most effective spokesman of the Muslims, and though he may not win a single seat, except his own in Kishanganj he can cause a swing of five to ten per cent votes in more than 100 constituencies in UP and Bihar. Muslims, who voted almost as one man for Rajiv Gandhi and added lustre to his phenomenal victory, are now in bulk for one party, but may use their discretion in choosing the party and the candidate. This cautious attitude is also not favourable to the Congress.

With no emotional issue involved, it is going to be a tough fight. It can be touch and go for both—the ruling party and the opposition.

Current, 28.10.1989.
pp. (1 + 2 + 3)

C. Congress on the Threshold of its 2nd Century

The turning point for the Congress

The Congress has completed 100 years and enters the second century of its dynamic existence with elan, faith and a sense of pride. It is an achievement for a political organisation; it has few parallels in the history of the democratic world.

It is not just an achievement for the party which has been at the helm of affairs for a century and in power for four decades with a brief interruption; it is also a tribute to the people who run the largest, most vibrant, most viable and most committed democracy in the world.

At this rare moment in our history, we bow in gratitude to the founders of this party. They never lost faith in the intrinsic national spirit of the people and the destiny of this great country.

The one man who stands out in the century like the tallest Himalayan peak is Mahatma Gandhi, a unique being who walked the length and breadth of the land and roused a people wallowing in colonial slavery. It was he who moulded our destiny more than anyone else, and instilled deep into our psyche the spirit of secular democracy. The venue of the centenary celebrations should have been named after him, the Father of the Nation.

The Congress has survived 100 years and it may hit yet another century, who knows. And the secret of its survival has been its capacity to rise above the sectarian, communal, linguistic, regional and rigid ideological barriers.

From its very inception, its leaders took a national view. They always thought and acted for the whole country and its people, irrespective of caste, creed or religion. Its doors remained open to all people, who in their millions flocked around it. The Congress leaders believed in the totality of the people and their collective wisdom.

A party like this may lose elections, but it cannot die. It may make mistakes, but it has an inbuilt flexibility to accept them and not to repeat them. It has always been a judicious mix of the old and the young, the radical and the liberal, the leftist and the rightist, the ultra and the traditionalist, the nationalist and the internationalist, the God-fearing and the atheist, the vegetarian and the non-veg.

The Congress had under one roof a Tilak and a Gokhale, Gandhi and Bose, Nehru and Patel, Madan Mohan Malaviya and Maulana Azad. It has survived because it has always absorbed fresh ideas even as it retained the old ones. Through the century, waves after waves of young men and women have swelled its ranks. Its leaders have come from among the people—all kind of people. From the rich and the poor, from the elite and commoner, from the south, north, east and west. It has been flowing like a mighty Ganga from the Himalayan to the Cape. And like the Ganga it did get polluted from time to time.

The party has no tradition of purge. It got divided. It got split. It expelled the recalcitrants, only to make them come back. It threw the rebels out, but kept the doors open for the repentent. It has believed in dialogue, discussion, deliberation and consensus, and it did not shut anybody's mouth. It believed in freedom of thought and action and gave maximum latitude to its members and followers to express themselves totally freely.

The Congress would not have survived so gloriously had it not believed in inner party democracy. The DCCs, the PCCs, the AICC, the Working Committee and the Parliamentary Board were always elected with the fullest participation of its thousands of members with millions of people witnessing the great game of democracy.

It was in a true sense a people's party though it always had its popular and equally dedicated opponents. It threw up giants. But the people have proved idol-breakers. They demolished their own idols whenever they found that their cherished dreams and values were endangered.

Standing on the threshold of its second century, the Congress can look back with pride on its past and the gifts to the nation—the Constitution, Parliament, the secular spirit and the commitment to freedom, social justice and equality.

But looking ahead, it finds itself at the cross-roads. A new turning point has come, and the Congress will never be the same again. It has to change. That is inevitable.

The change is visible. The Congress recreated by Indira Gandhi after the 1969 split was made up of young, committed men who reiterated their commitment to social justice and their will to forge ahead to build a new, vibrant India.

The party got a shot in the arm with the organisational elections in 1972 following the memorable parliamentary victory. Then something went wrong, somewhere, and degeneration set in. The first casualty was the voice of dissent and consequentially inner party democracy. The 1977 debacle was the culmination of this process of decay.

Even then, the Congress did not die. The spirit survived. In 1980 the party bounced back with tremendous vigour and with a new commitment to complete its unfinished tasks. By the beginning of 1985 it once again showed signs of cracking up. Fissiparous tendencies, regionalism and then terrorism posed a serious challenge. It took the martyrdom of Indira Gandhi to save the nation from a catastrophe. And the Congress was once again to the fore to safeguard the country's unity and integrity.

It ushers in a new era, a breakthrough, an entirely different phase under the leadership of young and forward-looking leader. Rajiv Gandhi heads the party which runs the government. The party has always been more important than the government and if it becomes weak it will be isolated from the people who sit in judgement every five years.

India has passed its most gruelling test with the assassination of Indira Gandhi and the events that followed. It is to the credit of Rajiv Gandhi that he steward the nation well enough through this trying period. Now he faces the formidable problems of transition. Both the government and the party will have to pass through this acid test of transition. The country is preparing to move from the industrial to a technological era. This is bound to generate new hopes and aspirations.

The Congress will have to be given a new orientation in tune with the technological revolution and it will have to keep pace with the fresh forces released by this rapid development. A large number of young men have come into the fold and they rightly reposed high hopes in him and faith in his promises. These promises will have to be kept and the policies implemented with vigour and zeal.

And in this crucial phase the party can be ignored at its own peril. Its democratic spirit will have to be kept intact. The Congress will have to remain a mass-based organisation and not a group of elitist functionaries. And the only way to keep its democratic fibre intact is to reinfuse into it the broadest possible participation by the people.

On the occasion of the centenary, a resolve will have to be made to restructure the Congress with the grass-roots elections. The party will have to be democratic from the bottom to the top. Only then will it acquire a new zeal and be ready to face the mighty challenge of building a new India in keeping with the times.

Rajiv Gandhi's one year in power and his unquestioned success on almost every political front is reassurance that he will turn the Congress into a powerful instrument of change.

Current, 28.12.1985
pp. (1 + 3)

**You said it Rajiv, it's time for. . .
operation clean-up**

If speeches could launch a revolution or save the Congress from certain moral collapse, then Rajiv Gandhi's presidential address was undoubtedly a brilliant piece of brave words. Even an incorrigible critic of the ruling party would not have come down so mercilessly as he did while launching his party into the second century. As he read his extremely well-written address in a voice bereft of emotions, a phalanx of well-dressed, well-oiled party bigwigs adorning the huge stage heard him with expressionless faces.

On the spacious ground below a few thousand party members listened to him staring in the vacuum. The stands of the Brabourne Stadium with a 60,000 capacity were almost empty. The mike did not work and the system outside failed. Hundreds of party activists and freedom fighters made desperate attempts to get in holding their badges and cards. The police would not listen to the pleas of Aruna Asaf Ali, heroine of the 1942 movement, and N.G. Ranga, the seniormost parliamentarian. The fate of lesser beings was worse.

It was a fiasco. A pathetic sight for those who expected a grand assemblage of party activists, pro-Congress intelligentsia, thinkers, academicians, poets, outstanding social workers, workers and peasant leaders and well-known well-wishers of the 100-year old party. It was meant to be an extraordinary occasion for the entire nation to watch and admire. What turned out looked like a requiem.

During my twenty years experience of covering the various sessions of the Indian National Congress, I have not seen partymen with so much gloom in their hearts, so much uncertainty oozing out of their long-drawn faces and so many of them hurling choicest invectives at the leadership. The Congress at the Brabourne Stadium appeared a dark shadow of its glorious past, with Rajiv Gandhi, trim in spotless white, as the only ray of hope. But average congressmen seemed doubtful even of this ray of hope. What was wrong? What was amiss? Why this cynicism? Why these abuses—not from ordinary workers but from important party functionaries?

Rajiv more than anyone else seemed to be aware of the decay setting in the sinews of a party which claims to run a country of seven hundred million with a massive majority in Parliament. No Congress President in the past did such an incisive post mortem of the party as he did and with ruthless frankness.

Congressmen, many of them, had allowed themselves to be influenced by "the brokers of power and influence who disposed patronage to convert a mass movement into a feudal oligarchy. . . For such persons, the masses do not count. Their lifestyle, their thinking or lack of it, their self-aggrandisement, their corrupt ways, their linkages with the vested interests in society, and their sanctimonious posturings are wholly incompatible with work among the people. They are reducing the Congress organisation to a shell from which the spirit of service and sacrifice has been emptied."

The tragedy was that, when Rajiv was making these shattering observations, a number of party MPs and AICC members displayed cynical smiles on their visage and they began to look around uncomfortably when he said the Congress which had blazed new trails "had shrunk, losing touch with the toiling masses. We are a party of social transformation, but in our preoccupation with governance we are drifting away from the people. Thereby we have weakened ourselves and fallen prey to the ills that the loss of invigorating mass contact brings."

The Congress of which he has been the chief for over a year and his mother for over a decade has "acquired the status of an heirloom, to be polished and brought out on special occasions," and it has been "faltering in talking the ideology of socialism, democracy and secularism to the masses."

Who can disagree with him in this year of its century that the 'revitalisation' of the ruling party is a historic necessity and that there is no other single party with a national base to keep the country intact and take it forward on the path of progress and prosperity?

The whole country will stand behind him like one man if he launches a "war on corruption and restore a clean social and political environment and introduce electoral laws to break the nexus between politicians and vested interests and make the political parties accountable for the funds they receive." When he uttered these very brave words he was reflecting not only his own feelings and aspirations but those of millions of honest countrymen.

He did think of the poor and the toiling people when he said that any "denial of justice to the poor and the weak is in itself a crime and that the Congress will be the shield of the oppressed and the sword of the poor."

When he was making these pronouncements many MPs and AICC members were loitering about enjoying the cool breeze of Marine Drive and he hit the bull's eye when he looked at the thin audience and said in a raised voice:

"Our lifestyle must change. Vulgar, conspicuous consumption must go. Simplicity, efficiency and commitment to national goals hold the key to self-reliance. The Congress ministers, Members of Parliament and state Assemblies, party functionaries and leaders at all levels must set the example for the millions to follow. Austerity and Swadeshi would galvanise the masses to grow more, to produce more and to serve more."

But what actually happened during the three historic days in Bombay he had better know. Many of his party bigwigs occupied huge suites in the city's five-star hotels and private and public sector guest houses. Bottles of scotch and champagne were uncorked and a number of them were seen in dazzling jewellery shops buying ornaments for their families. These were the leaders whom he was addressing.

At the Mahalaxmi camp where the bulk of the party workers were packed like sardines, there was no food, no drinking water and no basic amenities. They looted trucks carrying vegetables and bananas, cursed the leadership loudly. These people were humiliated so blatantly that the next day most of them stayed away and Rajiv had to deliver his concluding remarks to a frightfully empty house.

Rajiv's speeches in the last Lok Sabha and the Assembly elections had roused such hopes that the people overwhelmed him with their unstinted support. His centenary speech has created a sensation in the country and once again there is a surge of an avalanche of hope.

The question is whether he has the will and the capacity to rise to the expectations. Will he be launching the much-expected 'operation clean up', and how?

Will charity begin at home?

Now the oppressed whom he wants to 'shield' and the poor whose "sword" he would like to be, expect him to act, and act ruthlessly. The more he acts the greater approbation he will receive and the people themselves will rally round him as his "shield" and his "sword". He need not worry. He should . . .

1. Declare a moratorium on sycophancy.
2. Purge the party of all corrupt elements whom he knows too well. Chop the dead wood, the inept and the inefficient who have lost their relevance. Pick up the broom and clean the Augean stables of his party with a massive sweep; do it now, before it is too late. Do it before the proposed party elections. If these people are allowed to stay the polls which he wants to hold from February onwards will be a farce. With no mass base it is these people who pack the party with bogus members and rule the roast.

3. Reshuffle his cabinet which has people with corrupt records, get the confidential files on them and find out how much wealth each one of them has amassed, it cannot be hidden from him. Their lifestyle and the lifestyle of their sons and daughters and their hangers on is as clear as daylight. Catch them by the scruff and throw them out. Let the princelings and the 'feudals' about whom he has been talking take a back seat. They have had enough and they will not lose much if power is denied to them. Let him bring in his council of ministers representatives of the schedule castes and the weaker sections who constitute the backbone of his party and who form the majority in the country. He has a large number of young and relatively clean men in his parliamentary party. The few young men he has brought into his government have been doing excellent work. They will do still better if they are saddled with those whose only contribution to the party has been corruption.
4. Let the 'mighty' heads in his administration roll and let the young and spirited ones take their place. He aroused tremendous hopes when he said: "We have government servants who do not uphold the law but shield the guilty, tax collectors who do not collect taxes but connive with those who cheat the state, and whole legions whose only concern is their private welfare at the cost of society. They have no work ethic, no feelings for the public cause, no involvement in the future of the nation, no comprehension of national goals, no commitment to the values of modern India. They have only a grasping mercenary outlook, devoid of competence, integrity and commitment."

   Who are these officers? Identify them and denude them of all the powers and privileges. Sack them in thousands. Not a dog will bark. Not a tear will be shed. The country will be jubilant. There will be celebrations. He will earn the gratitude of the nation as no other leader ever did.

   But he must do it. How can he govern with these people about whom he has such low opinion? How in future will he have the confidence of the electorate if he keeps them in their cozy positions? He will have to act.

   He has other men around him of the highest integrity. The country is proud of people like Vishwanath Pratap Singh, Arun Nehru, Arun Singh and many like them who have risen to make his dream come true. Let them execute his policies and plans. Give them a free hand. Give them protection. Let them do the job the country wants them to do.

5. Let him launch a massive programme, a crash programme on a war footing, to eradicate poverty, hunger, ignorance, superstition, inefficiency and, above all, corruption.

   And let Rajiv Gandhi know that if he fails the country, its good, decent, honest people will not forgive him.

Current, 04.01.1986.
pp. (1 + 3)

And more zindabad

This was the most unusual Congress session I ever attended in the last 25 years. It lacked enthusiasm, sense, of direction, commitment, sobriety, move and thrust.

Nothing more could be expected from a body largely nominated and handpicked by the so called high command. The last election of the AICC was held in 1972, that is 16 years ago. Since then the party has witnessed scores of splits, desertions, expulsions and over 50 deaths.

The president of the party is himself not a properly elected member. Most of those who adorned the stage were either nominated or had left the party in the wake of its defeat and once again jumped back onto the bandwagon.

Such an amorphous body cannot be expected to live up to the expectations of the people or even throw up some new worthwhile ideas. It can merely indulge in sycophancy and slogan mongering.

All the 80 odd speakers who took to the podium either began or finished their speeches with an unabashed adulation of our beloved leader Rajiv Gandhiji. More the seniority, the greater was the sycophancy.

H.K.L. Bhagat was not an exception when he thundered: "No power on earth can stop Rajiv Gandhi from winning the next election and that is one of the hard realities of life". And Rajiv sat through the two days' session listening to the praises showered on himself, without batting an eyelid.

Every congressman gathered at Kamraj Nagar carried a larger question mark on his face. He was caught in a cess of uncertainty of his and his party's future. Those from the north and especially from Uttar Pradesh, Bihar, Rajasthan and Madhya Pradesh appeared to be seized by the spectre of Vishwanath Pratap Singh.

The freshly drafted political resolution let the cat out of the bag when it directed the party's tirade against V.P. Singh and his Jan Morcha. "They are once again dreaming of a new version of a grand alliance under a new prophet of untruth. Needless to say, the combination is reactionary to the core. Its feudal, casteist and communal underpinnings can hardly be concealed. It is from these forces that the country has to be rescued."

Rajiv drafted Buta Singh and Darbara Singh to mount a bitter, virulent attack against Zail Singh. Most of the senior congressmen were taken aback by the severity of the attack on a person whom they had elected as Head of state at the behest of Indira Gandhi. Home minister Buta Singh even suggested a CBI inquiry against him but did not disclose who had prevented him from ordering such an inquiry so far.

Most members, especially from the south, murmured in disapproval of the vicious remarks and some of them were heard saying it was in bad taste and that Rajiv should not have allowed the AICC platform to hurl abuses on the former Head of state.

A senior AICC member from the South reminded the other members sitting around him of how often the high command has bitten dust. Pointing at the huge cutout of Kamaraj he said it was the same Kamaraj the Congress had branded "traitor, a reactionary in league with other reactionaries" in the historic Bangalore session in 1969.

Till his death he remained persona non grata to the Congress leadership and died in stark misery in 1975. At this AICC meeting in the heart of Tamil Nadu a crude attempt was made to unwrap his memory and to resurrect him. Was it only to win elections in the state? Can these kind of cheap gimmicks fool the people permanently?

Another gimmick, which instantly boomeranged was the new slogan: *Garibi hatao, bekari hatao.* Who, who on earth, prevented the Congress from *hataoing garibi and bekari* in the last forty years. What have these congressmen been doing all this time." The soul stirring slogan was given to the nation in a most cavalier manner. There was no word on how *garibi* or *bekari* will be *hataoed* and when.

Rajiv, who coined the slogan, told the nation that the details would be announced the next day. But in his concluding remarks he did not even refer to the slogan.

The lapse was pointed out by some young congressmen and an on the spot decision was taken to appoint a committee headed by Finance minister N.D. Tiwari. He was asked to prepare a comprehensive plan to *hatao* these two evils. Will this plan be different from what we hear, year after year from the Planning Commission or read in every Congress manifesto on the eve of elections?

How lacklustre was the show was evident from the *bhashans* from the stage. Hardly any speaker referred to the Congress party. How can the house be put in order? How can it be given a new sense of direction? How can it be rejuvenated? How can it once again be made a symbol of the people's aspirations? How can it be made in a democratically elected body? What strategy should it adopt to save it from total disintegration in those states where it has lost power?

Few congressmen gathered at Kamaraj Nagar seem to bother about these basic issues. It was *zindabad* all the way from Delhi to Madras. Was it necessary to go all the way to Madras for merely shouting *zindabad.*

Current, 30.04.1988.
p. (3)

Danger signals

"Since the advent of Rajiv Gandhi, many have joined the Congress to make a quick buck or grab positions of power, Adhocism and sycophancy have thrived. The neo-rich and the mafia are ruling the roost. There is a greater need of glasnost and perestroika in the Congress than in the Soviet Union." This is not an indictment by any opposition leader but a cry of anguish from senior Gujarat MP, Chimanbhai Mehta. Surprisingly his is not a lone voice. Dozens of ruling party MPs have been using stronger words to criticise what is euphemistically called the High Command, which in actuality means Rajiv Gandhi.

It is an unusual situation. Never before had a Congress Prime Minister been criticised and ridiculed so bitterly and extensively by such a cross section of the ruling party MPs and senior functionaries. The 'love letters' being written to him by these agitated MPs appear to be the tip of an iceberg. The wave of despondency sweeping through the party rank and file has to be seen to be believed. Gone is the era of whispers. A strong feeling of uncertainty is discernible among most of the Congress MPs especially from the north.

The letter written by a group of ten senior MPs representing Bihar, UP, Rajasthan, Haryana, Gujarat and Andhra is the first collective effort to reflect the general feeling among party MPs but being a first missive, of is polite in tone yet firm in pointing to the failures of the leader. Their first point is that the leadership has not been able to convince the people if its non-involvement in cases of corruption and bribery; second, the party and its leaders have lost credibility and it has taken no tangible steps to refurbish its image; third, the party is no longer committed to any kind of an ideology, it lacks a sense of direction and has lost touch with the masses; fourth, it has been giving priority to purely elitist policies and squandering money on non-developmental programmes; fifth, it has adopted ad-hocism as a raison d'etre and has found it safe to run away from the pressing socio-economic problems; sixth, it has successfully instilled fear in the minds of the ranks and file and considers even fair and legitimate criticism as signs of disloyalty and revolt; seventh, the erosion of the mass base, once the strongest point of the party; eighth, it is infested with many more power brokers now than it ever was and some of his close friends have been taking the Prime Minister for a ride.

"We aspire for no position," these MPs try to impress upon their leader and "our only objective is to save the Congress and Parliamentary democracy from collapse." "It seems Rajiv has not seen the writing on the wall", a former UP Chief minister was heard remarking in the central Hall the day Parliament met for the monsoon session. He spoke for over 70 minutes at a stretch at the CLP meeting blaming the opposition for the defeat in the recent by-elections and large-scale rigging. It was a monologue. No party MP participated in the one-man debate and as soon as he finished speaking, they headed towards the Lok Sabha and the Rajya Sabha. Earlier the by-election debacle was discussed for less than fifteen minutes in the working committee. The CWC meetings have been reduced to a farce. Hardly any member opens up. There is no agenda and most of the time Rajiv does the talking.

"It is a pathetic situation," former Chief minister Abdul Ghafoor commented in sheer disgust and colleagues sitting around him in the central Hall agreed in silence. The post-Allahabad developments have unnerved most Congress MPs and so far the Prime Minister has done nothing to boost their morale. Strangely, he himself appears as usual charming, happy smiling and totally unconcerned about the appearance of the dark clouds.

Current, 06.08.1988.
p. (2)

The Congress is withering away

The one thing the democratic structure in the country cannot afford is the withering away of the Congress. It is facing the danger of disintegration as a secular democratic organisation with a deep, strong national base. It is a party with followers in almost every village of the country and despite its ignominious defeat in 1977 it could not be wiped out.

Three years later it staged a dramatic comeback. But for the last three years it has been receiving blow after blow at the hands of its traditional enemies in the left as well as the right. It lost Assam, Bengal, Punjab, Haryana, Kerala and it is most likely to lose Tamil Nadu. It had already lost Andhra and Karnataka. Kashmir has also gone out of its control. Farooq Abdullah cannot be considered a permanent ally. Similarly Sharad Pawar's loyalty cannot be taken for granted. The Congress is almost extinct in the states where it does not have its government.

What is disturbing is the state of the party in those states where it is in power, specially in the Hindi belt, the so-called High Command has withered away and the party president's moral writ is confined to his fortress of a house. It remains impregnable even to the party chief ministers and senior partymen and PCC chiefs. The situation is intractable specially in Bihar, Uttar Pradesh and Madhya Pradesh. In Bihar, Chief minister Bhagwat Jha Azad is involved in a grim battle with Governor Govind Narain Singh, speaker Shiv Chandra Jha and PCC president Tariq Anwar. All three have been conspiring to dislodge him knowing that he was handpicked by their supreme leader Rajiv Gandhi. None of his opponents have been restrained, not even asked to let him run the government as a responsible Chief minister.

The Congress as an organisation hardly exists, nor the faction leaders are interested in preventing the decay. The party president has hardly had any time from his increasing interest in foreign affairs to set the things right.

The situation is not better in UP where a seasoned Chief minister Narain Dutt Tiwari, waits for weeks to meet the Prime Minister, Balaram Singh Yadav, the PCC president, was foisted on him. From the very first day Yadav, a close confident of former Chief minister Vir Bahadur Singh opened a hostile camp against the chief minister. He has packed the PCC with men chosen by Vir Bahadur Singh. In Tiwari's cabinet, too, most senior members have divided loyalties.

Vir Bahadur and Yadav pull strings from Delhi giving the impression that Tiwari no more enjoys the confidence of the Prime Minister and that he may be changed any day. The Prime Minister has done nothing to remove this impression.

This is the situation in a state where the Congress is bound to face a massive challenge from Vishwanath Pratap Singh. He has been touring the state addressing mammoth crowds. According to reports in pro-establishment newspapers, including The *Times of India* and the *Hindustan Times,* from indications available, UP is in a foul mood. The situation has further deteriorated after Allahabad and the tragedy is, no corrective measures have been taken so far, it is being offered to V.P. Singh on platter.

Madhya Pradesh, the third most populous Hindi state is in a much more advanced stage of faction flight. Chief minister Arjun Singh has been fighting a single handed battle against his party adversaries. Two senior ministers in the centre—Motilal Vora and Madhav Rao Scindia—have been carrying a vigorous mass campaign against him and the impression has gone round that they enjoy tacit approval of the Prime Minister. PCC chief Chandulal Chandrakar holds press conferences to attack him. Almost all the MPs from the state, including former loyalists like Kamal Nath, have been demanding his removal as though it was not enough his sworn enemy Shyam Charan Shukla has been admitted in the party with freedom to stake his claim for the Chief ministership.

Arjun Singh too has lost his rapport with the Prime Minister. He is no more the blue-eyed boy. His access to the sanctum-sanctorum has been severely restricted. This is the condition in the three most populous states in the Hindi-belt which, incidentally, send over 180 members to Lok Sabha in the past few years. The Congress has been identified with the Hindi-belt. Having lost the south and the north-east, if it loses in its traditional stronghold, the country will be faced with an awkward situation of keeping itself intact. India needs a party with a national base. It is time for the senior leaders in the Congress to ponder over this very delicate and crucial issue.

Current, 14.01.1989.
p. (2)

Countdown begins

We wrote last week in this column that the situation is much worse in the Hindi heartland than it appeared in the South. The events in the country's two largest states, Bihar and MP, and the warning signals from Rajasthan and Gujarat are pretty strong indications of the total moral collapse of congressmen, especially the legislators. They are in panic and are up in arms. They have defied the High Command which, in fact, means Rajiv Gandhi. They knuckled down only at the final threat, that is the dissolution of the Assembly and imposition of President's rule.

It happened in Bhopal. The riotous, rebellious legislators who were against Rajiv Gandhi's choice of Madhav Rao Scindia were herded at Arjun Singh's bungalow at 4 in the morning with Buta Singh, Fotedar, Ghulam Nabi Azad and Vir Bahadur Singh holding the sword of Democles and threatening to impose President's rule. Some legislators were seen carrying pistols and were heard hurling the choicest invectives at the Prime Minister—the ugliest scenes the state capital has ever witnessed. The central team headed by Buta Singh was constantly in touch with the commander-in-chief at Delhi who was stunned at the defiance of his subalterns. His writ no longer ran beyond the Race Course Road fortress. The legislators capitulated only after their leader Arjun Singh was threatened with dire consequences by the members of the central team and agreed to have Motilal Vora and not Scindia as Chief minister, knowing fully well that the young prince was Rajiv's personal choice.

Having lost the battle in Bhopal, Arjun Singh did not want to lose the war in Delhi and within a couple of days issued a statement defending the Congress defeat in Tamil Nadu. Nobody had asked him to come out with the statement but he did it in typically V.P. Singh manner. "For us, congressmen, it is a moment of deep introspection, unity and determination. The effort by the opposition to portray these results as a verdict against the Congress and our supreme leader, Mr. Rajiv Gandhi, is totally untenable . . . Mr. Gandhi is the leader of the nation and his popularity can only be tested in a national election . . . The likes of V.P. Singh and other opportunists who are floating to find their moorings of power cannot even measure up to his knees." The same Arjun Singh was the motivator of the revolt and the ugly anti-Rajiv scene in Bhopal. The Congress is packed with dozens of Arjun Singhs at the top and they will pop up the moment the ship begins to sink.

They surfaced in Bihar where the bizarre incidents exposed the ruling party to sordid blackmail and skullduggery. The same Buta Singh, Fotedar team headed a large contingent of senior congressmen from Delhi to suppress the rebellion. Patna paled Bhopal into insignificance. Here the revolt against Chief minister Bhagwat Jha Azad rattled the nerves of even Buta Singh, known for his bulldozing tactics. When he tried to browbeat the defiant legislators they abused him on his face, told him to mind his business and pack off. "Why have you come to Patna. Who sent you. Who are you. Get out of Raj Bhavan," they were heard shouting at the second most powerful man in the country who had been assigned the task of putting down the revolt. When the legislators were heaping insults on him they knew he was Rajiv Gandhi's eyes and ears, his trouble shooter. The fear of being expelled or denied a ticket has melted away. A Congress legislator in normal situation is perhaps the most docile and meek politician who has lost the political virility needed to get back to power. He never revolts in periods of normalcy.

The situation may be repeated soon in Rajasthan and Gujarat. They too are perched on the tip of a volcano. Bhopal and Patna are likely to be repeated in Jaipur and Ahmedabad. The trepidation of facing the electorate under Rajiv's leadership is spreading like an epidemic. Congress MP Chimanbhai Mehta seems to have belled the cat. He has asked for a change in leadership. He stands expelled but he says at least hundred others like him are waiting in the wings. How long can Delhi be safe if challenges continue to be thrown from Bhopal and Patna. It is a disturbing situation for the country. The Congress has been identified with stability and gradual progress of the country. Its disintegration at this juncture will hurt the national cause. It is up to the senior and responsible Congress leaders to find a way out.

Current, 04.02.1989.
p. (2)

Dissidence or defiance?

Dissidence is an old disease in the ruling party. It was there during Nehru's time and Indira Gandhi spent considerable time putting it down. Dissent is the kernel of democracy but it has to be within certain parameters. It should not be allowed to take the form of a revolt or disobedience of the central authority. One cannot discipline democracy but no democracy can have its impact on the people without an element of inner discipline. Inner party democracy does not necessarily mean inner party chaos. Every norm of government is guided by a set of rules framed by its own promoters.

What is happening in the Congress is an entirely new phenomenon. The total disregard of the so-called High Command and the acts of defiance witnessed in various states are disturbing factors not only for the ruling party but for the country too. The Congress has indeed been very largely responsible for the flowering of democracy in this country. It has been in power for almost forty years and it can certainly take credit for the survival of the system based on a constitution considered to be one of the finest documents in the world. But what we see today is that the High Command, which once commanded tremendous respect not only among the party rank and file but also the country, has degenerated into a coterie of small insignificant people who themselves are leaders of one or the other faction in their own states.

The so-called High Command was humiliated and kicked around even in states like Rajasthan where the congressmen are known to be traditionally docile and meek. The two central Cabinet ministers, Bir Bahadur Singh and L.P. Sahi, who were sent to Jaipur to put down the uprising in the ruling party were abused, chased and booed by the Congress legislators. They were protected by the Seva Dal volunteers who were also punished around and finally the police had to be called to rescue them. They were demanding a change of the Chief minister who was handpicked by Prime Minister Rajiv Gandhi only last year. Similar ugly scenes took place in Patna where the central party observers, Home minister Buta Singh and Steel minister Fotedar, were abused on their face and asked to go back to Delhi. The dissidents here too were demanding the removal of Bhagwat Jha Azad who was handpicked by Rajiv Gandhi only a year back.

Earlier much worse had happened in Bhopal where central observers, including a very senior person like Darbara Singh, were pushed around and here even the police did not come to their rescue. In Bhopal the defiant legislators took out pistols and hurled abuses at Rajiv Gandhi for his decision to remove Arjun Singh, who again was his choice as Chief minister in place of Motilal Vora.

Both in Bhopal and Patna the CMs are once again the personal choice of the PM. In Jaipur, Ahmedabad and Bombay, where the insurgency is in various stages against his Chief minister, the PM is trying to buy time by adopting all kinds of dilatory tactics but the cat, he should know by now, is out of the bag. The newly acquired acts of defiance are a sequel to the debacle in Tamil Nadu. The average congressmen is becoming aware of the stark fact that his leader, who brought the party back to power with an unprecedented majority, is a shadow of his past. That he is no more a crowd puller and that he has lost his value as a vote catcher is becoming a painful reality. The simple fact is that in a democracy if a leader loses his charisma and is unable to get his party back to power, he is discarded. Dissidence in almost all the Congress-ruled states is a symptom of a gathering storm. Congressmen have always been after power. They just cannot think of being in public life without enjoying the fruits of power. A year ago they were arguing: But there is no alternative to him. For the last couple of months they have been looking around, though meekly and sheepishly, for a replacement, if the state legislature parties are in revolt now, the days are not far when the Congress Parliamentary Party, too, will begin to reflect the situation in the states.

Too much has been lost for Rajiv. He will find it difficult to retrieve the ground but politics is a game of imponderables. He can retrieve much of the lost ground by falling back on the party and making it an instrument of attaining his goals. One should not hope to run a Parliamentary democracy without a democratic, vibrant political party. Such a leader will not survive for a long. For him it is a question of survival.

Current, 01.04.1989.
p. (2)

The country going to the dons

"This V.P. Singh is just like a cobra. He was fed on milk by the Congress but is now injecting poison into the body politic of the country. Only a man like me can kill him." This is not the dialogues of a mafia don in one of those block-busters, but the vituperations of Union minister Kalpanath Rai during an interview to a newspaper against the leader of a political party aiming to replace the ruling party.

The 'cobra' can be the next Prime Minister, Kalpanath Rai's fulmination is not an isolated act of insinuation. It forewarns the country of the shape of things to come if a major effort is not launched by decent politicians, whose number is fast declining, public spirited men and women and all those who have developed a vested interest in the survival of democracy in the country.

Not that the ruling party is taken over by the *Kalpanath Rais* but if the conspiracy to hand over politics to people with criminal intentions or those believing only in muscle power or those who would like to intimidate their political adversaries with the language of the gun is allowed to prosper, India would soon pale the banana republics into shame. Something positive has to be done immediately at the national level to expose and isolate criminals and hoodlums who have gained control of public life.

The fearsome dimensions of the danger must be ruthlessly exposed by the media and stalwarts like Kamalapati Tripathi who warned his party bosses of the inherent danger of the criminalisation of politics. "I know about the kind of elements that have got the upper hand in the recent elections to the gram sabhas in UP. I have also got information that the Congress positions at many such places have been sold. And these have gone to people against whom are serious complaints, who are known for *goondaism*".

The veteran Congress leader was provoked to issue the statement a couple of days after the Prime Minister's Independence day speech in which he had vowed to clean public life by purging the body politic of criminals but a few days later the Congress admitted a number of notorious criminals—MLAs and MPs—among its ranks. It also took help of history-sheeters, smugglers, murderers, in an attempt to grab the mayorship in Allahabad and Lucknow.

The word 'nexus' between criminals and politicians has lost its meaning because most of the 'celebrated' criminals, specially in the Hindi heartland, no longer scurry about seeking political patronage. They have taken to politics as ducks to water. They have infiltrated almost all the political parties except, perhaps, the BJP.

The Congress has done nothing to prevent such an infiltration specially in the Hindi-belt of UP, Bihar and MP. Recent surveys in some newspapers on the criminalisation of politics have created a sense of horror among well meaning people.

Not many newspapers reported about Prime Minister Rajiv Gandhi's birthday celebrations by notorious history-sheeters in a number of cities and towns of UP. These functions were organised by the local Congress units and many ministers participated in them. For the first time people witnessed ministers and criminals sharing the same platform singing paeans of Rajiv Gandhi with the police watching them with remarkable passivity. The criminals were so predominant in Lucknow in these birthday functions that the 'crime bulletin' issued by the local police listed the event at the PCC headquarters on the Mail Avenue as an 'Incident of crime'. Hardened criminals with NSA records, and some of them implicated in dozens of murder charges, have been elected to local bodies, corporations, assemblies and parliament. Quite a few of them are ministers. Imagine a convict-becoming a minister and ordering about the same police officers who had nabbed him and the magistrate who had convicted him.

A week before the Prime Minister's much talked about 15th August speech, the Union Home Ministry had disclosed in Parliament that as many as 18 ruling party MLAs in UP were notorious criminals. The opposition too did not lag behind. It had ten of them. In Bihar 26 criminals had successfully contested the Assembly election in 1980 and their number trebled in 1985. In these two states, having criminal records is no more considered a disqualification. If the police sources are to be believed, every fifth MLA in Lucknow and Patna is a history-sheeter. As the elections edge closer, politics will inevitably get more brutalised with more criminals taking to the battle of hustings. Both the Congress and the Janata Dal will be found guilty of the heinous crime of handing over the country to the underworld.

The only way to put an effective stop to this rot is to bring some kind of a legislation preventing people with criminal records from contesting election either to the legislatures or local bodies. This has to be done before it is too late. Otherwise, in a few years the Parliament may even be taken by the dons.

Current, 09.09.1989.
p. (2)

Rajiv Gandhi's toughest challenge

The Congress party is at the crossroads. Despite being the single largest party in Parliament as also in the country, its future has never been so uncertain. The average congressman is passing through the most agonising phase of his political career. Caught as he is in a nut-cracker, he does not know what the new alliances and unpredictable postures the so-called High Command assumed without taking him in confidence. Never in the past did such a communication gap exist between him and the leadership or should we say the leader. Major policy decisions are taken by a small group sowing confusion in the rank and file while the established institutions like the Parliamentary Board or the Congress Working Committee have ceased to function—they seem to have lost their relevance. The pace of events is so fast and unpredictable that even Rajiv Gandhi, whose authority has yet to be questioned in party fora, hardly know what the new alliances and unpredictable postures the so-called High Command assumed without taking him in confidence. Never in the past did such a communication gap exist between him and the leadership or should we say the leader. Major policy decisions are taken by a small group sowing confusion in the rank and file while the established institutions like the Parliamentary Board or the Congress Working Committee have ceased to function—they seem to have lost their relevance. The pace of events is so fast and unpredictable that even Rajiv Gandhi, whose authority has yet to be questioned in party fora, hardly appears to be coherent and is unable to give direction to his vast flock.

First, his 'unconditional' support to Chandra Shekhar and his gang of opportunists and defectors has left congressmen speechless. How could he make common cause with a man who has been a sworn enemy of the party and its leaders for over two decades? How can they respect a man who was jailed by Indira Gandhi for conspiring against her regime and her dynasty and who was one of the main destroyers of Congress rule in 1977 as their leader? Congressmen do not know what the principles or issues were which compelled Rajiv Gandhi to catapult him on to the *gaddi*. And how long he will be allowed to rule the country and at what cost to the party they cannot guess. In this game Chandra Shekhar is not alone. He has brought in people like Mulayam Singh Yadav, Chimanbhai Patel, Devi Lal and his family. These people are not known for any discipline in their political life nor do they have any qualms about political morality. The stresses in this marriage of convenience are severe. The Congress is in turmoil in the Hindi belt, Gujarat and Maharashtra.

Soon Rajiv Gandhi will come face to face with the reality. If Chandra Shekhar succeeds in solving some of the major national problems, Rajiv's relevance in the country and in his own party will be open to question. Shekhar may be an opportunist but he is nobody's fool. He has got what he wanted after waiting for years and he will not give it up easily. He will fight a bitter battle to retain the Prime Ministership and in the process may cause a vertical split in the Congress. He has powerful allies in Sharad Pawar, Mulayam Singh Yadav and Chimanbhai Patel who will most likely challenge the existing leadership of the Congress taking alongwith them second rung leaders like Jagannath Mishra, Dinesh Singh, K.C. Pant, Arjun Singh, Bansi Lal, Siddharta Shankar Ray, Janaki Ballabh Patnaik, Shiv Shankar, etc . . .

To avoid this Rajiv will be left with no choice but to invite Shekhar and his coterie to merge with his party and also ask ex-Jan Morcha men to return to the Congress fold. In a recent interview, V.C. Shukla spilled the beans. But if Shekhar rejoins the Congress, what will be his condition. A close associate of Rajiv Gandhi, who often speaks for him, feels that within next year Gandhi will take over the Prime Ministership and make Shekhar the president of the party, provided the latter is agreeable to such a proposition. If he does not, then the Congress will withdraw support to him and stake its claim to form the government with the support of most of the men in the Janata Dal-S who are expected to switch their loyalty to Rajiv Gandhi.

The only deterrent is the threat of mid-term poll. Neither Rajiv nor Shekhar wants that for at least two more years. The polity has been totally polarised. The backwards and Muslims and a big chunk of the Harijans are lined up behind V.P. Singh who is making every effort to consolidate his position. Singh is not the kind of man who will let the grass grow under his feet. He has been drawing impressive crowds in Bihar, Maharashtra, Tamil Nadu, Kerala and is slated to storm Andhra and Karnataka. His coming tour of UP is also likely to prove a boon for him. In the north, Singh's formidable adversary will be the BJP and its leader Lal Krishna Advani. Here the Congress is in total disarray while the JD-S is mere flotsam. Rajiv is not left with any following in the vote banks his grandfather and mother had built among the minorities, Harjians and Brahmins. The upper castes in the north will prefer the BJP this time, and Kanshi Ram's Bahujan Samaj Party, if it does not become a part of the Congress alliance, will eat into large chunks of the Harijan vote.

In the unlikely event of something unpredictable happening, the Congress is in for a major drubbing. It will be a grievous loss to the country because it is a party with glorious traditions which also upheld democratic values except during the brief period of Emergency.

Current, 15.12.1990.
p. (2)

Index

H

T

U